New Ways of
Looking at Old Texts, V

Papers of the
Renaissance English Text Society
2007–2010

MEDIEVAL AND RENAISSANCE
TEXTS AND STUDIES

VOLUME 456

———————

RENAISSANCE ENGLISH TEXT SOCIETY
SEVENTH SERIES

SPECIAL PUBLICATION

New Ways of
Looking at Old Texts, V

Papers of the
Renaissance English Text Society
2007–2010

Edited by
Michael Denbo

ARIZONA CENTER FOR MEDIEVAL

 ACMRS

AND RENAISSANCE STUDIES

in conjunction with
Renaissance English Text Society
Tempe, Arizona
2014

THE ARIZONA CENTER FOR

MEDIEVAL & RENAISSANCE

STUDIES

Published by ACMRS (Arizona Center for Medieval and Renaissance Studies)
Tempe, Arizona
© 2014 Arizona Board of Regents for Arizona State University.
All Rights Reserved.

Library of Congress Cataloging-in-Publication Data

New ways of looking at old texts. V, Papers of the Renaissance English Text Society 2007-
2010 / edited by Michael Denbo.
    pages cm. -- (Medieval and Renaissance texts and studies ; Volume 456)
(Renaissance English Text Society, 7th series, special publication)
  Includes bibliographical references and index.
  ISBN 978-0-86698-507-9 (acid-free paper)
1. English literature--Early modern, 1500-1700--Criticism, Textual. 2. Transmission of
texts--England--History--16th century. 3. Transmission of texts--England--History--17th
century. 4. Manuscripts, Renaissance--England--Editing. 5. Manuscripts, English--
Editing. 6. Renaissance--England. 7. Paleography, English I. Denbo, Michael Roy, editor.
II. Renaissance English Text Society. III. Title: Papers of the Renaissance English Text
Society, 2007-2010.
  PR418.T48N4946 2014
  820.9'003--dc23

                                                                            2014034767

∞
This book is made to last. It is set in Adobe Minion Pro,
smyth-sewn and printed on acid-free paper to library specifications.
Printed in the United States of America

Table of Contents

Preface   ix

In Memoriam — W. SPEED HILL   xi
     P. G. STANWOOD
     MICHAEL DENBO

Early Modern Digital Editing

Underpinnings of the Social Edition? A Brief Narrative, 2004–2009,   3
     for the Renaissance English Knowledgebase (REKn)
     and Professional Reading Environment (PReE) Projects
     RAYMOND G. SIEMENS

Providing a Base for E-Editing: The Text Creation Partnership Project   47
     SHAWN MARTIN

The Emory Women Writers Resource Project: Teaching Students,   61
     Training Students
     SHEILA T. CAVANAGH

The Henslowe-Alleyn Digitisation Project: Past, Present, and Future   71
     GRACE IOPPOLO

Brave New World or Dumping Ground? Electronic Supplements   81
     and the Printing of Jonson's *Cynthia's Revels*
     ERIC RASMUSSEN

Mutability and Variation: A Digital Response to Complex Texts 91
MICHAEL BEST

Drawing Networks in the Devonshire Manuscript (BL Add. MS. 17492): 113
Toward Visualizing a Writing Community's Shared Apprenticeship,
Social Valuation, and Self-Validation
RAYMOND G. SIEMENS

Paratext and Pointy Brackets: How Early Modern Archives Can Inform 153
Digital Collections
ERIKA FARR

Textual Criticism

The Sense of a Letter: Brilliana Harley's Advice Manuscript (BL MS. 70118) 165
JOHANNA HARRIS

Reforming Sir Thomas More in the Court of Katherine Parr 181
SUSAN F. FELCH

Monastic Authorship, Protestant Poetry, and the Psalms Attributed to 193
Dame Clementia Cary
JAIME GOODRICH

"Who am I?": Exploring Questions of Authorship Using Digital Texts 209
IRENE J. MIDDLETON

The Woman in Black: The Patron of Antoine Vérard's Edition of the 219
Horloge de Sapience (PML 17591)
CAROLYN DISKANT MUIR

"All the Adulteries of Art": The Dramatic Excerpts of Margaret Bellasys's 235
BL MS. Add. 10309
LAURA ESTILL

The Autograph Manuscript of Mary Wroth's *Pamphilia to Amphilanthus* 247
ILONA BELL

Sixteenth-Century Artisanal Practices and Baconian Prose 259
    KEN HILTNER

Francis Bacon in Collaboration 277
    ALAN STEWART

Editing the Early Modern Text

Editing Richard Tottel's *Songes and Sonettes* 297
    PAUL A. MARQUIS

Cælivs Secvndus Curio His Historie of the Warr of Malta: Translated by 309
    Thomas Mainwaring, 1579
    HELEN L. VELLA BONAVITA

Editing "a mute inglorious Milton" of Gloucestershire: Nicholas Oldisworth 321
    JOHN GOUWS

On Textual Editing: MA 1057 335
    MICHAEL DENBO

Index 345

RETS Panels and Papers 355

Preface

For this, the fifth volume of *New Ways of Looking at Old Texts*, we will not have an Introduction but instead include two essays in tribute to our founding editor, W. Speed Hill. Speed actually passed away before the publication of our fourth volume, but at the time we were committed to honoring another late RETS council member, David Freeman, who was also Speed's friend and colleague. All of us at RETS and contributors to *New Ways* who follow these two fine early modern textual scholars must know that our work rests firmly on their great contributions. We have all done our best to follow their leadership.

Our readers will note that this volume is somewhat shorter than our last number. There are two reasons for this: as we know, MLA shifted its annual convention from December to the following January, thus there was no convention held in calendar 2011. Ultimately, I think this change will make things neater for *New Ways*. We will not be following the academic calendar of September one year to June the next for our volumes, but will instead be following the regular calendar, since all the academic meetings will occur in the same year. Also, several of our 2007-2008 meetings were based on digital editing, and, as such, some of the panels were devoted more to presentations rather than academic papers that did not lend themselves to publication in this journal.

And on a personal note, this volume of *New Ways* will be my last as its editor. I have enjoyed my work in this position and I am grateful to the many contributors who have helped me with this project. Our new editor will be Arthur F. Marotti, who surely needs no introduction to our readership. I wish him well in this new endeavor.

MICHAEL DENBO

W. Speed Hill

W. Speed Hill and the Folger Library Edition of Richard Hooker

P. G. STANWOOD

W. Speed Hill may be best known to many textual critics for his significant contribution to the affairs of the Renaissance English Text Society, for his ever-reliable advice, his mentorship of many younger scholars, and his numerous and outstanding publications. My knowledge of Speed confirms all of these achievements, but from the perspective of his collaborator in the great *Folger Library Edition of the Works of Richard Hooker*.

Speed's interest in Hooker began early, with his Harvard Ph.D. thesis (directed by Herschel Baker) on "The Doctrinal Background of Richard Hooker's Laws of Ecclesiastical Polity" (1964). And the edition of Hooker occupied the central and most essential part of Speed's career — more than thirty years from 1967 until the final index volume that appeared in 1998. In all there are seven numbered volumes though in fact eight bound books, for volume 6 of commentary appears in two separate parts — a remarkable shelf of books, all of them directed by the general editor, W. Speed Hill.

I first heard from Speed in his letter to me of October 1969 (the letter, with my own and other Hooker correspondence and materials, is now in the Folger Library archives), asking me to join the Hooker project. I had recently completed an edition of John Cosin's *A Collection of Private Devotions* for the Clarendon Press (in 1967), and Speed had asked Helen Gardner, who was then a Delegate to the Press, for her advice about an editor — I had previously been encouraged by Dame Helen (as she was to become) to undertake an edition of Jeremy Taylor's *Holy Living* and *Holy Dying*. Speed had already begun his ambitious project, the genesis of which he describes in his *Studies in Richard Hooker: Essays Preliminary to an Edition of His Works*, published in 1972 by the Press of Case Western

Reserve University. The project seemed intriguing, and I put Taylor aside for the time being to concentrate on Hooker.

Speed was building an editorial team, mostly complete by the end of 1969, with the edition now formally sponsored by the Folger Library, where O. B. Hardison was director and strong encourager of the Hooker project. So in the first half of 1972, I went to the Folger on a Senior Fellowship to proceed with work on the posthumous books of Hooker, and it was there that I met Speed for the first time — and incidentally, also the remarkable Fredson Bowers. There began the long association with Speed that developed into one of the happiest and most productive professional collaborations of my career, which also would ultimately grow into a personal friendship.

In his historical note in the 1972 *Studies in Richard Hooker,* Speed laid out the plan of the edition, which remained essentially the same to the end, designating as well almost all the editors, now firmly committed — one might say — for life. Speed wrote then that "a completion date of 1980 — or even sooner — is not impossible, even taking into account the inevitable delays that attend upon such a complex and far-flung effort." Such boldness! But we all remember Speed for his cheerful optimism, which, together with his talent for tenacity, was put to a twenty- or thirty-year test. In those distant days, textual editors knew W. W. Greg's essay on copy text almost by heart, and they were bound to develop stemmata, in accordance with Lachmann, and ultimately, it was presumed, to discover and record the author's intentions. Speed Hill's understanding and study of the first edition of Hooker's *Laws* is consequently irreproachable in terms of this traditional execution, and its theoretical underpinnings still make good sense, at least in terms of what had to be done in the editing of this or any work. One recognizes Speed's influence in Georges Edelen's excellent textual introduction to the first four books of the *Laws* and in the account of the composition, printing, and proofing of the 1593 folio, against which the Folger edition of these books is based. Edelen remarks in his acknowledgements that "only those closely associated with the Hooker edition know how much it depends, both in conception and in every detail, on the energy and acuity of . . . W. Speed Hill."

Speed would apply these special talents to his textual analysis of Hooker's fifth book, the longest of the *Ecclesiastical Polity,* exceeding the first four books combined. I remember meeting Speed in the old Bodleian (the Selden end) in 1973 where he was studying Benjamin Pullen's scribal copy — 225 folios — and carefully noting the many instances of Hooker's holograph corrections. This would become the printer's copy for the 1597 folio, the proof of which Hooker himself read, and occasionally corrected. In a dense and utterly convincing argument, Speed determined that the copy text should be based on a transcription of the Pullen copy of Hooker's autograph, corrected by Hooker, and collated with the text of the first printed edition. The resulting volume, the second of the Folger Library Edition, is perhaps the crowning achievement of Speed Hill's textual scholarship, and a major contribution to modern editorial theory and practice. This volume and Edelen's were published together in 1977 by the Belknap Press of the Harvard University Press, an occasion marked by a notable reception of Hooker editors, friends and Folger Library administrators at the British Embassy in Washington, where the Ambassador received the volumes on behalf of Her Majesty Queen Elizabeth II, in fitting memory of Hooker's dedication of his work to the first Elizabeth's Archbishop Whitgift.

Speed's own superb textual and critical study may be best or most obviously demonstrated in his edition of Hooker's Fifth Book of the *Laws*; but of course his guidance and influence is everywhere apparent in the *Folger Library Edition of the Works of Richard Hooker*, and especially in the third volume that presents the posthumous books Six, Seven, and Eight. This volume was my assignment, the complexity of which emerged slowly and overwhelmingly, the Eighth Book alone available in fifteen manuscript versions. And in the midst of this troublesome array of authorities, there turned up Hooker's own autograph notes and drafts for this book. Speed was often at my side as we studied these notes in the manuscript room of Trinity College, Dublin; and together we also explored the resources of the Chapter Library of Salisbury Cathedral. Meanwhile, meetings with him and the other editors, including Laetitia Yeandle, Curator of Manuscripts at the Folger, continued — at Oxford (Corpus Christi College and Queen's College); Cambridge University (Peterhouse and Trinity College); the British Library; Lambeth Palace Library; and of course the Folger itself — and I have given only a partial list of places that Speed and I visited. These great travels (and I do intend a pun) resulted at last in my long introduction to the edition of Hooker's last three books of *Ecclesiastical Polity* and the texts that follow. Only Speed and I would ever know how much discussion and anguish lay behind the stemmata displayed in this edition.

The third volume of the Folger Edition appeared in 1981, thus completing the *Laws* and bringing to a close one important stage of a cooperative endeavor, overseen at all times by the energy and intelligence of its general editor, W. Speed Hill. Still to come were the volumes containing *Attack and Response* (with *A Christian Letter*), edited by John Booty, in 1983; and *Tractates and Sermons,* edited by Laetitia Yeandle, in 1990. The final volumes of commentary appeared in 1993. Now except for the Index, the edition was complete. The occasion was marked by another great occasion in Washington, at the Folger Library and at the National Cathedral, at a conference held September 24-26, 1993. From this event came a collection of essays edited by Arthur Stephen McGrade, *Richard Hooker and the Construction of Chris-*

tian Community (MRTS, 1997), which begins with a lively and learned apologia by Speed, on "Richard Hooker in the Folger Edition: An Editorial Perspective."

Speed Hill's "perspective" is an eloquent review of Hooker's legacy presented through the Folger Edition of his works, and by implication of Speed's own legacy to textual criticism and more generally to Renaissance (or early modern) scholarship. The Folger Edition has encouraged renewed interest in Hooker, with an outpouring of articles and books about him over the past thirty years or so, and most recently in the publication of the magnificent Brill *Companion to Richard Hooker,* edited by Torrance Kirby, published in 2008. "Scholar, humanist, truth-seeker" are terms appropriately descriptive both of Speed and of the great author to whom he has brought new life. Because of his superb textual skills and his genius for collaborative editing, he was able to open the way for a new generation of students and critics of Richard Hooker — and more generally of textual criticism and editorial practice.

I have spoken of the professional collaboration I enjoyed over many years with Speed through a common scholarly pursuit, and earlier I referred to the personal friendship that developed out of this association. My wish is to end with a brief recollection of incidents not quite connected with the Folger Edition of Richard Hooker.

Through my encouragement, Speed gave, as a distinguished visiting professor, an extremely successful and fully enrolled summer seminar on textual bibliography at the University of British Columbia, in 1992, during my tenure as graduate chair. Moreover, he and I shared an active concern for the International Association of University Professors of English. During the time when he was Chairman of the Association and I was President, Speed introduced a section on textual criticism and theory that continues successfully. The triennial meetings of the Association took us to Copenhagen, Lausanne, Vancouver — we seem to have met, talked and argued over a wealth of literary, textual, and world problems in many of the major cities of Europe and North America. One of our most memorable encounters was in Berlin, in June 2002, where Speed, eager as always to seek new experiences, joined me in a friendly, informal long weekend of opera — neither his favorite nor most familiar art form. But as a good companion and a fast friend, Speed joined me for a performance at the Deutsche Oper of *Parsifal,* an event and production that left him more puzzled than even the construction of the posthumous books of Richard Hooker. Speed proved yet once more his tenacity and determination never to give up, even to Wagner.

UNIVERSITY OF BRITISH COLUMBIA

W. Speed Hill and New Ways of Looking at Old Texts

MICHAEL DENBO

W. SPEED HILL: I CANNOT TELL YOU HOW SURPRISED I WAS WHEN SPEED offered me the editorship of *New Ways*. He was so incredibly knowledgeable on virtually every aspect of scholarly editing. More than many times I asked him a question that I thought he would have to at least think about before he answered: I assumed there was some book somewhere that had all the answers. But Speed seemed to have that book memorized, or perhaps he himself had written it: his knowledge about texts, the nature of texts, their structure, their history, seemed to be woven into his fingertips. Nonetheless, as his student, he also taught me to say yes when something important was offered, so rather than rebel against his own teachings, I said yes, assuming that he knew something about me that I didn't. Only time will tell.

Speed explained the purpose of *New Ways* in his preface to volume I. (As you will see, I prefer to let him speak for himself.) His first concern was to contextualize and codify the editing of nondramatic Renaissance texts, but his approach was clearly pedagogic, an aspect of his scholarship not always known or recognized. He wrote:

> In the course of preparing a survey of scholarly editing of nondramatic texts of the English Renaissance . . . , I discovered that there was no coherent body of scholarly literature on the editing of these texts, as there is, for example, for editors of Renaissance play-texts. Editing skills, passed on from mentor to student and exemplified in the practices of individual editions published by particular university presses (especially Oxford and Harvard), were nowhere codified in a form that a beginning editor of texts

of the period might emulate or modify. To remedy that lack, my essay surveys these various practices.[1]

Speed followed his preface with the first complete essay ever to appear in *New Ways*, an essay that he himself wrote entitled "Editing Nondramatic Texts of the English Renaissance: A Field Guide with Illustrations." Unlike all other essays to appear in the series, this one was written exclusively for the volume and was — to my knowledge — never delivered at any panel or oral presentation. Its purpose was to survey the field and its history, and, if possible, to anticipate its future. Since I know how important this history was to Speed, I will summarize his remarks here.

Speed describes four types of scholarly editions: documentary, including diplomatic and photographic reprints; genealogical editions; copy-text editions; and multiple-version editions.

Since my own diplomatic edition of the Holgate Miscellany was created under Speed's tutelage, I have always been taken with the simplicity of his explanation for this primary category. "The rationale behind the documentary edition is to make more widely available scarce or unique texts whose inspection would otherwise necessitate a trip to the library."[2] In other words, make the text widely available and explain as much as possible. Among Speed's many qualities, his pragmatism may have been among the first. Whatever you do, have a purpose. That was his best lesson.

A far more idealistic editorial approach is the genealogical edition (Karl Lachmann, 1793-1851), one that posits by necessity that there must have been an original prototype and that the editor, through a careful examination of the genealogical trees, i.e., its stemmata, can describe — possibly even recreate — "a lost archetype." All of us know the problems with this idea, but it is impossible in a world of cause and effect that such an approach would not have a powerful influence on modern editing.

According to Speed, the third category, the copy-text edition, has its origins specifically in the editing of Renaissance texts. The genealogical edition focused on texts written long before any original copy-text could be identified, but a copy-text edition focused on texts published in and around the time of their creation. In other words, the printed version is the one we have: how do we get back to the original manuscript? As Speed describes these editors:

---

[1] W. Speed Hill, Preface to *New Ways of Looking at Old Texts, 1985-1991*, I, ed. W. Speed Hill (Binghamton, NY: Medieval & Renaissance Texts & Studies in conjunction with Renaissance English Text Society, 1993).

[2] W. Speed Hill, "Editing Nondramatic Texts of the English Renaissance: A Field Guide with Illustrations," in *New Ways I*, 3-24, at 4.

Their attentions . . . were turned to analyzing exactly how early Renaissance printers transformed their texts in the course of printing them. The 'new' (i.e. analytical) bibliography was to trailblaze 'the bibliographical way' for editions of printed texts, just as codicology and stemmatic analysis had for manuscript texts.[3]

New here is the concept of revision: how do we account for a text that was changed by its author? The modern textual editor had two choices:

. . . to base an edition either on the earliest text, the one closest to a (usually) lost authorial original, or on the last one over which the author demonstrably exercised his or her revisional prerogatives. If one chose the first, subsequent authorial revision must be disambiguated from transmissional corruption through collation of later printed texts. . . . If the second, the author is deemed to have approved the revised text in its entirety by having acquiesced in its publication, and that task of the editor is that of identifying and removing the more egregious forms of transmissional corruption from the last edition printed in the author's lifetime.[4]

It's ironic that the Renaissance text, so immersed as it was in revising (or re-visioning) the texts of its past, would, in the twentieth century, lead to the copy-text edition. In Speed's view, both the copy-text editor and the genealogical editor had the same goal: to discover or recreate a 'best' text, or a 'better' text, better, of course, than any critical edition could possibly be. The problems, of course, are many, and brought such words as 'accidentals' and 'substantives' into our vocabulary. Also the concept of 'copy-text' or 'base-text' is distinguished by the different types of editors. For the Lachmannian editor, more than likely it is the most complete text; but for the copy-text editor, it is implicit in his or her task that the text as it now appears is indeed the *best* text.

Speed's final category is the multiple-version edition. If you can't tell, print everything. Although there is enormous value to this type of edition, Speed, following the language of the *Donne Variorum* editors, indicates that they are still looking for the "earliest, least corrupted text." Be that as it may, multiple-version editions are expensive and generally restricted to the best-known of our writers.

However, after Speed's own anatomy of textual editing described above, he introduces a yet newer approach, one directly relevant to our practices today. It

---

[3] Hill, "Field Guide," 9.
[4] Hill, "Field Guide," 10.

is important to note that as early as 1985 he was able to describe the concerns of every writer in volume IV of *New Ways*. He writes:

> A fifth prototype is not fully articulated as a working model, nor has it as yet an authoritative exemplar to point to. It originates, as Arthur Marotti observes . . ., in the "cultural materialism . . . implicit in the interpretative practices of the New Historicism" as expressed in such works as McGann's *Critique* (1983) and D. F. McKenzie's *Bibliography and the Sociology of Texts* (1985). McGann's views especially have discomfited those who, having operated for a generation under the authoritative guidance of Greg, Bowers, and Tanselle, had grown to feel that the excavations of modern textual practice had at last reached bedrock and that they could safely build editions that would stand that test of time. However, they have provoked newer historicists such as Marotti to call for a literary history (and a concomitant textual program) that does not privilege the solitary author at the expense of the social milieu in which he or she wrote.[5]

I suspect that the 'working model' implicit in the earlier theories of textual editing has become a paradox. How can there be a model for a text whose influences are mainly cultural, or perhaps I should say even nonverbal? There are so many suggestions here, none of which could ever identify all the influences a particular writer explores or represents. Indeed, the very questions of revision, change, that dominate the earlier theories of editing are themselves determinate cultural markers. Where is the text, we might ask! Writing in our new period is often seen as a performance. Is performance a text, or text a performance; or are the markings on a Renaissance bowl a textual performance? It is ironic that Speed's original concern was the editing of nondramatic texts not created for performance. As much as anything, our language has shifted, not metaphorically as is sometimes supposed, but by a shift to cultural concerns. Nonetheless, were he here today I would ask him about the dramatic play texts and nondramatic written texts that he first classified, a classification which, according to him, led to this series.

So then, today, what is *New Ways*? Speaking as its present editor, it is itself a combination of performance and writing. All of us know the difference between delivering a paper and then adapting it to publication: every source must be accounted for, every edition recognized. But a performance text (as you see today) is uniquely sensitive to our present concerns, especially gender, which dominated Volume IV. Gone it seems are the theoretical questions that Speed asked when he first developed this series: each writer is concerned with a specific text, whether it

---

[5] Hill, "Field Guide," 20.

be one he or she edited or simply studied, it is the text itself — in whatever specific version — that has drawn the attention of the critic. Indeed, as I looked at the index of Volume IV, some very famous names are absent, among them W. W. Greg and G. Thomas Tanselle. This is not to say that these important theorists of modern editorial practices have lost their value — none of us would say that — but the reader/critic today is a very finely tuned instrument, one looking for evidence to prove his or her point, creating, ultimately, our own markers of identity. We were here. How ironic that I, after working so hard on the present volume, find his approach so remarkably psychological — new ways — old texts — as if we meet our forebears and remake them: editor as Oedipus! It is our time to find our own particular texts and then show the world why we individually think they are important, or perhaps, if I might be so bold, how we individually envision ourselves living in the English Renaissance. Regardless, it is ironic that Speed, who was so intensely interested in human psychology, should have described the *raison d'être* of this journal in what are ultimately psychological terms.

We should also consider why Speed was so fascinated by the history of scholarly editing. Some of you may know that Speed's original ambition was to be a chemist, and therefore it is not surprising that he was so careful in how he described editorial structure. But, as always, it is the context and the admixture of elements that allow us to go forward, what gives us, perhaps, the justification to believe in what we do. The models are not just old texts; they are also contexts, to some degree ignored (or unconscious) as we go about the business of scholarly editing. We have, in a sense, been taught how to think, which becomes the modus operandi of how we go about editing our texts.

But have we not also been taught how to read — reading old texts in the sense that *all texts* have been written at an earlier date? Although I never heard Speed say this, I suspect reading was his most important concern. My earliest recollection of Speed was at a conference held at the CUNY Graduate Center: students and faculty together in a vestibule awaiting entrance to some sort of plenary session, the subject of which I don't remember. Since the doors to the session were yet to open, all of us were jammed together in a rather small space awaiting — probably — the person who would unlock the door of the auditorium. Speed was sitting on a table, dressed — then to my surprise — in a tennis sweater, which is how he often dressed. Since he was chatting with two of my classmates, I walked over to introduce myself and to ask a question: why do we make mistakes in reading; why is it we read one word and see another? Speed had thought a lot about this question and was ready with his answer. As we read along, we make certain expectations about what is being said. Often we misread by reading what we would have said — the mind actually goes faster than the eye, leading us to mistakes. At the time I did not realize that Speed had already published an essay on much the same question, "The Calculus of Error, or Confessions of a General Editor," referring, obviously, to his experience as the General Editor of the Hooker project. The "two orders of evidence" discussed in the paper refer to the impossibility of a 100% accurate transcription and the problem of editing an error first made by the author, who, in truth, was unaware of the mistake.

> But there is a difference between the two orders of evidence here yoked together. On the one hand we have the physical evidence of print or script: it can be recorded, analyzed, collated, weighed, verified. On the other, we have mental acts. There is a crucial difference — more a barrier than a veil — between the two. Intentions change: they have conscious as well as unconscious components; they are not finally subject to verification, especially across the space of four centuries. It is accepted that the interpretative bias of a literary critic enters into his inferences as to authorial intention in his criticism, but editors — at least under the aegis of contemporary bibliographers — have aspired to the objectivity of scientists, and editing is to be logical, objective, and, by virtue of these, definitive. Yet, in the absence of direct evidence, I do not see how one can infer authorial intention without a substantial input of editorial intention. An editor could normalize all scribal spellings to their corresponding authorial forms — so long as he was willing to admit that it was his own intention that was at issue. But to father such a text on a sixteenth-century author who rarely cared about such things is duplicitous. My own image of Hooker is that, if asked, he could scarcely understand what was at issue; he would certainly not have felt that anything very essential inhered in his personal orthography, and I suspect that he would have been more in sympathy with the modernized texts of Keble, the culmination of a long and honorable tradition, than the old-spelling ones of our edition, which is so distinct from it, although Keble himself acknowledged "that he should himself prefer an exact reprint of the original, excepting of course palpable errors of the press," for "as a specimen and monument of language, ancient books lose very much of their value by the neglect of ancient orthography."[6]

No matter how expressive of our own visions we may be, editors transform texts, and part of that transformation is created by error, by how we misread, both accidentally and otherwise, for whatever reason. If it is our intention to recreate

---

[6] John Keble was the nineteenth-century editor of Hooker. He corrected Hooker's mistakes. W. Speed Hill, "The Calculus of Error, or Confessions of a General Editor," *Modern Philology* 75.3 (Feb. 1978): 247-60, here 257-58.

the texts of the seventeenth century, it is our mistake as well, and whatever that mistake is it will inform each and every editorial decision we make. As a scholar, teacher, mentor, and I hope friend, Speed was unique, far more so than many appreciated. In all his endeavors, in all his concerns, it was always the individual who came first, as we see in his brief portrait of Hooker in the previous example. Simply put, he was fascinated by the human mind. No doubt there will always be a call for this series. We honor the unique scholar who created it.

BRONX COMMUNITY COLLEGE
CITY UNIVERSITY OF NEW YORK

Early Modern Digital Editing

Underpinnings of the Social Edition? A Brief Narrative, 2004–2009, for the Renaissance English Knowledgebase (REKn) and Professional Reading Environment (PReE) Projects[1]

RAY SIEMENS, MIKE ELKINK, ALASTAIR MCCOLL,
KARIN ARMSTONG, JAMES DIXON, ANGELSEA SABY,
BRETT D. HIRSCH and CARA LEITCH, with MARTIN HOLMES,
ERIC HASWELL, CHRIS GAUDET, PAUL GIRN, MICHAEL JOYCE,
RACHEL GOLD, and GERRY WATSON,
and members of the PKP, ITER, TAPoR, and INKE teams.

Introduction and Overview

THE RENAISSANCE ENGLISH KNOWLEDGEBASE (REKn) IS A PROTOTYPE research knowledgebase consisting of a large dynamic corpus of both primary (15,000 text, image, and audio objects) and secondary materials (some 100,000 articles, e-books, etc.). Each electronic document is stored in a database along with its associated metadata and, in the case of many text-based materials, a light encoding. The data is queried, analyzed, and examined through a stand-alone prototype document-centered reading client called the Professional Reading Environment (PReE).

---

[1] This paper was first presented by Raymond G. Siemens at the 2007 Modern Language Convention, Chicago, IL, at the Josephine Roberts Forum: E-Editing in Corpora, Michael Denbo presiding. As the title reflects, this paper has been updated for its present publication. It was originally entitled "Prototyping a 'Knowledge' Approach to Texts and Secondary Resources in Renaissance Studies."

This is an abridged version of a longer article, the full text of which can be found at http://cnx.org/content/m34335/latest/.

Recently, both projects have moved into new research developmental contexts, requiring some dramatic changes in direction from our earlier proof of concept. For the second iteration of PReE, our primary goal continues to be to translate it from a desktop environment to the Internet. By following a web-application paradigm, we are able to take advantage of superior flexibility in application deployment and maintenance, the ability to receive and disseminate user-generated content, and compatibility with a variety of computing environments. As for REKn, experimentation with the prototype has seen the binary and textual data transferred from the database into the file system, affording gains in manageability and scalability as well as the ability to deploy third-party index and search tools.

This article offers a brief outline of the development of both REKn and PReE at the Electronic Textual Cultures Laboratory (ETCL) at the University of Victoria, from proof of concept through to their current iterations, concluding with a discussion about their future adaptations, implementations, and integrations with other projects and partnerships. This narrative situates REKn and PReE within the context of prototyping as a research activity, and documents the life cycle of a complex digital humanities research program that is itself part of larger, ongoing, iterative programs of research.[2]

Conceptual Backgrounds

The conceptual origins of REKn may be located in two fundamental shifts in literary studies in the 1980s — the emergence of New Historicism and the rise of the sociology of the text — and in the proliferation of large-scale text-corpus humanities computing projects in the late 1980s and early 1990s.

New Historicism

New Historicism situated itself in opposition to earlier critical traditions that dismissed historical and cultural context as irrelevant to literary study, and proposed instead that "literature exists not in isolation from social questions but as a dynamic participant in the messy processes of cultural formation." Thus, New Historicism eschewed the distinction between text and context, arguing that

---

[2] Much of the content of the present article has been presented in other forms elsewhere. See Appendix 1 for a list of addresses and presentations from which the present article is drawn. Appendix 1 can be found as part of the longer article, available online here: http://cnx.org/content/m34336/latest/.

both "are equal partners in the production of culture" (Hall 2007: vii). In Renaissance studies, as elsewhere, this ideological shift challenged scholars to engage not only with the traditional canon of literary works but also with the whole corpus of primary materials at their disposal. As New Historicism blurred the lines between the literary and non-literary, its proponents were quick to illustrate that all cultural forms — literary and non-literary, textual and visual — could be freely and fruitfully "read" alongside and against one another.[3]

The Sociology of Text

A concurrent paradigm shift in bibliographical circles was the rise of the social theory of text, exemplified in the works of Jerome J. McGann (1983) and D. F. McKenzie (1986). "If the work is not confined to the historically contingent and the particular," the social theory of text posited, "it is nevertheless only in its expressive textual form that we encounter it, and material conditions determine meanings" (Sutherland 1997: 5). In addition to being "an argument against the notion that the physical book is the disposable container," as Kathryn Sutherland has suggested, "it is also an argument in favor of the significance of the text as a situated act or event, and therefore, under the conditions of its reproduction, necessarily multiple" (1997: 6).

In other words, the social theory of text rejected the notion of individual literary authority in favor of a model where social processes of production disperse that authority. According to this view, the literary "text" is not solely the product of authorial intention, but the result of interventions by many agents (such as copyists, printers, publishers) and material processes (such as revision, adaptation, publication). In practical terms, the social theory of text revised the role of the textual scholar and editor, who (no longer concerned with authorial intention) instead focused on recovering the "social history" of a text — that is, the multiple and variable forms of a text that emerge out of these various and varied processes of mediation, revision, and adaptation.[4]

---

[3] It is outside the purview of this article to evaluate the claims of New Historicism. Interested readers are directed to the following early critical assessments of New Historicism: Erickson (1987), Howard (1986), and Pechter (1987).

[4] As with New Historicism, it is outside the purview of this article to critically evaluate the claims of social textual theory. Interested readers are directed to critical assessments by Tanselle (1991) and Greetham (1999: 397–418).

Knowledgebases

The proliferation of Renaissance text-corpus humanities computing projects in North America, Europe, and New Zealand during the late 1980s and early 1990s[5] might be considered the inevitable result of the desire of Renaissance scholars, spurred on by the project of New Historicism, to engage with a vast body of primary and secondary materials in addition to the traditional canon of literary works; the rise of the sociology of text in bibliographical circles; and the growing realization that textual analysis, interpretation, and synthesis might be pursued with greater ease and accuracy through the use of an integrated electronic database.

A group of scholars involved in such projects, recognizing the value of collaboration and centralized coordination, engaged in a planning meeting towards the creation of a Renaissance Knowledge Base (RKB).[6] Consisting of "the major texts and reference materials [...] recognized as critical to Renaissance scholarship,"[7] the RKB hoped to "deliver unedited primary texts," to "allow users to search a variety of primary and secondary materials simultaneously," and to stimulate "interpretations by making connections among many kinds of texts" (Richardson and Neuman 1990: 1–2). Addressing the question of "Who needs RKB?" the application offered the following response:

> Lexicographers [need the RKB] in order to revise historical dictionaries (the *Oxford English Dictionary*, for example, is based on citation slips, not on the original texts). Literary critics need it, because the RKB will reveal connections among Renaissance works, new characteristics, and nuances of meaning that only a lifetime of directed reading could hope to provide.

---

[5] Representative examples include: the Women Writers Project; the Century of Prose Corpus; the Early Modern English Dictionaries Database; the Michigan Early Modern English Materials; the Oxford Text Archive; the Riverside STC Project; Shakespeare Database Project; and the *Textbase of Early Tudor English*.

[6] Richardson and Neuman (1990). In addition to the authors of the application itself, other investigators involved with the group included David A. Bank, Jonquil Bevan, Lou Burnard, Thomas N. Corns, Michael Crump, R. J. Fehrenback, Alistair Fox, Roy Flannagan, S. K. Heniger Jr., Arthur F. Kinney, Ian Lancashire, George M. Logan, Willard McCarty, Louis T. Milic, Barbara Mowat, Joachim Neuhaus, Michael Neuman, Henry Snyder, Frank Tompa, and Greg Waite.

[7] As outlined in the application, the materials intended for inclusion and integration in the RKB were "old-spelling texts of major authors (Sidney, Marlowe, Spenser, Shakespeare, Jonson, Donne, Milton, etc.), the *Short-Title Catalogue* (1475–1640), the *Dictionary of National Biography*, period dictionaries (Florio, Elyot, Cotgrave, etc.), and the *Oxford English Dictionary*" (Richardson and Neuman 1990: 2).

> Historians need the RKB, because it will let them move easily, for example,
> from biography to textual information. The same may be said of scholars
> in linguistics, Reformation theology, humanistic philosophy, rhetoric, and
> socio-cultural studies, among others. (1990: 2)

The need for such a knowledgebase was (and is) clear. Since each of its individual
components was deemed "critical to Renaissance scholarship," and because the
RKB intended to "permit each potentially to shed light on all the others," the
group behind the RKB felt that "the whole" was "likely to be far greater than the
sum of its already-important parts" (1990: 2).

Recommendations following the initiative's proposal suggested a positive
path, drawing attention to the merit of the approach and suggesting further ways
to bring about the creation of this resource to meet the research needs of an even
larger group of Renaissance scholars. Many of the scholars involved persevered,
organizing an open meeting on the RKB at the 1991 ACH/ALLC Conference in
Tempe to determine the next course of action. Also present at that session were
Eric Calaluca (Chadwyck-Healy), Mark Rooks (InteLex), and Patricia Murphy,
all of whom proposed to digitize large quantities of primary materials from the
English Renaissance.

From here, the RKB project as originally conceived took new (and largely
unforeseen) directions. Chadwyck-Healy was to transcribe books from the *Cambridge Bibliography of English Literature* and publish various full-text databases
now combined as *Literature Online*. InteLex was to publish its *Past Masters* series
of full-text humanities databases, first on floppy disk and CD-ROM and now
web-based. Murphy's project to scan and transcribe large numbers of books in
the *Short-Title Catalogue* to machine-readable form was taken up by *Early English Books Online* and later the *Text Creation Partnership*. In the decade since
the scholars behind the RKB project first identified the need for a knowledgebase of Renaissance materials, its essential components and methodology have
been outlined (Lancashire 1992). Moreover, considerable related work was soon
to follow, some by the principals of the RKB project and much by those beyond
it, such as R. S. Bear (*Renascence Editions*), Michael Best (*Internet Shakespeare
Editions*), Gregory Crane (*Perseus Digital Library*), Patricia Fumerton (*English
Broadside Ballad Archive*), Ian Lancashire (*Lexicons of Early Modern English*),
and Greg Waite (*Textbase of Early Tudor English*); by commercial publishers such
as Adam Matthew Digital (*Defining Gender, 1450–1910*; *Empire Online*; *Leeds
Literary Manuscripts*; *Perdita Manuscripts*; *Slavery, Abolition and Social Justice, 1490–2007*; *Virginia Company Archives*), Chadwyck-Healy (*Literature Online*), and Gale (*British Literary Manuscripts Online, c.1660–c.1900*; *State Papers*

Online, 1509–1714), and by consortia such as *Early English Books Online–Text Creation Partnership* (University of Michigan, Oxford University, the Council of Library and Information Resources, and ProQuest) and *Orlando* (Cambridge University Press and University of Alberta).

As part of the shift from print to electronic publication and archiving, work on digitizing necessary secondary research materials has been handled chiefly, but not exclusively, by academic and commercial publishers. Among others, these include Blackwell (*Synergy*), Cambridge University Press, Duke University Press (*eDuke*), eBook Library (*EBL*), EBSCO (*EBSCOhost*), Gale (*Shakespeare Collection*), Google (*Google Book Search*), Ingenta, JSTOR, netLibrary, Oxford University Press, Project MUSE, ProQuest (*Periodicals Archive Online*), Taylor & Francis, and University of California Press (*Caliber*). Secondary research materials are also being provided in the form of (1) open access databases, such as the *Database of Early English Playbooks* (Alan B. Farmer and Zachary Lesser), the *English Short Title Catalogue* (British Library, Bibliographical Society, and the Modern Language Association of America), and the *REED Patrons and Performance Web Site* (Records of Early English Drama and the University of Toronto); (2) open access scholarly journals, such as those involved in the *Public Knowledge Project* or others listed on the *Directory of Open Access Journals*; and (3) printed books actively digitized by libraries, independently and in collaboration with organizations such as Google (*Google Book Search*) or the Internet Archive (*Open Access Text Archive*).

Even with this sizeable amount of work on primary and secondary materials accomplished or underway, a compendium of such materials is currently unavailable, and, even if it were available, there is no system in place to facilitate navigation and dynamic interaction with these materials by the user (much as one might query a database) and by machine (with the query process automated or semi-automated for the user). There are, undoubtedly, benefits in bringing all of these disparate materials together with an integrated knowledgebase approach. Doing so would facilitate more efficient professional engagement with these materials, offering scholars a more convenient, faster, and deeper handling of research resources. For example, a knowledgebase approach would remove the need to search across multiple databases and listings, facilitate searching across primary and secondary materials simultaneously, and allow deeper, full-text searching of all records, rather than relying on indexing information alone — which is often not generated by someone with field-specific knowledge. An integrated knowledgebase — whether that integration were actual (all files stored in a single repository) or virtual (access through a portal that searches the distributed files) — would also encourage new insights, allowing researchers new ways to consider relations between texts and materials and their professional, analytical contexts. This is accomplished by facilitating conceptual and thematic searches across all pertinent materials, via the incorporation of advanced computing search and analysis tools that assist in capturing connections between the original objects of contemplation (primary materials) and the professional literature about them (secondary materials).

Critical Contexts

Knowledge Representation

Other important critical contexts within which REKn is situated arise out of theories and methodologies associated with the emerging field of digital humanities. When considering a definition of the field, Willard McCarty warns that we cannot "rest content with the comfortably simple definition of humanities computing as *the application of the computer to the disciplines of the humanities*," for to do so "fails us by deleting the agent-scholar from the scene" and "by overlooking the mediation of thought that his or her use of the computer implies" (1998: n. pag.). After McCarty, Ray Siemens and Christian Vandendorpe suggest that digital humanities or "humanities computing" as a research area "is best defined loosely, as the intersection of computational methods and humanities scholarship" (2006: xii).[8]

A foundation for current work in humanities computing is *knowledge representation*, which John Unsworth has described as an "interdisciplinary methodology that combines logic and ontology to produce models of human understanding that are tractable to computation" (2001: n. pag.). While fundamentally based on digital algorithms, as Unsworth has noted, *knowledge representation* privileges traditionally held values associated with the liberal arts and humanities, namely: general intelligence about human pursuits and the human social/societal environment; adaptable, creative, analytical thinking; critical reasoning, argument, and logic; and the employment and conveyance of these in and through human communicative processes (verbal and non-verbal communication) and other processes native to the humanities (publication, presentation, dissemination). With respect to the activities of the computing humanist, Siemens and Vandendorpe suggest that *knowledge representation* "manifests itself in issues related to archival representation and textual editing, high-level interpretive

---

[8] See also Rockwell (1999).

theory and criticism, and protocols of knowledge transfer — all as modeled with computational techniques" (2006: xii).

Professional Reading and Modeling

A primary protocol of knowledge transfer in the field of the humanities is reading. However, there is a substantial difference between the reading practices of humanists and those readers outside of academe — put simply, humanists are professional readers. As John Guillory has suggested, there are four characteristics of professional reading that distinguish it from the practice of lay reading:

> First of all, it is a kind of *work*, a labor requiring large amounts of time and resources. This labor is compensated as such, by a salary. Second, it is a *disciplinary* activity, that is, it is governed by conventions of interpretation and protocols of research developed over many decades. These techniques take years to acquire; otherwise we would not award higher degrees to those who succeed in mastering them. Third, professional reading is *vigilant*; it stands back from the experience of pleasure in reading [...] so that the experience of reading does not begin and end in the pleasure of consumption, but gives rise to a certain sustained reflection. And fourth, this reading is a *communal* practice. Even when the scholar reads in privacy, this act of reading is connected in numerous ways to communal scenes; and it is often dedicated to the end of a public and publishable "reading" (2000: 31–32).

Much recent work in the digital humanities has focused on modeling professional reading and other activities associated with conducting and disseminating humanities research.[9] Modeling the activities of the humanist (and the output of humanistic achievement) with the assistance of the computer has identified the exemplary tasks associated with humanities computing: the representation of archival materials; analysis or critical inquiry originating in those materials; and the communication of the results of these tasks.[10] As computing humanists, we assume that all of these elements are inseparable and interrelated, and that all processes can be facilitated electronically.

---

[9] On the importance of reading as an object of interest to humanities computing practitioners and a brief discussion of representative examples, see Warwick (2004). For a discussion of professional reading tools, see Siemens et al. (2006); and the forthcoming "It May Change My Understanding of the Field."

[10] On modeling in the humanities, see McCarty (2004). On modeling as it pertains to literary studies in particular, see McCarty (2008).

Each of these tasks will be described in turn. In reverse order, the communication of results involves the electronic dissemination of, and electronically facilitated interaction about the product of, archival representation and critical inquiry, as well as the digitization of materials previously stored in other archival forms.[11] Communication of results takes place via codified professional interaction, and is traditionally held to include all contributions to a discipline-centered body of knowledge — that is, all activities that are captured in the scholarly record associated with the shared pursuits of a particular field. In addition to those academic and commercial publishers and publication amalgamator services delivering content electronically, pertinent examples of projects concerned with the communication of results include the *Open Journal Systems* and *Open Monograph Press* (Public Knowledge Project) and *Collex* (NINES), as well as services provided by Synergies and the Canadian Research Knowledge Network / Réseau Canadien de Documentation pour la Recherche (CRKN/RCDR).

Critical inquiry involves the application of algorithmically facilitated search, retrieval, and critical processes that, although originating in humanities-based work, have been demonstrated to have application far beyond.[12] Associated with critical theory, this area is typified by interpretive studies that assist in our intellectual and aesthetic understanding of humanistic works, and it involves the application (and applicability) of critical and interpretive tools and analytic algorithms on digitally represented texts and artifacts. Pertinent examples include applications such as *Juxta* (NINES), as well as tools developed by the Text Analysis Portal for Research (TAPoR) project, the Metadata Offer New Knowledge (MONK) project, the Software Environment for the Advancement of Scholarly Research (SEASR), and by Many Eyes (IBM).

Archival representation involves the use of computer-assisted means to describe and express print-, visual-, and audio-based material in tagged and searchable electronic form. Associated as it is with the critical methodologies that govern our representation of original artifacts, archival representation is chiefly bibliographical in nature and often involves the reproduction of primary materials such as in the preparation of an electronic edition or digital facsimile.[13] Key issues in archival representation include considerations of the modeling of

---

[11] See Miall (2001).

[12] Representative examples include Lancashire (1995) and Fortier (1993–94).

[13] For a detailed discussion of electronic archival forms, see Hockey (2000). In addition to the projects mentioned above (such as the English Broadside Ballad Archive) and others, pertinent examples of projects concerned with archival representation include digitization projects undertaken by the Internet Archive and Google, and by libraries, museums, and similar institutions.

objects and processes, the impact of social theories of text on the role and goal of the editor, and the "death of distance."

Ideally, object modeling for archival representation should simulate the original object-artifact, both in terms of basic representation (e.g. a scanned image of a printed page) and functionality (such as the ability to "turn" or otherwise "physically" manipulate the page). However, object modeling need not simply be limited to simulating the original. Although "a play script is a poor substitute for a live performance," Martin Mueller has shown that "however paltry a surrogate the printed text may be, for some purposes it is superior to the 'original' that it replaces" (2005: 61). The next level of simulation beyond the printed surrogate, namely the "digital surrogate," would similarly offer further enhancements to the original. These enhancements might include greater flexibility in the basic representation of the object (such as magnification and otherwise altering its appearance) or its functionality (such as fast and accurate search functions, embedded multimedia, etc.).

Archival representation might then involve modeling the process of interaction between the user and the object-artifact. Simulating the process affords a better understanding of the relationships between the object and the user, particularly as that relationship reveals the user's disciplinary practices — discovering, annotating, comparing, referring, sampling, illustrating, representing.[14]

The Scholarly Edition

The recent convergence of social theories of text and the rise of the electronic medium has had a significant impact on both the function of the scholarly edition and the role of the textual scholar. As Susan Schreibman has argued, "the release from the spatial restrictions of the codex form has profoundly changed the focus of the textual scholar's work," from "publishing a single text with apparatus which has been synthesized and summarized to accommodate to the codex's spatial limitations" to creating "large assemblages of textual and non-textual lexia, presented to readers with as little traditional editorial intervention as possible" (2002: 284). In addition to acknowledging the value of the electronic medium to editing and the edition, such "assemblages" also recognize the critical practice of "unediting," whereby the reader is exposed to the various layers of editorial

---

[14] See Unsworth (2000).

mediation of a given text,[15] as well as an increased awareness of the "materiality" of the text-object under consideration.[16]

Perfectly adaptable to, and properly enabling of, social theories of text and the role of editing, the electronic medium has brought us closer to the textual objects of our contemplation, even though we remain at the same physical distance from them. Like other enabling communicative and representative technologies that came before it, the electronic medium has brought about a "death of distance." This notion of a "death of distance," as discussed by Paul Delany, comes from a world made smaller by travel and communication systems, a world in which we have "the ability to do more things without being physically present at the point of impact" (1997: 50). The textual scholar, accumulating an "assemblage" of textual materials, does so for those materials to be, in turn, re-presented to those who are interested in those materials. More and more, though, it is not only primary materials — textual witnesses, for example — that are being accumulated and re-presented. The "death of distance" applies also to objects that have the potential to shape and inform further our contemplation of those direct objects of our contemplation: namely, the primary materials.[17]

We understand, almost intuitively, the end-product of the traditional scholarly edition in its print codex form: how material is presented, what the scope of that material is, how that material is being related to us and, internally, how the material presented by the edition relates to itself and to materials beyond those directly presented — secondary texts, contextual material, and so forth. Our understanding of these things as they relate to the *electronic* scholarly edition, however, is only just being formed. We are at a critical juncture for the scholarly edition in electronic form, where the "assemblages" and accumulation of textual archival materials associated with social theories of text and the role of editing meet their natural home in the electronic scholarly edition; and such large collections of primary materials in electronic form meet their equivalent in volume in the world of secondary materials, that ever-growing body of scholarship (Siemens 2001: 426).

To date, two models of the electronic scholarly edition have prevailed. One is the notion of the "dynamic text," which consists of an electronic text and integrated advanced textual analysis software. In essence, the dynamic text presents a text that indexes and concords itself and allows the reader to interact with it in

---

[15] On this sense of "unediting," see Marcus (1996); on "unediting" as the rejection of critical editions in preference to the unmediated study of originals or facsimiles, see McLeod (1982).

[16] On the materiality of the Renaissance text, see De Grazia and Stallybrass (1993), and Sutherland (1998).

[17] See also Siemens (2001).

a dynamic fashion, enacting text analysis procedures upon it as it is read.[18] The other, often referred to as the "hypertextual edition," exploits the ability of encoded hypertextual organization to facilitate a reader's interaction with the apparatus (textual, critical, contextual, and so forth) that traditionally accompanies scholarly editions, as well as with relevant external textual and graphical resources, critical materials, and so forth.[19]

Advances over the past decade have made it clear that electronic scholarly editions can in fact enjoy the best of both worlds, incorporating elements from the "dynamic text" model — namely, dynamic interaction with the text and its related materials — while at the same time reaping the benefits of the fixed hypertextual links characteristically found in "hypertextual editions."[20] At present, there is no extant exemplary implementation of this new *dynamic edition*, an edition that transfers the principles of interaction afforded by a dynamic text to the realm of the full edition, comprising of that text and all of its extra- and paratextual materials — textual apparatus, commentary, and beyond.[21]

Prototyping as a Research Activity

In addition to the aforementioned critical contexts, it is equally important to situate the development of REKn and PReE within a methodological context of prototyping as a research activity. The process of prototyping in the context of our work involves constructing a functional computational model that embodies the results of our research, and, as an object of further study itself, undergoes iterative modification in response to research and testing. A prototype in this context is an interface or visualization that embodies the theoretical foundations our work establishes, so that the theory informing the creation of the prototype can itself be tested by having people use it.[22]

Research prototypes, such as those we set out to develop, are distinct from prototypes designed as part of a production system in that the research prototype focuses chiefly on providing limited but research-pertinent functionality

---

[18] Lancashire (1989). See also the exemplary illumination of three early "dynamic text" Shakespeare editions in Bolton (1990).

[19] The elements of the hypertextual edition were rightly anticipated in Faulhaber (1991).

[20] Indeed, scholarly consensus is that the level of dynamic interaction in an electronic edition itself — if facilitated via text analysis in the style of the "dynamic text" — could replace much of the interaction that one typically has with a text and its accompanying materials via explicit hypertextual links in a hypertextual edition.

[21] See the discussion of these issues in Siemens (2005).

[22] For example, see Sinclair and Rockwell (2007); see also the discussion of modeling in this context in McCarty (2004, 2008).

within a larger framework of assumed operation.[23] Production systems, on the other hand, require full functionality and are often derived from multiple prototyping processes.

The Proof of Concept

REKn was originally conceived as part of a wider research project to develop a prototype textual environment for a *dynamic edition*: an electronic scholarly edition that models disciplinary interaction in the humanities, specifically in the areas of archival representation, critical inquiry, and the communication of results. Centered on a highly encoded electronic text, this environment facilitates interaction with the text, with primary and secondary materials related to it, and with scholars who have a professional engagement with those materials. This ongoing research requires (1) the adaptation of an exemplary, highly encoded and properly imaged electronic base text for the edition; (2) the establishment of an extensive knowledgebase to exist in relation to that exemplary base text, composed of primary and secondary materials pertinent to an understanding of the base text and its literary, historical, cultural, and critical contexts;[24] and (3) the development of a system to facilitate navigation and dynamic interaction with and between materials in the edition and in the knowledgebase, incorporating professional reading and analytical tools; to allow those materials to be updated; and to implement communicative tools to facilitate computer-assisted interaction between users engaging with the materials.

The electronic base-text selected to act as the initial focal point for the prototype was drawn from Ray Siemens' SSHRC-funded electronic scholarly edition of the Devonshire Manuscript (BL MS. Add. 17492). Characterized as a "courtly

---

[23] An example of a prototypical tool that performs an integral function in a larger digital reading environment is the Dynamic Table of Contexts, an experimental interface that draws on interpretive document encoding to combine the conventional table of contents with an interactive index. Readers use the Dynamic Table of Contexts as a tool for browsing the document by selecting an entry from the index and seeing where it is placed in the table of contents. Each item also serves as a link to the appropriate point in the file. See Ruecker (2005); Ruecker et al. (2007); and Brown et al. (2007).

[24] An important distinction between REKn and the earlier RKB project is the scope of the primary and secondary materials contained. While RKB set out to include "old-spelling texts of major authors (Sidney, Marlowe, Spenser, Shakespeare, Jonson, Donne, Milton, etc.), the *Short-Title Catalogue* (1475–1640), the *Dictionary of National Biography*, period dictionaries (Florio, Elyot, Cotgrave, etc.), and the *Oxford English Dictionary*" (Richardson and Neuman 1990: 2), REKn is not limited to "major authors" but seeks to include all canonical works (in print and manuscript) and most extra-canonical works (in print) of the period.

anthology" (Southall 1964) and as an "informal volume" (Remley 1994: 48), the Devonshire Manuscript is a poetic miscellany consisting of 114 original leaves, housing some 185 items of verse (complete poems, fragments, extracts from larger extant works, and scribal annotations). Historically privileged in literary history as a key witness of Thomas Wyatt's poetry, the manuscript has received new and significant attention of late, in large part because of the way in which its contents reflect the interactions of poetry and power in early Renaissance England and, more significantly, because it offers one of the earliest examples of the explicit and direct participation of women in the type of literary and political-poetic discourses found in the document.[25]

While editing the Devonshire Manuscript as the base text was underway, work on REKn began by mapping the data structure in relation to the functional requirements of the project, selecting appropriate tools and platforms, and outlining three objectives: to gather and assemble a corpus of primary and secondary texts to make up the knowledgebase; to develop automated methods for data collection; and to develop software tools to facilitate dynamic interaction between the user(s) and the knowledgebase.

Data Structure and Functional Requirements

We felt that the database should include tables to store relations between documents; that is, if a document includes a reference to another document, whether explicitly (such as in a reference or citation) or implicitly (such as in keywords and metadata), the fact of that reference or relation should be stored. Thus, the document-to-document relationship will be a many-to-many relationship.

In addition to a web service for public access to the database, it was proposed that there should be a standalone data entry and maintenance application to allow the user(s) to create, update, and delete database records manually. This application should include tools for filtering markup tags and other formatting characters from documents; allow for automating the data entry of groups of documents; and allow for automating the data entry of documents where they are available from web services, or by querying electronic academic publication amalgamator services (such as *EBSCOhost*).

Finally, a scholarly research application to query the database in read-only mode and display documents — along with metadata where available (such as

---

[25] On the editing of the Devonshire Manuscript in terms of modeling and knowledge representation, see Siemens and Leitch (2008). See also the forthcoming Siemens et al., "Drawing Networks in the Devonshire Manuscript."

author, title, publisher) — was to be developed. The appearance and operation of the application should model the processes of scholarly research, with many related documents visible at the same time, easily moved and grouped by the researcher. The application should display the document in as many different forms as are available — plain text, marked-up text, scanned images, audio clips, and so forth. Users should also be able to easily navigate between related documents; to easily search for documents that have similar words, phrases or word patterns; and to perform text analysis on the document(s) — word list, word frequency, word collocation, word concordance — and display the results.[26]

Gathering Primary and Secondary Materials

The gathering of primary materials for the knowledgebase was initially accomplished by harvesting content from open-access archives of Renaissance texts, and by requesting materials from various partnerships (researchers, publishers, scholarly centers) interested in the project. These materials included a total of some 12,830 texts in the public domain or otherwise generously donated.[27] The harvesting and initial integration of these materials took a year, during which time various file formats were standardized into the same format.

The bulk of the primary material was so substantial that harvesting the secondary materials manually would be too onerous a task — clearly, automated methods were desirable and would allow for continual and ongoing harvesting of new materials as they became available. Ideally, these methods should be general enough in nature so that they can be applied to other types of literature, requiring minimal modification for reuse in other fields. This emphasis on transportability and scalability would ensure that the form and structure of the knowledgebase could be used in other fields of scholarly research.

---

[26] 'Tools and Platforms' are discussed in the larger article, which can be found at section 3.2, http://cnx.org/content/m34335/latest/.

[27] The texts discussed here were donated by the following organizations: EEBO-TCP (9,533), Chadwyck-Healy (1,820), *Text Analysis Computing Tools* (311), the *Early* and *Middle English Collections* from the University of Virginia Electronic Text Centre (273 and 27 respectively), the Brown Women Writers Project (241), the *Oxford Text Archive* (241), the *Early Tudor Textbase* (180), *Renascence Editions* (162), the *Christian Classics Ethereal Library* (65), *Elizabethan Authors* (21), the Norwegian University of Science and Technology (8), the Richard III Society (5), the University of Nebraska School of Music (4), *Project Bartleby* (2), and *Project Gutenberg* (2).

A master list of the primary text titles and their sources is included in the longer article as Appendix 2. It can be accessed at the following URL: http://cnx.org/content/m34337/latest/.

Initially, the strategy was to assemble a sample database of secondary materials in partnership with the University of Victoria Libraries, gathering materials harvested automatically from electronic academic publication amalgamator services (such as *EBSCOhost*). An automated process was developed to retrieve relevant documents and store them in a purpose-built database. This process enabled us to search a number of remote databases, weed out erroneous and duplicate entries, separate metadata from text, and store both in a database. The utility of our harvesting methods would then be demonstrated to the amalgamators and other publishers with the intent of fostering partnerships with them.

Building a Professional Reading Environment

At this stage REKn contained roughly 80 gigabytes of text data, consisting of some 12,830 primary text documents and an ongoing collection of secondary texts in excess of 80,000 documents. Text data in the knowledgebase was roughly 80 gigabytes; text and image data combined was estimated to be in the two to three terabyte range. Given its immense scale, development of a document viewer with analytical and communicative functionality to interact with REKn was a pressing issue. The inability of existing tools to accurately search, navigate, and read large collections of data in many formats, later coupled with the findings of our research into professional reading, led to the development of a Professional Reading Environment (PReE) to meet these needs.

The first proof of concept included a number of useful features. Individual users were able to log in, open as many separate instances of the graphical user interface (GUI) as they desired, and perform search, reading, analytical, composition, and communication functions. These functions were drawn on our modeling of professional reading and other activities associated with conducting and disseminating humanities research. Searches could be conducted on document metadata and citations (by author, title, and keyword) for both primary and secondary materials (Figure 1). A selected word or phrase could also spawn a search of documents within the knowledgebase, as well as a search of other Internet resources (such as the *Oxford English Dictionary Online* and *Lexicons of Early Modern English*) from within PReE. Similarly, the user could use TAPoR Tools to perform analyses on the current text or selected words and phrases in PReE (Figure 2).

The proof-of-concept build could display text data in a variety of forms (plain-text, HTML, and PDF) and display images of various formats (Figures 3 and 4). Users could zoom in and out when viewing images, and scale the display when viewing texts (Figure 5). If REKn contained different versions of an

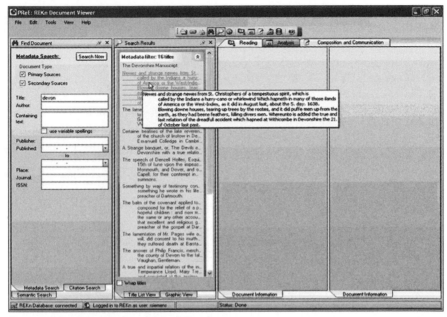

Figure 1. Metadata Search and Search Results

Figure 2. Spawned Search and Analytical Functions

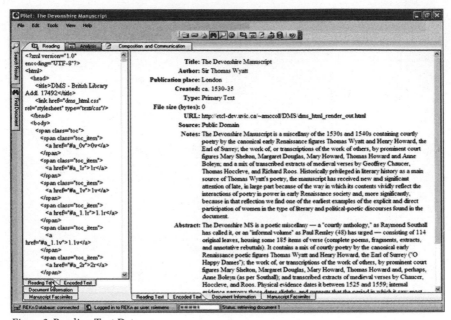

Figure 3. Reading Text Data

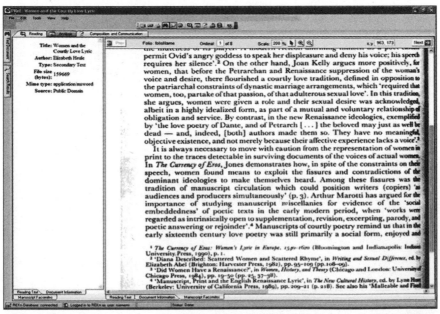

Figure 4. PDF Display

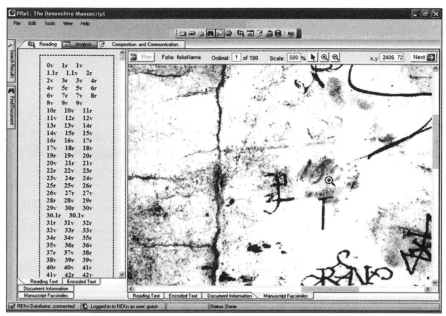

Figure 5. Zoom and Pan Images

object — such as images, transcriptions, translations — they were linked together in PReE, allowing users to view an image and corresponding text data side-by-side (Figure 6).

This initial version of PReE also offered composition and communication functions, such as the ability for a user to select a portion of an image or text and to save this to a workflow, or the capacity to create and store notes for later use. Users were also able to track their own usage and document views, which could then be saved to the workflow for later use. Similarly, administrators were able to track user access and use of the knowledgebase materials, which might be of interest to content partners (such as academic and commercial publishers) wishing to use the data for statistical analysis.

A demonstration of REKn/PReE proof of concept is available as **Movie 1** in the longer version of this article. To view it, go to the following URL: http://cnx.org/content/m34335/latest/#movie1.

Research Prototypes: Challenges and Experiments

After the success of our proof of concept, we set out to imagine the next steps of modeling as part of our research program. Indeed, growing interest amongst

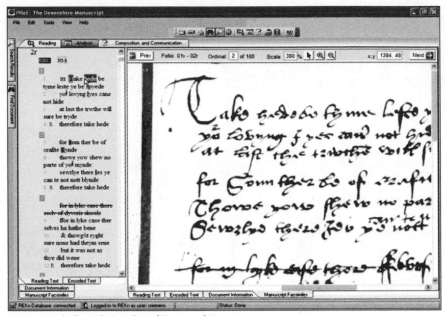

Figure 6. Side-by-Side Display of Texts and Images

knowledge providers in applying the concept of a professional reading environment to their databases and similar resources brought us to consider how to expand PReE beyond the confines of REKn. After evaluating our progress to date, we realized that we needed to take what we had learned from the proof of concept and apply that knowledge to new challenges and requirements. Our key focus would be on issues of scalability, functionality, and maintainability.

Challenge: Scalable Data Storage

In the proof-of-concept build, all REKn data was stored in a database. While this approach had the benefit of keeping all of the data in one easily accessible place, it raised a number of concerns — most pressingly, the issue of scalability. Dealing with several hundred gigabytes is manageable with local infrastructure and ordinary tools. However, we realized that we had to reconsider the tools when dealing in the range of several terabytes. Careful consideration would also have to be given to indexing and other operations which might require exponentially longer processing times as the database increased in size.

Even with a good infrastructure, practical limitations on database content are still an important consideration, especially were we to include large corpora (the larger datasets of the Canadian Research Knowledge Network were discussed, for example) or significant sections of the Internet. Setting practical limitations required us to consider what was essential and what needed to be stored — for example, did we have to store an entire document, or could it be simply a URL? Storing all REKn data in a database during the proof-of-concept stage posed additional concerns. Incremental backups of the database required more complicated programming to identify new data that had been added since the previous backup. Full backups would require exporting all of the data in the database, a server-intensive process. This, of course, could present performance issues should the total database size reach the terabyte range.

Indexing full text in a relational database does not give optimum performance or results: in fact, the performance degradation could be described as exponential in relation to the size of the database. Keeping both advantages and disadvantages in mind, it was proposed that all REKn data be stored in a file system rather than in the database. File systems are designed to store files, whereas the database is designed to store information about the relationships between files. To mix the two approaches defeats the advantages of each. Moreover, in testing the proof of concept, users found speed to be a significant issue. Many were unwilling to wait five minutes between operations. In its proof-of-concept iteration, the computing interaction simply could not keep pace with the cognitive functions it was intended to augment and assist. We recognized that this issue could be resolved in the future by recourse to high-performance computing techniques. In the meantime, we decided to reduce the REKn data to a subset, which would allow us to imagine and work on functionality at a smaller scale.

Challenge: Document Harvesting

The question of how to go about harvesting data for REKn, or indeed any content-specific knowledgebase, turned out to be a question of negotiating with the suppliers of document collections for permission to copy the documents. Since each of these suppliers (such as the academic and commercial publishers and the publication amalgamator service providers) has structured access to the documents differently, harvesting those documents would require tailored programming for each supplier. Designing an automated process for harvesting documents from suppliers could be accomplished by combining all of these program variations together with a mechanism for automatically detecting the custom access requirements in a given case and customizing the program accordingly.

Experiment: Shakespeare's Sonnets

As outlined above, to facilitate faster prototyping and development of both REKn and PReE it was proposed that REKn should be reduced to a limited dataset. Work was already underway on an electronic edition of Shakespeare's Sonnets, so limiting REKn data to materials related to the Sonnets would offer a more manageable dataset.

Modern print editions of the Sonnets admirably serve the needs of lay readers. For professional readers, however, print editions simply cannot hope to offer an exhaustive and authoritative engagement with the critical literature surrounding the Sonnets, a body of scholarship that is continually growing. Even with the considerable assistance provided by such tools as the World Shakespeare Bibliography and the MLA International Bibliography, the sheer volume of scholarship published on Shakespeare and his works is difficult to navigate. Indeed, existing databases such as these only allow the user to search for criticism related to the Sonnets through a limited set of metadata, selected and presented in each database according to different editorial priorities, and often by those without domain-specific expertise. Moreover, while select bibliographies such as these have often helped to organize specific areas of inquiry, the last attempt to compile a comprehensive bibliography of scholarly material on Shakespeare's Sonnets was produced by Tetsumaro Hayashi in 1972. Although it remains an invaluable resource in indicating the volume and broad outlines of Sonnet criticism, Hayashi's bibliography is unable to provide the particularity and responsiveness of a tool that accesses the entire text of the critical materials it seeks to organize.

Without the restrictions of print, an electronic edition of Shakespeare's Sonnets could be both responsive to the evolution of the field, updating itself periodically to incorporate new research, and more flexible in the ways in which it allows users to navigate and explore this accumulated knowledge. Incorporating the research already undertaken toward an edition of Shakespeare's Sonnets, we sought to create a prototype knowledgebase of critical materials reflecting the scholarly engagement with Shakespeare's Sonnets from 1972 to the present day.

The first step required the acquirement of materials to add to the knowledgebase. A master list of materials was compiled through consultation with existing electronic bibliographies (such as the *MLA International Bibliography* and the *World Shakespeare Bibliography*) and standard print resources (such as the *Year's Work in English Studies*). Criteria were established to dictate which materials were to be included in the knowledgebase. To limit the scope of the experiment, materials published before 1972 (and thus considered already in Hayashi's bibliography) were excluded. It was also decided to exclude works pertaining to translations of the Sonnets, performances of the Sonnets, and non-academic discussions of the Sonnets. Monograph-length discussions of the Sonnets were also excluded on the basis that they were too unwieldy for the purposes of an experiment.

The next step was to gather the materials itemized on the master list. Although a large number of these materials were available in electronic form, and therefore much easier to collect, the various academic and commercial publishers and publication amalgamator service providers delivered the materials in different file formats. A workable standard would be required, and it was decided that regularizing all of the data into Rich Text format would preserve text formatting and relative location, and allow for any illustrations included to be embedded. Articles available only in image formats were fed through an Optical Character Recognition (OCR) application and saved in Rich Text format. Materials unavailable in electronic form were collected, photocopied, and scanned. The images were then processed through an OCR application and saved in Rich Text format.

The next step will involve applying a light common encoding structure on all of the Rich Text files and importing them into REKn. The resulting knowledgebase will be responsive to full-text electronic searches, allowing the user to uncover swiftly, for example, all references to a particular sonnet. License agreements and copyright restrictions will not allow us to make access to the knowledgebase public. However, we will be exploring a number of possible output formats that could be shared with the larger research community. Possibilities might include the use of the Sonnet knowledgebase to generate indices, concordances, or even an exhaustive annotated bibliography. For example, a dynamic index could be developed to query the full-text database and return results in the form of bibliographical citations. Since many users will come from institutions with online access to some or most of the journals, and with library access to others, these indices will serve as a valuable resource for further research.

Ideally, such endeavors will mean the reassessment of the initial exclusion criteria for knowledgebase materials. The increasing number of books published and republished in electronic format, for example, means that the inclusion of monograph-length studies of the Sonnets is no longer a task so onerous as to be prohibitive. Indeed, large-scale digitization projects such as Google Books and the Internet Archive are also making a growing number of books, both old and new, available in digital form.

Experiment: The REKn Crawler

We recognized that the next stages of our work would be predicated on the ability to create topic- or domain-specific knowledgebases from electronic materials. The work, then, pointed to the need for a better Internet resource discovery system, one that allowed topic-specific harvesting of Internet-based data, returning results pertinent to targeted knowledge domains, and that integrated with existing collections of materials (such as REKn) operating in existing reading systems (such as PReE), in order to take advantage of the functionality of existing tools in relation to the results. To investigate this further, we collaborated with Iter, a not-for-profit partnership created to develop and support electronic resources to assist scholars studying European culture from 400 to 1700 CE.[28]

Premises

We thought we could use existing technologies, such as Nutch, combined with models from more complex harvesters (such as *Data Fountains* and the *Nalanda iVia Focused Crawler*)[29] to create something that would suit our purposes and be freely distributable and transportable among our several partners and their work. In using such technologies, we hoped also to explore how best to exploit representations of ontological structures found in bibliographic databases to ensure that the material returned via Internet searches was reliably on-topic.

Method

The underlying method for the prototype REKn Crawler is quite straightforward. An Iter search returns bibliographic (MARC) records, which in turn provide the metadata (such as author, title, subject) to conduct a web search, the results of which are returned to the knowledgebase. In the end, the original corpus is complemented by a collection of pages from the web that are related to the same subject. While all of these web materials may not be directly relevant, they may still be useful.

The method ensures accuracy, scalability, and utility. Accuracy is ensured insofar as the results are disambiguated by comparison against Iter's bibliographic records — that is, via a process of domain-specific ontological structures. Scalability is ensured in that individual searches can be automatically sequenced, drawing bibliographic records from Iter one at a time to ensure that the harvester covers all parts of an identified knowledge domain. Utility is ensured because the resultant materials are drawn into the reading system and bibliographic records are created.

---

[28] On the mandate, history, and development of Iter, see Bowen (2000, 2008). For a more detailed report on this collaborative experiment, see Siemens et al. (2006).

[29] See also Mitchell (2006).

The method described above is illustrated in the following example: A user views a document in PReE; for instance, Edelgard E. DuBruck, "Changes of Taste and Audience Expectation in Fifteenth-Century Religious Drama."[30] Viewing this document triggers the Crawler, which begins processing the document's Iter MARC metadata (record number, keywords, author, title, subject headings). Search strings are then generated from this data.[31] The Crawler conducts searches with these strings and stores them for the later process of weeding out erroneous returns.

In the example given above, which took under an hour, the Crawler generated 291 unique results to add to the knowledgebase relating to the article and its subject matter. In our current development environment, the Crawler is able to harvest approximately 35,000 unique web pages in a day. We are currently experimenting with a larger seed set of 10,000 MARC records, which still amounts to only 1% of Iter's available bibliographical data.

The use of the REKn Crawler in conjunction with both REKn and PReE suggests some interesting applications, such as: increasing the scope and size of the knowledgebase; being able to analyze the results of the Crawler's harvesting to discover document metadata and document ontology; and harvesting blogs and wikis for community knowledge on any given topic, and well beyond.

Moving into Full Prototype Development: New Directions

Rebuilding

Our rebuilding process was primarily driven by the questions generated from our earlier proof of concept. The proof of concept pointed us toward a web-based user interface to meet the needs of the research community. Building human knowledge into our application also becomes more feasible with a web environment, since we can depend on a centralized storage system and an ability to easily share information. The proof of concept also suggested that we rethink our document storage framework, since exponential decline of full-text searching speed

---

[30] DuBruck (1983).

[31] In this particular instance the search strings will include: DuBruck, Edelgard E.; DuBruck, Edelgard E. Changes of Taste and Audience Expectation in Fifteenth-Century Religious Drama; DuBruck, Edelgard E. Religious drama, French; DuBruck, Edelgard E. Religious drama, French, History and criticism; Changes of Taste and Audience Expectation in Fifteenth-Century Religious Drama; Religious drama, French; Religious drama, French, History and criticism.

quickly renders the tool dysfunctional in environments with millions of documents. For long-term scalability a new approach was needed.

We decided to focus on moving toward a web-based environment for the tool. This approach will allow us, among other things, to add new features via "plug-ins" that can be layered on top of the existing infrastructure (rather than requiring us to rebuild again). In this way, we will have the agility to respond to emerging ideas and visions, such as "Web 2.0" and social networking tools.[32]

New Directions: Social Networking

Users are beginning to expect more from web applications than ever before. Social networking tools and the "Web 2.0" pattern of design has given web application developers many new ways of building knowledge into their applications. By adopting a web-application model for PReE, we could tie into existing social networking tools and begin to innovate with the creation of new tools designed specifically for the professional reader. The decision to include social networking capabilities in the PReE design was based on research conducted by the Public Knowledge Project (PKP) into the reading strategies of domain-expert readers (a subset of professional readers).[33] Like PReE, the goal for the reading tools developed by PKP was to provide access to research and scholarship and to support critical engagement with those materials. During interviews conducted by PKP and ETCL researchers, expert readers identified the ability to communicate with other researchers as an important benefit of an online reading environment. These readers also expressed interest in contextual information that would help them judge the value of an author's work. From these observations, researchers concluded that future online reading environments would need to provide the kind of communication and profile-management features currently offered by social networking tools.

Before adding social networking components to the PReE features list, we researched existing social networking tools and their use by expert readers (Leitch et al. 2008). Based on evidence gathered during the PKP study we determined that as expert readers became adept at using online tools, they would demand a higher level of sophistication from an online reading environment. In order to

---

[32] The decision to move PReE to a web-based environment was followed by a a survey of the relevant applications, platforms, and technologies in terms of their applicability, functionality, and limitations. The results of that survey can be found in Appendix 3 in the longer version of this paper, and is available at http://cnx.org/content/m34338/latest/.

[33] See Siemens et al. (2006) and "It May Change My Understanding of the Field," forthcoming.

respond to this increasing awareness of the potential of social networking tools for scholarly research, a successful online reading environment should integrate social networking tools in such a way that it extends the readers' existing research strategies. We identified three key strategies that readers used as part of their research: *evaluating, communicating,* and *managing.* Our survey found that no single social networking tool supported all three of these strategies. An environment able to facilitate all three strategies would be of immense value to the expert reader, who would not be forced to use a variety of disjointed social networking tools. Instead, he or she would be able to perform the same tasks from within the reading environment.

How could we incorporate these findings into PReE? In answering that question we were effectively reconceptualizing PReE as *social software,* "loosely defined" by Tom Coates as software that "supports, extends, or derives added value from, human social behaviour" (2005: n. pag.). If we could outline the common elements of the social networking tools we wished to incorporate, the task of combining them could be more streamlined. For Ralph Gross and Alessandro Acquisti, the feature common to all social networking applications is the ability to create a user-generated *identity* (or "profile") for other users to peruse "with the intention of contacting or being contacted by others" (2005: 71). Acknowledging the importance of identity, Judith Donath and danah boyd have proposed that "a core set of assumptions" underlie all social networking applications, all of which emphasize the notion of making *connections,* that "there is a need for people to make more connections, that using a network of existing connections is the best way to do so, and that making this easy to do is a great benefit" (2004: 71).

Identity and Evaluation

The "Digital Footprints" report prepared by the Pew Internet and American Life Project found that "one in ten internet users have a job that requires them to self-promote or market their name online," and that "voluntarily posted text, images, audio, and video has become a cornerstone of engagement with Web 2.0 applications" to the point that "being 'findable and knowable' online is often considered an asset in participatory culture where one's personal reputation is increasingly influenced by information others encounter online" (Madden et al. 2007: iii, 4). Similar assertions have been made by other scholars: Andreas Girgensohn and Alison Lee suggest that one of the benefits of creating an maintaining a profile on a social networking site is the opportunity to create a "persistent and verifiable identity" (2002: 137), whereas danah boyd and Nicole B. Ellison note that "what makes social network sites unique is not that they allow individuals to meet strangers, but rather that they enable users to articulate and make visible their social networks" (2007: n. pag.).

Given the importance expert readers place on markers of authority such as credentials and past publications, it is in the individual's best interest to exert some control over his or her online identity. The ability to create and maintain an online profile as part of PReE allows users to include the kind of information expert readers look for when evaluating the value of research material.

Connections and Communication

Expert readers learn about new ideas and develop existing ones by engaging in scholarly communication with their peers and colleagues. Online, these readers participate in discussion forums, mailing lists, and use commenting tools on blogs and other social networking sites. As Kathleen Fitzpatrick observes:

> Scholars operate in a range of conversations, from classroom conversations with students to conference conversations with colleagues; scholars need to have available to them not simply the library model of texts circulating amongst individual readers but also the coffee house model of public reading and debate. This interconnection of individual nodes into a collective fabric is, of course, the strength of the network, which not only physically binds individual machines but also has the ability to bring together the users of those machines, at their separate workstations, into one communal whole. (2007: n. pag.)

Likewise, Christopher M. Hoadley and Peter G. Kilner have asserted that *conversation* is the method by which information becomes knowledge, suggesting that "knowledge-building communities are a particular kind of community of practice focused on learning," where the "explicit goal [is] the development of individual and collective understanding" (2005: 32). Adopting this definition, PReE models a knowledge-building community of practice by combining content with communication through the use of social networking tools.

User and Content Management

Searching, retrieving, classifying, and organizing research material is a primary activity of professional readers. Expert readers employ a variety of strategies ranging from simple filing systems to elaborate systems of classification and storage. Reference management tools allow users to find, store, and organize research materials online. The use of *folksonomy* tagging in reference management tools can improve on a reader's existing research strategies by providing him or her with a flexible and easily accessible way of organizing research according to his or her own criteria.[34] These tools also allow users to share research collections with colleagues and find material relevant to their interests in other collections. Moreover, as Bryan Alexander has observed, social bookmarking functions in a higher education context as a tool for "collaborative information discovery" (2006: 36). As Alexander suggests, "finding people with related interests" through social bookmarking "can magnify one's work by learning from others or by leading to new collaborations," and that "the practice of user-created tagging can offer new perspectives on one's research, as clusters of tags reveal patterns (or absences) not immediately visible" (2006: 36). User incentives for tagging include the ability to quickly retrieve research material, to share relevant material with colleagues, and to express an opinion or make a public statement about one's interests (Marlow et al. 2006: 34–35). The planned inclusion of similar tools in PReE extends expert readers' existing management strategies by simplifying the organization process and creating new opportunities for collaborative categorization.

Designing the PReE Interface

When the original interface was designed for the proof of concept of REKn, very little consideration was given to further use of the code. The focus was solely on producing a down-and-dirty prototype. The decision to translate PReE from a desktop application to a web application promised a whole host of new benefits: superior flexibility in application deployment and maintenance, the ability to receive and disseminate user-generated content, and multi-platform compatibility. These new benefits, however, came with new challenges.

Migrating the application from desktop to Internet also offered us an opportunity to completely rethink the appearance and functionality of the interface. This gave us the chance to consult with prominent researchers working in the field of professional reading and designing such interfaces, as well as the opportunity to conduct our own usability surveys in order to better accommodate professional readers of various disciplinary backgrounds and levels of expertise.

---

[34] For the origin of the term folksonomy and its use to describe the practice of socially derived content tagging, see Vander Wal (2007).

User Needs: Analyzing the Audience

Before embarking on a new interface design, it was pertinent to identify the features and functions that users would expect and desire from PReE. Surveys and interviews were conducted, and the results led to our distinguishing between users of PReE in terms of their backgrounds, goals, and needs. Of course, it was recognized that the usefulness of these user profiles was limited, particularly with respect to the needs of interdisciplinary users and users from less text-centric disciplines (such as Fine Arts). These limitations notwithstanding, this initial discussion allowed us to identify three general user profiles: graduate students ("students"), teaching professors ("teachers"), and research professors ("researchers").

"Student" users were characterized as coming from potentially broad disciplinary backgrounds. Their goals were to conduct self-directed research for the purposes of acquiring a thorough knowledge of a particular field; to complete their doctoral or masters theses; and to build their scholarly reputations. Needs and desires dictated by these goals included access to citations and bibliographies; a way of assessing the impact-factor of a given article, topic, or researcher in a particular field; and a system to facilitate both formal and informal peer review of their research.

"Teacher" users were characterized as potentially belonging to broad disciplinary backgrounds (such as history) and/or specific fields (such as late medieval English military history). Their goals included recommending readings to students, and undertaking self-directed research for the purpose of compiling knowledge-area bibliographies (often annotated), and writing and delivering lectures. These goals required access to citations and surveys of new and recent research in their particular field(s).

"Researcher" users were similarly characterized as potentially coming from a broad field and/or a more specific field of research expertise. Their goals included self-directed research for the purpose of building knowledge-area bibliographies (often annotated), writing and presenting conference papers, writing and delivering lectures, engaging in scholarly publication, and building and maintaining their scholarly reputations.

As a whole, these results suggested three key user requirements: the facilitation of high-level research, the facilitation of collaboration, and the achievement of recognition in their field of study. Although additional features were suggested, meeting these key requirements would be the driving force behind the design of the new PReE interface.

Design Principles, Processes, and Prototypes

A series of design principles were also agreed upon, which dictated that the interface design should focus on providing efficient ways to complete tasks (*efficiency*), on managing higher and lower priority objects (*visual balance*), on testing usability (*prototyping*), and on the ability to rapidly execute tasks in an agile work environment (*flexibility*). These principles suggested a design process of four steps. The first step was to conduct environmental scans in order to survey successful features offered by other web applications and assess their applicability for our present needs. The next step was to construct workflow sketches. The third step was to develop simple prototypes, and the fourth, to develop initial designs.

Design Processes of the PReE User Interface

Environmental scans focusing on the search and display functions of existing web applications highlighted a number of useful user features. A useful feature of some applications is the suggestion of search terms to the user, either by way of a drop-down list or by auto-completion of the search string. Other applications offer "bookshelves" of saved search items, allowing their users to group items together and to tag, rate, and comment on them (Figure 7). The survey of reader and display functions similarly suggested useful features that we could implement in the PReE user interface. As outlined in more detail above (see 5.2), there is growing interest in the research application of social annotations and annotation tools (Figure 8).[35] Other web applications enrich their content through the inclusion of user-contributed data, such as comments, tags, links, ratings, and other media (Figure 9). As in the original proof-of-concept, the capacity for viewing images and texts side-by-side was also expected to be included (Figure 10). In the longer version of this article, *Movie 2* (available at the URL http://cnx.org/content/m34335/latest/#movie2) illustrates the features of PReE. As indicated in the movie, all of these features were included in the PReE workflow sketches, simple prototypes, and initial designs of the user interface.

---

[35] For a useful survey and assessment of existing annotation tools and their implementation in electronic editions of literary texts, see Boot (2009).

Figure 7. Interface design: bookshelves

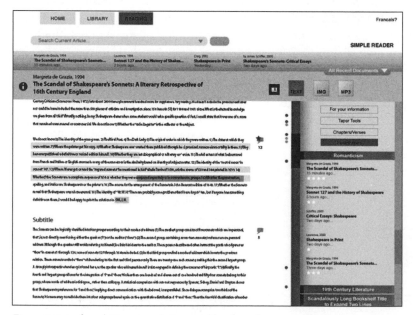

Figure 8. Interface design: annotations and bookmarks

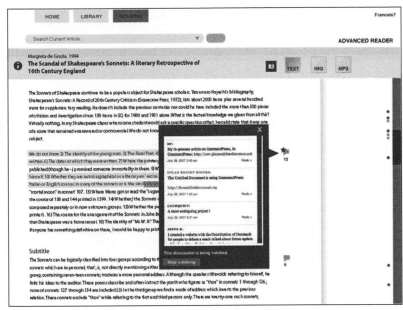

Figure 9. Interface design: annotations, bookmarks, and user comments

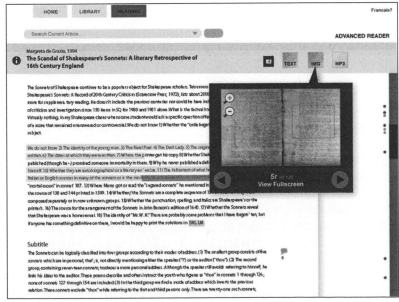

Figure 10. Interface design: side-by-side text and image display

New Insights and Next Steps

Research Insights and the Humanities Model of Dissemination

While we have learned much about humanistic engagement with the technologies under consideration, we recognize also that we have gained significant experience and understanding about the nature of the work itself from a disciplinary perspective.

One unexpected insight involved the nature of where the research lies in our endeavor. Our original approach to the project was to work toward a reading environment that suited the needs of professional readers, with the belief that we understood our own needs best and could therefore contribute to the development of professional reading tools through our active participation in pertinent research processes. Conceptualizing and theorizing the foundations of and rationales for humanist tools and their features was an important part of our role, as was modeling the features and functions computationally so that it was clear that what we wished to do could be done. Indeed, we had particular success in amalgamating previously unconnected (but research-pertinent) database contents so that a researcher could speed workflow by not having to enter search terms across several unconnected databases and interfaces. By modeling these processes we were better able to understand the problems and to suggest possible solutions. From our perspective as researchers, developing the prototype that proved the concept was our primary goal — anything beyond this was more production- than research-oriented, and it was unclear to us whether production was part of our endeavor.

In the second instance, we found that the most valuable point of impact for our research work manifested in ways that our humanities disciplines could not readily understand, evaluate, and appreciate. Our research-related successes often involved (1) the identification of a key area of intervention pertaining to our larger program of research; (2) understanding this area and modeling it with the computer; (3) testing and refining the model until we achieved acceptable functionality in proof of concept; (4) delivering a conference paper on this as quickly as possible (because computational fields, their tools, and the possibilities they enable advance rapidly) and engaging in further discussions with those who were interested in carrying this work further; and either (5a) working with a partner who was interested in putting our research into production within their own work; (5b) watching others involved in adjacent programs of research implement similar features in their own work and advancing our own research in that way;

or (5c) noting the adoption of our procedures without our involvement by other area stakeholders. As a progression from idea to point of impact, this is ideal in every way except one: our home disciplines in the humanities find it difficult to document this impact in professional terms. It simply does not fit the article- and book-focused publication and dissemination model favored by humanities scholarship, and most digital humanities venues do not integrate conference presentation and publication in a way that provides immediate publication on presentation (as is common in the sciences). As a result, work related to this project has, for the most part, been disseminated without publication, and is therefore largely unquantifiable in humanities disciplinary terms.

Partnerships and Collaborations

The second phase of our development of both REKn and PReE is at a crossroads. Over the course of some five years, we have been working on REKn and PReE in various ways. During this time we have presented our findings at conferences and discussed our methodology of modeling and prototyping with other research groups. The professional and pedagogical exercise of this work has been immense, driven at its core by a consistent aim to explore document-centered reading environments, and to work toward the production of a functional tool for a variety of professional readers. As with any project of this nature, our research experience has been (and continues to be) attended by successes and fraught with apparent dead-ends. However, as the preceding project narrative has made clear, even these seemingly inconclusive pursuits are in fact evidence of an active pedagogical process and a professional evolution in design and implementation — something privileged in all academic pursuit — where each step has led to a better understanding of how our overall research goals could be accomplished.

In light of the insights gained and lessons learned, our next steps are firmer and more secure, and we bring our experience to a series of very fruitful partnerships in which elements of our research are being extended in ways not initially considered. Moreover, we are incorporating our research experience into a large collaborative initiative, Implementing New Knowledge Environments (INKE), sponsored by the Social Sciences and Humanities Research Council of Canada MCRI program, as well as contributing to further developments associated with the Text Analysis Portal for Research (TAPoR).

Our research on interfaces, annotation, social interaction, and document-centered reading environments has also been incorporated into more focused research partnerships with groups like the Public Knowledge Project (PKP) and

Synergies. Our collaboration with PKP has seen work toward the integration of professional reading tools into the PKP Open Journal Systems (OJS). As outlined briefly above, our partnership began with conducting user experience surveys to identify and assess elements of users' engagement with texts and the OJS interface.[36] Work was then undertaken towards the identification of basic principles for an OJS interface redesign to respond to needs identified by the study; the carrying out of more precise user analysis and profiling; the design of wireframes (sketch prototypes) to emulate workflows; and consultation about technological facilitation for interaction that was imagined (including the integration of social networking technologies). These processes led to iterative computational modeling and testing, aimed at the creation of a proof-of-concept prototype. This prototype was presented to PKP in early 2008, in order that they might consider integrating it into their current development cycle — and also in more traditional research dissemination.[37] The next step of this conjoint research program is to build on earlier work carried out toward provision of a knowledgebase approach to speed professional readers' workflow through better access to pertinent critical textual resources. In turn, this new work draws on earlier and ongoing work with Iter, another of our research partners, to further develop the concept of enriched domain-specific knowledgebases, as well as ongoing research as part of a collaboration with the Transliteracies and BlueSky working groups at the University of California, Santa Barbara, towards the prototyping of an interface with document-centered professional reading tools and advanced social networking capabilities.

Works and Resources Cited

Alexander, Bryan. "Web 2.0: A New Wave of Innovation for Teaching and Learning?" *Educause Review* 41.2 (2006): 32–44.

Austin, David. "How Google Finds Your Needle in the Web's Haystack." *Feature Column*. American Mathematical Society. Dec. 2006. Web. 24 Apr. 2009. http://www.ams.org/featurecolumn/archive/pagerank.html.

Bolton, Whitney. "The Bard in Bits: Electronic Editions of Shakespeare and Programs to Analyze Them." *Computers and the Humanities* 24.4 (1990): 275–87.

---

[36] The results of this process have been published in Siemens et al. (2006) and "It May Change My Understanding of the Field," forthcoming, and presented at a number of conferences and symposia.

[37] See the list of presentations delivered in 2008 in Appendix 1 (available at http://cnx.org/content/m34336/latest/), in particular those presented in June 2008.

Boot, Peter. "Mesotext: Digitised Emblems, Modelled Annotations and Humanities Scholarship." Ph.D. Diss., University of Utrecht, 2009.

boyd, danah. "The Significance of Social Software." In *BlogTalks Reloaded: Social Software Research and Cases*. ed. Thomas N. Burg and Jan Schmidt, 15–30. Norderstedt: Books on Demand, 2007.

———, and Nicole B. Ellison. "Social Network Sites: Definition, History, and Scholarship." *Journal of Computer-Mediated Communication* 13.1 (2007): n. pag. Web, 24 Apr. 2009.

Bowen, William R. "Iter: Building an Effective Knowledge Base." In *New Technologies and Renaissance Studies*, ed. William R. Bowen and Ray Siemens, 101–9. New Technologies in Medieval and Renaissance Studies 1. Toronto and Tempe: Iter and Arizona Center for Medieval and Renaissance Studies, 2008.

———. "Iter: Where Does the Path Lead?" *Early Modern Literary Studies* 5.3 (2000): 2.1–26. Web, 24 Apr. 2009. http://extra.shu.ac.uk/emls/05–3/bowiter.html

Brown, Susan, Stan Ruecker, Jeffrey Antoniuk, Sharon Balasz, Patricia Clements, and Isobel Grundy. "Designing Rich-Prospect Access to a Feminist Literary History." *Women Writing and Reading* 2.1 (2007): 12–17.

Canadian Research Knowledge Network / Réseau Canadien de Documentation pour la Recherche (CRKN/RCDR). Web, 24 Apr. 2009. http://researchknowledge.ca/

Coates, Tom. "An Addendum to a Definition of Social Software." *Plasticbag.org*. 5 Jan. 2005. Web, 24 Apr. 2009. http://www.plasticbag.org/archives/2005/01/an_addendum_to_a_definition_of_social_software/.

Collex. NINES. Web, 24 Apr. 2009. http://www.collex.org/

Data Fountains. iVia Project. University of California, Riverside. Web, 24 Apr. 2009. http://datafountains.ucr.edu/.

De Grazia, Margreta, and Peter Stallybrass. "The Materiality of the Shakespearean Text." *Shakespeare Quarterly* 44 (1993): 255–83.

Delany, Paul. "Virtual Universities and the Death of Distance." *TEXT Technology* 7 (1997): 49–64.

Donath, Judith, and danah boyd. "Public Displays of Connection." *BT Technology Journal* 22.4 (2004): 71–82.

Drucker, Johanna, and Geoffrey Rockwell. "Introduction: Reflections on the Ivanhoe Game." *TEXT Technology* 12.2 (2003): vii-xviii.

DuBruck, Edelgard E. "Changes of Taste and Audience Expectation in Fifteenth-Century Religious Drama." *Fifteenth-Century Studies* 6 (1983): 59–91.

Early Modern English Dictionaries Database. Ed. Ian Lancashire. University of Toronto. Web, 24 Apr. 2009. http://www.chass.utoronto.ca/~ian/emedd.html.

Erickson, Peter. "Rewriting the Renaissance, Rewriting Ourselves." *Shakespeare Quarterly* 38 (1987): 327–37.

eXist. Wolfgang Meier, et al. Web, 24 Apr. 2009. http://exist.sourceforge.net.

eXist XML-RPC API. Mike Elkink and James Dixon. Web, 24 Apr. 2009. http://www.rubyforge.org/projects/exist-xml-rpc/.

Faulhaber, Charles B. "Textual Criticism in the 21st Century." *Romance Philology* 45 (1991): 123–48.

Fedora. Fedora Commons. Web. 24 Apr. 2009. http://www.fedora-commons.org/.

Fitzpatrick, Kathleen. "CommentPress: New (Social) Structures for New (Networked) Texts." *Journal of Electronic Publishing* 10.3 (2007): n. pag. Web, 24 Apr. 2009. http://dx.doi.org/10.3998/3336451.0010.305.

Fortier, Paul. "Babies, Bathwater, and the Study of Literature." *Computers and the Humanities* 27 (1993–94): 375–85.

Girgensohn, Andreas, and Alison Lee. "Making Web Sites Be Places for Social Interaction." In *Proceedings of the 2002 ACM Conference on Computer Supported Cooperative Work*, 136–45. New York: ACM, 2002.

Google Book Search. Google. Web, 24 Apr. 2009. http://books.google.com/.

Greetham, D. C. *Theories of the Text*. Oxford: Oxford Univ. Press, 1999.

Gross, Ralph, and Alessandro Acquisti. "Information Revelation and Privacy in Online Social Networks." In *Proceedings of the 2005 ACM Workshop on Privacy in the Electronic Society*, 71–80. New York: ACM, 2005.

Guillory, John. "The Ethical Practice of Modernity: The Example of Reading." In *The Turn to Ethics*, ed. Marjorie Garber, Beatrice Hanssen, and Rebecca L. Walkowitz, 29–46. New York: Routledge, 2000.

Hall, Kim F. "About This Volume." In *Othello: Texts and Contexts*, ed. Kim F. Hall, vii–xii. New York: Bedford/St. Martin's, 2007.

Hayashi, Tetsumaro. *Shakespeare's Sonnets: A Record of Twentieth-Century Criticism*. Metuchen, NJ: Scarecrow Press, 1972.

Hoadley, Christopher M., and Peter G. Kilner. "Using Technology to Transform Communities of Practice into Knowledge-Building Communities." *SIGGROUP Bulletin* 25.1 (2005): 31–40.

Hockey, Susan. *Electronic Texts in the Humanities: Principles and Practice*. Oxford: Oxford Univ. Press, 2000.

Howard, Jean E. "The New Historicism in Renaissance Studies." *English Literary Renaissance* 16 (1986): 13–43.

Internet Shakespeare Editions. Coordinating ed. Michael Best. University of Victoria. Web. 24 Apr. 2009. http://internetshakespeare.uvic.ca/.

Iter. Renaissance Society of America, University of Toronto Centre for Reformation and Renaissance Studies, Arizona Center for Medieval and Renaissance Studies. Web, 24 Apr. 2009. http://www.itergateway.org/.

Juxta. NINES. Web, 24 Apr. 2009. http://www.juxtasoftware.org/

Lancashire, Ian. "Bilingual Dictionaries in an English Renaissance Knowledge Base." In *Historical Dictionary Databases*, ed. T. R. Wooldridge. *CCH Working Papers* 2 (1992): 69–88.

———. "Computer Tools for Cognitive Stylistics." In *From Information to Knowledge: Conceptual and Content Analysis by Computer*, ed. Ephraim Nissan and Klaus M. Schmidt, 28–47. Oxford: Intellect, 1995.

———. "Working with Texts." IBM Academic Computing Conference. Anaheim, California. June 1989. Address.

Leitch, Cara, Ray Siemens, James Dixon, Mike Elkink, Angelsea Saby, and Karin Armstrong. "Social Networking and Online Collaborative Research with REKn and PReE." Society for Digital Humanities/Société pour l'étude des médias interactifs, Congress of the Canadian Federation of Humanities and Social Sciences. University of British Columbia, Vancouver. 3 Jun. 2008. Poster presentation.

Lemon8-XML. Public Knowledge Project. University of British Columbia, Stanford University, and Simon Fraser University. Web, 24 Apr. 2009. http://pkp.sfu.ca/lemon8.

Lexicons of Early Modern English, ed. Ian Lancashire. University of Toronto Library and University of Toronto Press. Web, 24 Apr. 2009. http://leme.library.utoronto.ca/.

Literature Online. Chadwyck-Healy Literature Online. ProQuest. Web, 24 Apr. 2009. http://lion.chadwyck.com/.

Lucene. Apache Software Foundation. Web, 24 Apr. 2009. http://lucene.apache.org/.

Machan, Tim William. "Late Middle English Texts and the Higher and Lower Criticisms." In *Medieval Literature: Texts and Interpretation*, ed. idem, 3–16. Medieval and Renaissance Texts and Studies 79. Binghamton: Center for Medieval and Renaissance Studies, 1991.

Madden, Mary, Susannah Fox, Aaron Smith, and Jessica Vitak. "Digital Footprints: Online Identity Management and Search in the Age of Transparency." *Pew Internet and American Life Project.* 16 Dec. 2007. Web, 24 Apr. 2009. http://pewinternet.org/Reports/2007/Digital-Footprints.aspx.

Many Eyes. IBM Collaborative User Experience Research Group, Visual Communication Lab. Web, 24 Apr. 2009. http://manyeyes.alphaworks.ibm.com/manyeyes.

Marcus, Leah S. *Unediting the Renaissance: Shakespeare, Marlowe, Milton*. New York: Routledge, 1996.

Marlow, Cameron, Mor Naaman, danah boyd, and Marc Davis. "HT06, Tagging Paper, Taxonomy, Flickr, Academic Article, To Read." In *Proceedings of the Seventeenth Conference on Hypertext and Hypermedia*, 31–40. New York: ACM, 2006.

McCarty, Willard. "Modeling: A Study in Words and Meanings." In *A Companion to Digital Humanities*, ed. Susan Schreibman, Ray Siemens, and John Unsworth, 257–70. Malden, MA: Blackwell, 2004.

———. "Knowing . . . : Modeling in Literary Studies." In *A Companion to Digital Literary Studies*, ed. Ray Siemens and Susan Schreibman, 391–401. Malden, MA: Blackwell, 2008.

———. "What is Humanities Computing? Toward a Definition of the Field." Address. Reed College, Portland. Mar. 1998. Web, 24 Apr. 2009. http://staff.cch.kcl.ac.uk/~wmccarty/essays/McCarty, What is humanities computing.pdf.

McLeod, Randall. "Information on Information." *Text* 5 (1991): 240–81.

———. "UnEditing Shakespeare." *Sub-Stance* 33–34 (1982): 26–55.

McGann, Jerome J. *A Critique of Modern Textual Criticism*. Chicago: Univ. of Chicago Press, 1983.

———, and Johanna Drucker. "The Ivanhoe Game: An Introduction." 2000–1. Web. 24 Apr. 2009. http://jefferson.village.virginia.edu/~jjm2f/old/IG-amehtm.html.

———, and Lisa Samuels. "Deformance and Interpretation." *New Literary History* 30 (1999): 25–56.

McKenzie, D. F. *Bibliography and the Sociology of Texts*. London: British Library, 1986.

Miall, David S. "The Library versus the Internet: Literary Studies Under Siege?" *PMLA* 116 (2001): 1405–14.

Michigan Early Modern English Materials, ed. Richard W. Bailey, Jay L. Robinson, James W. Downer, and Patricia V. Lehman. University of Michigan. Web, 24 Apr. 2009. http://quod.lib.umich.edu/m/memem/.

Mitchell, Steve. "Machine-Assisted Metadata Generation and New Resource Discovery: Software and Services." *First Monday* 11.8 (2006): n. pag. Web, 24 Apr. 2009. http://firstmonday.org/issues/issue11_8/mitchell/.

Metadata Offer New Knowledge (MONK) Project. Web, 24 Apr. 2009. http://monkproject.org/

Mueller, Martin. "The Nameless Shakespeare." *TEXT Technology* 14.1 (2005): 61–70.

Nalanda iVia Focused Crawler. iVia Project. University of California, Riverside. Web, 24 Apr. 2009. http://ivia.ucr.edu/projects/Nalanda.

Nutch. Apache Software Foundation. Web, 24 Apr. 2009. http://lucene.apache. org/nutch/.

Open Access Text Archive. Internet Archive. Web, 24 Apr. 2009. http://www. archive.org/details/texts.

Open Journal Systems. Public Knowledge Project. University of British Columbia, Stanford University, and Simon Fraser University. Web, 24 Apr. 2009. http:// pkp.sfu.ca/ojs.

Open Monograph Press. Public Knowledge Project. University of British Columbia, Stanford University, and Simon Fraser University. Web, 24 Apr. 2009. http://pkp.sfu.ca/omp.

Oxford English Dictionary Online. Oxford Univ. Press. Web. 24 Apr. 2009. http:// dictionary.oed.com/.

Oxford Text Archive. Oxford University Computing Services, Oxford University. Web, 24 Apr. 2009. http://www.ota.ox.ac.uk/.

Pechter, Edward. "The New Historicism and Its Discontents: Politicizing Renaissance Drama." *PMLA* 102 (1987): 292–302.

PostgreSQL. PostgreSQL Global Development Group. Web, 24 Apr. 2009. http:// www.postgresql.org/.

Public Knowledge Project. University of British Columbia, Stanford University, and Simon Fraser University. Web, 24 Apr. 2009. http://pkp.sfu.ca/.

Remley, Paul. "Mary Shelton and Her Tudor Literary Milieu." In *Rethinking the Henrician Era: Essays on Early Tudor Texts and Contexts*, ed. Peter C. Herman, 40–77. Urbana: University of Illinois Press, 1994.

Richardson, David A., and Michael Neuman. "Application for NEH Funding: A Planning Conference for a Renaissance Knowledge Base." Funding Application, 1990.

Rockwell, Geoffrey. "Is Humanities Computing an Academic Discipline?" Address at Humanities Computing Seminar, University of Virginia, Charlottesville. 19 Nov. 1999. Web, 24 Apr. 2009. http://www.iath.virginia.edu/ hcs/rockwell.html.

Ruby on Rails. David Heinemeier Hansson. Web, 24 Apr. 2009. http://www. rubyonrails.org/.

RubyFedora. MediaShelf. Web, 24 Apr. 2009. http://yourmediashelf.com/ruby-fedora/.

Ruecker, Stan. "The Electronic Book Table of Contents as a Research Tool." Address at Congress of the Humanities and Social Sciences: Consortium for

Computers in the Humanities / Consortium pour Ordinateurs en Sciences Humaines (COCH/COSH) Annual Conference. University of Western Ontario, London. 30 May 2005.

———, Milena Radzikowska, Susan Brown, Thomas M. Nelson, Isobel Grundy, Patricia Clements, Sharon Balasz, Jeff Antoniuk, and Stéfan Sinclair. "The Dynamic Table of Contents: Extending a Venerable List in a Digital Context." Address at The Potential and Limitations of a List: An International Transdisciplinary Workshop. Prague, Czech Republic. Nov. 2007.

Schreibman, Susan. "Computer-Mediated Texts and Textuality: Theory and Practice." *Computers and the Humanities* 36 (2002): 283–93.

Shakespeare Database Project. Dir. H. Joachim Neuhaus. Westfälische Wilhelms-Universität, Münster. Web, 24 Apr. 2009. http://www.shkspr.uni-muenster.de/.

Siemens, Ray. "Text Analysis and the Dynamic Edition? Some Concerns with an Algorithmic Approach in the Electronic Scholarly Edition." *TEXT Technology* 14.1 (2005): 91–98.

———. "Unediting and Non-Editions: The Death of Distance, the Notion of Navigation, and New Acts of Editing in the Electronic Medium." *Anglia* 119.3 (2001): 423–55.

———, and Cara Leitch. "Editing the Early Modern Miscellany: Modeling and Knowledge [Re]Presentation as a Context for the Contemporary Editor." In *New Ways of Looking at Old Texts IV*, ed. Michael Denbo, 115–30. Tempe: Arizona Center for Medieval and Renaissance Studies, 2008.

———, and Christian Vandendorpe. "Canadian Humanities Computing and Emerging Mind Technologies." In *Mind Technologies: Humanities Computing and the Canadian Academic Community*, ed. Ray Siemens and David Moorman, xi–xxiii. Calgary: University of Calgary Press, 2006.

———, William R. Bowen, Jessica Natale, Karin Armstrong, Alastair McColl, and Greg Newton. "Iter Database: Research Report on the Inclusion of Electronic Resources." Whitepaper. Electronic Textual Cultures Laboratory, University of Victoria. 2006. Web, 24 Apr. 2009. http://etcl-dev.uvic.ca/public/iter-report/.

———, Johanne Paquette, Karin Armstrong, Cara Leitch, Brett D. Hirsch, and Eric Haswell, "Drawing Networks in the Devonshire Manuscript (BL Add MS 17492): Toward Visualizing a Writing Community's Shared Apprenticeship, Social Valuation, and Self-Validation." *Digital Studies/Le Champ Numérique*. In press.

———, John Willinsky, Analisa Blake, Karin Armstrong, Lindsay Colahan, and Greg Newton. "A Study of Professional Reading Tools for Computing Humanists." Report. Electronic Textual Cultures Laboratory, University of Victoria. May 2006. Web, 24 Apr. 2009. http://etcl-dev.uvic.ca/public/pkp_report/.

———, John Willinsky, Cara Leitch, and Analisa Blake. "It May Change My Understanding of the Field: Understanding Reader Tools for Scholars and Professional Readers." *Digital Humanities Quarterly.* In Press.

Sinclair, Stéfan, and Geoffrey Rockwell. "Reading Tools, or Text Analysis Tools as Objects of Interpretation." Address at Digital Humanities 2007. University of Illinois at Urbana-Champaign, Illinois. June 2007.

Solr. Apache Software Foundation. Web, 24 Apr. 2009. http://lucene.apache.org/solr/.

Southall, Raymond. "The Devonshire Manuscript Collection of Early Tudor Poetry, 1532–41." *Review of English Studies,* n. s. 15 (1964): 142–50.

———. *The Courtly Maker: An Essay on the Poetry of Wyatt and His Contemporaries.* Oxford: Blackwell, 1964.

Sutherland, Kathryn. "Introduction." In *Electronic Text: Investigations in Method and Theory,* ed. eadem, 1–18. Oxford: Oxford Univ. Press, 1997.

———. "Revised Relations? Material Text, Immaterial Text, and the Electronic Environment." *Text* 11 (1998): 17–30.

Synergies. Web, 24 Apr. 2009. http://www.synergiescanada.org/

Tanselle, G. Thomas. "Textual Criticism and Literary Sociology." *Studies in Bibliography* 44 (1991): 83–143.

TAPoR Tools. Text Analysis Portal for Research (TAPoR) Project. Web, 24 Apr. 2009. http://portal.tapor.ca/.

Textbase of Early Tudor English, eds. Alistair Fox and Greg Waite. Universsity of Otago. Web, 24 Apr. 2009. http://www.hlm.co.nz/tudortexts/.

Unsworth, John. "Knowledge Representation in Humanities Computing." Address at eHumanities NEH Lecture Series on Technology and the Humanities. Washington. Apr. 2001. Web, 24 Apr. 2009. http://www.iath.virginia.edu/~jmu2m/KR/KRinHC.html.

———. "Documenting the Reinvention of Text: The Importance of Failure." *Journal of Electronic Publishing* 3.2 (1997): n. pag. Web, 24 Apr. 2009. http://http://dx.doi.org/10.3998/3336451.0003.201.

———. "Scholarly Primitives." Address at Humanities Computing: Formal Methods, Experimental Practice. King's College, London. May 2000. Web, 24 Apr. 2009. http://www.iath.virginia.edu/~jmu2m/Kings.5-00/primitives.html.

Vander Wal, Thomas. "Folksonomy Coinage and Definition." *Off the Top.* 2 Feb. 2007. Web, 24 Apr. 2009. http://www.vanderwal.net/folksonomy.html.

Warwick, Claire. "Print Scholarship and Digital Resources." In *A Companion to Digital Humanities*, ed. Susan Schreibman, Ray Siemens, and John Unsworth, 366–82. Malden, MA: Blackwell, 2004.

Women Writers Project. Women Writers Project. Brown University. Web, 24 Apr. 2009. http://www.wwp.brown.edu/.

Zotero. Center for History and New Media, George Mason University. Web, 24 Apr. 2009. http://www.zotero.org/.

UNIVERSITY OF VICTORIA

Providing a Base for E-Editing:
The Text Creation Partnership Project[*]

SHAWN MARTIN

A
S THE DIGITAL HUMANITIES COMMUNITY THINKS ABOUT HOW IT SHOULD
build infrastructure to support and continue scholarship in the field, it
will become increasingly important to define clearly the various roles
that libraries, scholars, funding agencies, and other interested parties form in the
increasingly complex world of online research. In 2005, the American Council of
Learned Societies (ACLS) published a report that stated "In considering how best
to organize the publishing side of scholarly communication, it will also be important to be open to new business models."[1] More recently other foundations have
amplified the recommendation of ACLS. The Ithaka Foundation issued Sustaining Digital Resources: An On-the-Ground View of Projects Today (July 2009) by
suggesting that a variety of different routes had to be considered depending on
the type of resource. The solutions included creating revenue streams through
subscriptions, foundation money, institutional subsidies, and other means.[2] Additionally the Scholarly Publishing and Resources Coalition (SPARC) issued
Income Models for Open Access, An Overview of Current Practice (September 2009) which investigated how people are funding open access publications

[*] This paper was first delivered at the 2007 Modern Language Association convention,
Chicago, IL, at the Josephine Roberts Forum: "E-Editing in Corpora," Michael Denbo presiding.
[1] John Unsworth et al., *Our Cultural Commonwealth: The Report of the American Council of Learned Societies' Commission on Cyberinfrastructure for Humanities and Social Sciences*
(for complete citation, see Reference List at end of paper).
[2] *Sustaining Digital Resources: An On-the-Ground View of Projects Today* (Ithaka Foundation, 2009), full report available at http://www.ithaka.org/ithaka-s-r/research/ithaka-case-
studies-in-sustainability.

including article processing fees and other payment options.[3] Though all of these reports discuss the importance of business models and how to make money, they leave one important component largely neglected: how to build production models that sustain digital projects.[4]

Currently many digital humanities projects try to do everything. Staff funded by various grants create content by digitizing or transcribing books and manuscripts. Other staff build tools to mine and utilize that content, and still others may do outreach for the project. In the meantime, faculty, who often are best qualified to be doing research rather than project management, find themselves attempting to do two (or more) jobs as project managers, salespeople, and researchers. Clearly a more equitable division of labor is required.[5]

The Text Creation Partnership (TCP) has begun to develop a distributed model in cooperation with over one hundred libraries and institutions around the world that may help to define some of these roles. At the Universities of Michigan and Oxford, the TCP has production staff that transcribes texts which can be used in a variety of different ways. TCP collaborates with publishers, particularly ProQuest, Readex, and Gale to distribute that content. Finally, and perhaps most interestingly, TCP works with scholarly projects throughout the world in which the projects use TCP content as a base on which they can build tools to accomplish particular scholarly goals. In the future, it would seem likely that this is a more sustainable and better model to follow. Rather than one project creating content, publishing that content, and creating tools for that content, it would seem better that these roles are divided. That way, libraries can create a base of content to be used in any number of scholarly projects, and scholars can then build tools for their areas which utilize that content most effectively.

The Technological Base

First, some background on what the technical specifications of the TCP are. TCP staff ensures that their transcriptions are done to a 99.995% accuracy rating (most commercial products guarantee only around 99% accuracy). In practice this means that everyone involved with the TCP uses a common procedure (with

---

[3] Full SPARC report available at http://www.arl.org/sparc/publications/papers/imguide.shtml.

[4] Another good source for the general picture of humanities scholarship and its future is Kathleen Fitzpatrick, *Planned Obsolescence: Publishing, Technology, and the Future of the Academy* (New York: New York University Press, 2011).

[5] A good history of the field and where it began, including some of the infrastructural requirements, can be found in Willard McCarty, *Humanities Computing* (New York: Palgrave Macmillan, 2005).

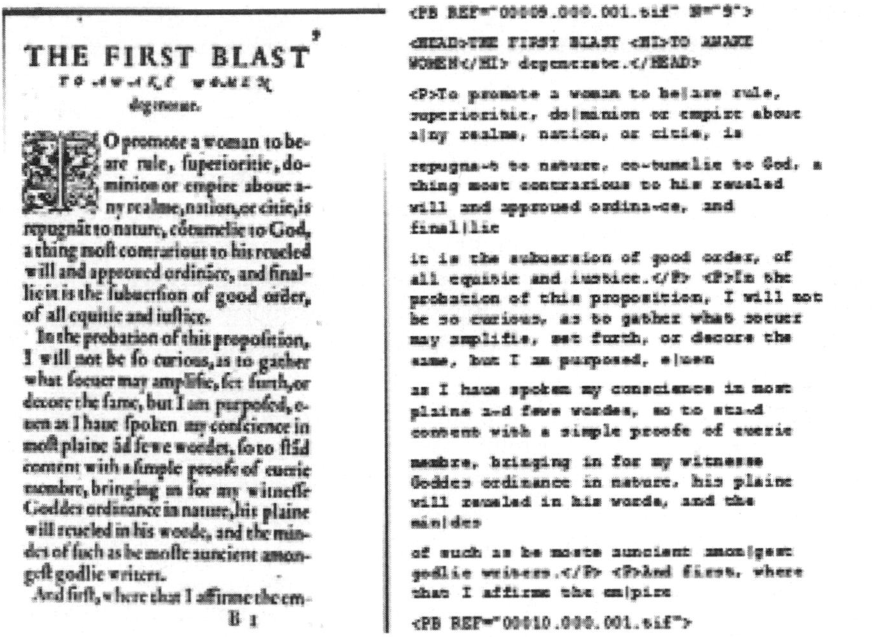

<PB REF="00009.000.001.tif" N="9">

<HEAD>THE FIRST BLAST <HI>TO AWAKE WOMEN</HI> degenerate.</HEAD>

<P>To promote a woman to be|are rule, superioritie, do|minion or empire aboue a|ny realme, nation, or citie, is

repugna-t to nature, co-tumelie to God, a thing most contrarious to his reueled will and approued ordina-ce, and final|lie

it is the subuersion of good order, of all equitie and iustice.</P> <P>In the probation of this proposition, I will not be so curious, as to gather what socuer may amplifie, set forth, or decore the same, but I am purposed, e|uen

as I haue spoken my conscience in most plaine a-d fewe wordes, so to sta-d content with a simple proofe of euerie

membre, bringing in for my witnesse Goddes ordinance in nature, his plaine will reueled in his worde, and the min|des

of such as be moste auncient amon|gest godlie writers.</P> <P>And first, where that I affirme the em|pire

<PB REF="00010.000.001.tif">

Figure 1. Example of original image on left and TCP text with structural tagging on the right.

some variations). Each transcription is typed out twice (by different people); discrepancies between the two transcriptions (if any) are resolved by a third person. This part of the process is usually performed by transcription companies. The final transcription these companies provide is then reviewed by professional librarians at Michigan and Oxford with the help of the University of Toronto and the National Library of Wales (for Latin and Welsh texts respectively). Of course mistakes do happen, but essentially the final text is as accurate as is possible to create given the constraints of a large project.

Perhaps even more important, though, TCP adds basic structural tagging marking according to Text Encoding Initiative (TEI) guidelines. TCP likes to call the kind of structural tagging staff does "TEI lite with additions." In other words, the basic structure of text is there with some additional elements added (eg. colophons, typeface changes, quotations, etc.). TCP does try to avoid making too many editorial decisions. Reviewers at TCP are charged to create a basic file and leave more difficult (orthographic or typographical) decisions to those with more experience in advanced textual analysis. It is hoped that scholars may at a later point create enhanced editions using TCP text as a base for their work.

The Social Base

TCP is a project founded on the idea that publishers, librarians, and scholars should collaborate (rather than compete) in order to produce scholarly information. Thus, ideally, all three can capitalize on their strengths. Libraries are often best at organizing information. Publishers are best at disseminating information. Scholars are best at analyzing information. TCP tries to harness the strengths of all of these groups and create a corpus of text useful to a wide variety of different audiences.

In 1998, ProQuest Information and Learning produced a database of scanned images from their microfilm collection which they called Early English Books Online (EEBO) containing images of English books printed between 1470 and 1700, around 125,000 titles. EEBO contained works listed in the Short Title Catalogs I (Pollard and Redgrave) and II (Wing), the Thomason Tracts, and the English Tract Supplement. EEBO greatly increased the availability of primary source titles. Yet in many ways EEBO replicated the holdings of libraries like the University of Michigan. EEBO had the advantage of viewing individual titles from one's home computer, have multiple views of the same book, and so forth, but many librarians at Michigan and elsewhere felt that the potential for EEBO was the possibility of full text searching. Such an upgrade would allow researchers and students to search individual words or concepts across titles and engage with the sources in ways previously unimaginable. ProQuest, however, felt that the cost of adding text searching to the EEBO collection would be too costly, and libraries would be unwilling to pay the additional costs involved. Librarians at the University of Michigan and other members of the academic library community, on the other hand, believed that there would be enough support for the creation of full text versions for at least a subset of the EEBO collection within research libraries. Under the leadership of Mark Sandler, then collection development officer at the University of Michigan Library, ProQuest agreed to partner with the University of Michigan Library for the purpose of creating full text for a subset of 25,000 titles in the initial phase, with the understanding that the project might continue depending on the support it got.[6]

---

[6] Mark Sandler, "New Uses for the World's Oldest Books: Democratizing Access to Historic Corpora," *Association of Research Libraries (ARL) Bimonthly Report* 232 (Febuary 2004). http://www.arl.org/resources/pubs/br/br232.shtml, 4 – 6.

What is unique about the TCP initiative, though, is its unique structure and new prototype for cooperation among university libraries, the academic community, and commercial publishing. TCP allowed both commercial publishers and academic libraries to compromise and create an entirely new e-publishing venture. For libraries, it was important that these texts become publicly available to the world, not just paying subscribers. So, all of the texts that TCP creates will enter the public domain after a period of five years. During those five years, the commercial publishers have exclusive sales rights and the ability to develop specific tools to search the text that TCP creates. This creates a great opportunity for them to recoup their investment and generate new sales because of increased functionality. TCP, unlike many scholarly projects, does not utilize grant funding but rather utilizes funds from partner libraries and hopes to build a community around TCP texts. So, in essence, universities are taking ownership of the texts which they help to create. The TCP model has been largely successful with nearly 25,000 texts available. In fact, it has been successful enough to be extended to two other similar commercial databases. These additional collections include Evans Early American Imprints (Evans), a collection of every work printed in Britain's American colonies and later the United States between 1639 and 1800 (based on the Evans Bibliography) available from Readex Incorporated; additionally, TCP works with Eighteenth Century Collections Online (ECCO), a database containing over 150,000 titles printed in Britain between 1700 and 1800 available from Thomson-Gale. Also, the EEBO-TCP has also begun a second round of funding to complete the remaining 25,000 unique titles in EEBO.

In all, the TCP model has allowed the project to sustain a budget of about $1.4 million per year over approximately seven years, far more than any grant-funded or institutional model would be able to do. It is hoped that the TCP model can be extended even further to other collections and other academic areas and perhaps eventually create a cross-searchable, public domain collection from EEBO, Evans, ECCO, and perhaps other databases that will form a vast base of material for digital library development for many years to come. It is worth considering, for instance, whether Google Books, the Digital Library of America, or other similarly ambitious digital library projects might utilize a TCP-like model for their potentially vast holdings.

The Fruits of the TCP Model: Collaborative E-editing Projects

One of the goals of the TCP project has always been to spawn further investigations of TCP text. Fortunately for both TCP and the digital humanities profession as a whole, scholars have come along to do more advanced work with TCP texts. There are many examples of scholarly projects using TCP texts.[7] Yet there are three particularly striking examples of how TCP text can be enhanced for better scholarship. These include the Spenser Archive (Washington University – St. Louis), the Holinshed Project (Oxford University), and the Virtual Modernization Project (Northwestern University). All of these projects are focused on specific aspects of early modern literature and hope to create their own projects with their own websites using TCP as a basis for their work.[8]

Spenser Archive (Washington University – St. Louis)
http://spenserarchive.org/web_pages/about.html

The Spenser archive is is a digital component of a print volume *Collected Works of Edmund Spenser* from Oxford University Press. The Spenser archive is endeavoring to create an electronic archive of the works of Edmund Spenser that will take the basic text from TCP and add tagging of particular value to Spenser scholars. Such tagging will include signatures, form (placement of text relative to the page), textual issues such as "mech" (mechanical error), "ink" (inking problem), "hand": (handwritten correction), "comp" (compositorial error), and "press" (press-alteration). Such tags would generally not be of use to scholars outside of Spenser studies but are incredibly important if one hopes do research across printings of various editions. Because of the basic text TCP has created, the Spenser project does not need to re-type all of the basic text again. It will simply use TCP's texts and add the appropriate tags, saving significant amounts of time and money.

Holinshed Project (Oxford University)
http://www.cems.ox.ac.uk/holinshed/

Similarly, the Holinshed Project at Oxford University will do more detailed tagging of two editions of Holinshed's *Chronicle* using TCP texts. In this case, the textual editing will focus specifically on markup that will help to map variants between editions. These markup additions would include things such as "rdg" (introduces an individual reading), "type" (occasionally the editors will view a

---

[7] For a complete list of all projects using TCP texts see http://www.lib.umich.edu/tcp/eebo/scholarship.html.

[8] Aaron McCullough, formerly TCP project outreach librarian, has also written a good summary of such editing projects in "Bedfellows in Mass Digital Conversion: Ten Years of Text Creation Partnership(s)," *New Knowledge Environments* Vol. 1 No. 1 (2009) http://journals.uvic.ca/index.php/INKE/article/view/160/166.

variant from another edition as relevant), "inter" (for variants between various editions, and "intra" for intraeditional ones), "wit" (each copy of the text that includes a reading of the variant is called a witness and has its own unique alphanumeric identifier, also called a "siglum"), and "cause" (notes the reason for a variant, which is determined by an editor from a list of options). Again, such tagging is incredibly useful when comparing editions, though less useful if one is doing other types of research. So the Holinshed Project hopes to use the base TCP has created and enhance it for its own projects.

Virtual Modernization – Northwestern University
http://panini.northwestern.edu/mmueller/vospos.pdf

The Virtual Modernization project in some ways shows the true power of how publishers, librarians, and scholars can all work together to provide tools previously unimaginable. This project is based on the work of Prof. Martin Mueller as part of a larger project called Virtual Orthographic Standardization (particularly for early modern texts). Prof. Mueller sought to map variant spellings that are common in early modern printed works to their modern counterparts (e.g., saynte, sainct, : saint. See Figure 2). In order to find instances of words and how they changed their meanings over time, Prof. Mueller looks for every instance of words like "saint" over 400 years and compares the context of those words throughout the entire corpus. [9]

By mapping TCP texts to modern spellings, Prof. Mueller can then create a further collaboration with PhiloLogic (a linguistics interface tool developed at the University of Chicago), load his TCP texts with their mapped variant spellings, and perform more accurate searches. Furthermore, this mapping of variant spellings allowed for a collaborative project between ProQuest and the Committee for Institutional Cooperation (CIC), a consortium of twelve universities, to create a tool in Early English Books Online that allowed users (particularly novice searchers like undergraduates) to search on a word and then check off variant spellings they would also like to search under (see Figure 3). So in essence Prof. Mueller's work was able to foster collaborations with over a dozen universities and create further tools that had not been previously imagined.

Furthermore, because of the development of these tools, Mueller and scholars like him have the ability to ask entirely new kinds of questions. For instance

---

[9] More information about this project is available in Martin Mueller. "The TCP texts and the query potential of the digital surrogate" Project Bamboo Website, November 28, 2011 http://www.projectbamboo.org/the-tcp-texts-and-the-query-potential-of-the-digital-surrogate.

one can pick a word such as "God" or "Man" and generate distributions of that word in particular kinds of literature or at certain periods of time. With those distributions, a scholar can speculate on why people would have referred to God more frequently at certain times than at others. One might then begin to speculate that during times of calamity, crop failures, or plague it might be more common to plead for God's help. During the Scientific Revolution, one might expect to hear praise of Man's achievements. Computers allow scholars to test these hypotheses by displaying frequency of words according to particular variables. They also allow scholars to map words in geographical locations to see if one location uses a particular word more than others. They also allow scholars to trace ideas geographically to see if a word like "God" is more common in one part of the world than in another, and whether that usage migrates from one place to another.[10]

So What Does All of This Mean?

Collaborative projects are nothing new in the digital humanities, but what the TCP is doing is unique in several ways. First, one must recognize that "access" to primary resource materials (like EEBO, Evans, and ECCO) is really a multifaceted issue. There are records of individual books (already provided online by the *English Short Title Catalog*), there are digital facsimile images of the works (provided by EEBO), there are full text transcriptions allowing searchability (provided by TCP), and finally, perhaps most importantly to scholars, there is editorial work which help to interpret materials in ways that are particular to specific disciplines. In order for scholars to truly do their work well, all of the other layers (record, image, text) need to be built beforehand.

The American Council of Learned Societies (ACLS) report on cyberinfrastructure in the humanities discussed the benefits of collaboration and the need for further development for particular tools.[11] Nonetheless, the report also seemed to rest on a certain assumption common to many digital humanities projects today that scholars should create an entire project (including scanning documents, hiring staff, creating transcriptions, and any number of other functions)

---

[10] Such uses begin to truly put into action the theories provided by scholars like Jerome McGann in his work *Radiant Textuality: Literature after the World Wide Web* (New York: Palgrave. 2001).

[11] "Our Cultural Commonwealth," *The Report of the American Council of Learned Societies Commission on Cyberinfrastructure for the Humanities and Social Sciences.* Washington, D.C.: American Council of Learned Societies. http://www.acls.org/cyberinfrastructure/OurCulturalCommonwealth.pdf.

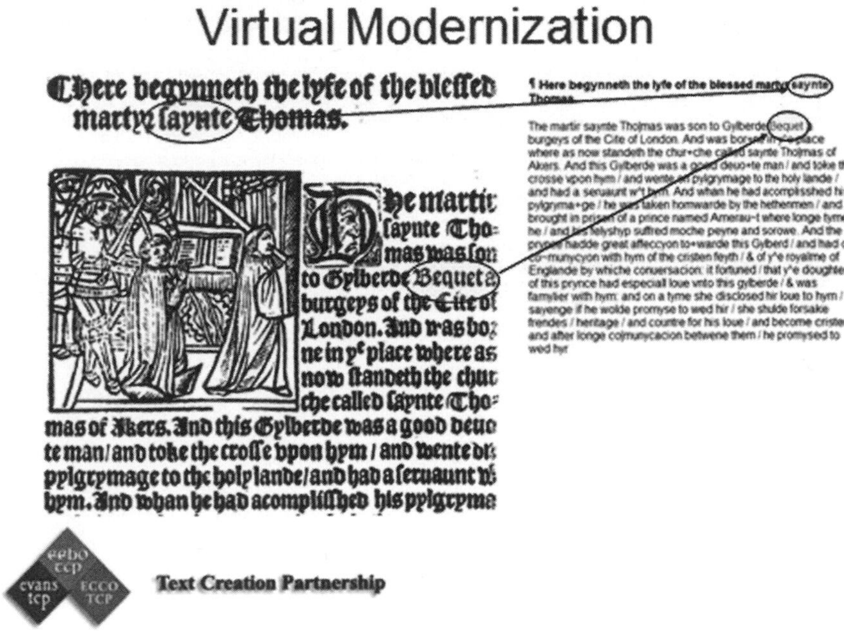

Virtual Modernization

Figure 2. Comparison of original text with variant spellings of "saint" and "Beckett".

from beginning to end. Libraries may collaborate with such projects in terms of providing server space or other infrastructural support, but are not always key partners. It would seem that it might be worth examining this division of labor from a different perspective.

Libraries, traditionally, have been very good at providing basic access to print materials. They have always provided cataloging and made things available in the print world. In the digital world, libraries are increasingly digitizing their collections, and in some cases providing transcriptions of difficult-to-read materials. So in some ways it would seem that this kind of basic work should fall to libraries. Nonetheless, no library has the monetary resources to create a resource as massive as EEBO. Even in collaboration with partners, the cost of digitizing and mounting a database of 125,000 books would likely prove too daunting. Publishers are at least in this case a natural ally in creating content on a large scale.

Scholars have generally concerned themselves with research rather than production of infrastructure for scholarship. Libraries and publishers have done that work for them, and should likely continue to do so in the digital world. In other words, the first three levels of access (records, images, and texts) to primary

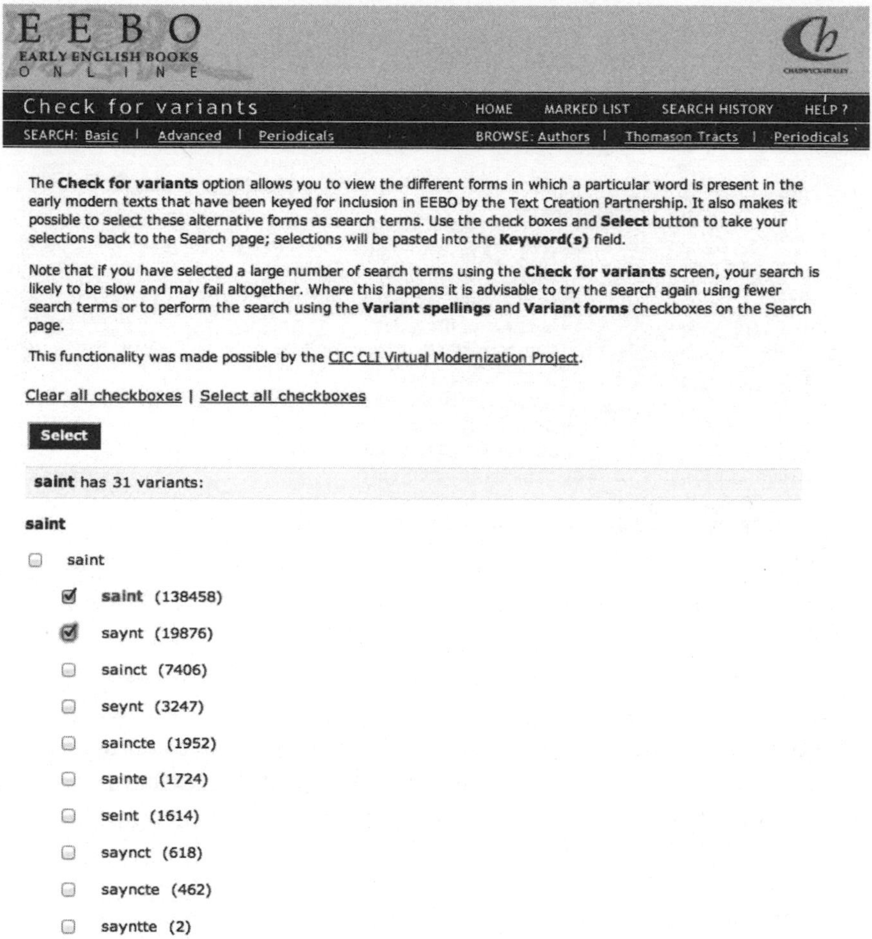

Figure 3. Screenshot of ProQuest's Interface showing variant spelling check list.

resource materials could be provided by libraries and publishers. This base of material should, in turn, be given to scholars in a standardized way (like TEI encoded texts) for them to utilize in whatever way is best for their discipline.

As the humanities community faces the daunting prospect of having the largest corpus of material ever imaginable with Google Books with images (and some text), might it be imaginable for the entire community (librarians, scholars, publishers, and funders) to determine what is a seminal corpus of material and deliver it for the purposes of scholarship? [12]

Conclusions

Rather than following the traditional model for humanities scholarship, that is, asking for a grant from the NEH (or a similar funder), digitizing materials (which may already have been digitized for a different project), doing the editorial work, and making such a project available on the internet, perhaps a new model is called for: a model where publishers (such as ProQuest or Google) provides a basic level of access (to images and OCR text), libraries band together to improve a corpus of those items to a level that would be useful for scholars, and scholars take that improved material to build their own scholarly projects. Rather than spending millions of dollars to build the same basic level of infrastructure over and over again for different scholarly projects, it would seem a more beneficial use of resources to collaborate and agree on some basic parameters of what will be most useful to humanities scholarship in the future.[13]

In all, it would seem that the digital humanities community has a tremendous opportunity. Now, with large amounts of data, images, and text suddenly available, it would be a great time to think about guidelines for what kinds of materials will be valuable for scholarship and to create a joint effort of librarians, scholars, and publishers to create an infrastructure like TCP. TCP is a community effort built around a corpus of early modern text. What other communities could be built around different corpora? Could these communities build efforts similar to the TCP? How could these various communities band together to create a large effort around projects like Google Books? What standards would need to be developed? All of these questions remain to be answered, but TCP may provide an interesting way of answering them. The community of scholars currently is divided among different disciplines. By banding together and working to build some common cores of primary resource material (however one might wish to

---

[12] To see examples of how this might work out specifically in the context of the Google digitization project, see Shawn Martin, "To Google or not to Google, that is the question: Supplementing Google Books to make it more useful for scholarship," *Journal of Library Administration* 47 (2008): 141–50.

[13] TCP is not the only entity to attempt such a project (even in early modern studies): projects like ITER have also effectively garnered support from different communities to build a large knowledgebase. See William Bowen, "Iter: Building an Effective Knowledge Base," in *New Technologies in Medieval and Renaissance Studies*, Volume 1, Iter and the Arizona Center for Medieval and Renaissance Studies, 2008 http://cf.itergateway.org/ntmrs/pdf/NTMRS1bowen.pdf.

define that) one could create a TCP-like project that upgrades many thousands of books in a cost-effective way. The only way of doing that, however, is to have a concerted effort to cooperate between commercial entities, universities, and scholarly communities. TCP has done it in a small scale. The question is, can it be done on a larger scale?

Reference List

Bowen, William. 2008. "Iter: Building an Effective Knowledge Base." In *New Technologies in Medieval and Renaissance Studies*, Volume 1, Iter and the Arizona Center for Medieval and Renaissance Studies http://cf.itergateway. org/ntmrs/pdf/NTMRS1bowen.pdf.

Crow, Raym. 2009. *Income Models for Open Access: An overview of current practice.* Washington, DC: Scholarly Publishing and Resource Coalition, http:// www.arl.org/sparc/publications/papers/imguide.shtml.

Fitzpatrick, Kathleen. 2011. *Planned Obsolescence: Publishing, Technology, and the Future of the Academy.* New York: New York Univ. Press.

Guthrie, Kevin, Rebecca Griffiths, and Nancy Maron. 2008. *Sustainability and Revenue Models for Online Academic Resources.* New York: Ithaka Foundation, http://www.jisc.ac.uk/media/documents/themes/eresources/sca_itha-ka_sustainability_report-final.pdf.

Maron, Nancy L. Smith, K. Kirby Smith, and Matthew Loy. 2009. *Sustaining Digital Resources: An On-the-Ground View of Projects Today,* New York: Ithaka Foundation. http://www.ithaka.org/ithaka-s-r/research/ithaka-case-stud-ies-in-sustainability/report/SCA_Ithaka_SustainingDigitalResources_Re-port.pdf.

Martin, Shawn. "To Google or not to Google, that is the question: Supplementing Google Books to make it more useful for scholarship." *Journal of Library Administration* 47 (2008): 141–50.

McCarty, Willard. 2005. *Humanities Computing.* New York: Palgrave Macmillan.

McCullough, Aaron. 2009. "Bedfellows in Mass Digital Conversion: Ten Years of Text Creation Partnership(s)." *New Knowledge Environments* http://journals. uvic.ca/index.php/INKE/article/view/160/166

McGann, Jerome. 2001. *Radiant Textuality.* New York: Palgrave Macmillan.

Mueller, Martin. 2011. "The TCP texts and the query potential of the digital surrogate." *Project Bamboo Website,* November 28. http://www.projectbamboo. org/the-tcp-texts-and-the-query-potential-of-the-digital-surrogate/.

Sandler, Mark. 2004. "New Uses for the World's Oldest Books: Democratizing Access to Historic Corpora." *Association of Research Libraries Bi-Monthly Report* 232 (February, 2004): 4. http://www.arl.org/newsltr/232/textcreation. html.

Unsworth, John, Paul N. Courant, Sarah E. Fraser, Michael F. Goodchild, Margaret Hedstrom, Charles Henry, Peter B. Kaufman, Jerome McGann, Roy Rosenzweig, and Bruce Zuckerman. 2006. "Our Cultural Commonwealth." *The Report of the American Council of Learned Societies Commission on Cyberinfrastructure for the Humanities and Social Sciences Report from the American Council of Learned Societies.* Washington, D.C.: American Council of Learned Societies. http://www.acls.org/cyberinfrastructure/OurCulturalCommonwealth.pdf.

UNIVERSITY OF PENNSYLVANIA

The Emory Women Writers Resource Project: Teaching Students, Training Students

SHEILA T. CAVANAGH

THE EMORY WOMEN WRITERS PROJECT (EWWRP)[1] HAD AN INAUSPICIOUS, but probably appropriate, start in 1995. After completing a computer-assisted instruction program the previous year, I decided that a web project would be a good way to build instructional resources about women writers (supplementing those available through the Brown Women Writers Project), while providing fifth-year funding for a graduate student (at that point, funding extended for only four years). Accordingly, I applied for an internal grant from the Emory Instructional Computing Committee. Unfortunately, I do not have my initial rejection letter, but I remember its substance quite well. It said that the committee had determined that I was interested only in performing my own research and that the proposal had no instructional merit. Copies of the letter went to my chair and dean. I was outraged, not so much for the rejection as for the perceived attack on my integrity. At that point, I had not published a word on any woman writer and was appalled that a letter was circulating that claimed I was being self-serving in support of research that did not even exist. I promptly sent a copy of my c.v. to my chair, the dean, and the committee, circling my research record and expressing my fury at the accusation. Shortly thereafter, the proposal was funded. A couple of years later, I was turned down by the "Superfund," which was part of the Emory Digital Information Resources Council, because my proposal did not look like the successful grant applications, which predominantly came from the sciences. I wanted to fund people, not machines, which Emory's

---

[1] This paper was delivered at the 2007 MLA convention in Chicago, IL, at a panel entitled "E-Editing in Corpora," Michael Denbo presiding.
http://womenwriters.library.emory.edu/

Library had already offered to supply. More calmly this time, since my honesty was not being impugned, I requested reconsideration. Once again, the money was approved, this time for three years.

I start with these anecdotes because they illustrate the kind of bumps new work often encounters, before the collaboration I will describe begins to flourish. I call these obstacles "appropriate" since they reflect the re-education process that many of us have participated in as we worked to fashion women in the archives and digital humanities into recognizable and recognized academic endeavors. It has been relatively recently that either field has gained whatever academic credibility it now enjoys, and research on women and academic computing in the humanities still face hurdles that more established fields do not. As one prominent early modern scholar asked me shortly after my book on Mary Wroth appeared in 2001: "Did your book on a woman writer sink like a stone to the bottom of the ocean? Mine did. Of all my books, my work on women writers receives the least recognition." For a long time, those of us working digitally and on women's studies have faced similar responses.

Fortunately, however, the EWWRP has enjoyed numerous collaborative accomplishments since its rocky start. Collaboration has been essential over the past fifteen years, as countless graduate students, librarians, undergraduates, computer staff and administrators, grant specialists, deans, provosts, colleagues, and friends have brought their intellectual and financial support, as well as their physical labor and problem-solving skills, to create and sustain a project that continually measures its success through both process and product. Relying heavily on serendipity as well as serious planning, the EWWRP has helped shape careers and long-term partnerships while building its archive.

The EWWRP operates predominantly through three organizing foci: faculty needs, student interests, and library resources. The project contains several discrete units. The largest of these, the Women's Genre Fiction Project, includes approximately 240 nineteenth- and early twentieth-century popular novels. Funded by the NEH, with a generous subsidy from Emory, this collection makes available numerous yellow-back novels, many of which are hard to find elsewhere. By digitizing these novels and making them openly available, we expand their accessibility, while reducing the numbers who handle the original books. We also have collections in texts from the early modern period to the early twentieth century, World War I poetry, Native American writers, Abolition, Freedom and Human Rights writers, and writers on Women's Advocacy. In addition, several graduate students have contributed edited texts, contextualizing essays, and study guides to the site. We have also made available the full text of Ruth Hughey's early twentieth-century Cornell dissertation entitled *Cultural In-*

terest of Women in England from 1524 to 1640. In short, the EWWRP represents
an eclectic mix of texts, gathered together and processed by an even more eclectic
group of collaborators.

As director, my main goal is teaching and training students, while building
an archive that can aid pedagogy and research locally and globally. Since the project requires significant technological expertise in a realm that is continually in
flux, it offers graduate students the opportunity to gain practical as well as intellectual skills and content knowledge. In several cases, this experience has led directly to post-Ph.D. employment. Dr. Erika Farr, for example, who has an essay in
this volume, is now working as a digital librarian helping forge the field of "born
digital archives," through crafting procedures for dealing appropriately with Sir
Salman Rushdie's computers (several of Rushdie's personal computers are included in his archive at Emory). In other cases, students have given conference papers
and published print or electronic articles about their work with the EWWRP and
some have discovered texts that provided important, but hitherto unknown, material for their dissertations. Students have also gained invaluable experience in
learning how to create an archive, as they have been integrally involved in the selection and organization of the texts included. Several have also acquired expertise in the intimidating, labyrinthine world of grant proposals. Still others have
learned how to select and edit early modern texts for digitization. The pedagogical
benefits of creating this archive, therefore, have been considerable.

Those of us working in the varied worlds of women's studies — particularly
in earlier periods — know all too well, however, that not everyone shares our passion for these subject areas. As my opening anecdotes suggest, even before the
current economic crisis struck, digital humanities and scholarship on women
writers do not always feature as priorities in the broader university community.
The evolution of the EWWRP has not depended on widespread consensus about
the significance of its specific aims, however. Instead, the collaborative efforts
that have led to its success have enabled other units of the university to meet
their independent goals, using the EWWRP as a mechanism. Providing support
for this digital archive, in other words, is just as often the result of working with
those pursuing disparate outcomes, as it is likely to come from people who believe that the specific subject area of the project is important. As we move forward, it is likely to become increasingly critical that we recognize and take advantage of the ways that this situation can work to our advantage.

Here I would like to offer a few examples. In 2007, the Association of Ameri-
can Colleges and Universities released a report entitled *College Learning for the
New Global Century*, also known as the LEAP report, from its genesis with the
National Leadership Council for Liberal Education and America's Promise. The

report challenges American higher education to reassess what students of today
need to be learning in college and how institutions of tertiary education can better serve their diversifying population. In the current environment of strategic
plans, measurable outcomes, and proliferating models of goals and assessments,
reports such as this play a significant role in determining how colleges and universities present themselves publicly. Not surprisingly, the LEAP report does not
contend that all students in the new millennium need to demonstrate proficiency
in the study of women's texts. It does, however, make a strong case for the importance of integrative learning and collaboration, advising academic "institution[s]
[to] create an intellectual commons where faculty and staff work together to connect the essential outcomes with the content and practices of their educational
programs."[2] It also recommends that universities help students gain "intellectual
and practical skills, including inquiry and analysis, critical and creative thinking, written and oral communication, quantitative literacy, information literacy,
teamwork and problem solving."[3]

The report speaks additionally about the importance of collaborative projects:

> Collaborative Learning combines two key goals: learning to work and
> solve problems in the company of others, and sharpening one's own
> understanding by listening seriously to the insights of others, especial-
> ly those with different backgrounds and life experiences. Approaches
> range from . . . team-based assignments and writing, to cooperative
> projects and research.[4]

The LEAP report, like the 1998 Boyer Report *Reinventing Undergraduate Education: A Blueprint for America's Research Universities*, offers colleges and universities benchmarks for assessing their progress in improving the quality of American higher education. It provides the foundation for measurable results that these
institutions can use to increase their standing in the academic community, while
strengthening the education received by their students. Collaborative, digital projects like the EWWRP provide avenues for the students who create the archive and
for students who encounter it in the classroom to achieve the kinds of goals promul-
gated in the LEAP report. In accordance with the report's directives, these students
encounter each of the desirable components mentioned above, from intellectual

---

[2] Association of American Colleges and Universities, *College Learning for the New Global
Century: A Report from the National Leadership Council for Liberal Education & America's
Promise* (Washington, DC: Association of American Colleges and Universities, 2007), 51.

[3] *College Learning for the New Global Century*, 12.

[4] *College Learning for the New Global Century*, 54.

and practical skills to information literacy, teamwork, and problem solving. In accordance with the tenets of the Boyer Report, moreover, such projects involve students directly in the research that creates the archive:

> Undergraduates need to benefit from the unique opportunities and resources available in research universities. . . . The Research Universities need to be able to give their students a dimension of experience and capability they cannot get in any other setting.[5]

Once again, while the Boyer Report does not mandate the creation of collaborative archives of women's writings, projects like the EWWRP help further its primary recommendations.

As such examples illustrate, these kinds of reports provide initiatives like the Emory Women Writers Resource Project with an invitation to align themselves with broader institutional priorities. Successful grant proposals sustain projects such as this one, while bringing joy to the hearts of university administrators. In many cases, the content of the project can be less important to those who support it institutionally than its ability to further broader aims. Provosts, Directors of Information Technology, and Development personnel, for example, may never have given any thought to early modern women's writing (however preposterous that sounds), but they have devoted considerable attention to ways they can showcase the achievement of their institution's faculty and students. Linking projects we cherish to the framework of broad institutional goals, therefore, can entice key members of the university into supporting an initiative they have no intrinsic interest in. From a university perspective, furthering the study of woman writers is insignificant. Creating an archive that brings in outside funding, trains students, publicizes library holdings, and enhances the reputation of the university, on the other hand, catches administrative attention. For those of us who value research on women over the plethora of other topics that could generate institutional support, it is important that we remember this principle and use it to our advantage.

At Emory, for example, like many other universities, we recently completed the monumental endeavor of creating strategic plans for the university overall and for each individual unit. While the EWWRP was in place long before these plans were finished, we certainly intend to remind the institution of our vital role

---

[5] The Boyer Commission on Educating Undergraduates in the Research University, *Reinventing Undergraduate Education: A Blueprint for America's Research Universities* (http://naples.cc.sunysb.edu/Pres/boyer.nsf, 1998), 38.

in the attainment of their stated goals. The five-year strategy for Emory Libraries, for instance, states the following:

> To fulfill its vision, build on areas of great strength, and assume a leadership position among university libraries, the Library seeks to pursue the following goals and strategic initiatives.
> Goal 1: Digital Innovations
> Innovative and robust digital information services and resources will establish Emory as a leader in the development and deployment of digital information resources and services, and among the top tier digital libraries in the country by 2012.[6]

While elaborating upon this goal, the plan continues:

> The digital production and management of information is central to the redefinition of university libraries. Through digitization and the development of new tools and systems for information management, libraries are poised to play a pivotal role in the production of knowledge, replace university presses as 21st century disseminators of knowledge, and contribute to the internationalization of scholarship . . . Emory seeks to advance this evolution through digital initiatives that increase connections between people and build on the Library's role as a meeting ground for scholars.[7]

Although scholarship on women does not appear in this statement, the EWWRP can readily situate itself in the context of Goal 1. Since we are housed in the Library and depend on library support for our endeavors, the way that our project coincides with the predominant aim of the Library for the next five years is something we can capitalize upon as we work to strengthen our academic goals. Similarly, Goal 2 of the Library's strategic plan correlates with our mission, with its strong support for Emory's Special Collections:

> Renowned special collections and world-class facilities differentiate Emory from peer institutions and establish Emory as one of the top five destinations in the country for research and teaching in modern literature, African

---

[6] Robert Woodruff Library Emory University Strategic Plan, http://web.library.emory.edu/about/mission-and-strategic-plan

[7] Woodruff Library Strategic Plan, http://web.library.emory.edu/about/mission-and-strategic-plan

American history and culture, theological studies, and other emerging areas of institutional priority.[8]

Goal 2 rightly praises Emory's Special Collections, now known as the Manuscripts, Archives, and Rare Books Library or MARBL. As we have worked to expand our archive, members of the EWWRP have met regularly with MARBL staff, combing through their catalogues in order to identify texts and collections that can further our goals as well as support the strategic aims of the Library. The Women's Genre Fiction Project, for instance, which received the NEH support, arose from our collaborative conviction that digitizing a significant proportion of the yellow-back novels Emory had collected, starting in the 1960s, would provide a valuable resource for scholars and students of women's fiction, while promoting an under-utilized segment of our print collection. Similarly, our African-American and Women's Advocacy collections arose from collaborations with MARBL and other area libraries designed to make accessible texts dealing with topics of great concern to scholars. Although we have not always received the grants we've applied for, by linking our aspirations with those of the Library we enhance our mutual ability to move forward with our individual goals. As the University strategic plan proclaims: "Our aspirations as a university can best be reached within overarching, university-wide strategic goals."[9] While many faculty understandably bemoan the current primacy of such strategic efforts, the common association between financial support and stated institutional missions makes it prudent to acknowledge that cooperation with these rhetorical assertions can promote individual scholarly and pedagogical initiatives that the university may not otherwise value. Accordingly, when Emory's Office of Information Technology asserts that it is guided by University strategic initiatives when it supports digital scholarship and IT-Enabled Research, it behooves the Emory Women Writers Resource Project to remind the Vice-Provost of Information Technology that the project exists in order to further the university's initiatives as well as its own academic mission. Few, if any, of those who wrote these strategic plans gave any thought to women's writing during their deliberations. It is up to those of us who value this research to let them know how critical women's archives can be in their quest to achieve their strategic goals.

At the same time, projects such as the EWWRP continue to provide intellectual, technical, and financial support for students of all levels, make women's texts

---

[8] Woodruff Library Strategic Plan, http://web.library.emory.edu/about/mission-and-strategic-plan

[9] Emory University Strategic Plan, http://www.emory.edu/strategicplan/

available to interested readers throughout the world, and enhance the pedagogical and research agendas of those who work in related fields. The students and others who work on the project have acquired substantial content knowledge in areas that were largely new to them. They have learned how to determine which texts cry out to be digitized and which have already been made available electronically. They also learn how to prioritize during text selection when resources are inevitably limited. Those involved in editing learn to visualize the needs of their audiences as they determine what kind of annotations and introductions to create for their texts. They also figure out what texts might be most usefully edited, both for their own professional and educational advancement and for the betterment of the field. Those whose primary focus is pedagogical gain experience in bringing these kinds of electronic documents into the classroom, endeavors that have also resulted in print publications for several current and former Emory graduate students. Most of those engaged with the project also acquire technical experience that helps fund their education, while enhancing their marketability for academic computing projects and positions in the future. Over the years of the project, many of the students involved have become faculty; several have followed their new expertise into librarianship. All of us have learned a great deal about women's writing, computers, collaboration, and the vagaries of human nature. The EWWRP has been fortunate in attracting a wide range of talented, congenial people into its realm. The one disastrous partnership we've experienced was not formed with someone at Emory and several of us gained valuable experience in moving forward productively despite the poor behavior of others. This is a useful skill to cultivate.

As we move forward through the current precarious financial circumstances, I believe that it will be even more important to work collaboratively if we are going to advance our work in women's writing. Fortunately, organizations like the MLA are taking steps to support this kind of joint effort, which has traditionally been devalued in the humanities. In their statement on reforming current tenure and promotion criteria, the MLA recommends that:

> Departments and institutions should recognize the legitimacy of scholarship produced in new media, whether by individuals or in collaboration, and create procedures for evaluating these forms of scholarship.[10]

In addition, since the 2008 convention, there have been a series of workshops, officially sponsored by the MLA, dedicated to addressing the issues surrounding

---

[10] Report of the MLA Task Force on Evaluating Scholarship for Tenure and Promotion (2006) http://www.mla.org/tenure_promotion, 11.

digital scholarship in promotion and tenure decisions. This kind of institutional endorsement for the work we are doing will be a critical factor in determining whether such projects can survive and thrive in the long-term. As those working in the field of digital humanities know, there is much important work that has already been done and we will all suffer unless we make deliberate, concerted, and collaborative efforts toward sustainability.

EMORY UNIVERSITY

The Henslowe-Alleyn Digitisation Project: Past, Present, and Future[1]

GRACE IOPPOLO

First: The Past

THE ARCHIVE OF DULWICH COLLEGE IN LONDON, ENGLAND, HOLDS thousands of pages of manuscripts left to the College by its founder, the eminent actor Edward Alleyn (1566–1626). This archive includes his personal and professional papers and those he inherited from his father-in-law, Philip Henslowe (d. 1616). As a group, these manuscripts comprise the largest and most important single extant archive of material on the professional theatre and dramatic performance in early modern England. Henslowe and Alleyn ran several of the most successful acting companies of the time, including the Lord Strange's Men and the Lord Admiral's Men, for which Alleyn performed such famous roles as Dr Faustus and Tamburlaine. The sole surviving actor's 'part', or script, from the period, for the play *Orlando Furioso* (http://www.henslowe-alleyn.org.uk/images/MSS-1/Article-138/01r.html) is in the Dulwich archive, as is the 'plot', or backstage outline, of the play *The Seven Deadly Sins, Part II*, one of only four plots known to survive in their entirety. Henslowe and Alleyn built and expanded several London public theatres, including the Rose and the Fortune (http://www.henslowe-alleyn.org.uk/images/Muniments-Series-1/Group-022/01r.html), the foundations of some of which have recently been discovered or excavated by Museum of London staff. Named by King James I as Joint 'Masters of the Royal Game of Bears, Bulls and Mastiff Dogs', Henslowe and Alleyn

---

[1] This paper was first delivered at a panel entitled "New Technologies and Renaissance Studies II: RETS, The Henslowe-Alleyn Digitisation Project," held at the 2008 Renaissance Society of America Annual Meeting, Chicago, IL, Michael Denbo presiding.

also staged such blood sports as bull- and bear-baiting at the Bear Gardens and other venues, including royal palaces.

Remarkably, Henslowe's and Alleyn's papers provide extensive, detailed, dated, and unique information about their daily, weekly, or annual employment of dramatists and actors such as Ben Jonson, Thomas Middleton, George Chapman, Thomas Heywood, Philip Massinger, Thomas Dekker, Cyril Tourneur, John Webster, Richard Burbage, Will Kemp, and Nathan Field, among numerous others (http://www.henslowe-alleyn.org.uk/images/MSS-1/Article-068/01r.html and http://www.henslowe-alleyn.org.uk/images/MSS-1/Article-070/01r.html). Although Shakespeare is not mentioned, he belonged to acting companies for which Henslowe commissioned plays, and box office receipts for Easter 1594 for *Titus Andronicus* can be found here (http://www.henslowe-alleyn.org.uk/images/MSS-7/009r.html). As Henslowe's famous 'Diary', or account book (http://www.henslowe-alleyn.org.uk/images/MSS-7/011r.html), makes clear, he comissioned or staged over three hundred and fifty plays, the texts of most of which are now lost. The information he provides about these plays, even in listing their titles and identifying their authors, greatly enlarges our knowledge of the canon of particular dramatists such as Jonson, Heywood, Chettle, and Dekker, and establishes which authors wrote plays alone and how and when they collaborated with others. In his own transcription of two poems, for example, you see what Jonson did in his spare time (http://www.henslowe-alleyn.org.uk/images/MSS-1/Article-135/01r.html).

Henslowe also notes the rehearsal and performance dates and histories of many of these plays, occasionally detailing their box-office receipts. In doing so, he provides, in most cases, our most significant records for early modern performance schedules in general and in particular, especially in allowing us to establish exactly when acting companies performed in the provinces due to official closures of London theatres in times of plague. Henslowe and Alleyn fully document their costs and revenues, and those of stockholders, for all aspects of London theatre production and provincial touring, even including the commission and purchase of costumes, properties, and sets from a variety of named tradesmen, as well as the loss of income by those whose businesses depended on theatre attendance, such as Thames ferrymen (http://www.henslowe-alleyn.org.uk/images/MSS-1/Article-017/01r.html). In fact, most of what modern scholars know about the early modern English theatre, both as financial enterprise and artistic endeavour, comes from the study of the Henslowe and Alleyn papers at Dulwich College.

More broadly, these rich and extraordinary manuscripts also explore the intersection between theatre and the political, cultural, religious, and social spheres of early modern England. Henslowe and Alleyn document their personal and professional dealings with many of the most powerful figures from the 1570s to the 1620s, including monarchs: Queen Elizabeth I, King James I, Queen Anne, Prince Henry, and King Charles I; chancellors, Privy Councillors, and courtiers: Sir Robert Cecil (Secretary of State), Sir Thomas Howard (Lord Treasurer), Charles Howard (Lord High Admiral), and William Herbert (Earl of Pembroke), as well as Sir Francis Bacon (Lord Chancellor), Sir Edward Coke, Sir Christopher Hatton, Ferdinando Stanley (Lord Strange), Thomas Sackville (Lord Buckhurst), George Villiers (Duke of Buckingham), and Henry Carey (the Lord Chamberlain and patron of Shakespeare's acting company). Also included are the Master of the Rolls, Sir Julius Caesar; church leaders: various Bishops of London, and John Donne, Dean of St Paul's; foreign ambassadors: Count Gondomar among them; local London officials: various Lord Mayors and Sheriffs; and the Masters of the Revels: Sir Edmund Tilney and George Buc. Other notable figures whose autograph papers are in the archive include Stephen Gosson, the polemicist and scourge of the early modern stage.

In addition to their theatrical enterprises, Henslowe and Alleyn were shrewd and successful investors in a number of other businesses. As property developers, they purchased numerous parcels of land and leased commercial buildings throughout London, particularly in Southwark, Bishopsgate, Cripplegate, Shoreditch, and Dulwich, as well as in York and Surrey; these records provide a virtual map of several early modern London neighbourhoods. Henslowe particularly excelled in what we call now venture capitalism, earning income through banking, pawnbrokerage, mining iron ore, forestry, and the marketing of Ashdown forest timber. All the detailed financial records of these enterprises, which illuminate a wide range of early modern economic, regional, architectural, and archaeological history, are also housed at Dulwich College.

In sum, this manuscript archive is a rich, invaluable, and unique part of English culture and heritage, but for over 250 years most of the Henslowe-Alleyn papers remained unbound and stored in the chest in which they had lain since the founding of the College by Edward Alleyn in 1619. Many individual documents, both large and small, were left in their original condition: folded up into small packets (a form of storage which preceded the use of envelopes). The volume comprising Henslowe's Diary began to be borrowed from the library during the 18th and 19th centuries by the scholars Edmond Malone, John Payne Collier, and J. O. Halliwell-Phillips, among others. In fact, during this time some of its pages were removed or otherwise destroyed. Some of its fragments have since been sold or auctioned and are now at the British Library, Belvoir Castle, and the Folger Shakespeare Library, among other places.

In the early 19th century, staff at Dulwich were successful in reclaiming the play *The Telltale* and the plot of *The Second Part of the Seven Deadly Sins* from an auction, but over the years many other items were dispersed and have not yet been definitively identified, including about one hundred play manuscripts and a number of printed books bequeathed to the College in 1687 by the actor and bibliophile William Cartwright the younger. In the 1870s, the Governors of Dulwich College asked George Warner, an expert at the British Museum, to catalogue the manuscripts. Warner spent many years assessing the contents of the archive as he found it, expertly opening, repairing, and ordering the documents in the archive, finally having them bound into a set of 36 volumes which he named the 'Alleyn Papers'. He left the muniments, some of which are extremely large in size, unbound. In 1881, he published *The Catalogue of the Manuscripts and Muniments of Alleyn's College of God's Gift at Dulwich*.[2] Further discoveries at the archive were listed by Francis Bickley in the Second Series of *The Catalogue of the Manuscripts and Muniments of Alleyn's College of God's Gift at Dulwich*.[3]

Half of these manuscript volumes and most of the muniments concern the private affairs and non-theatrical businesses of the Henslowe and Alleyn families, as well as the history of Dulwich College since its inception. It is the other half of these volumes, representing the theatrical affairs of Henslowe and Alleyn, which are the subject of this website and electronic archive. Less than half of the theatrical items in the Henslowe-Alleyn Papers have ever been transcribed, and these transcriptions are largely available only in out-of-print editions. R. A. Foakes's 1977 photographic facsimile edition of two volumes of manuscripts (*The Henslowe Papers*) had a limited printing and covers only 20% of the relevant archive.[4] The 2002 reprinting of Foakes's standard 1961 edition of *Henslowe's Diary* has widely encouraged scholars to pursue other material in the Dulwich archive.[5] The archive has also been of tremendous value also to Museum of London archaeologists, who are now using new technology, such as radar scanning, to examine the original sites in Southwark and Shoreditch of various early modern playhouses, including the Theatre, the Globe, the Curtain, and the Rose, and who are radically re-evaluating their data about the building of these playhouses.[6]

---

[2] G. Warner, *The Catalogue of the Manuscripts and Muniments of Alleyn's College of God's Gift at Dulwich* (London: Longmans, Green, and Co., 1881).
[3] F. Bickley, *The Catalogue of the Manuscripts and Muniments of Alleyn's College of God's Gift at Dulwich* (London: privately printed, 1903).
[4] R. A. Foakes, *The Henslowe Papers*, 2 vols. (London: Scolar Press, 1977).
[5] *Henslowe's Diary*, ed. R. A. Foakes and F. T. Rickert (Cambridge: Cambridge Univ. Press, 1960, repr. 2002).
[6] See Julian Bowsher and Pat Miller, *The Rose and the Globe: Playhouses of Tudor Bankside, Southwark Excavations 1988–91* (London: Museum of London, 2009).

Second: The Present

Although transcriptions of the over 2200 pages of manuscripts are not yet available in this electronic archive and website, the members of the Henslowe-Alleyn Digitisation Project hoped that making the manuscripts themselves available as photographic images would encourage further study and use of this very rich resource. This website and electronic archive were not primarily designed to suit the needs of specialist scholars, however, but to enrich and enhance the study of all those interested in early modern English drama, theatre history and historiography, as well as social, economic, regional, architectural, and legal history, besides palaeography and manuscript studies. It is the hope of the Henslowe-Alleyn Digitisation Project members that the use of these manuscripts will not be confined to students and scholars but to a wide-ranging and ever-changing community of online readers in a variety of ways. In short, the website and electronic archive will appeal to anyone interested in the greatest age of English professional drama and theatrical production.

Thus, this Digitisation Project, founded in 2002, had two aims and objectives: first, to protect and enhance the increasingly fragile manuscripts in Dulwich College, and second, to make their contents much more widely and freely available in an electronic format online. I am the Founder and Director of the Project; David Cooper, formerly librarian at Corpus Christi College, Oxford University, is the Project Photographer, and Paul Vetch is the Computer Manager. The members of our advisory board are Peter Beal (University of London), Julian Bowsher (Museum of London), S. P. Cerasano (Colgate), R. A. Foakes (UCLA), John Lavagnino (King's College London), H. R. Woudhuysen (University College London), and Jan Piggott (former Keeper of Archives, Dulwich College) and Calista Lucy (Keeper of Archives, Dulwich College).

These theatrical manuscripts include the following 'Alleyn Papers':

MSS 1: Alleyn's Letters/Papers on English Drama and Stage and the Fortune Theatre, 1559–1662 (all documents);
MSS 2: Henslowe's and Alleyn's Letters and Papers as Joint Masters of the Royal Game of Bears, Bulls and Mastiff Dogs, 1598–1626 (all documents);
MSS 3: Alleyn & Henslowe's General Correspondence, 1577–1626 (selected documents);
MSS 5: Legal and Miscellaneous Papers of Edward Alleyn and his Family, 1612–1626 (selected documents);
MS 7: Henslowe's Diary and Account-Book 1592–1609 (all pages);

MS 8: Alleyn's Memorandum Book, 1594–1616 (all pages);
MS 9: Alleyn's Diary and Account-Book, 1617–1622 (all pages);
MS 19: 'Plott' (or outline) of *The Seven Deadly Sins, Part II* (all)
MS 20: Text of the play *The Telltale* (all).
Muniments, Section I: The Theatre and Bear Garden documents, 1546–1662 (all)
Muniments, Section II: Leases and other documents (selected muniments).

One brief discussion of why these manuscripts need digitisation and the stunning information they can finally reveal to us can concentrate on Alleyn's Diary, which has been published only once, as the second volume in a very limited printing of *The History of Dulwich College* (1889).[7] As S. P. Cerasano and I have discovered in preparing a modern critical edition of this diary from the manuscript for Oxford University Press, while Philip Henslowe's Diary records an extraordinary professional life, Edward Alleyn's Diary records a largely ordinary, and occasionally extraordinary, private life. In his Diary, Alleyn documents nearly every day from September 29, 1617 to October 1, 1622, long after his retirement from acting. He illustrates how he lived his life on a daily basis: where he travelled, whom he knew and dealt with, what he ate, as well as how and where he ate it, what he and his wife Joan wore, and even what medicines they took. Thus the Diary reveals aspects of his domestic life and household, his social and political circle, his personal friends and professional contacts, and how he spent his considerable weath.

Alleyn lists expenses for an astonishingly wide variety of goods and services, including the acquisition and maintenance of land, buildings, and gardens, the care of livestock, including pigeons, and the purchase and preparation of food, especially for dinner parties and social events, as well as the costs of everyday household items. His purchase of screws, binding rods, leather stirrups, herbs and seeds appear alongside those of various types of clothing and textiles — including whalebone for his wife Joan's bodices. On May 7th, he has itemised his expense of £1 17s 11d for the coats to be worn by the 'poore schollers', probably at the opening of Dulwich College, where Alleyn will provide them with with a free education. His wife's red petticoat with expensive black velvet and his cloth jerkin and a cloak with silk basting may also have been ordered for the College's opening. Joyous celebrations of birthdays, wedding anniversaries, and religious feast days are particularly noted in the Diary, as on May 16, Whitsunday (i.e.,

---

[7] William Young, *The History of Dulwich College: Down to the Passing of the Act of Parliament Dissolving the Original Corporation, 28th August 1857,* 2 vols. (London: Morrison & Gibb, 1889).

Pentecost), when he and his wife invited to dinner the poor, for whom he provided almshouses, which still stand today alongside Dulwich Chapel, in which
Alleyn and Joan are buried.

Alleyn also itemises his frequent travel to London from his home in Dulwich, including the cost of crossing the Thames by ferry from the south to the
north bank. Extra expenses for 'horse-standing' (i.e. holding a horse) are also
noted. Alleyn itemizes meals at a number of named pubs, whose locations, often
near the playhouses, he specifies, providing a kind of map of London. Yet other
entries record his receipt of rent for the Fortune Theatre and other leased properties, as well as visits to theatres such as the Red Bull, where on October 3, 1617
he received the sum of £3 6s 4d as his share in the play *The Younger Brother*. He
maintained contact with his colleagues and collaborators in the theatre, for example dining frequently over the years with the actor Charles Massey.

Not least of Alleyn's expenditure was on the writing and use of manuscripts.
He often lists the full costs of having various documents copied, engrossed, and
enrolled in Chancery and elsewhere, with prices ranging from 8 to 12 pence per
page, as well as what he has paid for a ream of paper (4s 4p on one occasion). He
also refers to the 'fayer copies' that he is having made, adding yet one more example of the contemporary use of the term, as distinct from 'foul papers'.[8] Alleyn's
friendship and compassion stretched beyond his former theatrical colleagues, for
he names at least one scrivener, 'Bowlton', who has been incarcerated for debt in
the Marshalsea prison and has appealed to Alleyn for relief. Alleyn eases Bowlton's 'great povertye' by sending him 10 shillings.

In fact, Alleyn's Diary suggests that he possessed the sort of prestige and stature that ambassadors and clerics as well as government officials recognised and
perhaps sought to share. At the very least, he was a popular companion or guest,
whether of the Mayor of London or the notorious Count Gondomar, Spanish Ambassador to England. Alleyn records his acquisition of books on theology, witch-
craft, and languages, for example, and paintings of Plantagenet kings, as well as his
visits to the collections of others, including Thomas Howard, Earl of Arundel, who
on April 17, 1618 showed Alleyn 'all His statues & picktures that came from Italy'
(http://www.henslowe-alleyn.org.uk/images/MSS-9/014r.html).

Alleyn's other invitations, either in his official capacity as the master of blood
sports or as a private individual, were to even more prestigious places — not merely the Bishop of Westminster's palace in the Clink, but to Greenwich and Whitehall

---

[8] For a full discussion of authorial foul papers and authorial and scribal fair copies of play-
texts, see Grace Ioppolo, *Dramatists and their Manuscripts in the Age of Shakespeare, Jonson,
Middleton and Heywood: Authorship, Authority and the Playhouse* (London: Routledge, 2006).

Palaces and other residences of James I. On July 13, 1618, Alleyn rode 'to wansted wher ye markques off buckinghame [George Villiers, the King's favourite] vndertooke ye Kings hand' for him on the letters patent for Dulwich College (http://www.henslowe-alleyn.org.uk/images/MSS-9/018r.html). Alleyn still had to negotiate the College's tax status with Sir Francis Bacon, but finally on May 27, 1619 Alleyn reported that he 'rode to grenewich & gott ye King's Hand' (http://www.henslowe-alleyn.org.uk/images/MSS-9/032v.html). Bacon's signature as a Dulwich College Governor on the Foundation Deed (http://www.henslowe-alleyn.org.uk/images/Muniments-Series-3/Group-584/01r.html) and his frequent presence in the Diary on less formal occasions testify to Alleyn's ability to negotiate personal and professional relationships with some of the King's most trusted officials.

The Diary was also a place for Alleyn to record those remarkable historical events to which he had a personal, and familiar, connection, as on January 12, 1619 when Whitehall Palace burned down; he had often performed in its Banqueting Hall. On March 1, 1619, he tersely writes in the margin, '4 in ye morning Q. Ann died'. On April 6, he explains: '[I went] with my wife to somersett Howse to see ye Hearse of Queen Anne' (http://www.henslowe-alleyn.org.uk/images/MSS-9/031v.html). In On May 13th he writes: 'memorandum; the quens funeral was this day, after diner my wife & I went to see itt' (http://www.henslowe-alleyn.org.uk/images/MSS-9/032r.html). Given Alleyn's role as actor-manager of the Queen's Men, and his frequent performances at court over the years in front of Anne, this would have been a poignant day for him. But also apparent here is Alleyn's sense that his Diary was, in some way, a witness to history.

Numerous other notable figures come to life in the pages of Alleyn's Diary, including John Taylor the Water Poet, Sir Robert Sidney, and John Donne, whom Alleyn heard preach in Camberwell on three occasions. Alleyn also records going to dinner on September 4, 1622 with a group of friends including Donne's daughter Constance. About a year later, and five months after the death of Joan, Alleyn married Constance, who was nearly forty years his junior. Donne's apparent refusal to pay Constance's dowry, which Alleyn in a draft letter to Donne called an 'vnkind vnexspeckted and vndeserved denial of that common curtesie afforded to a frend' (http://www.henslowe-alleyn.org.uk/images/MSS-3/Article-102/01r.html), caused a breach between Alleyn and Donne. Even such breaches allow us to connect the world of the early modern theatre with the world outside it, bringing both of them into vivid focus. With its minutiae and richness of detail, Alleyn's Diary is a remarkable bridge between and testament to those worlds. If you have never heard of this magnificent volume or the many others besides Henslowe's Diary in this archive, you will undertand why I and the other members of the Project want you to know about these manuscripts.

Third: The Future

In our Project, we have made available access to each of the 2200 pages, as well as digital essays by project members on fifteen of the most important documents in the Alleyn Papers, including the contracts for the Rose and Fortune Theatres, Alleyn's 'part' in *Orlando Furioso*, the 'Plot' of *The Seven Deadly Sins, Part II*, representative pages from Henslowe's 'Diary' and Alleyn's 'Diary' and from their correspondence with privy councillors, dramatists, and actors, as well as Ben Jonson's transcription of two poems. These digital essays offer expert commentary on their contents and contexts; the authors of these essays include members of the Advisory Board.

This Digitisation Project is designed for research purposes only. For contractual and copyright reasons, images and content are not downloadable or printable from the website or the electronic archive, nor can any material be used, copied, or reproduced in any fomat without permission and acknowledgement. The Project has been graciously supported by grants from The Leverhulme Trust, The British Academy, The Thriplow Charitable Trust, The Pilgrim Trust, the Henry E. Huntington Library, the Folger Shakespeare Library, the Newberry Library, the British and American Bibliographical Societies, and The University of Reading, for which the members of the Project remain very grateful.

I will conclude by very briefly outlining the various stages of the Henslowe-Alleyn Digitisation Project. But first a simple distinction for some and a complex distinction for others — a digitisation project is not a computer database; databases are a collection of data, for example a catalogue or index, that are accessible online; digitisation projects reproduce through digital photography or scanning particular sets of documents which then can be viewed online.

The first stage was development, including hiring David Cooper as Project Photographer and bringing John Lavagnino and Paul Vetch at King's College London's Centre for Computing in the Humanities into the Project as computer managers.

The second stage was fundraising (still ongoing) — we have thus far raised £70,000 — UK trusts are very generous in giving money for archival work, preservation, and heritage.

The third stage was the photography, using very high-quality professional camera and lighting equipment as well a custom-built cradle, and computer software. David Cooper, not only a former Oxford librarian but a conservation chemist by training, is now a freelance manuscript photographer. I have assisted him in photographing these 2200 pages, and I delivered the images on a portable disk to Paul Vetch, who stored them on the server at King's College London's Centre for Computing in the Humanities. Paul and his colleagues designed and continue to update the website and electronic archive which displays and stores these 2200 photographs. The photography took over 1½ years, working 2–3 days a week at Dulwich College with wonderful support from the archivists, first Jan Piggott and then his successor Calista Lucy. Each photograph could take from five minutes to one-half hour to set up and do, requiring from sixteen to thirty-two flashes and photographs, which the software integrated into one main photograph. This was often a physically arduous process, at least for David, me, and the porters who assisted us in carrying very heavy photographic equipment up four flights of stairs at Dulwich College into the stuffy, dusty, and wasp-laden attic in which we photographed the documents. For insurance reasons, we could not remove the manuscripts from Dulwich College and had to photograph them there, where David set up a makeshift studio.

The fourth stage was processing the images using Adobe Photoshop, which enhances and refines the photographs and their backgrounds, thereby removing obscurities; most of this work was done by Gill Cooper, David's wife and partner in Digital Lightforms, which I took over when we ran out of funding to pay Gill.

The fifth stage was marking up the prefatory material, the fifteen digital essays and the supporting documents, with XML language; I did this work after taking a one-day course in using Oxygen XML editor, taught by two of Paul Vetch's colleagues at King's College London

The sixth stage is design and implementation of the website which continues long after the Project's official launch at a gala party, hosted by Dulwich College, on November 25, 2009. While the 2000 or so digital images of manuscript pages are currently available through the use of the 'Zoomify' tool, we hope in this next, but not final, stage will attempt to acquire enough funding to upload transcriptions of nearly all the documents and to introduce search and indexing functions to the website and archive.

We still have a great deal to do in the Henslowe-Alleyn Digitisation Project, but we believe that Henslowe and Alleyn, who so carefully began the process of preserving their remarkable, unique, and invaluable archive for four hundred years, would appreciate our efforts thus far.

UNIVERSITY OF READING, UK

Brave New World or Dumping Ground? Electronic Supplements and the Printing of Jonson's Cynthia's Revels[1]

ERIC RASMUSSEN

PHILOSOPHERS FROM ROUSSEAU TO DERRIDA HAVE ALERTED US TO THE curiously dual nature of the *supplement*: often seen as an inessential extra, added to something complete in itself, the supplement is also added in order to complete, to compensate for a lack in what was supposed to be complete in itself. The advent of what are known in the publishing trade as "hybrid titles," print editions with electronic supplements, has recently brought this duality into sharp focus. Every major edition of early English drama published in the last few years — *The New Variorum Shakespeare, The Oxford Works of Thomas Middleton*, the 5th edition of David Bevington's *Complete Works of Shakespeare, The RSC Complete Works of Shakespeare*, the 2nd edition of *The Norton Shakespeare*, and *The Cambridge Works of Ben Jonson* — has included an electronic supplement. Dismissed by many as frivolous add-ons, unnecessarily "bundled" with serious scholarship in order to appeal to a generation of students that demands pixelated bells and whistles, electronic supplements are viewed by others as heralding a brave new era in publishing in which the virtues of the codex can be maintained and its limitations simultaneously transcended by providing virtually limitless numbers of relevant textual, audio, and visual records in a digital database. However, this celebration of the hybrid edition must be tempered by the realization of a somewhat disturbing trend: many publishers have come to treat the accompanying website as a sort of dumping ground for material that they would rather

[1] This paper was first delivered at the 2008 International Congress on Medieval Studies, Kalamazoo, MI, at a panel entitled "Electronic Shakespeare<s>," Michael Denbo presiding.

not print; consequently, over time users may come to view the electronic supplements not as rich repositories of contextual material but as archives of data that is inherently worth less than that in print editions.

The CD-ROM included with the New Variorum edition of *The Winter's Tale*, published by the Modern Language Association in 2005, represents the electronic supplement in its simplest form. The disk contains a PDF file of the book, which enables searches of this magisterial 974-page volume, but provides no additional material. The 2nd edition of *The Norton Shakespeare* (2008) provides users with a registration code to a password-protected website on which they can access multimedia resources, advertised as "the ideal tool for tying text to context in ways uniquely flexible and imaginative," including "audio clips and stills from classic productions, etchings, photographs, and costume design illustrations." David Bevington's 2008 *Complete Works of Shakespeare* offers students "study-on-the-go" guides for each play, which can be downloaded to an iPhone.

The edition of the *Complete Works of Shakespeare* that Jonathan Bate and I prepared for the Royal Shakespeare Company in 2007 contains the maximum number of pages, 2486, that a hardcover book of its size can physically include without danger of the binding falling apart. In an edition commissioned by a major acting company, we wanted to include substantial stage histories for each play, but having "maxed out" the print edition, we decided to put these materials on an open website. Given that bibliographies of suggested readings are one of the features of print editions that tend to become dated most quickly, we included an annotated list of the "100 best books on Shakespeare" on the website, where it can be updated as needed. Users can also access audio files of RSC actors and directors discussing the ways in which performers treat iambic pentameter, end-stopped lines versus run-on lines, and so on. In an editors' blog, Jonathan kept interested readers apprised of the edition's progress in the years leading up to its publication, and he has since posted entries responding to reviews as they come forth, providing a lively record of the edition's reception history.

The most ambitious electronic component of a scholarly edition to date is the one planned for the *Cambridge Works of Ben Jonson*, which will include the complete modernized text of the print edition along with digitized texts of Jonson's manuscripts and all early quarto and folio editions; a variety of legal documents and extracts from court records, parish registers, and guild archives; a range of visual and documentary material relating to the masques and entertainments, encompassing iconography, dance, eyewitness accounts, and records of payment; illustrations relevant to the stage history and masque records such as theater, costume, and stage designs; portraits of Jonson from his own time to the nineteenth century, and portraits of selected contemporaries; plans and drawings of great houses mentioned in Jonson's work (e.g. Penshurst, Bolsover); maps and other illustrations from the period; and musical scores of known arrangements of Jonson's songs. This promises to be an extraordinary database that will enrich future Jonsonian studies beyond measure.

On the downside, Cambridge University Press made a policy decision that strikes me as untenable: certain elements standardly included in critical editions, which may be of interest only to specialist readers, such as textual introductions, will not appear in the print edition but only in the electronic supplement. Full disclosure: I am one of the contributing editors to the Cambridge Jonson; a team of graduate students and I spent four years traversing the globe in order to collate press variants in all extant copies of the 1601 quarto of *Cynthia's Revels*; our research revealed that one sheet of the quarto had been completely reset and reprinted *circa* 1604; this suggested that at some point after the original printing of *Cynthia's Revels*, a bookseller, whose warehoused stock of pages had run short in one sheet, took the unprecedented step of reprinting the entire sheet in another printing-house, presumably because he believed that the market for the play would justify the not inconsiderable expense; thus, the reprinting may attest to the continuing popularity and marketability of *Cynthia's Revels* in the early years of James' reign. But this exciting new discovery, with its seemingly important implications for the reception history of the play, is not part of the seven-volume CUP edition of Jonson's works. It will be on the accompanying website, rusticated there because bibliographical discussions are assumed to be uninteresting to "most readers." One might puckishly ask who these readers are, and wonder whether purchasers, having spent many hundreds of dollars for this definitive scholarly edition, will not feel downright cheated when they discover that detailed textual analysis has been excluded in order, in the words of the press, "to make Jonson's works altogether more easily and attractively accessible, to ensure that the print edition is simple and pleasurable to use." But do serious students really want critical editions to be easy, attractive, accessible, and simple? Or do such readers actually take pleasure in difficult, messy, impenetrable, and complex textual questions? One also wonders about the longevity of the website database. David Scott Kastan has observed that

> as electronic texts are dependent upon technologies that a reader does not
> own, the reader has distressingly little control over them. That is, Columbia
> University cannot remove a book that I own from my bookshelf, but it can

easily remove the electronic version from a website that it maintains and that I have bookmarked for future access.[2]

Thus, a purchaser of the *Cambridge Works of Ben Jonson* will have access to the textual introductions to each play only so long as CUP continues to support the website. Although we have been assured that the site will be maintained for as long as Cambridge University Press remains in business, the untimely demise of other high-profile electronic databases in recent years, such as the Arden Shakespeare Online, must give one pause.

A recent review in *Shakespeare Quarterly* reinforces my point. Given the page restrictions for the *RSC Complete Works*, Jonathan Bate and I could include only a seven-page summary of textual and editorial issues in the general introduction; we directed readers to the "longer and more technical discussion of the textual question and our editorial procedures" available on the edition's website, where one can access a PDF file entitled "The Case for the Folio" that runs to sixty-nine pages.[3] However, in reviewing the edition for *Shakespeare Quarterly*, it appears that Anthony Dawson did not consult that expanded textual discussion. Dawson, for example, questions our emendation of "sledded Pollax" to "steelèd pole-axe" and complains that "No grounds are given, nor is the source of the emendation provided."[4] In fact, we provided quite a substantial discussion of the process whereby we arrived at that emendation, which I'll quote in the footnote below.[5]

---

[2] David Scott Kastan, *Shakespeare and the Book* (Cambridge: Cambridge Univ. Press, 2001), 310–11.

[3] See http://www.rscshakespeare.co.uk/pdfs/Case_for_Folio.pdf.

[4] *Shakespeare Quarterly* 59 (2008): 486.

[5] "A famous pair of lines about Old Hamlet:

> So frown'd he once, when in an angry parle
> He smot the sledded Pollax on the Ice.

(No significant variations between early texts, though the adjective is spelt 'sleaded' in Q1 and Q2, 'sledded' in F and the noun 'pollax' is lower-case in the quartos.) Problem for editors: what is a 'sledded pollax'? Commonest solution proposed by editors: emend to 'sledded Polacks', i.e. Polish soldiers fighting on sledges. The Oxford *Complete Works* adopts this emendation without any justificatory discussion in its *Textual Companion*, despite the fact that no one has ever found examples of Polish (or any other) soldiers on sledges in the literature of the period. Problem with the solution: Old Hamlet is combating 'Ambitious Norway', not Poland. A 'parle' is a 'parley', a peace negotiation, not a battle. An iced-over river on the border between Denmark and Norway is an appropriate setting for the negotiation of a treaty, whereas the notion of a battle fought on ice is colourful but wildly implausible. Problem with retaining 'sledded pole-axe': search of databases reveals no other usage of the word 'sledded' or 'sleaded' in the period. Inference: surely the problem is with 'sledded', not 'pollax'. Action: search early modern databases for occurrences of 'pollax' (and its variant spellings), to see

One could argue that a reviewer exercising due diligence should have perused the electronic supplement before making (demonstrably false) statements about the edition's deficiencies. But the fact is that Dawson either chose to ignore the electronic textual introduction or simply overlooked it. Either way, what seems clear is that textual essays on websites — despite being arguably more accessible than their print counterparts — may not find their way to a great variety of readers. This being the case, I am delighted to take the opportunity to publish a portion of my *Cynthia's Revels* essay here, supplementing the electronic supplement, as it were, with print.

Jonson's reputation as a textbook example of a "ruthless" reader of proofs rests largely on the remarkable number of press variants in the first quarto (1601) of *Cynthia's Revels*.[6] Fresh collation of the fourteen known copies of Q1 — nine more

---

what adjectives customarily qualify it. Discovery: many usages in Shakespeare's time refer to a 'steele-pollax' or 'pollax well-steeled'. Furthermore, there is an abundance of steeled weaponry in Shakespeare's other plays, and a 'steeled coat' in *Henry VI Part 1* (1.1.85). Further discovery from contexts thrown up by the databases: the pole-axe was primarily a ceremonial implement rather than a weapon used in battle. It was literally a steel axe on a pole, analogous to the halberds carried by the Yeomen of the Guard and the 'Switzers' who still form the ceremonial guard in the Vatican. Conclusion: the absence of other occurrences of 'sledded' strongly suggests compositorial error; the occurrence of 'steeled' with pole-axe suggests the emendation 'steeled pole-axe'. During a parley with the Norwegians, angry Old Hamlet grabs the steel-headed pole-axe from the Switzer who stands guard beside him and bangs it emphatically on the ice. Check with editorial tradition: *Hamlet* has been edited so many times and discussed in such minute detail for so many years that one is unlikely to find new solutions to the old problems. Most strong emendations will have been proposed before. And so it proves: a search of the online variorum edition, www.hamletworks.org, yields this from Friedrich August Leo's *Shakespeare-Notes* of 1885: 'I never heard of a battle called a 'parle,' and I cannot suppose that a parliamentary negotiation between two monarchs would end in a row. No! Horatio speaks of two positions he has seen the dead king in: the first, when he went to war against Norway — Horatio remembers the very armour the king had on; the second, when he became angry in the course of a discussion, and — to vent his anger — smote his steeled pole-axe on the ice. (For 'to smite' in the same sense, see *Lucrece*, 176.) You must see him how he frowned, how he tried to overcome his passion, and how at last this grew upon him, and he lifted his arm, and battered the axe down on the ice! There is more life, more action and nature in this picture, than in the poor Polack, who tumbles down and falls on his nose.'"

   [6] Joseph Lasky comments on how serious Jonson was as a proofreader. "The brilliant Ben Jonson was an assiduous proofreader of his printed work, his attitude toward a *dirty* compositor was ruthless. It is known that when proofs were read by Jonson of his *Cynthia's Revels* in 1601, he made 192 changes in the text, many of which indicated much more than a cursory

than were collated for the Herford and Simpson edition — now reveals 275 press variants, more than are found in any other early English dramatic quarto.[7] However, only about a dozen of these variants were the result of stop-press correction; the vast majority are minor changes that resulted when three formes were completely reset into type. Moreover, renewed scrutiny of the type used for one of the reset sheets reveals that it was produced by a second print shop, perhaps years after the original printing. In the case of *Cynthia's Revels,* then, press-variant analysis is significant not for what it tells us about an author's proofreading habits, but rather for what it may reveal about the early reception history of his play.

Cynthia's Revels was entered in the Stationers' Register by Walter Burre on 23 May 1601 as "a booke called Narcissus, the Fountaine of Self Love," oddly invoking Narcissus, who does not figure in the title of the play as printed (the Latin quotations are from Juvenal, *Sat.* 7. 90 and 93). A quarto appeared in the same year with the title-page:

> THE | FOVNTAINE | *OF SELFE-LOUE.* | *Or* | CYNTHIAS | REVELS. | As it hath beene sundry times | *priuately acted in the* Black- | Friers *by the* Children | *of her* Maiesties | *Chappel.* | Written by BEN: IOHNSON. | Quod non dant Proceres, dabit Histrio. | Haud tamen inuideas vati, quem pulpita pascunt. | [double rule] | Imprinted at London for *Walter Burre,* and are to be | *solde at his shop in Paules Church-yard, at the signe* | of the Flower de-Luce and Crowne. 1601.

This is the first time that the Blackfriars theatre is mentioned on the title page of a play quarto. The printer was unidentified until 1970, when J. A. Lavin observed that the ornamental initials on B1r and B1v were part of the stock used by Richard Read and subsequently by George Eld.[8] Read is a rather shadowy figure: although he apparently printed more than thirty books, his name is never mentioned on any of their title pages. Apprenticed to Richard Jugge, the Queen's printer, and freed on 18 January 1580, Read eventually acquired the shop of Gabriel Simson — one of his fellow apprentices with Jugge — following Simson's death. We know that Read married the widowed Frances Simson in 1601, but the precise date at which he took over the shop is uncertain; therefore, some books printed in

---

knowledge of professional proofreading": Lasky, *Proofreading and Copy-Preparation: A Textbook for the Graphic Arts Industry* (New York: Mentor Press, 1941), 20.

[7] Collation of the fourteen extant copies was undertaken *in situ* by Donald L. Bailey, Dee Anna Phares, Karen Britland, and Eric Rasmussen, with the assistance of Lara Hansen, Mark Dunagan, and Sonia Massai.

[8] J. A. Lavin, "Printers for Seven Jonson Quartos," *The Library,* 5th ser., 25 (1970): 331–38.

that year, including *Cynthia*, should perhaps be assigned to Frances Simson. In any event, Read's tenure as owner of the shop was short-lived: George Eld took over following Read's death in 1603 — by marrying the twice-widowed Frances.

The quarto, which collates A-L⁴ M², consists of forty-six unnumbered pages. All pages have thirty-six lines of type save for D2r, D3v, and D4r, which have thirty-seven; the last line of text and the catchword on D4r are cropped off in many of the extant copies. There are two copies in which special dedications have been inserted on a single leaf added after A1: the Huntington copy has a dedication to William Camden; the Clark copy at the University of California has a dedication to Lucy Countess of Bedford. Cancel slips with the words "Cᴙɴᴛʜɪᴀs Reuells" were pasted over the running-titles on outer forme B where the original running-title had been mistakenly printed as "The Fountaine of Selfe-loue." Three formes exist in two distinct settings: the resetting of outer C is preserved in the Huntington, British Library (copy 1), Victoria & Albert, University of California at Los Angeles, Yale, Harvard, Smith, Pierpont Morgan, Library of Congress, National Library of New Zealand, and Petworth House copies; the reset inner and outer F are preserved only in the Victoria & Albert copy.

Percy Simpson accounted for the large number of press variants in Q1 *Cynthia* by assuming that the inexperienced Read produced a text riddled with errors. In Simpson's vivid fantasy, the printer, "unless he was a very earnest Christian," must have "made the printing-house ring with his curses when he got the proofs,"[9] since Jonson had insisted that hundreds of changes be made, including "such minutiae as setting right wrong-font colons and marks of interrogation" (*H&S* 4:5). The discovery of a proof-sheet of *Neptune's Triumph*, possibly in Jonson's hand, in which a mere handful of literals are corrected, may call for a rethinking of the view of Jonson as a manic reader of proofs who would demand that wrong-font marks of punctuation be corrected.[10] Moreover, Q1 *Every Man in his Humour* (1601), printed by Read in the same year as *Cynthia* and for the same publisher,[11] affords no evidence of the printer's ineptitude or the playwright's fastidiousness: no one imagines that Jonson hovered over the proofs of Q1 *Every Man in his Humour*, in which there are only five minor press variants, and he may not have done so with Q1 *Cynthia* either.

---

[9] Percy Simpson, *Proof-reading in the Sixteenth, Seventeenth, and Eighteenth Centuries* (London: Oxford Univ. Press, H. Milford, 1935), 10–11.

[10] See Johan Gereitsen, "A Jonson Proof-Sheet — *Neptune's Triumph*," in *Studies in Seventeenth-Century English Literature, History, Bibliography*, ed. G.A.M. Janssens and F.G.A.M. Aarts (Rodopi, 1984), 107–17.

[11] Read printed signatures A², H-L⁴, M² and Simon Stafford printed B-G⁴. See Robert Miola's Revels edition of *Every Man in his Humour* (Manchester: Manchester Univ. Press, 2000), 40.

Of the 275 press variants in *Cynthia*, 261 appear in the three reset forms. Of these variants, only a very few, confined to outer C, appear to represent corrections ("*States-men*" is corrected to "*States-man*" C1r25, "satified" to "satisfied" C2v1, "bnrning" to "burning" C2v25, "Ssr" to "Sir" C3r4). There are no corrections whatsoever in the reset sheet F of any errors in the original — and the resetting actually introduces a number of errors. Given the meticulous care taken over the running-titles in Read's shop, in which many hours must have been spent pasting delicate cancel slips over the incorrect running-titles on outer B, it is surprising to find the egregious running-title error "*CYMTHIAS*" in reset F (F1v and F2v), along with the equally glaring errors at the foot of the reset pages: the signature error "E2" (for "F2") and "*Fxit*" for "*Exit*" (F2v35). Moreover, the three substantive variants in sheet F all appear to be errors in the resetting: "Houres" for "Houers" (F2v13), "take" for "talke" (F2r3), and "*Cart*" for "*Court*" (F4v1).

The question of whether the readings in the unique sheet F preserved in the V&A copy represent the first or the second state of the text particularly vexed Percy Simpson, and his filling and backfilling on the issue is an unfortunate embarrassment in the great Herford and Simpson edition. In the textual introduction to the play, Simpson asserted that the majority of the readings in the V&A sheet F represented the corrected state of the text, and the accompanying distribution charts listed the first- and second-state readings in separate columns (*H&S* 4:8–11). But in the wake of a withering review by W. W. Greg, who asserted that "the tables as printed make bibliographical nonsense," Simpson reversed himself. A bizarre erratum printed in the subsequent volume stated that all of those readings originally listed as representing the second state "should be transposed to the first column" and now be understood as representing the first state (*H&S* 5:552). Greg was not amused:

> In sheet F the great majority (in all 138) of what were previously declared to be corrections are now classed as original errors. If literary judgment is prepared thus to reverse its verdict in textual matters, one cannot help wondering what authority it can claim.

Although Greg had initially agreed with Simpson that "the minute correction" of Q1 *Cynthia* was done "presumably by Jonson himself," he later came to believe that the reset pages proved that "Jonson had nothing whatever to do with these variants" and, in fact, called into question the "myth" of "the care which Jonson is alleged to have bestowed upon his proofs." Greg concluded, "[t]he simple fact is that for some reason sheet F was set up in duplicate and that the differences are mere printer's errors and irregularities."[12]

The specific reason for the resetting, as Greg noted, is not immediately obvious. Forme replacements were occasionally necessitated by printing-shop accidents such as a dropped chase or pied type;[13] the resetting of outer C seems to be an instance of this. Whole-sheet replacements were less common, and the resetting of sheet F is proved to be unique by the discovery that it was printed not by Read but by a second printer, Valentine Simmes. Font analysis reveals that whereas Read's identifiable type is used throughout the original sheet, Simmes' distinctive Guyot pica italic M's and P's appear on the reset sheet.[14] If sheet F had been ruined in Read's shop, presumably Read himself would have undertaken the reprinting. How, then, can we explain the fact that the resetting of a complete sheet was done at another printing-house — a practice unprecedented in early modern English printing?[15]

A possibly analogous case may be the Shakespeare Fourth Folio (1685), where seventeen sheets of the book were reprinted in a different shop; the reprinted sheets are easily identified by the absence of side rules and foot rules. Giles Dawson conjectured that some years after the original printing of F4, it was noticed that seventeen of the warehoused stacks of ungathered sheets were nearly exhausted, while the vast majority of stacks had a few hundred sheets remaining. In Dawson's scenario, a calculation of costs and of the probability of future sales indicated that it would be profitable to go to the expense of reprinting the seventeen sheets required to make the remaining stock good.[16]

---

[12] See W. W. Greg's reviews of Volumes IV and V of the Herford & Simpson *Works of Ben Jonson, Review of English Studies* 9 (1933): 103; 14 (1938): 218.

[13] See, for instance, Fredson Bowers' analysis of the resetting of inner forme I of Q1 *The Roaring Girl*, in *The Dramatic Works of Thomas Dekker* (Cambridge: Cambridge Univ. Press, 1961–68), 3: 4–5.

[14] I am pleased to acknowledge, with gratitude, Adrian Weiss' assistance in identifying the printer of the reset pages. For the characteristics of the type, Read-S, used in Q1 *Cynthia*, see Weiss, "Elizabethan Play-Quarto Printers and Compositors," *Studies in Bibliography* 43 (1990): 95–164, esp. 109–12. For the characteristics of Simmes' Guyot pica italic, see Weiss, "Printers and Compositors," n. 44.

[15] Henry de Vocht, in a self-proclaimed "momentous" solution to the problem, proposed that F represented a proof-sheet. But the discovery that sheet F was printed in another shop causes the proof-sheet hypothesis to lose most of its momentum. See *Comments on the Text of Ben Jonson's Cynthia's Revels* (Louvain: Librairie universitaire, 1950).

[16] Giles Dawson, "Some Bibliographical Irregularities in the Shakespeare Fourth Folio," *Studies in Bibliography* 4 (1951): 93–103; for a collation of the reset pages, see E. Rasmussen, "Anonymity and the Erasure of Shakespeare's First Eighteenth-Century Editor," in *Reading*

Could a similar scenario help to explain the resetting of Q1 *Cynthia*? If Read had short-sheeted Burre (intentionally or accidentally) and Burre had noticed the discrepancy in the pile of F sheets when the print-job was first delivered to him, he no doubt would have insisted that Read reprint the sheets to fulfill the contract. The fact that F was reprinted by Simmes suggests that Read may have been out of the picture, which would have been the case if the sheet was reprinted in 1603 or after; and there is evidence of collaboration between the two print-shops during this period: Simmes and Eld shared the printing of Jonson's *Entertainment through London* in 1604. It is worth observing that the V&A copy preserves the first state of the outer forme of K and the first of three states of outer L; if one assumes that the earlier states of a forme (having been printed first) would be found towards the bottom of a warehoused stack of sheets,[17] the early states of outer K and L may provide evidence that the V&A copy was gathered from some of the remnants of the warehoused stock supplemented by the reprinted sheet F.

We do not know whether Burre commissioned Simmes to undertake the reprinting, or whether, as Adrian Weiss has suggested to me, Burre sold the incomplete books to Simmes, who then went to the trouble of making up the lacking sheets himself. What we do know is that at some point after the original printing of Q1 *Cynthia*, a bookseller took the unprecedented step of reprinting an entire sheet of the quarto in another printing-house, presumably because he believed that the market for the play would justify the not inconsiderable expense. Thus, the reprinting may attest to the continuing popularity and marketability of *Cynthia's Revels* — a manifestation, perhaps, of the wave of nostalgia for Queen Elizabeth that seems to have pervaded early Jacobean England.[18]

UNIVERSITY OF NEVADA

Readings: Essays in Shakespeare Editing in the Eighteenth Century, ed. Joanna Gondris (London: Associated University Presses, 1998), 318–22.

[17] For a detailed study of the evidence that early states tended to be bound with other sheets containing early states, see Joseph A. Dane, "Perfect Order and Perfected Order: The Evidence from Press-Variants of Early Seventeenth-Century Quartos," *Publications of the Bibliographical Society of America* 90 (1996): 272–320.

[18] See Curtis Perry, *The Making of Jacobean Culture: James I and the Renegotiation of Elizabethan Literary Practice* (Cambridge: Cambridge Univ. Press, 1997), esp. 153–87.

Mutability and Variation:
A Digital Response to Complex Texts[1]

MICHAEL BEST

FLUELLEN
By your patience, Aunchient Pistol, Fortune is painted blind, with a muffler afore his eyes, to signify to you that fortune is blind; and she is painted also with a wheel, to signify to you, which is the moral of it, that she is turning and inconstant, and mutability, and variation; and her foot, look you, is fixed upon a spherical stone, which rowls and rowls and rowls. In good truth, the poet makes a most excellent description of it. Fortune is an excellent moral.[2]

MUTABILITY AND VARIATION ARE TRADITIONALLY SEEN AS RATHER threatening reminders of the transience of life and the vagaries of fortune, as Fluellen carefully explains. My contention, in contradistinction to this anxiety, is to argue that in the instability of Shakespeare's text we can discover a richness of texture that exceeds the capacity of print technology to display. In the complex world of Shakespeare's texts, one aim of the Internet Shakespeare Editions is to explore the capacities of the electronic interface to find ways of visually displaying variation more informatively.[3] The problem, faced by both print and electronic editions, is that for several plays the base texts vary, at times

---

[1] This paper was first presented at the 2008 International Congress on Medieval Studies, Kalamazoo, MI, at a panel entitled "Electronic Shakespeare<s>," Michael Denbo presiding. The paper was originally titled "Variation and Mutabilities: Representing Variants in Shakespeare's Texts."

[2] *Henry V*, ed. James Mardock, *Internet Shakespeare Editions*. TLN 1480–89.

[3] Two sibling sites will use the same software infrastructure, and have access to the same methods of displaying texts: The Queen's Men Editions, and Digital Renaissance Editions.

substantially. The result is a series of puzzles and difficulties: what Paul Werstine appropriately calls "mysteries" (Werstine, "Mystery"). The degree of variation in some of Shakespeare's plays raises important and teasing questions: is it the result of revision, corruption, or (most likely) both? If both, how do we separate the deliberate from the accidental? If the changes are both extensive and deliberate, how do we most effectively record variation for the modern reader of the play, given that the text "is turning, and inconstant, and mutability, and variation"? The important theoretical work done by critics like D. F. McKenzie and Jerome McGann has given us a label for the kind of texts we work with: they are "social" texts, contributed to not only by the author, but also by actors, scribes, compositors, proofreaders, and others. But to give the text a label does not solve the mysteries, nor give us a clear direction on how to publish the texts in a form convenient to the wide range of modern readers interested in Shakespeare's works.

Among Shakespeare's most widely variant texts are the great tragedies, *Hamlet* and *King Lear*, which I will focus on in this discussion. *Hamlet* was published in two remarkably dissimilar quartos (1603 and 1604). Both described the play as a "Tragicall Historie"; the Folio (1623), in keeping with its careful distinctions of genre, described it as simply a "Tragedie." Though the Folio text largely follows the second quarto (Q2), it omits significant passages (two of Hamlet's soliloquies, for example), and adds some passages that exist in neither of the earlier versions. *King Lear* was published in 1608 as the "True Chronicle Historie of the life and death of King Lear" (Q1); the Folio of 1623 describes it as "The Tragedie of King Lear" (F). The two versions are significantly different in more than their titles: Q1 includes some 300 lines not in F, and F records about 100 lines not in Q1; in addition there are a large number of individually varying readings in words, phrases, and speech assignments. In each case the texts present a challenge to editors: what should they present to their readers as *Hamlet* or *Lear*?

Tom Berger, in a review of the Oxford *Works* published in 1986, commented that "Just as we create fictions to get through the day, bibliographers and editors create fictions to get through texts" (161); Paul Werstine similarly warns against the seductive power of narratives to provide convenient simplification of the puzzles and mysteries variant texts present ("Narratives," passim). But of course editors need a reason for any emendations they make, and the process of justification inevitably creates a narrative, even if it is as simple as suggesting that an obscurity was caused by compositorial eye-skip. The larger narratives that seek to explain the causes of widely variant texts have come to focus on a key question: do the texts represent different reflections of a single Shakespearean original, or are they separate snapshots of a play that was in constant motion, being rewritten by Shakespeare or other agents?

The traditional answer: conflation

The traditional response to the problem of widely variant texts has been to assume that Shakespeare, in the words of his contemporary Ben Jonson, "never blotted out line": in other words, that he did not revise his plays, and that therefore any differences between versions were not created by him. The logical corollary of this position was to create a conflated edition, in which the editor attempted to recreate an ideal original — the play that Shakespeare wrote, which had for whatever reasons become corrupted in one or more of these published versions. Editors were accordingly free to make more or less eclectic decisions on which variant reading to adopt. The narratives editors have developed to justify an attempt to reconstitute a lost ideal original have focused on theories of transmission, most commonly explaining wide variation as the result of memorial reconstruction by actors or others of lost originals, shorthand transcriptions,[4] or as part of the process of acquiring unauthorized access to the play. The fundamental arguments did not change with the advent of the New Bibliography, despite its aim to make the editorial process grounded less on an editor's critical and interpretive judgment, more on objective data derived from knowledge of practices in the theater and print shop, and evidence in the printed text as to the nature of the manuscript that lay behind it. Despite some debate about details, the assumption that variant texts were derived from a single lost original was generally accepted, and even reinforced, largely by the invention of a new category of variant texts, the "bad quarto" theory.[5]

Steven Urkowitz ("Growth") and Sonia Massai have extensively explored the long editorial tradition that culminated in the full conflation in the Globe edition of 1863–66, which has become the default public domain version accessible on the Web. Alexander Pope was the first editor to consult the quarto in his edition of the play;[6] interestingly enough, he prefigured the modern reassessment by making a practicing writer's natural assumption that the quartos represented earlier drafts that Shakespeare had revised,[7] and as a self-confident poet, his awareness of variant readings provided a convenient rationale for his generally

---

[4] The case for shorthand was trenchantly dismissed by Duthie in 1977, but has recently been re-opened by Adele Davidson; see, however the refutation of her arguments by Knowles ("Shakespeare and Shorthand").

[5] For a discussion of the self-reinforcing nature of this theory, see Werstine, "Narratives," passim.

[6] Though in fairness it should be noted that Nahum Tate consulted both folio and quarto as he created his radical rewriting of the play.

[7] Urkowitz quotes Pope's energetic dismissing of the claim that Shakespeare "scarce ever *blotted a line*": "This they [his fellow actors] industriously propagated. . . . there never was a

high-handed tendency to improve Shakespeare whenever he found the originals lacking in taste or decorum. The debate about including quarto-only passages continued until the magisterial edition of Malone in 1790, which published a full conflation and collation; Malone's text became the basis for nineteenth- and twentieth-century editions, variously and eclectically conflated.[8]

Two late twentieth-century theoretical discussions have significantly complicated this deceptively neat solution. As our understanding of the processes of the theater and print shop has deepened, we have become more keenly aware of the production of a work as a social and collaborative activity; a corollary of this increasing awareness has been a willingness to look at each text as a separate record of a play that was in continuing change both on stage and in varying manuscript manifestations. The most important result of this approach has been a sustained argument that Shakespeare did in fact revise his plays. Discussion has focused on *King Lear*, though editions of *Hamlet*, *Henry V*, and (to a lesser extent) *Troilus and Cressida* and *Othello* thus far have been influenced by the shift in attitude. In 1978, Michael Warren published an essay ("Quarto and Folio *King Lear*") that set out a case for considering the Folio text a later Shakespearean revision of the play; two years later Steven Urkowitz followed with a book-length study (*Shakespeare's Revision*), and soon after Warren and Gary Taylor published a collection of essays that argued strongly that the Folio *Lear* represents a conscious revision by Shakespeare (*The Division of the Kingdoms*). Three years later, the new Oxford *Complete Works* edited by Taylor and Stanley Wells published two separate versions of *Lear*, one based on Q1, the other on the Folio; since the Oxford editors organized the plays according to their sense of the chronological composition of the plays, these two versions of *Lear* appear widely separated in the volume. The rationale behind this choice is set out in *The Division of the Kingdoms*, and in *William Shakespeare: A Textual Companion*, the volume accompanying the *Complete Works*.

The question of revision

The question of revision is central to arguments for and against conflation. That there was extensive revision of some kind is clear; even so determined a proponent of conflation as Richard Knowles comments: "The question is not whether

---

more groundless report, or to the contrary of which there are more undeniable evidences" ("Growth," 5).

    [8] In an essay in *The Division of the Kingdoms*, Randall McLeod wrote of these later editions that "the more [they] changed superficially the more they became the same — testimonials to eclectic conflation" ("No more," 153).

there was revision — of course there was — but who did it, and when, and why" ("Two *Lears*?" 58). The writers of *The Division of the Kingdoms* for the most part rely on arguments that the Folio was revised by Shakespeare specifically to improve stage-worthiness, and to make deliberate changes in characterization. More recent critical debate about the relative theatrical value of the Quarto and Folio texts, however, has illustrated the way that arguments of this kind can be made to work in both directions (compare Urkowitz, *Revision* and Clare, "Who is it"). It is also worth noting A. R. Braunmuller's astute judgment that academic editors are "at best only intermittently . . . equipped to understand matters of performance" (148), however perceptive the arguments of critics like Michael Warren and Steven Urkowitz are in their detailed discussions.[9] It is also the case that productions of the play vary enormously in the kinds of cuts and modifications that directors have historically made; one actor's/director's/critic's high point is another's candidate for the axe. The empirical test of production over many years argues rather against the clear superiority of the Folio text in the theater, since only those directors who have deliberately decided to produce a Folio version have followed its cuts. Michael Dobson, in a review of the Bate/Rasmussen RSC edition of the Folio, commented unkindly that "Even now Ian McKellen is performing *King Lear* in Stratford using a text including the mock-trial scene, here relegated to an appendix. . . . Perhaps Bate and Rasmussen would have preferred McKellen to perform the mock-trial scene in *King Lear* only as an encore." In all fairness, someone should have directed Dobson to Rasmussen's more strictly bibliographical argument that cuts in F *Lear* are different in nature from those in F *Hamlet* (Rasmussen, "Revision of Scripts," passim).

In a similar vein, there is reason for skepticism about arguments for consistent revision based on character rather than role. Character, as conceived in current criticism, is largely a construct of late nineteenth-century critics and twentieth-century acting traditions (see, for example, the discussion by Slights, "Character and Conscience"). A number of arguments in favor of revision detail changes in characterization between the two versions. Many of these critics are subtle in their analyses, but their critical approach tends to over-value small changes in wording over the kinds of variation a good actor can instill into any passage by shifting emphasis. Lukas Erne astutely points out the profound influence that punctuation — of necessity very largely the responsibility of the compositor and/or editor — can have on meaning, and hence of the construction of character (18–19). In a modern production of *Lear*, a director can cut significant

---

[9] While it is true that both these critics have extensive experience in the theater, it is also true that modern production values differ significantly from those of Shakespeare's time.

parts of a character's role without inducing changes in the interpretation of the character, since both the director and actor will have read the entire play (probably in a conflated version) and can thus adduce motive to actions that are only obliquely referred to in the redacted stage version. Changes in roles, however, can be more consistently defended as the result of revision. The roles of Kent, Albany, the Fool, and Lear are significantly changed in the Folio;[10] Ioppolo also argues that Cordelia's role changes, as she becomes a stronger character in F (*Revising*, 167–83). The motives for the changes, by Shakespeare or some other hand, may be the result of something as arbitrary as a change in theater personnel, but the argument for revision is not necessarily dependent on the motives that lie behind the changes. An interesting parallel can be made with the kind of revision undertaken by Mozart when he adapted his Oboe Concerto (K314) for the flute; in addition to transposing the work into the key of D, he altered many passages to take advantage of the flute's higher range and technical agility. In a sense the music remains the same, but it is at the same time clearly different; the effect is arguably similar to the kind of change a new actor would bring to a part. It is also important to recognize that it is possible, even probable, that revision may have been undertaken at different times, and that other hands than Shakespeare's may well have contributed modifications.

An argument for revision not pursued in *The Division of the Kingdoms* relies more on critical than historical or bibliographical arguments. It begins with the central, fundamental, and quite shocking change that Shakespeare made in the plot he inherited from both his historical and literary sources: the substitution of a tragic for a comic ending. If any members of his original audience came to the play with a preconceived notion from the earlier anonymous *History of King Leir*, they would have expected Cordelia to win the final battle and to place her father back on the throne. *Leir* is a play that depends for its happy ending on a deeply providential view of the world. In his Introduction to his edition of *King Leir* for the online Queen's Men Editions, Andrew Griffin writes:

> Characters such as Cordella, Leir, and Perillus . . . often point out that God
> ordains their fates, and audiences regularly witness God's implausible in-

---

[10] Michael Warren discusses the reduction in the importance of Kent's role in the Folio ("Diminution," 59–74), and explores changes in both Kent's and Albany's roles ("Quarto and Folio," passim); Urkowitz also discusses Albany's role (*Revision*, 80–128); after analyzing surviving examples of different modes of revision and adaptation in the period, John Kerrigan ("Revision," 218–30) argues that the character of the Fool was consciously revised between Quarto and Folio versions; Thomas Clayton ("Revision," 128–38) puts the case for a revision of Lear's character, especially in his last moments.

terventions, as when he appears in the form of thunder, for instance, in order to protect the virtuous. (Paragraph 8)

The change that Shakespeare made is so striking that he must have had some kind of deeply negative response to *Leir*'s convenient view of the world where virtue is rewarded, sins punished — a world Albany vainly echoes in the final scene of Shakespeare's play, where he pronounces optimistically (in both versions), "All friends shall / Taste the wages of their virtue, and all foes / The cup of their deservings" (TLN 3274–6). Typically for *King Lear*, this optimism is ironically undercut immediately: the next speech (in the Folio) is Lear's last, as he dies grasping a desperate hope that the dead Cordelia yet lives; in the Quarto he lives just long enough to plead — successfully — that his heart break.[11]

One way of reading the series of dark reverses of this kind in the play is to see in them a determination by Shakespeare to present a world in which appeals to a providential god are shown to be as pointless as they were seen to be effective in the earlier play. In these terms the Folio represents a further step in the darkening of the narrative. At least two passages the Folio omits are moments where in the Quarto the tragedy is illuminated by a shaft of gentler light: the two servants speaking compassionately of Gloucester after his blinding, and the scene in which a Gentleman speaks to Kent of the absent Cordelia in lines few readers (if not directors) would want to cut: "You have seen / Sunshine and rain at once; her smiles and tears / Were like a better way" (TLN 2347.17–47.21). Not all the changes in the Folio follow this pattern, but the overall emotional vector from *Leir* to Q1 *Lear* to F *Lear* is steadily towards a darkening of the tone.[12] This consistency of direction suggests that the Folio is, at least in part, a further Shakespearean revision.

There is no doubt that the text records other kinds of revisions, well documented in *The Division of the Kingdoms*; I am especially persuaded by the statistical tests applied by MacDonald P. Jackson and the similar conclusion reached by Paul Werstine in the same collection, using quite different methods of analysis. While I accept the general position of Gary Taylor's argument that very little revision is likely to have been caused by outright censorship, it is striking that one significant change is the modification of many of the references to the invasion from France, some resulting in awkwardness in the revised version. For whatever

---

[11] Unless, of course, the editor chooses to emend the speech prefix to conform to the Folio, where Kent speaks the line.

[12] The omission of the mock trial in F seems to be neutral in terms of the darkening of the tone. Few modern productions omit it entirely, so it is not likely to have been omitted because of unstageworthiness, *pace* Roger Warren.

reason this revision was undertaken, it is not difficult to imagine Shakespeare, asked to make the change, looking afresh at the play and restructuring it to sharpen its distinction from the optimistically providential *Leir*, at the same time unable to resist the impulse to "tinker" (Kerrigan, "Revision," 195) with words, phrases, and perhaps roles as he re-read and re-worked the play. Halio similarly suggests that the process of adapting the play to the Blackfriars stage might have had the same result (*First Quarto*, 82). The date of revision (if the play was only revised once) is not easy to determine. Taylor ("Date and Authorship") and Clegg ("Print Culture") make various arguments, but the evidence remains slender. In the process of discussing Shakespeare and the concept of "late writing," Gordon McMullan makes an important contribution to this debate, effectively complicating and questioning the precision of dating Shakespeare's chronology, or of separating the authorial components in collaborative work — which, in one sense or another, *King Lear* certainly was. On balance, it seems likely that the Folio reflects changes by hands other than Shakespeare as well as any he made himself; Knowles, for example, argues that the number of "rare words" in the additions casts doubt on Shakespeare's authorship, even as he dismisses arguments for the authorship of Massinger ("Transforming") or John Day ("Two *Lears*?" 60–61). On the other hand, Arthur Kinney's computer analysis suggests that Shakespeare was more likely to have written the additions than any of the usual suspects (Chapman, Fletcher, Jonson, Massinger, Webster). The sheer number of small changes makes the suggestion that they would have been made by a scribe rather than by Shakespeare or another dramatist called on to revise the play extremely unlikely (see Knowles, "Two *Lears*?" 76). On the other hand, though revision is the most likely explanation for many changes between Q1 and F, it is unlikely that all revisions were uniquely Shakespeare's, and it is the critic's task rather than the editor's to determine whether the revisions produced a markedly improved play. The two texts are different in a number of demonstrable and important ways, but each — like many that have been distilled from some form of extended text for production — has its own integrity and interest.

Since the publication of the Oxford *Works*, the debate about the legitimacy of conflated texts in general has continued and has been extended to include *Hamlet*, *Troilus and Cressida*, *Othello*, and possibly other plays where Quarto and Folio versions differ considerably.[13] Grace Ioppolo put the case against conflation trenchantly:

---

[13] James Mardock's edition of *Henry V* for the *Internet Shakespeare Editions* includes modern versions of both Quarto and Folio.

Any edition of *King Lear* which conflates the Quarto and Folio texts, . . . produces an inconsistent treatment of themes such as war and familial conflict, a confused presentation of the play's structure and form, and, most important, a falsely conflated version of Cordelia and so many other characters, creating a counterfeit and non-Shakespearean foundation upon which only the most limited literary interpretation and meaning can be built. (*Revising*, 181)

The enterprise of recreating a single ideal text has become increasingly suspect as our knowledge of the instability of manuscript transmission and the vagaries of practices in the print-shop have increased. In considering the related case of *Hamlet*, Paul Werstine adapts Foucault's comments on the futility of the search for origins, remarking that

. . . assertions of Shakespeare's agency alone in the production of first the Q2 and then the F text of *Hamlet* translate these printed versions out of the realm of history, where things are fabricated in piecemeal fashion . . . through accident and succession, into the world of metaphysics, where timeless and tireless genius produces and then reproduces the essence of *Hamlet*. ("Mystery," 26)

Conflation is thus characterized as the pursuit of a metaphysical and unattainable object. The Oxford editors seem to avoid this chimera by their decision to print editions of the two versions separately. Oddly, however, they did not entirely abandon the concept of an ideal original: for the ideal concept of an author's authoritative manuscript lying behind the printed text, they substituted an imagined authorized performance, privileging what they argued were playhouse-influenced versions of the plays.[14] In justification, they claimed that "The theatrical version is, inevitably, that which comes closest to the 'final' version of the play" (*Complete Works*, xxxiii). Their use of the word "inevitably" is confident but unsupported, and the scare quotes around the word "final" are teasing: what is "final"? Is it the most important? The most useful? The most polished? Should one publish only the final version and ignore earlier, less final versions? The admirable caution of R. B. McKerrow is salutary here: in 1939 he made the salient observation that "it is very doubtful whether, especially in the case of the earlier plays, there ever existed any written 'final form'" ("Problem," 6). More recently, Barbara Mowat has convincingly argued that manuscript practice in the period was such that even authorial

---

[14] "This edition chooses, when possible, the more theatrical version of each play" (*Complete Works*, xxxv).

manuscripts were subject to wide variation and that the discovery of a single manu-script exemplar of one of the plays would not solve the many problems we face in finding a single text we can call *King Lear* or *Hamlet*.[15]

Print responds to de-conflation

King Lear again led the way in the response of print to the debate between confla-tion and de-conflation. The most radical and inventive solution was provided by Michael Warren's boxed publication of *The Complete King Lear*, which provides a variety of different graphic facsimiles; parallel texts, including all variant pas-sages, and loose-leaf facsimiles of Q1, Q2, and F, all waiting for the reader to re-arrange them in whatever format they choose. René Weis has published a more traditional parallel-text edition. A simpler response is to edit and print separate versions of Q1 and F, following the lead of the Oxford editors: thus Jay Halio and Stanley Wells have published texts based on Q1, and folio-based texts have been published by Halio again, and Eric Rasmussen and Jonathan Bate as part of their edition of the Folio for the Royal Shakespeare Company. Halio's Folio text in-cludes a series of parallel passages where Q1 and F differ (though through a print-ing oddity, the differing passages appear on following pages rather than togeth-er), and an appendix of passages unique to Q1; his Quarto text also includes an appendix of passages unique to the Folio. Rasmussen/Bate also include passages unique to Q1 in an appendix. In his Q1 text, Wells makes no concession to the reader interested in passages Shakespeare — by Wells's own argument — added later, since they appear nowhere in the edition, and are only sporadically noted in the collations or commentary.

De-conflated texts for *Hamlet* are consistent in providing the reader with sec-tions of the play not included in the version that is the focus of the edition. Like their edition of *King Lear*, the Rasmussen/Bate Folio edition de-conflates by edit-ing only the Folio of 1623. For the reader of *Hamlet* who wants the 224 lines the Folio omits, their edition includes the missing Quarto passages, again in an appen-dix. The Arden 3 *Hamlet*, edited by Ann Thompson and Neil Taylor is a more am-bitious and complex endeavor, involving all three versions of the play edited (more or less) separately. Volume 1 is the Q2 edited in its own right — but it thoughtfully includes appendices so you can get the 77 lines unique to the Folio, so long as you are alert to the very quiet signals in the collation of Q2 that indicate where the passages fit. Since volume 1 will inevitably be more widely bought and read, this

---

[15] Barbara Mowat, "The Problem of Shakespeare's Text(s)," *Shakespeare-Jahrbuch* 132 (1996): 26–43.

text will become the default Arden of the current iteration of the series. Volume 2 includes the complete Folio and Q1 texts, with detailed commentary only in those sections of the plays that have not already had the full treatment in volume 1. This means, oddly, that the strange (if not outright "bad") Q1 gets much fuller treatment than the Folio text. Again, it takes very experienced readers to spot where the Folio offers unique passages, and where they should put down volume 2 and find — in volume 1, not in an appendix — the quarto-only material.

Both Thompson/Taylor and Rasmussen/Bate de-conflate, but almost apologetically provide the additional passages.[16] Unfortunately, despite this compromise, neither the Rasmussen/Bate nor the Thompson/Taylor edition makes it easy for a reader to undertake a continuous, fully aware reading of the variations, or for a reading of all the words generally agreed to have been written by Shakespeare. In terms that would be applied to a computer program, their interface is awkward and non-intuitive, and the overall effect is oddly like the much-criticized fashion in which Pope relegated passages he considered inferior to footnotes.

The problem with de-conflation: a "play function"

In part because of the difficulty I have just flagged — that readers are accustomed to a simpler print interface through consulting a conflated text — not all scholars agree that de-conflation is desirable or necessary. Ernst Honigmann points out astutely that even those editors who attempt to produce a "pure" modern text of Q1 or F end up, in effect, conflating, since they invariably use readings from the other text in their solutions to various cruces: "Conflation appears to be unavoidable: the question is not whether to conflate or not, but rather how much to conflate" (Honigmann, "New Bibliography," 87–88).[17] When Norton used the Oxford texts for its *Works*, they published Quarto and Folio versions in parallel texts and added a third, conflated, version. R. A. Foakes's edition for the Arden 3 series prints a conflated version with readings and passages from Quarto and Folio clearly indicated by small superscript letters; Paul Werstine and Barbara Mowat's Folger *Lear* uses

---

[16] Urkowitz comments on the habit of editors to "save from obscurity all lines of the poet's composing, even those he seems to have discarded" ("Growth," 31).

[17] In their edition of *King Lear*, Mowat and Werstine choose to create "an *edition* of the Folio" but offer a rather disarming rationale for the conflations they accept: "Q1 words are *added* when their omission seems to leave a gap in our text. . . . Sometimes Q1 readings are *substituted* for F words when a word in F is unintelligible (i.e. not a word) or is incorrect according to the standards of that time for acceptable grammar, rhetoric, idiom, or usage . . . Finally we print a word from Q1 rather than from F when a word in F seems at odds with the story that the play tells and Q1 supplies a word that coheres with the story" (lxi–lxiii); emphasis in the original.

variously-shaped brackets to distinguish the origin of different readings. In each case, the editors acknowledge the importance of providing readers with a version of the play that includes the widest possible range of information about what Shakespeare wrote, however different the extant versions may be. It is instructive to realize that Dr. Johnson, an editor usually seen as generally lacking in rigor, chose to create a more informative interface, taking the path more recently espoused by the Folger Shakespeare Series by using brackets and alternative typefaces to indicate the varying origins of the text he published (Urkowitz, "Growth," 32).

In his remarkable experiment in movable text in the medium of print, *The Complete King Lear*, Michael Warren concludes the first paragraph of his General Introduction with a fundamental question: "What is the work called *King Lear*?" (xi). Foakes picks up the same terminology in his Introduction, where he defines *King Lear* as a "work" divided into two separate versions: "There is every reason to think that we have two versions of the same play, not two different plays" (119). It does seem that editors tacitly or openly acknowledge that in cultural terms *Lear* has become a single concept rather than two separate texts, even if this is the result of an editorial tradition that evolved many years after the play was written, rewritten, and published.[18] If we accept the narrative—as I do—that several of the Folio plays represent revisions that are for the most part by Shakespeare, the question then becomes how an editor is to represent a revised text. The normal process of privileging an author's final revision and relegating earlier readings to collations will not comfortably apply (as it fails to apply, for example, to Wordsworth's revisions of *The Prelude*), because readers, critics, and directors may reasonably wish to work with everything Shakespeare wrote, whether the words are his final thoughts or not.

At the base of this problem is the fact that Shakespeare's works have become more than texts; they have become culturally constructed entities that reverberate far beyond the scholar's desktop. A simple example will illustrate. Most (nonspecialist) readers coming across this quotation:

No grave upon the earth shall clip in it
A pair so famous.

would assume immediately that it is from *Romeo and Juliet*. It is in fact the surprisingly generous epitaph spoken by Caesar over the body of Cleopatra, as he concedes that she should "be buried by her *Antony*" (TLN 3628–30). Today we would not say of a passionate lover, "He's a real Antony"; we may, however, say

---

[18] Knowles attempts to find a physical manifestation of the "work"; he writes of a possible "'Maximal' record of all the lines approved by the Master of the Revels (whether acted or not)" kept in the playhouse ("Evolution," 143).

"he's a real Romeo," and even those who have never read a word of Shakespeare will understand because *Romeo and Juliet* has assumed a life of its own, certainly in this instance eclipsing the love-interest in *Antony and Cleopatra*. This example makes clear that at least some of Shakespeare's plays have acquired a kind of "play-function" — analogous to Foucault's author-function — in performance, in translation, and in the expectation of the general reader ("What Is an Author?").[19] While de-conflation produces a neat solution for the scholar, it is thus less pragmatically useful for the critic, the actor, or the general reader, since none of the resulting texts will present the play as it has come to be received, and none of them will include all the passages an actor or critic may wish to use or to refer to. If the most recent scholarly orthodoxy has come to eschew conflation and to edit texts separately, how can editors respond to a legitimate need from those who access their texts to view a fully functioning *Hamlet* or *Lear*? The nature of the critical and bibliographical debate on the issue suggests that there is a strong ideological component to the apparent desire of editors to have readers think of the separate texts as independent; the truth is that no modern critic will risk basing an argument on a single version of the play,[20] and few theatre practitioners are likely to choose to put on a version of the play limited to a single text. The pressing question becomes how to manage the complexity of two (or three) texts so that a reader can read it all, but will know at all times which text they are reading. When the Oxford text was adopted by Norton, the problem with de-conflation became evident. Faced with the inexorable demands of the marketplace, Norton decided to add a conflated *King Lear* text to the volume already weighted down by two versions: a traditional conflated text. This is a lot of pages to spend on a single play.

In 2000, Cambridge University Press published a CD-ROM of *King Lear in Performance* edited by Christie Carson and Jackie Bratton, with texts supplied by Jay Halio. The electronic space of the CD-ROM allowed the editors to include both Quarto and Folio texts, separately edited, as well as a number of

---

[19] Foucault comments: "It is not enough, however, to repeat the empty affirmation that the author has disappeared. . . . Instead, we must locate the space left empty by the author's disappearance, follow the distribution of gaps and breaches, and watch for the openings that this disappearance uncovers" ("Author," 145). Extending the analogy to the play-function, it becomes the task of the digital edition to highlight and illustrate the "gaps and breaches."

[20] The situation has changed significantly since Urkowitz wrote that the possibility of revision "has had little observable consequence in printed editions, in literary criticism, or in stage productions" ("Growth," 23). Critics are generally more aware of the fallacy of working only with a conflated edition; Erne, however, does note some quite surprising lapses, though he tactfully mentions only in a footnote those who cheerfully reach critical conclusions by citing variant passages without differentiating the texts (*Collaborators*, 95; see 123, nn. 192 and 193).

later adaptations. To solve the navigational problem of moving between these variant texts they included — conceptually at the top level of the layers the medium makes possible — what they called a "finder" text that provided access to all instances of the play. In this case the finder text was actually a conflation. The simple usefulness of this text requires us to ask whether it is still possible to publish conflated texts despite the strength of the arguments against them. Paul Werstine, in "Textual Mystery," argues against conflation, but nonetheless concedes that "Combining Q2 and F is hardly an unreasonable strategy" (2 n. 5). In contrast, H.R. Woudhuysen more pessimistically comments that in *Lear* "all the bickering and squabbling over whether Shakespeare did revise *King Lear* has led to a too rarely articulated sense that *Lear* as a work can never be recovered (because it never was a single work), and that only the relevant documents which preserve versions of it can be edited" ("Editors and Texts," 43). The awkward fact remains that, from a user's point of view, a finder text is the navigational aid missing from the de-conflated print editions of both *Hamlet* and *King Lear*; at the same time, the finder text will look remarkably like the culturally constructed work that many readers expect.

The digital text: some possible answers

A first step in finding a finder text is to create ways of displaying the variations and ambiguities that we find in the original texts. In 1997, when browsers first began to display colored text, I suggested (Best, "*Othello* 3.4.462–78") that a text with multiple variants, like *Othello*, could be displayed with colors to flag the different sources of readings the editor has chosen (the page now looks remarkably ugly with the colors then available). I was picking up the work done by Bernice Kliman in her *Enfolded Hamlet*, which was originally a print version of the play using different-shaped brackets to indicate the different sources of readings, and has now been extended to the electronic medium as *hamletworks.org*, a web site that uses both colors and brackets to distinguish the various bits and pieces of a *Hamlet* that "enfolds" all three texts, Q1, Q2, and F. Since my early suggestion, web display has become almost bewilderingly capable of variation and sophistication in display, with the result that the digital space provides a perfect medium for multi-text, multi-faceted plays like *Hamlet* and *King Lear*.

David Bevington has begun the daunting task of preparing the multiple texts of *Hamlet* for the *Internet Shakespeare Editions*. His solution to the challenge of the multiple versions of the play is to create full and separate modern-spelling texts for Q1, Q2, and F, then to create what we have termed an "Editor's Choice" text, on the analogy of a movie's director's cut. Without attempting a conflated edition, his text uses Q2 as a base, adding, where he believes there is additional material that will be of value to the reader, passages and readings from the Folio, and giving an occasional nod to the rather anomalous Q1. The effect is to make visible the traditionally silent and bashful presence of the editor as constructor of the texts, and correspondingly to encourage readers to think in terms of their own choices.

The capacity of the reader to choose will be extended in two ways by the planned edition of *King Lear*, which I will be undertaking for the Internet Shakespeare Editions (ISE). As with all texts on the site, my edition will start with facsimiles and accurate old-spelling texts. Q1 *Lear* is unusual in that it exists in a number of variant versions, apparently because there were an exceptional number of "stop-press" corrections as it was being printed; for this reason, the old-spelling text will (uniquely for our series to date) provide collations for the various readings, with the attendant opportunity for readers of the text to see all variants simultaneously, color-coded. The online edition will provide full modern-spelling editions for Q1 and F, complete with annotation and collation; in each case I will retain readings for both Q1 and F where they are defensible, though I am aware that I run the risk of making the doubtful assumption that the merely defensible is correct.[21]

In editing the work that is *King Lear*, I plan to provide the reader with a range of texts to explore. Rather than a conflated text, my intention is to provide three ways of viewing the "complete" *Lear*, building them from the fully edited versions of Q1 and F:

1. An *inclusive* text, generated from the collations along the lines of our current display of variants, but limited to Q1 and F. This will include everything from both versions, color-coded. The one major challenge here there is no simple way of showing the multiple changes in lineation between the texts; there is ample opportunity here for experimentation.[22]
2. An *extended* text, based on Q1, but including all additional F passages, which will be distinguished (to provide uncomplicated reading) by typography rather than color: sans-serif to contrast with the default serif font.
3. A similarly extended text based on F.

---

[21] Honigmann quotes A. E. Housman's acerbic comment that to "bring it to pass that the readings of a [text] are right whenever they are possible and impossible wherever they are wrong . . . needs divine intervention" ("New Bibliography," 87).

[22] In a pedagogical extension of this method of displaying the text, I plan to include a kind of "do it yourself" facility for selected scenes of particular interest: visitors to these pages will be able to select variants from pull-down menus and compile their own eclectic version of the text. Randall McLeod invokes the felicitous term "infinitive" ("Marriage") to describe the multiplicity of choices the texts stimulate; the inclusive text perhaps comes close to this ideal form.

The basic navigation will be through either of the extended texts, from which readers will be able to glean most of what Shakespeare wrote in the two versions. The more curious, or scholarly, reader will be able to peel back layers to see what the play looked like in old spelling and in facsimile; or, indeed, to sift through an inclusive text that records all major variants on a single interface.

One interesting challenge in the two extended texts will be how to handle the several passages that are not only different, but incompatible. Urkowitz shows, for example, how the two versions of the angry interchange between Goneril and Cornwall (TLN 1472–80), each eminently dramatic, lose pungency when combined (*Revision,* 36–38):

Quarto

  Lear. This is a slaue, whose easie borrowed pride
Dwels in the fickle grace of her a followes,
Out varlet, from my sight.
  Duke. What meanes your Grace?
Enter Gon.
  Gon. Who struck my seruant, *Regan* I haue good hope
Thou didst not know ant.
  Lear. Who comes here? O heauens!
If you doe loue old men, if you sweet sway allow
Obedience, if your selues are old, make it your cause,

Folio

  Lear. This is a Slaue, whose easie borrowed pride
Dwels in the sickly grace of her he followes.
Out Varlet, from my sight.
  Corn. What meanes your Grace?
         Enter Gonerill.
  Lear. Who stockt my Seruant? *Regan*, I haue good hope
Thou did'st not know on't.
Who comes here? O Heauens!
If you do loue old men; if your sweet sway
Allow Obedience; if you your selues are old,
Make it your cause:

In instances like this, each extended text will record only its own version, but since this is a digital edition an icon in the margin will allow a reader to switch to the alternate reading.

The digital medium will also allow me to include a number of additional ways of visualizing variants. In an earlier article (Best, "Standing"), I have suggested applying animation to words that have acquired in modern spelling an ambiguous or complex "semantic field" of meaning.[23] An example is the ambiguously spelled "weyard" sisters in *Macbeth*, where the meanings "wayward" and "weird" were arguably both available to an early modern reader (and where the meaning of "weird" meant "fated" rather than simply "strange"). There are many such places where it is difficult for a modern text to recapture the original range of available meanings: a familiar example is the divergence that has occurred since Shakespeare's time in the word "travel" ("travail"/"travel"); and there is the lovely example of the multiple shades of meaning available as we add modern apostrophes to the title of *Love[']s Labor[']s Lost* (see Wells and Taylor, *Modernizing*). I have to admit that applying animation to these kinds of readings might only serve to confuse, and probably to irritate, readers. There are, however, some instances in Shakespeare's text where there is an irreducible ambiguity that is of genuinely significant critical import, and where animation might provide the most visually accurate way of recording a modern text. In *King Lear*, for example, the question of the speaker in the Folio at TLN 176 and 204 with the prefix "*Cor*," variously ascribed by editors to Cornwall or Cordelia (see Goldring, "Rescue," passim), is a perfect opportunity for an animated text moving between the two. In other instances where a reading from the current text is defensible but the alternative text provides a reading that can be seen as interestingly different (the "hit" / "sit" variant at TLN 328, for example), it will be possible for the reader to hover the mouse over the word to see the alternative, without having to click on it to open a commentary or collation window.

Multiplicity in texts leads inevitably to the need for an elegant way to indicate similar variability in interpretation. The structure of digital critical essays can be made carefully to distinguish conclusions that can be reached through readings common to both texts, unique to Q1, and to F through hypertextual branching (rather like the old children's "choice" stories). The existence of two "snapshots" of the play invites the metaphor of vision: one eye (Q1, say) offers a specific view, while the other eye (F) provides a subtly different perspective.

---

[23] The term comes from Margreta de Grazia and Peter Stallybrass, "Materiality," 264. In my article I take the example de Grazia and Stallybrass explore, the "weyard" witches in Macbeth, to animate a reading among "weyard," "weird," and "wayward."

Looking at a given moment or character in the play first through one, then the other, can provide a rich experience in critical analysis, as several of the essays in *The Division of the Kingdoms* attest. More challenging, perhaps, is the possibility of looking with both eyes at once, where the differing views can, as in stereoscopic vision, provide greater depth of understanding — or a blurring of meaning if the separate views conflict; thus in my edition of *King Lear* I will provide interlinked discussions, for example of Cordelia[F], Cordelia[Q], and Cordelia[QF].

The ISE's challenge is to find ways of recording and making visually apparent as much as possible both of the separate instances of the plays and of their complete play-function. In performance, we have begun already to provide representative snapshots of the range of ways in which the plays are transformed on stage in our database of Shakespeare in performance. The mutability and variation of the texts become a different kind of performance as they play their parts on the screen, in a fashion simply impossible for print. Indeed, the architecture of the underlying encoding will allow more views to be added if we so wish: it is entertaining to think of the equivalent to Google's "I'm feeling lucky" button, where a randomized set of variants would be loaded each time the button is clicked — very much the situation of the lucky owner of an original quarto or folio, since each copy will inevitably have different sets of proofed and unproofed pages bound into it. As Fluellen says in my epigraph, "Fortune is an excellent moral."

Works Cited

Berger, Thomas L. "The Oxford Shakespeare." *Analytical & Enumerative Bibliography* 3.3–4 (1989): 139.

Best, Michael. "*Othello* 3.4.462–78." Web page. http://internetshakespeare.uvic.ca/Annex/archives/OthSample4.html. Accessed October 2011.

———. " 'Standing in Rich Place': Electrifying the Multiple-Text Edition, Or, Every Text is Multiple." *College Literature* Special Issue 36.1 (Winter 2008): 26–39.

Blayney, Peter W. M. *The Texts of King Lear and Their Origins.* Vol. 1. Cambridge: Cambridge Univ. Press, 1979.

Braunmuller, A. R. "On Not Looking Back: Sight and Sound and Text." In *From Performance to Print in Shakespeare's England*, ed. P. Holland and S. Orgel, 135–51. Basingstoke and New York: Palgrave Macmillan, 2006.

Clare, Robert. "Quarto and Folio: A Case for Conflation." In *Lear from Study to Stage: Essays in Criticism*, ed. J. Ogden and A. H. Scouten, 79–108. Madison, NJ: Fairleigh Dickinson Univ. Press, 1997.

————. "'Who is it that can tell me who I am?': The Theory of Authorial Revision between the Quarto and Folio Texts of *King Lear*." *The Library*, Series 6, 17.1 (1995): 34–59.

Clayton, Thomas. "'Is This the Promis'd End?': Revision in the Role of the King." In *The Division of the Kingdoms: Shakespeare's Two Versions of King Lear*, ed. G. Taylor and M. Warren, 121–42. Oxford: Clarendon Press, 1983.

Clegg, Cyndia, S. "*King Lear* and Early Seventeenth-Century Print Culture." In *King Lear: New Critical Essays*, ed. J. Kahan, 104–23. New York and London: Routledge, 2008.

Craig, Hugh, and Arthur Kinney. *Shakespeare, Computers, and the Mystery of Authorship*. Cambridge: Cambridge Univ. Press, 2009.

Davidson, Adele. *Shakespeare in Shorthand: The Textual Mystery of 'King Lear'*. Newark, DE: Univ. of Delaware Press, 2009.

de Grazia, Margreta, and Peter Stallybrass. "The Materiality of the Shakespearean Text." *Shakespeare Quarterly* 44.3 (1993): 255–83.

Digital Renaissance Editions. General Editor, Brett D. Hirsch. http://dre.internetshakespeare.uvic.ca. University of Victoria.

Dobson, Michael. "For His Nose Was as Sharpe as a Pen, and a Table of Greene Fields." *London Review of Books* 29.9 (2007). http://www.lrb.co.uk/v29/n09/dobs01_.html.

Duthie, George Ian. *Elizabethan Shorthand and the First Quarto of King Lear*. Norwood, PA: Norwood Editions, 1977.

Erne, Lukas. *Shakespeare's Modern Collaborators*. New York and London: Continuum, 2008.

Foucault, Michel. "What Is an Author?" In *Textual Strategies: Perspectives in Post-Structuralist Criticism*, ed. J. V. Harari, 141–60. Ithaca: Cornell Univ. Press, 1979.

Goldring, Beth. "*Cor.*'s Rescue of Kent." In *The Division of the Kingdoms: Shakespeare's Two Versions of King Lear*, ed. Taylor and Warren, 143–52.

Griffin, Andrew. "Introduction." In *The Chronicle History of King Lear*. Victoria, BC: *Internet Shakespeare Editions*, 2011. http://qme.internetshakespeare.uvic.ca/Library/Texts/Leir/intro/GenIntro/default/.

Honigmann, E. A. J. "The New Bibliography and Its Critics." In *Textual Performances: The Modern Reproduction of Shakespeare's Drama*, ed. L. Erne and M. J. Kidnie, 77–93. Cambridge: Cambridge Univ. Press, 2004.

Internet Shakespeare Editions. Michael Best, Coordinating Editor. http://internetshakespeare.uvic.ca/. University of Victoria, 1996–2011. Accessed October 2011.

Ioppolo, Grace. *Revising Shakespeare*. Cambridge, MA: Harvard Univ. Press, 1991.

Jackson, MacDonald P. "Fluctuating Variation: Author, Annotator, or Actor?" In *The Division of the Kingdoms: Shakespeare's Two Versions of King Lear*, ed. Taylor and Warren, 313–50.

Kerrigan, John. "Revision, Adaptation, and The Fool in King Lear." In *The Division of the Kingdoms: Shakespeare's Two Versions of King Lear*, ed. Taylor and Warren, 195–246.

Kinney, Arthur F. "Transforming *King Lear*." In *Shakespeare, Computers, and the Mystery of Authorship*, ed. Craig and idem, 181–201.

Knowles, Richard. "The Evolution of the Texts of *Lear*." In *King Lear: New Critical Essays*, ed. Kahan, 124–54.

———. "Two *Lears*? By Shakespeare?" In *Lear from Study to Stage: Essays in Criticism*, ed. Ogden and Scouten, 57–78.

———. "Shakespeare and Shorthand Once Again." *Papers of the Bibliographical Society of America* 104.2 (2010): 141–80.

Kliman, Bernice, Frank Nicholas Clary, Hardin Aasand, Eric Rasmussen, and Jeffery A. Triggs. *Hamlet Works*. http://hamletworks.org. Accessed October 2011.

Massai, Sonia. *Shakespeare and the Rise of the Editor*. Cambridge: Cambridge Univ. Press, 2007.

McGann, Jerome J. *A Critique of Modern Textual Criticism*. Chicago: Univ. of Chicago Press, 1983.

———. *The Textual Condition*. Princeton: Princeton Univ. Press, 1991.

McKenzie, D. F. *Bibliography and the Sociology of Texts*. London: British Library, 1986.

McLeod, Randall. "*Gon*. No more, the text is foolish." In *The Division of the Kingdoms: Shakespeare's Two Versions of King Lear*, ed. Taylor and Warren, 153–94.

———. ["Random Cloud"]. "The Marriage of Good and Bad Quartos." *Shakespeare Quarterly* 33.4 (1982): 421–31.

McMullan, Gordon. *Shakespeare and the Idea of Late Writing: Authorship in the Proximity of Death*. Cambridge: Cambridge Univ. Press, 2007.

Mowat, Barbara. "The Problem of Shakespeare's Text(s)." *Shakespeare-Jahrbuch* 132 (1996): 26–43.

Queen's Men Editions. General Editor Helen Ostovich. http:qme.internetshakespeare.uvic.ca. University of Victoria. Accessed October 2011.

Rasmussen, Eric. "The Revision of Scripts." In *A New History of Early English Drama*, ed. J. D. Cox and D. S. Kastan, 441–60. New York: Columbia Univ. Press, 1997.

Shakespeare, William. *The Cambridge King Lear CD-ROM: Text and Performance Archive*. 2000. CD-ROM. Cambridge Univ. Press.

———. *The Complete King Lear, 1608–1623*. Ed. M. Warren. Berkeley: Univ. of California Press, 1989.

———. *The First Quarto of King Lear*. Ed. J. L. Halio. Cambridge and New York: Cambridge Univ. Press, 1994.

———. *The History of King Lear*. Ed. S. Wells. Oxford and New York: Oxford Univ. Press, 2000.

———. *King Lear*. Ed. R. A. Foakes. London: Thomas Nelson and Sons Ltd, 1997.

———. *King Lear*. Ed. B. Mowat and P. Werstine. New York: Washington Square Press, 1993.

———. *King Lear: A Parallel Text Edition*. Ed. R. Weis. London and New York: Longman, 1993.

———. *The Tragedy of King Lear*. Ed. J. L. Halio. Cambridge: Cambridge Univ. Press, 1992, 2005.

Slights, Camille. "When Is a Bastard Not a Bastard? Character and Conscience in *King John*." In *Shakespeare and Character: Theory, History, Performance and Theatrical Persons*, ed. P. Yachnin and J. Slights, 214–31. Basingstoke: Palgrave Macmillan, 2009.

Taylor, Gary and Michael Warren, eds. *The Division of the Kingdoms: Shakespeare's Two Versions of King Lear*. Oxford: Clarendon Press, 1983.

Taylor, Gary. "King Lear, The Date and Authorship of The Folio Version." In *The Division of the Kingdoms: Shakespeare's Two Versions of King Lear*, ed. idem and Warren, 351–451.

Urkowitz, Steven. "'The Base Shall to th' Legitimate': The Growth of an Editorial Tradition." In *The Division of the Kingdoms: Shakespeare's Two Versions of King Lear*, ed. Taylor and Warren, 23–44.

———. *Shakespeare's Revision of King Lear*. Princeton: Princeton Univ. Press, 1980.

Warren, Michael J. "Quarto and Folio *King Lear*: The Interpretation of Albany and Edgar." In *Shakespeare, Pattern of Excelling Nature*, ed. D. Bevington and J. L. Halio, 95–105, Newark, DE: Univ. of Delaware Press, 1978.

———. "The Diminution of Kent." In *The Division of the Kingdoms: Shakespeare's Two Versions of King Lear*, ed. Taylor and Warren, 59–74.

Warren, Roger. "The Folio Omission of the Mock Trial: Motives and Consequences." In *The Division of the Kingdoms: Shakespeare's Two Versions of King Lear*, ed. Taylor and Warren, 45–58.

Wells, Stanley W., and Gary Taylor. *Modernizing Shakespeare's Spelling: With Three Studies in the Text of Henry V [by] Gary Taylor.* Oxford: Clarendon Press, 1979.

Wells, Stanley W., et al. *William Shakespeare: A Textual Companion.* Oxford: Clarendon Press, 1986.

Werstine, Paul. "Folio Editors, Folio Compositors, and The Folio Text of King Lear." In *The Division of the Kingdoms: Shakespeare's Two Versions of King Lear,* ed. Taylor and Warren, 247–312.

———. "Narratives about Printed Shakespeare Texts: 'Foul Papers' and 'Bad' Quartos." *Shakespeare Quarterly* 41 (1990): 65–86.

———. "The Continuing Importance of New Bibliographical Method." *Shakespeare Survey* 62 (2009): 30–45.

———. "The Textual Mystery of *Hamlet.*" *Shakespeare Quarterly* 39 (1988): 1–26.

Woudhuysen, H. R. "'Work of Permanent Utility': Editors and Texts, Authorities and Originals." In *Textual Performances: The Modern Reproduction of Shakespeare's Drama,* ed. Erne and Kidnie, 36–48.

UNIVERSITY OF VICTORIA

Drawing Networks in the Devonshire Manuscript (BL Add. MS. 17492): Toward Visualizing a Writing Community's Shared Apprenticeship, Social Valuation, and Self-Validation[1]

RAYMOND G. SIEMENS, JOHANNE PAQUETTE, KARIN ARMSTRONG, CARA LEITCH, BRETT D. HIRSCH, ERIC HASWELL, GREG NEWTON, with DANIEL POWELL

1. Introduction

MISCELLANIES AND COMMONPLACE BOOKS ARE INHERENTLY SOCIAL documents, and the task of mapping out the complex social interactions involved in the processes of manuscript composition and transmission—both material and authorial—is one that traditional scholarship has found difficult to facilitate. The challenge of representing manuscript works, especially miscellanies, lies partially in the limitation of traditional scholarly tools to render interactions in and between material and authorial space in manuscripts, and partially in the conceptual struggle to detach manuscript texts "from

---

[1] This paper was first presented by Raymond G. Siemens, with Johanne Paquette, at the Josephine Roberts Forum: "Digital Technology and Manuscript Study," held at the 2008 Modern Language Association convention, San Francisco, CA. The paper was entitled "Variants, Visualization, and Analysis in the Devonshire MS (British Library Add. MS. 17492)."

the fixed systems of valuation and comprehension belonging to conventions of the book and the book trade."[2]

Recent work has emphasized the need to approach manuscripts as "'living' text[s] open to transformations," reflecting the appropriative "creative and re-creative" attitude with which early Renaissance readers and writers considered (and indeed, produced and re-produced) texts,[3] as in the case of commonplace books. Further, the need to approach manuscripts cognizant of their fluidity should be coupled with sensitivity to their social components, that is, to address the private and public, communal and individual natures of these works.[4]

All of these concerns can be readily addressed by embracing the electronic medium, since it is, in and of itself, dynamic and fluid. As part of a joint pilot project with Iter and Medieval and Renaissance Texts and Studies (MRTS), we are working on print and electronic scholarly editions of the Devonshire Manuscript (BL Add. MS. 17492) that will be published concurrently. The electronic edition of the Devonshire Manuscript offers a valuable opportunity to evaluate the applicability and reliability of digital visualization tools, since the results of our electronic analysis can be measured against existing knowledge derived by traditional means.[5] It is our hope that this undertaking will allow us to be more confident in the results that these tools can readily deliver when we encounter an unfamiliar object. This paper begins with a description of the composition and transmission of the Devonshire Manuscript, continues with a discussion of its reception by literary scholars, and ends with a discussion of our methodology and results.

---

[2] Melinda Alliker Rabb, "The Work of Women in the Age of Electronic Reproduction: The Canon, Early Modern Women Writers and the Postmodern Reader," in *A Companion to Early Modern Women's Writing*, ed. Anita Pacheco (Malden, MA: Blackwell Publishing, 2002), 339–60, at 353.

[3] Tatjana Chorney, "Interactive Reading, Early Modern Texts and Hypertext: A Lesson from the Past," *Academic Commons* (2005). http://academiccommons.org/commons/essay/early-modern-texts-and-hypertext.

[4] See also Margaret Ezell, *Social Authorship and the Advent of Print* (Baltimore: Johns Hopkins Univ. Press, 1999); Jean Klene, "'Monument of an Endless affection': Folger MS V.b.198 and Lady Anne Southwell," *English Manuscript Studies 1100–1700* 9 (2000): 165–86; and Jonathan Gibson, "Anne Southwell and the Construction of MS Folger V.b.198," address at the Renaissance Society of America Annual Conference, Cambridge University, Cambridge, 7 Apr. 2005.

[5] For a discussion of the encoding and prototyping of the electronic edition, see Raymond G. Siemens, "The Devil is in the Details: An Electronic Edition of the Devonshire MS (British Library Additional MS 17492), Its Encoding and Prototyping," in *New Technologies and Renaissance Studies*, ed. William R. Bowen and Raymond G. Siemens, New Technologies in Medieval and Renaissance Studies 1 (Tempe: Arizona Center for Medieval and Renaissance Studies, 2008), 261–99.

2. The Devonshire Manuscript

2.1 Significance

The Devonshire Manuscript *is usually* discussed as a sixteenth-century poetic miscellany; Raymond Southall has called it a "courtly anthology," [6] while Paul Remley has defined the document as an "informal volume."[7] It is bound in quarto, and, although physical evidence from the embossed leather binding dates its production to between 1525 and 1559, internal, topical evidence narrows the dates of greatest activity to the mid-1530s.[8]

Maintained as an informal volume and most likely circulated amongst a small circle of friends for private use, the document comprises 114 original leaves, containing approximately 194 items of verse, verse fragments, excerpts from longer works, annotations, anagrams, names, ciphers, and various jottings. The majority of the items found in the manuscript are lyrical, including courtly poetry by the canonical early Renaissance poets Thomas Wyatt (129 items) and Henry Howard, the Earl of Surrey (1 item: "O Happy Dames"); transcriptions of the work of others or original works by prominent court figures such as Mary Shelton, Margaret Douglas, Mary Howard, Thomas Howard, and, perhaps, Anne Boleyn (Southall, "Devonshire," 143); verses identified as written by Anthony Lee (1 item ["AI" has 3]), Richard Hatfield (2 items), Edmund Knyvet (2 items), Thomas Howard (3 items), Mary Howard (1 item), and Henry Stuart, Lord Darnley (1 item); transcriptions of portions of medieval verses by Chaucer (11 items), Hoccleve (3 items), and Roos (2 items); and some 30 unidentified or unattributed pieces.

The text of the manuscript reflects the interests, activities, and opinions of a dynamic group of men and women operating in and around Anne Boleyn's circle. At the time during which most of the interactions were recorded, Thomas Wyatt was already an experienced courtier who had introduced his own brand of politic translation of Petrarchan and contemporary Italian models into courtly

---

[6] Raymond Southall, *The Courtly Maker: An Essay on the Poetry of Wyatt and His Contemporaries* (Oxford: Blackwell Publishing, 1964), 15.

[7] Paul Remley, "Mary Shelton and Her Tudor Literary Milieu," in *Rethinking the Henrician Era: Essays on Early Tudor Texts and Contexts*, ed. Peter C. Herman (Urbana: Univ. of Illinois Press, 1994), 40–77, at 48.

[8] See the discussion of these theories in Richard Harrier, *The Canon of Sir Thomas Wyatt's Poetry* (Cambridge, MA: Harvard Univ. Press, 1975); Raymond Southall, *Courtly Maker* and idem, "The Devonshire Manuscript Collection of Early Tudor Poetry, 1532–41," *Review of English Studies* n.s. 15 (1964): 142–50; and Remley, "Mary Shelton."

poetics. Mary Howard, in her mid-teens in 1534, was married to Henry VIII's son Henry Fitzroy and had entered into Boleyn's circle, possibly bringing the initial manuscript with her since the original bindings bear the initials "MF," Mary's married name. Mary would also enter her brother Henry's poem "O Happy Dames" into the manuscript in the 1540s, well after the previous decade's intense period of composition. In the mid-1530s, Anne Boleyn's cousin Mary Shelton was in the same circle; indeed, Shelton was chastised in 1535 by Boleyn for entering into a book of prayers the sort of lyrical-poetical "trifles" one finds in the manuscript.[9] Thomas Howard, half-brother to the Duke of Norfolk, would die in the Tower in 1537 after being imprisoned for his private betrothal in 1536 to Margaret Douglas, a lady of the court and part of the Boleyns circle (in addition to being the niece of Henry VIII). Lastly, the initial center of the circle involved was Anne Boleyn, at the time just recently married to Henry VIII. While activity in the manuscript relating to the circle that surrounded Boleyn would, of course, lessen after her execution in 1536, the fact that the latest datable entry is that of Douglas' son, Lord Darnley, suggests that the manuscript stayed in Douglas' possession after its creation.

Literary history has privileged the Devonshire Manuscript as a main source of Thomas Wyatt's poetry since G. F. Nott borrowed it from the Devonshire collection to prepare his influential edition of the works of Wyatt and Surrey.[10] Early critics like Nott tended to situate Wyatt's poetry topically, with little interest in the other contributors to the manuscript,[11] who were regarded as copyists practicing a mechanical task "on the order of a handwriting exercise."[12] The manuscript's importance remained couched in these terms until the middle of the twentieth century, when scholars such as Raymond Southall, John Stevens, Ethel Seaton, and Richard Harrier took an interest in the manuscript as the product of multiple authors, as individuals representing their private and public concerns in ways allowed by the social context of Henry VIII's later court.[13] While Wyatt's presence was by no means diminished by this new focus, the contributions to the

---

[9] Remley, "Mary Shelton," 65 n. 19.

[10] The British Library acquired the manuscript from Nott's collection, through a Thomas Rodd, in 1848.

[11] The best-known examples of this approach to Wyatt's works, as represented in the Devonshire Manuscript and elsewhere, are those that championed a reading of the poems as topical allegories about Wyatt's alleged illicit relationship with Anne Boleyn.

[12] Remley, "Mary Shelton," 57.

[13] Representative studies include Southall, *Courtly Maker* and "Devonshire Manuscript"; John Stevens, *Music and Poetry in the Early Tudor Court* (London: Methuen, 1961); Ethel Seaton, *Sir Richard Roos: Lancastrian Poet* (London: Hart-Davis, 1961); and Harrier, *Canon.*

manuscript by Mary Shelton, Margaret Douglas, Thomas Howard, and others were increasingly recognized as important and worthy of scholarly attention.

Topicality continues as a unifying factor in the treatment of the Devonshire Manuscript in our edition, although the circle of critically acknowledged contributors is enlarged to incorporate more than just the poems of Wyatt and Surrey. Scholarly research of the later twentieth century situated more firmly such critical focal points on topicality: movements in both literary criticism and bibliography[14] demonstrated a renewed interest in the social context of Renaissance literature and a concomitant concern with the conditions of literary and textual production. Scholars accepted that an understanding of the rich and diverse connections that existed between poetry and power in English Renaissance society was central to a critical comprehension of its literature. At the same time, critics demonstrated that the focus of such literary study needed to be broadened beyond attention to canonical figures alone.[15] Further, scholars acknowledged that the key to determining the poetic-political significance of literary works lay in their currency within the very circles that the contents of those works addressed. Thus, courtly manuscript miscellanies and poetic anthologies such as the Devonshire Manuscript are viewed as "represent[ing] the meeting ground of literary

---

[14] That is, the social theory of text as exemplified in the work of McGann and McKenzie, among others. See Jerome J. McGann, *A Critique of Modern Textual Criticism* (Chicago: Univ. of Chicago Press, 1983) and D. F. McKenzie, *Bibliography and the Sociology of Texts* (London: British Library, 1986).

[15] Exemplary studies include Stephen Greenblatt, *Renaissance Self-Fashioning: From More to Shakespeare* (Chicago: Univ. of Chicago Press, 1980); David Norbrook, *Poetry and Politics in the English Renaissance* (London: Routledge & Kegan Paul, 1984); Steven W. May, *The Elizabethan Courtier Poets: The Poems and Their Contexts* (Columbia: Univ. of Missouri Press, 1991); Alistair Fox, *Politics and Literature in the Reigns of Henry VII and Henry VIII* (Oxford: Blackwell, 1989); and Jonathan Goldberg, *James I and the Politics of Literature: Jonson, Shakespeare, Donne, and Their Contemporaries* (Baltimore: Johns Hopkins Univ. Press, 1983). See also the following more recent studies: Remley, "Mary Shelton"; Helen Baron, "Mary (Howard) Fitzroy's Hand in the Devonshire Manuscript," *Review of English Studies* n.s. 65 (1994): 318–35; and Elizabeth Heale, *Wyatt, Surrey and Early Tudor Poetry* (London: Longman, 1994); eadem, "Women and the Courtly Love Lyric: The Devonshire MS. (BL Additional 17492)," *Modern Language Review* 90 (1995): 296–313; and eadem, "'Desiring Women Writing': Female Voices and Courtly 'Balets' in Some Early Tudor Manuscript Albums," in *Early Modern Women's Manuscript Writing: Selected Papers from the Trinity/Trent Colloquium*, ed. Victoria E. Burke, Jonathan Gibson, and Elizabeth Clarke (Aldershot: Ashgate, 2004), 9–31. On the importance of the Devonshire Manuscript specifically, see Julia Boffey, *Manuscripts of English Courtly Love Lyrics in the Later Middle Ages* (Cambridge: D. S. Brewer, 1985), and eadem, "Women Authors and Women's Literacy in Fourteenth- and Fifteenth-Century England," in *Women and Literature in Britain, 1150–1500*, ed. Carol M. Meale (Cambridge: Cambridge Univ. Press, 1993), 159–82.

production and social practices,"[16] and are understood to have the potential to reveal as much about the dynamics of poetry and politics as they do about the conditions of literary production in the early Renaissance — a process that Seth Lerer has shown to encompass the realms of public and private, blurring many preconceived notions about literary materials by exposing "confusions and conflations among poetry and drama, private letters and public performances."[17]

In addition to receiving new and significant attention because of the way in which its contents were seen to reflect the interactions of poetry and power in early Renaissance society, the Devonshire Manuscript was also recognized as a document that reflected the concerns associated with gender and literary production of the time.[18] The Devonshire Manuscript is one of the earliest examples of explicit and direct participation of women in political-poetic exchanges, and much of the recent work on the manuscript has focused on it as the product of a multi-gendered coterie, a primary site of women's involvement in the poetic-political world reflected in the early Tudor lyric.[19] Work such as this suggests the continuing significance of the Devonshire Manuscript for modern readers.

2.2 People and Networks

While we assume and appreciate its importance to Wyatt and his canon, our focus in preparing an edition of the Devonshire Manuscript has extended to all of

---

[16] Arthur F. Marotti, *Manuscripts, Print, and the English Renaissance Lyric* (Ithaca: Cornell Univ. Press, 1995), 212.

[17] Seth Lerer, *Courtly Letters in the Age of Henry VIII* (Cambridge: Cambridge Univ. Press, 1997), 38.

[18] Southall's work is traditionally cited as the central discussion of the manuscript and its import. See also Boffey, "Women Authors," at 180 and *Manuscripts*, passim.

[19] Representative examples include Heale, "Women"; Baron, "Mary (Howard) Fitzroy's Hand"; and Remley, "Mary Shelton." Heale explores the roles of Margaret Douglas, Mary Shelton, and Mary (Howard) Fitzroy and discusses "the evidence [the manuscript] yields of the parts women might have played as copiers, audiences, respondents, and, in a variety of senses, producers of love poetry in the early Tudor court" ("Women," 297). Baron confirms that Surrey's sole contribution to the manuscript, the poem "O Happy Dames," is in the hand of his sister Mary (Howard) Fitzroy, and also provides the very valuable service of making public her work with the various hands of the manuscript in a convenient table, identifying the personal hands of Margaret Douglas, Mary Shelton, Thomas Howard, Mary Howard, and others. Remley focuses specifically on Shelton's role in the manuscript and her use of a deliberate method that "attempt[s] to recast poetry written by others as a new and proprietary sort of literary text" to the end of, for example, documenting "the sense of outrage felt by her circle at the unjust imprisonment of two close acquaintances (Margaret Douglas and Thomas Howard) and [...] to protest the mistreatment of women by self-serving lovers" ("Mary Shelton," 42).

the identified and unidentified hands and social authors as represented in the manuscript — that is, those copyists, annotators, and arrangers associated with Boleyn's circle in the mid-1530s. In other words, we are interested in the manuscript not only as a document that contains the poetry of Wyatt, typically for use in a collation of witnesses found in Wyatt's Egerton Manuscript and elsewhere, but as a document whose contents vividly reflect the interactions of a number of important members of the courtly community that produced it. This is especially resonant since neither Wyatt nor Surrey penned their own verses within the manuscript; instead, their work is recorded by other hands — primarily the women associated with the text. Just as some early critics worked diligently towards interpreting Wyatt's early works within the context of his life at the time in which he wrote them — chiefly as circulated poetic responses (a type of epistolary politics) to aspects of his relationship with Anne Boleyn[20] — so too have studies from the middle of the twentieth century to our own time sought to identify how the various poetic utterances of the several identifiable contributors to the Devonshire Manuscript resonated with the events of their lives.

The best known of the interactions recorded in the manuscript is the love poetry exchanged between Margaret Douglas and Thomas Howard during the period of time when they were threatened, separated, and imprisoned for their marriage contract. The exchange takes place over several poems[21] that may well be original, combined with what has been characterized as "a pastiche of lines from Chaucer's *Troilus and Criseyde*."[22] Less well documented by recent work, however, is the way in which the majority of the individual entries in the Devonshire Manuscript have the potential to relate to one another, as well as to contemporary events beyond the borders of the manuscript itself.[23]

---

[20] See Greenblatt, *Self-Fashioning*, 115–56, and R. G. Siemens, "Thomas Wyatt, Anne Boleyn, and Henry VIII's Lyric 'Pastime with Good Company'," *Notes & Queries* 44. 1 (1997): 26–27.

[21] The significance of their choices and an analysis of the ways in which they adapted such verses to their own situations represent one way of exploring the social and political dynamics of courtly poetry, as is attention to the content and presentation of the poems they composed as inscribed in the manuscript.

[22] Remley, "Mary Shelton," 51.

[23] Such may be the case with Wyatt's "If yt ware not" (78v), which contains a burden that echoes a motto employed by Anne Boleyn in 1530, in turn echoing a line from Henry VIII's "Pastime With Good Company" (ca. 1509) which is itself an echo of one of the mottos employed by the Burgundian court in which Henry likely first met Boleyn. While often referred to as "If it ware not," the title of the piece as derived from the Devonshire Manuscript is "my yeris be yong even as ye see," with the incipit and burden "Grudge one who liste this ys my lott / no thing to want if yt ware not." See Siemens, "Thomas Wyatt."

Perhaps the most noteworthy aspect of the text, quickly apparent to those who come into contact with it, is that the Devonshire Manuscript is not a professional manuscript but, rather, the product of what we might call "educated amateurs." The manuscript text lacks many of the features that one would expect from professional copyists: some pages are ruled, but many are not (though a good number certainly might have benefited from the practice); some of the roughly 20 hands are even and regular,[24] while others are regular only in their irregularity.[25] Indeed, one of the major reasons why more research has not been done on the Devonshire Manuscript is that accurate transcription has proven quite difficult. While some 140 entries are copies of extant or contemporary works (129 attributed or attributable to Wyatt) and bear signs of copying, the majority of the pieces may reflect the work of local amanuenses and scribes with little professional regard for the standards we expect in a presentation-copy manuscript.[26] A full half of the manuscript's scribes (Hands 1, 3, 4, 5, 6, 8, 9, 10, 11, and MF) dedicate themselves to copying extant pieces, while another five (Hands 1.1, 2, 7, TH2, and MD) enter a mix of extant material and material that appears to be unique to the manuscript, with the remaining five (Hands 12, 13, HS, MS, and TH1) entering original materials alone.[27] The work of those ten hands entering material that has the potential to be original to the manuscript amounts to some 45 pieces (15 identified and/or attributed, 30 not).[28]

Save for the work of Mary Fitzroy, it is chiefly those identified amateur hands that have entered original work into the manuscript—namely, the group consisting primarily of Margaret Douglas, Thomas Howard, and Mary Shelton. One finds many features that suggest the personal engagement, immediacy, and spontaneity of this group in the original pieces, in the original responses to work known to be extant at the time of the manuscript's main period of activity, and also in some of the extant works that this group excerpts and adapts from others to fit personal circumstances. There are a number of examples of these personal qualities: the manuscript refers directly to Mary Shelton, for instance, as an audience to the text, and attributes various annotations to her;[29] Margaret Howard, too, is mentioned as a participant,

---

[24] Baron has documented 18 hands plus two slight examples, 6 of which have been identified thus far.

[25] Baron, "Hand."

[26] See Appendix 1B for a list of selected indications of nonprofessional scribal usage, including instances of overwriting and corrections.

[27] See Appendix 1A for a list of hands and their abbreviations in the Devonshire Manuscript. Our work follows that of Baron, "Hand."

[28] See Appendix 1C for a list of original entries by hand.

[29] See 1r, 7r, 22v, and also 6v-7r.

contributor, and audience.[30] The manuscript contains a direct address and plea by Margaret Douglas to her uncle and guardian, Henry VIII;[31] an implied association by Thomas Howard between Margaret Douglas and Chaucer's Criseyde;[32] and a poem ("My heart is set nat to remoue") by Douglas that exists in two versions, one express-ing undying love for (presumably) Thomas Howard, and the other containing an ad-ditional stanza indicating acceptance of the heartbreaking influence on this love of those who oppose the secret romance.[33] Other personal elements in the manuscript include a cryptic suggestion of allegiance (as tradition has it) from Anne Boleyn to Thomas Wyatt;[34] and a notation reflecting the solidarity between erstwhile sisters-in-law Mary Howard and Margaret Douglas.[35] Less personal, but equally important, are the attributions of this group's copying of original pieces to "anthony lee" (10v; "A. I." [22r]), "Rychard Hattfeld" (18v), Thomas Howard ("T h ho" [1r]; "T. h." [29r], "T. H. / T hou" [46r]; "T. H." [47v]), Edmund Knyvett ("E knywett" [59v]; "E K" [63v]), the less specific "Ihon" (22v), and the mysterious "s a i r" (24v).

In short, the contributors to (and participants in) the manuscript speak to one another in the poems and to those beyond their select circle. Often this conversa-tion takes place in extant verses adapted to a purpose; other times it unfolds in what we must (for lack of any external evidence) assume are original pieces. At times, specific topical, personal, and situational references can be cryptic. In addition to the poem "am el men," which requires the first and fourth characters of each line to be switched for it to make sense (so the first line reads "a lemmen"), there is the poem "Sum*m* say I love," which appears connected to Mary Howard:

---

[30] These include: "margayg" (1r); "[mar] garet how" (1r); "mar h" (26v, after the so-called "marriage" poem); and "m h" and "m h̶" (58v, one by MD). On the so-called "marriage" poem, see Boffey, "Women Authors."

[31] This occurs in "Now that ye be assembled here," where Margaret Douglas addresses her "ffather Dere / that off my blud ar the nerest" (88r).

[32] Here, Criseyde's name in the transcription is deliberately elided: blank space is intention-ally left in the text to substitute another name with similar scansion, i.e., Margaret. ³Syns ye [ ] [ ] / & me haue fully brought² (29v); ³and folowe always [ ] [ ] thy lady dere² (29v). See http://en.wikibooks.org/wiki/The_Devonshire_Manuscript/O_very_lord_/_o_loue_/_o_god_alas .

[33] See Bradley J. Irish, "Gender and Politics in the Henrician Court: The Douglas-Howard Lyrics in the Devonshire Manuscript (BL Add. 17492)," *Renaissance Quarterly* 64.1 (2011): 79–114.

[34] One of the most popular of these, raised often in discussions of the manuscript, is a riddle Southall has suggested was entered by Anne Boleyn. It reads: "am el men / an em e / as I haue dese / I ama yours an" (67v). This riddle, Southall observes (*Courtly Maker*, 17–18), is of the sort posed by Wyatt in his "What word is that that changeth not though it be turned." The answer (possibly a reply by Boleyn to Wyatt) is ANNA, solved by transposing the second and fourth letter of each line resulting in the following: "a lemmen / amene / ah I saue dese / I ama yours an."

[35] "Madame / Madame d / Madame margeret / et madame de Richemont" (68r).

Sum su*mm* say I love sum say I moke
su*mm* say I can not my selfe refrane
Sum say I was wraped in ~~myn~~in a whoman *semoke*
sun some say I hau plesu*re sun* I hau payn
yt yet on my fayth yf^{yow} wel be lewf me
non knw so wel as I wher my shwe grewe me (58v)

It is not entirely clear what this verse refers to, but it appears in a place in the
manuscript where there is a great convergence of identified hands. Less cryptic is
a reference in Thomas Howard's "To yowr gentyll letters an answere to resyte," in
which those who interfere in the speaker's relationship with (presumably) Margaret Douglas are wished to be on "goodwyn sandys" (29r). The Goodwin Sands
refers to a large bank of sand shoals, famous as a site of shipwrecks, off the coast
of Kent. To "set up shop on Goodwin Sands" was proverbial for hopeless endeavor and running aground,[36] thus Howard expresses the hope for the efforts of
those seeking to hinder his relationship with Douglas to be thwarted.

In addition to the verse entries described above, contributors to the Devonshire Manuscript interacted with one another through scribal annotation. These
marginal responses are, at times, quite personal in nature. For example, in the
margins of Wyatt's "Suffryng in sorow in hope to attayn" (6v–7r), Douglas writes
"fforget thys," to which Shelton responds, "yt ys wor[t]hy." Just above her attribution on the facing page Shelton adds, "ondesyard sarwes requer no hyar." Likewise, in the final lines of an unattributed poem, "The pleasaunt beat of swet delyte dothe blynd / our eyes" (66r), which read "whereas wysdome the soft Iudge
doth raign / prove wyt avoyed*es* all daunger breding pain," Douglas writes the
word "doutt," crosswise on the word "danger".

In stark contrast to the impersonal and detached engagement of the professional, the examples given above and others like them suggest the personal interaction and engagement of a small, select group, intending a small, select readership — one that would understand the nature of the document, the allusions
made, and the interplay of the several dominant scribal voices therein.[37] Indeed,
there is a chief allusion-maker and presiding voice over the manuscript, and that
voice is Margaret Douglas, who acts as scribe for 17 pieces across 19 pages and
has an identifiable presence — as annotator, corrector, and demarcator for half

---

[36] Morris Palmer Tilley, *A Dictionary of the Proverbs in England in the Sixteenth and
Seventeenth Centuries* (Ann Arbor: Univ. of Michigan Press, 1950), S393; W. G. Smith and F. P.
Wilson, *Oxford Dictionary of English Proverbs*, 3rd ed. (Oxford: Clarendon Press, 1970), S393.

[37] See Appendix 1D for a list of further examples of personal engagement through scribal
annotation.

the hands present in the manuscript (H1, H2, H3, H4, H7, H7.1, H8, H13, and MF) — on at least 50 leaves of the total 114. While she copies only five poems by Wyatt, Douglas marks 29 of his poems with the letter "s," and another 17 with the annotation "and thys," which, as Remley has suggested, may relate to another in-text annotation of hers, "lerne but to syng it" (81r). Her own scribal contributions are treated similarly in turn: they are corrected — albeit, only a very few times — by an unidentified hand which is possibly Thomas Howard's, and they are also annotated twice. "In the name of god amen" is added to her rendition of Wyatt's "to my meshap alas I ffynd" (42r), and on her poem "the sueden ghance ded mak me mves / off hym that so lat was my ffrend" (67v), Mary Shelton comments "hape hawe bedden / my happe a vaning," adding a stylized monogram with her own initials ("S" overwriting the middle descenders of a capital "M").

In writing both original and familiar verse to one another, annotating and distorting entries, and teasing each other, those responsible for the works in the Devonshire Manuscript interact in ways that capture our attention and literary-critical imagination. For those in manuscript studies this may not seem to be such a shattering observation; indeed, on the surface, it is not earthshaking to report on this type of scribal interaction. That said, what is notable is not that those participants interacting with one another in the Devonshire Manuscript do it well but, rather, that this unique group of men and women were able to do it at all.

As fascinating as these exchanges are, our current concern has little to do with listing about the details about what, how, when — and eventually perhaps why — these interactions take place. Rather, our focus is on determining how one might best approach this sort of scribal interaction analytically. Those engaging in traditional literary studies might be content with the task of identifying these scribal interactions and expounding upon their significance, but there is much more that can be done. For these new directions, as digital humanists, we turn to other fields of inquiry that have sought to analyze different materials that feature similar patterns of exchange.

3. Methodology

3.1 Overview

As suggested above, the traditional method of approaching social interaction in manuscripts involves listing instances of interaction and then expounding on their significance. However, other fields of inquiry have already sought to analyze different sorts of materials with similar patterns of exchange, and these have the potential to offer insights that could complement ways in which we already approach our analysis of social interactions. The study of communication networks in online chat-rooms or forums, spaces that bear a striking resemblance to that of the culture of early manuscript miscellanies, provides one such approach. In fact, modern writing environments and older ones are structurally similar: the patterns of annotation and response in the Devonshire Manuscript resemble a conversation among a circle of friends and relatives in written form, not unlike an archive of a series of discussions on an electronic mailing list.

As an experiment, we applied existing tools for visualizing communication networks to the Devonshire Manuscript. The manuscript contents were transformed into an XML-encoded text that could be easily manipulated to satisfy our particular analytical needs,[38] and the visualization tools were adapted to a technical structure that would best suit the requirements of the experiment. The first tool we tested was PieSpy, an analysis tool originally designed for use on an active IRC (Internet relay chat) channel in which a real-time conversation is taking place between channel users. Our strategy was to simulate the conditions of a real-time chat room by injecting the manuscript text from the transcript file, line by line, into the IRC channel, with each hand of the manuscript seeming to "speak" to the rest of the group.[39] PieSpy operates by interpolating channel activity into diagrams designed to reflect the strength of relationship between each user in the channel. The diagrams generated contain clusters of nodes joined together with lines, with each node corresponding to a user active within the channel. Through the progression of the Devonshire Manuscript, the blue lines connecting the hands to one another grow thicker or slowly fade away. The connections between the nodes, and the position of each node relative to the others, form the crux of the analysis. Those users who seem to be addressing one another are shown to have a stronger relationship to each other than to others in the channel, indicated by the proximity of their respective nodes and the thickness of the line joining them together. Similarly, those users who participate more in the ongoing conversation are given a more dominant role in the channel than those users who say relatively little, and are shown to be nearer the center of the cluster of user nodes. The end product of using PieSpy to analyze the manuscript

---

[38] For example, XML may be transformed through XSLT into a different XML file, a PDF file, a HTML web page, a delimited text file that can be imported into a spreadsheet application such as Calc or Excel, or any other appropriate format that is needed to generate the representations employed here.

[39] Technical details about applying IRC analysis tools to an encoded text are provided as Appendix 2.

transcript is a collection of roughly 200 diagrams that can be strung together into an animation to demonstrate visually the interaction between the contributors to the manuscript as it evolves and progresses from leaf to leaf.

The second tool tested was Simile Timeline, a web-based resource developed by the Simile group at MIT for the visualization of time-based events. Timeline allows users to physically manipulate a two-dimensional chronology by moving forwards and backwards in time by dragging with the mouse. Events can be represented as a single point (such as a date of birth) or as a bar (such as the amount of time working on a project). We adapted Timeline to visually represent a continuum of pages rather than dates: bars were modified to represent a continuing hand over multiple pages, while single points were tailored to denote hand markings of less than one line or annotations. We have also modified the software so that a simple mouse-click on a bar can show the first line of the verse it represents, and a click on a point reveals that particular annotation made by a scribe.

The last tool tested, TextArc, was designed and developed by interaction designer W. Bradford Paley (Columbia) as a Structuralist text analysis tool to visualize the distribution of words in texts. It draws the entire text in two concentric circles: the first is a line-by-line rendition of the entire text positioned around the outside of the screen in a one-pixel font; the second is a word-by-word representation of the text just inside the first circle of lines.[40] Even at this scale, the typographic layout of the lines conveys some of the structure of the text and gives context to the individual words found in the space created by the circle.[41]

The result of the experiments with these three visualization tools was to highlight particular features of the manuscript.[42] As outlined above, the visualization tools emphasize the shared apprenticeship of the group — especially the women — in creating the manuscript miscellany, as the various corrections, emendations, and annotations of the different participants are brought to the fore. The visualization tools also draw attention to aspects of social valuation in the manuscript, as the interaction of the contributors seems to focus on shared personal and political concerns in a court where privacy was often lacking. The continual vying for patronage and the omnipresence of spies and rivals made

---

[40] See Figure 7 for an image of TextArc.

[41] For example, words that have a higher rate of occurrence are rendered brighter in color, drawing the eye to potentially significant focal points of the text. Any word that appears more than once is drawn at its average position, exposing the structure implied by word distribution. In other words, the visualization reveals, at a glance, the distribution of words used throughout the text or only in a particular section.

[42] The combined operation of the tools is captured in a movie, available at: http://digitalstudies.org/ojs/public/site/DS-CN_published_media/DMS_FINAL.avi

the concealment and revelation of personal information to a select group an important concern. Furthermore, the communal space created by the manuscript encouraged women to reply freely to and interweave their voices with those of male contributors. The visualization tools also reveal the importance of self-validation in the Devonshire Manuscript. In the printed miscellanies that emerge later in the period, contributions by women to the conservation and creation of works — either through their epistolary correspondence, their effort in preserving oral or written texts, or their appropriation of text for their own use — become silenced. Applying visualization tools to the Devonshire Manuscript draws attention to the participation of women by positioning their contributions on the screen in relation to one another and in relation to the men with whom they interacted. Through the application of these digital tools, researchers are able to make information that has disappeared with the printed page resurface, represent information that would be time-consuming and even impossible to render manually and, to quote Kathryn Shevelow, provide for "a more encompassing view of writing as a broadly cultural process."[43]

3.2 Shared Apprenticeship

PieSpy and Simile Timeline, when applied to the Devonshire Manuscript, draw attention to the social interaction at work on the pages of the manuscript and to the involvement of women in its composition and circulation. Though there is indication of cooperation between the sexes, those who circulated and compiled the Devonshire Manuscript were mostly women who belonged to the circle surrounding Anne Boleyn. The movement toward a new humanist scholarship and the growing interest in the education of young people, especially of women, as well as the courtly fashions of the day — pageants, lyrics, and love games — created the backdrop to the stage on which Anne Boleyn, Margaret Douglas, Mary (Howard) Fitzroy, and Mary Shelton evolved. The education of the female circle of compilers of the Devonshire Manuscript was privileged in comparison to that of most women during the Tudor period.[44] These women had access to the

---

[43] Kathryn Shevelow, *Women in Print Culture: The Construction of Femininity in the Early Periodical* (London: Routledge, 1989), 19.

[44] Anne Boleyn completed her education at the court of Margaret of Austria where she sought to acquire "continental manners and good French" so that she could be secured a position at home with the French-speaking Queen, Katherine of Aragon (E. W. Ives, *Anne Boleyn* [Oxford: Blackwell, 1986], 23). Anne had surely heard or read some of Margaret's prescriptive lyrics advising the young ladies sent to her for grooming on how one should behave in courtly games of love. Margaret Douglas arguably received an excellent education since she resided

best women's schooling of their day, but despite these advantages, they were still subject to constraints that dictated their roles as both private and public figures. The new humanist education, championed by such figures as Juan Luis Vives, proposed a programme to focus women's attention on principled spiritual works. As Valerie Wayne has noted, Vives' image of a literate woman is not one who writes lyrical verse, but one who copies "some sad, prudent, and chaste saying from the Bible or a philosophical treatise [. . .] writing it over and over again."[45] According to Wayne, "the purpose of [such an] activity was not to communicate but [for a woman] to learn better her duty, and Vives did not suggest a larger purpose for handwriting elsewhere in his book."[46] Thus, despite their exceptional education, this group of women required guidance and direction when creating their court album.

Evidence of apprenticeship — members of this select coterie correcting one another and annotating one another's work, with Margaret Douglas acting as the *grande dame* of the endeavor — is revealed in the "snapshots" of the conversation in the Devonshire Manuscript created with PieSpy. Figure 1 is a snapshot of the conversation as it has progressed up to folio 70r as generated by PieSpy. This particular example demonstrates Margaret Douglas' involvement with many of the participating hands (unnamed scribes are numbered whereas identified scribes are referred to by initials). The snapshot clearly locates Douglas as a central point in the interaction at this point; as outlined above, palaeographical analysis has confirmed that she acts as scribe for 16 pieces (across 9 pages), and has an identifiable presence as annotator, corrector, and demarcator of half of the hands present in the manuscript (as outlined above), and on at least 50 leaves of the total 114.[47]

The Simile Timeline demonstrates the frequency of Douglas's interactions by placing the annotations ascribed to her hand as dots along a solid line that represent the activity of the principal hand employed in entering text over several

---

during her adolescence in the household of Princess Mary who was instructed in consultation with the Spanish scholar Juan Luis Vives. Mary Howard was the niece of Lord Thomas Howard and first cousin to Anne Boleyn. She was therefore connected to one of most powerful noble families of England and almost certainly had had an exceptional education. Her brother, the earl of Surrey, was a poet and she transcribed one of his poems in the Devonshire Manuscript. Mary Shelton's mother was governess to Princess Mary who was very well educated, which might account for Mary Shelton's high degree of literacy (Remley, "Mary Shelton," 43).

[45] Valerie Wayne, "Some Sad Sentence: Vives' *Instruction of a Christian Woman*," in *Silent But For The Word: Tudor Women as Patrons, Translators, and Writers of Religious Works*, ed. Margaret Patterson (Kent, OH: Kent State Univ. Press, 1985), 15–29, at 21.

[46] Wayne, "Vives' *Instruction*," 22.

[47] See Appendix 1D for additional examples of personal interaction via scribal annotation, including those of Douglas.

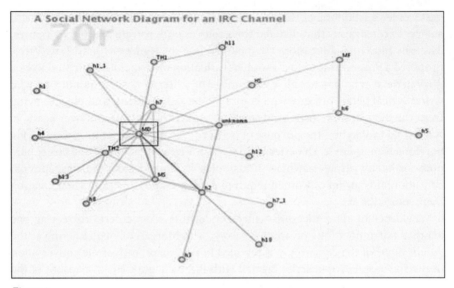

Figure 1.

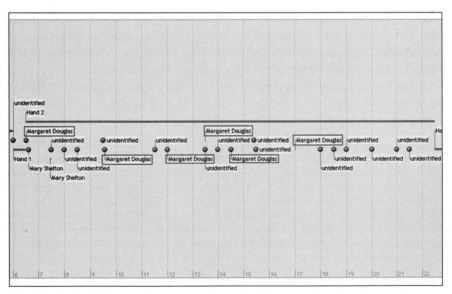

Figure 2.

pages. Figure 2 illustrates Margaret Douglas's several interventions on the pages where Hand 2 is very active. Other instances of corrections and annotations by other hands are also apparent. Whereas PieSpy focuses on the strength of relationships between participants, Simile Timeline focuses on the interactions themselves, identifying the kind of text produced as well as positioning and qualifying the participant's involvement. For instance, we can determine how many times a scribe intervenes as an annotator and, in turn, who intervenes in this scribe's entries.[48]

In Figure 3, we see that Margaret Douglas's entry, "Fanecy fframed my hart ffurst" (61v–62r), has at least five corrections made by an unidentified hand. By clicking on the node, we can make a quick assessment of the kind of annotation made by this unknown hand.[49] Though these tools cannot tell us who these unidentified hands are, they can give us a better understanding of the relatively complex relationship between the different scribes.

PieSpy can render the intricate representation of entries and annotations as illustrated in Figure 3 into a simple diagram that demonstrates the relationship between Margaret Douglas and various scribes (Figure 4). Textual analysis confirms that Margaret Douglas and Hand 2 are strongly linked in this section of the manuscript, and this is reflected in Figure 4 where the frequency of their interactions are indicated with a heavier line weight connecting them. Indeed, this relationship extends beyond this section: a snapshot generated by Simile Timeline (Figure 5) demonstrates that Douglas and Hand 2 remain strongly linked throughout the manuscript, which suggests that Hand 2 should be part of the historical record of Douglas' circle.

---

[48] For instance, the following corrections and insertions can be quickly uncovered in this way: Thomas Howard inserts "that I have lost" into H1's poem "O cruell causer of vndeserrved change" (2v) and adds "as semyth me" to H8's rendition of Wyatt "To cause accorde or to agree" (69r). H10 declares "finis" to H3's excerpt of Wyatt's "The knot which fyrst my hart dyd strayn" (22v), possibly as a separation to his/her own poem following. H5 writes the cryptic "s a i r" after H3's "finis quod" to "Hey Robyn Ioly Robyn tell me" (24v) and an unknown hand (possibly H5) continues "O hart aprest" transcribed by H11 but breaks off after two lines (47v).

[49] Two other entries by Margaret Douglas are annotated: "In the name of god amen" is added to her rendition of Wyatt's "to my meshap alas I ffynd" (42r); and Mary Shelton comments on Margaret's poem "the sueden ghance ded mak me mves / off hym that so lat was my ffrend" (67v), with "hape hawe bedden / my happe a vaning" and then the annotator adds a stylized monogram with her own initials ("S" overwriting the middle descenders of a capital "M").

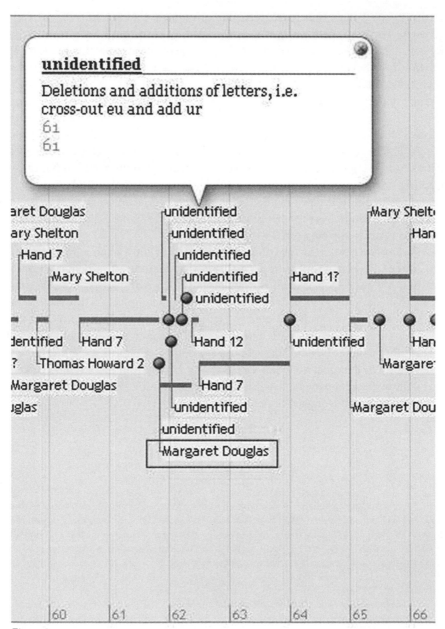

Figure 3.

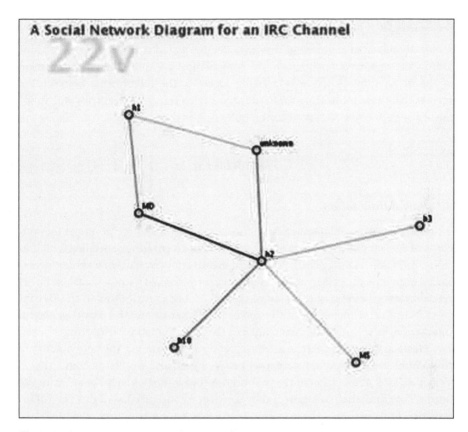

Figure 4.

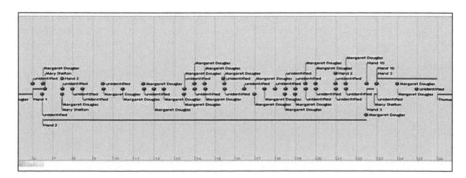

Figure 5.

3.3 Social Valuation

So far, these visual representations have demonstrated the types of interactions among the various participants in the composition, compilation, and circulation of the manuscript. Another interesting aspect of the relationship between the scribes that these tools bring forward is the circle's response to entries and annotations, a response which is, at times, quite personal in nature.

4. The Social Circle

4.1 Playful Interaction

The examples of social interaction in the Devonshire Manuscript reflect the concerns of a select group of court members living in an environment filled with tensions. As Heale has suggested, "poems in manuscript circulation were not necessarily, or primarily, valued as biographical expressions of a known author, but as reusable texts, belonging to a shared culture."[50] The contributors to the Devonshire Manuscript make use of the verses they enter in creative ways: as playful interaction, as serious reflection, and as a space for personal expression.

Heale argues that there is a "shared enjoyment" among the contributors of this album, even a playful interaction between men and women in some parts.[51] When we look at a section of the manuscript that is particularly "busy" with the Simile Timeline (such as Figure 5 above), we see a confirmation of this playful interaction in a portion of the text limited to just a few contributors (including two identified women) that has concentrated participation. PieSpy (Figure 6) gives an uncluttered view, highlighting Margaret Douglas' and Mary Shelton's involvement with four hands — H2, H3, H10, and Unknown.

When applied to this section, TextArc demonstrates that some key words of the playful interchange — for instance, "offend," "displease," "unkind," "falsehood," "foresworn," "husband," "shrewdness," "complaint," "prudence," "patience," "folly," "cruelte," and "meekness" — appear mainly in this section of the manuscript. TextArc provides data here that would be difficult to compile manually — for instance, the plural form "women" is particularly linked to this section (Figure 7) whereas the singular "woman," as well as "man" and "men," has a central position on the TextArc screen indicating that these words have a more general distribution throughout the manuscript. Why do the contributors to this

---

[50] Heale, *Wyatt*, 4.
[51] Heale, *Wyatt*, 312.

A Social Network Diagram for an IRC Channel

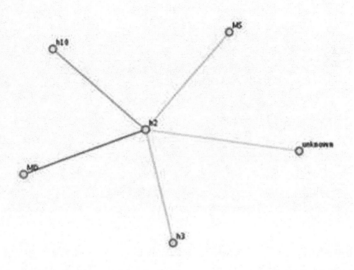

Figure 6.

section refer to the plural "women" — thus implying reference to "womankind" and not to a particular woman — more specifically here? And why are these particular nouns and adjectives, which should be found more evenly distributed in a commonplace book filled with lyrics of the courtly love tradition, instead linked strongly to this section of the manuscript?

Though the trope of the unrelenting, cruel, and unkind mistress and the patient, yet complaining, lover is found throughout the Devonshire Manuscript, seen through these digital tools this section seems particularly bent on a misogynistic perception of women in general. Textual analysis confirms the section's misogyny: H2's rendition of Wyatt's "Farewell all my welfare" (9v), a poem from a woman's perspective about the faithlessness of a male lover and lamenting false pledges, is followed by a text attributed to Anthony Lee about a cruel, unrelenting woman beginning "May not thys hate from the estarte" (10v). This is fol-

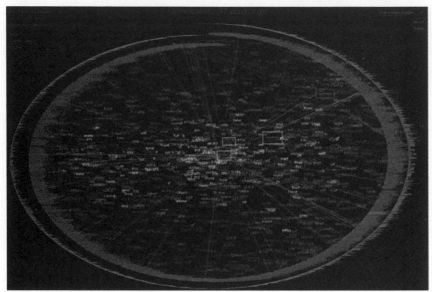

Figure 7.

lowed in turn by several other pieces copied from Wyatt about unkind female lovers — "Yff I had sufferd thys to yow vnware" (11r), "At most myscheffe" (12r), and "My lute awake performe the last labor" (15v) for instance — with an interesting punctuation poem appearing a few pages later attributed to Richard Hattfield ("All women have vertues noble & excellent") which plays on the double entendre of blame and praise of women (18v).

The visualizations produced by Simile Timeline (Figure 8) highlight the abundance of a symbol resembling the letter "S" in the hand of Margaret Douglas in the margins of this section. Though we do not yet know the significance of this marginal annotation, it indicates to us that Douglas read and seemed particularly interested in the verses on these pages.[52] Heale may be right in believing that the women who read and wrote in this manuscript "seem to have stomached, with spirit, some highly misogynist entries."[53]

---

[52] There are other instances of playful interactions between the scribes. Several poems are entered as answers to another. For instance, H8 enters Wyatt's "Patiens for my devise" (71r) and adds an explicit link to the earlier entry, "Pacyence tho I have not" (13v) transcribed by H2. H8 writes "to her that saide this patiens was not for her but that the contrarye of myne was most metiste for her porposse" (71r). Evidently, H8 teasingly pays homage to a woman's point-of-view about patience with a poem about the hardships of being unfaithful.

[53] Heale, "Women and the Courtly Love Lyric," 313.

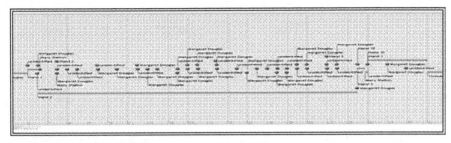

Figure 8.

4.2. The Douglas-Howard Affair

As Henry's niece, Lady Margaret Douglas was part of the court and a target for an advantageous marriage. When Queen Anne's court was established, Douglas was appointed as a lady-in-waiting, where she met and was courted by the Queen's uncle, Lord Thomas Howard. By the end of 1535, Thomas and Margaret had agreed to wed. (There is controversy over the nature of the marriage — whether it was indissoluble [consummated], or formally contracted.) When Anne Boleyn was charged with adultery and treason in May 1536, her daughter, the Princess Elizabeth, became illegitimate. Earlier, Princess Mary had been rendered illegitimate by the annulment of Katherine of Aragon's marriage to Henry VIII. This turn of events transformed Douglas from simply a good marriage prospect for the Howards into the heir presumptive to the throne. While Henry may have encouraged the original courtship between Howard and Douglas, the discovery of their marriage contract in July 1536 resulted in their arrest and imprisonment in the Tower of London. Howard was attainted — condemned by decree without trial — on 18 July 1536. He was sentenced to death, although the sentence was not carried out. By the end of the year, Douglas had been removed to confinement at Syon Abbey, where she eventually renounced her erstwhile husband. The King released her on 29 October 1537, while Thomas remained in the Tower where he died of an illness two days later. With the birth of Edward VI as a legitimate male heir and the death of Howard, Henry felt that Douglas was no longer a "valuable and dangerous pawn in the succession."[54]

Though earlier studies of courtly love games (such as Stevens, *Music and Poetry in the Early Tudor Court*) hinted at the desperate lack of privacy at court and the need for poems of the sort found in the Devonshire Manuscript to

---

[54] David M. Head, "'Beyng Ledde and Seduced by the Devyll': The Attainder of Lord Thomas Howard and the Tudor Law of Treason," *Sixteenth Century Journal* 13. 4 (1982): 1–16, at 15.

communicate by concealing information from certain individuals, later critical attention was focused resolutely on the subversive agenda of courtly poetry. Harold Love, for example, maintained that manuscripts were the media of choice for making available privileged information meant for a select audience, with the additional effect of promoting allegiances within groups of individuals with similar values and ideals.[55] There is little doubt that an extensive, even elaborate, interaction spanning forty-two poems between Douglas and Howard was such a correspondence, a conversation conducted in verse and coded with poetic metaphor between the pair of unlucky lovers. For instance, Howard draws an implied comparison between Margaret Douglas and Chaucer's Criseyde. In Chaucer's *Troilus and Criseyde*, the name "Criseyde" appears in the line "Iff I forgo that I so dere haue bought / Syns ye Criseyde and me haue fully brought" (Book IV, 289–90) and "Flee forth out of myn herte, and lat it breste, / And folwe alwey Criseyde, thy lady dere" (Book IV, 805–6). In his transcription of the same verses in the Devonshire Manuscript, Howard leaves a gap instead of entering the name "Criseyde," rendering the lines as "Syns ye _____ / & me haue fully brought" and "and folowe alwaye _____ thy lady dere" (29v). The metre and sense requires the reader to insert a name and, given Howard's circumstances as we know of them, the name "Margaret" fits. If we accept that this indeed is the case, Douglas is represented in these intentional omissions — these deliberate gaps and silences demonstrating the close association between her life and the circumstances of the inscription, compilation, and circulation of the manuscript.

Another poem, "My heart is set nat to remoue," this time by Douglas, exists in two versions: one an expression of undying love (presumably) for Howard (58v), the other containing an additional stanza suggesting acceptance of the heart breaking influence of those who oppose the secret romance (65r). As with the example of the adaptation of Chaucer by Howard to demonstrate his love for Douglas during their separation, here Douglas demonstrates the same for him. Again, the meaning of the poem is sharpened by an awareness of the biographical circumstances that may have prompted its composition. In the poems, Douglas seems to be vowing her constancy to her mésalliance with Howard in the face of the disapproval of her uncle and guardian, King Henry VIII. Political reality may have dictated the first line of the fourth stanza, "do what they wyll and do ther warst," and the additional stanza in the variant entry completes the

---

[55] Harold Love, *Scribal Publication in Seventeenth-Century England* (Oxford: Clarendon Press, 1993), 177.

symmetry of the poem poetically, demonstrating her understanding of the affair's consequences.[56]

To reflect her difficult situation, Margaret also adapts an unattributed poem. In "the pleasaunt beat of swet delyte dothe blynd / our eyes" (66r), as discussed above, she writes the word "doutt," crosswise, on the word "daunger" in the final lines of the poem, which reads: "whereas wysdome the soft Iudge doth raign / there wyl avoyedes all daunger breding pain." Where delight blinds and makes one embrace a foe, yet "will" should make one avoid the disdainful lover ("daunger") that breeds pain. Douglas changes "daunger" to doubt and thus changes the last line to mean the will should be wary of doubt that causes pain. This significant change might be interpreted as characterizing her feelings during the affair with Howard — her principal care seems to be with continued certainty of her lover's steadfastness.[57]

Considering the textual evidence, one might assume that the hands of Margaret Douglas and Thomas Howard would be directly linked frequently. However, the visualizations of the manuscript interactions generated by PieSpy reveal that these links are not as numerous as might be anticipated. In Figure 9, Howard is surrounded by H3, H4 and unknown, whereas Douglas interacts with H2, H3 and indirectly with H10, hands which are seen throughout the visualizations as part of her circle. Perhaps Howard may not have had the same physical access to the places where the manuscript resided since, as far as biographical research has established, the scribal circle seems to have centered on the women of the court, and the manuscript may have been circulated primarily among them.

However, the verse entered by Howard on the pages leading up to this point focus on his predicament, and on the fact that the lovers' situation is well known to this coterie. In fact, Howard makes it clear in his poem "Who hath more cawse for to complayne" that the injustice he and Douglas are suffering is well known to others around him. He makes obvious his concern with being powerless in this instance: "I can not optayne that ys my none / Wych cawsyth me styll to make

---

[56] The last two lines of the recovered stanza return poetically to the last line of the first stanza, "nor never chaung hes ffantesy." The poem ends with her reciprocal assertion of her loyalty: "ffor a sunder my hart shall borst / sow[n]er then change my ffantesy." The actions of the foe(s), though in vain, lead to heartbreak; only the "bursting" of her heart will be able to change the fantasy of the female lover's experience.

[57] Douglas also modifies entire lines of Howard's poems which, according to Remley, suggests that she had received his verse ("Mary Shelton," 52). For example, Howard wrote, "My loue truly shall not decay / For thretnyng nor for punysment " (27r), to which Douglas responds, "From me his loue wyll not decay" and "Wyth thretnyng great he hath ben payd / Off payne and yke off punnysment" (28v).

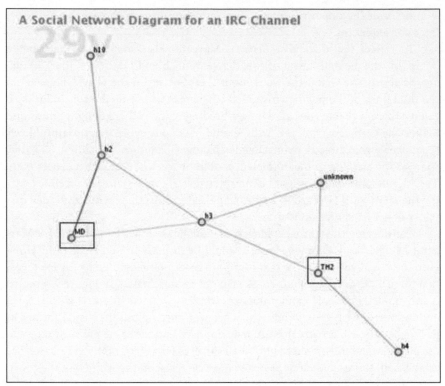

Figure 9.

great mone / To se thus ryght with wronge ouerthrowne / as not vnknowne / It ys not vnknowen how wrongfully / The wyll me hyr for to deny" (28r). Other members of the coterie seek to protest the unjust treatment of the lovers. One annotation is particularly resonant when read in this light: an unidentified hand adds "amen" after H1's transcription of a poem ("I lowe lovyd and so doithe she") about a couple in love but kept apart by others. The last lines read, "but they that causer is of thes / of all owr cares god send then part / that they may knowe what greve it es / to lowe so will and leve in smart" (6r). Apparently the members of the coterie involved with the Devonshire Manuscript were responsive to the plight of Douglas and Howard, which is suggested by the hands surrounding Howard on the PieSpy visualizations.

Shelton's and Douglas' verses together on 58r to 59r, and again on 65r to 68v, appear to support one another in similar themes. They lament the passing of happier times ("When I bethink my wontet days" [58r, 59r]), profess steadfast

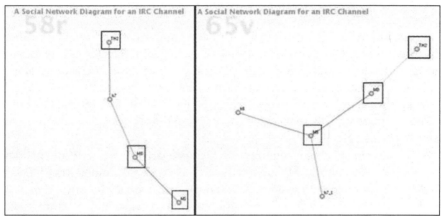

Figure 10.

love in the face of adversity ("My hart is set not to remove" [58v, 65r]; and "Lo in thy ha[r]t thow hast be gone" [59r]), and express the need to conceal (and perhaps the difficulty of concealing) one's true feelings ("I am not she be prowess off syt" [65r]; "Myght I as well within my song be lay" [65v]; and, "To cowntarfette a mery mode" [65v]). Interestingly, Douglas and Shelton copy the same poem, "When I bethink my wontet days" (58r, 59r), almost identically except for spelling variations, as if they were echoing one another's poignant sorrow over the loss of happier times and the "wery days / that [were] apoyntyt to be" theirs (58r).

The PieSpy visualization of folios of 58r and 65v (Figure 10) shows the strong link between Douglas and Shelton and the more distanced link between Douglas and Howard. Though there are many instances in which Douglas and Howard are connected, it is interesting to notice the supportive network that is revealed clearly in the visualizations.[58] Thus, by demonstrating the intensity of interactions between certain individuals, the types of interactions in certain sections, as well as the themes that are particularly conspicuous, these digital tools can visually highlight areas that might be of interest for further investigation.

---

[58] Many of these individual poems work as responses to one another, playing off attitudes and sentiments expressed in an epistolary manner. When we consider the striking parallels between the social context in which the verse was created and copied and the content of this verse, it can be argued that the contributors to the Devonshire Manuscript were "writing *about* the King, *despite* him, and in many ways *against* him": Greg Walker, *Writing Under Tyranny: English Literature and the Henrician Reformation* (Ann Arbor: Univ. of Michigan Press, 1950), 416.

3.4 Personal Validation

The networking images generated with PieSpy and Timeline visually manifest the links between the various individuals engaging with the Devonshire Manuscript materials as well as highlight salient features of those interactions. However, these visualizations also position the nodes that represent these individual participants at the core of analysis: by bringing forward the participants' individuality, these visualizations draw attention not only to *textual* interaction, but also to the interplay of *people*.

In addition to being recognized as a literary space where poetry and politics interact, the Devonshire Manuscript is recognized as a document that reflects concerns associated with gender and literary production at the time. However, as Kim Walker has cautioned, the notion of lyric-as-personal-expression must be tempered: rather than naively reading texts from personal albums such as the Devonshire Manuscript as "transparent accounts of the self or of experience," one should approach these commonplace books as "a space for constructing a personal voice, constituting the self, shaping a self-image, and articulating an identity within and against available structures of meaning."[59] Adopting this model, the Devonshire Manuscript might be better conceptualized as a space where the compilers could construct their personal view of the world around them and share these views with their entourage. In order to do so, however, the contributors had to feel free to express themselves in a political and social context that was fraught with tension, where friends were also courtiers and rivals, and where social and political advancement were dispensed capriciously. These sentiments are resoundingly expressed in h8's transcription of Wyatt's "My nowne Iohn poynt" (85v–87r), and many instances of descriptions of the thin line separating friends and foes are found throughout the manuscript. When these instances are examined using TextArc, the mention of friend ("frend" and "ffrynd") appears more localized, yet correlates with the mention of foes ("foo"). "Foo" is found near the center of the TextArc screen, demonstrating that it is somewhat evenly distributed throughout the lyrics (Figure 11). This can undoubtedly be explained by the concern of courtly love poetry with rivals and opponents. However, this visual representation of the text highlights a noteworthy subversive use of the social and personal space provided by the manuscript.

Women were particularly disadvantaged in finding a space in which they felt free to reply and appropriate courtly literary language for their own purposes. Publication was particularly problematic for women, even well into the

---

[59] Kim Walker, *Women Writers of the English Renaissance* (New York: Twayne, 1996), 26.

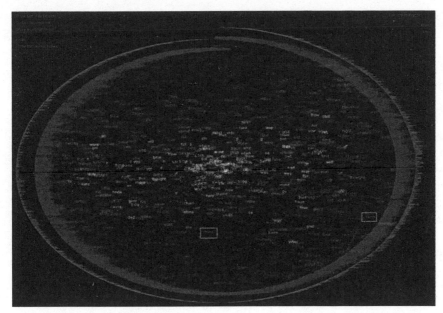

Figure 11.

sixteenth century, and remained a rare occurrence until Lady Margaret Cavendish published her poems in the mid-seventeenth century.[60] Coterie circulation being relatively private and print culture being an unsympathetic medium, women continued to produce verse in manuscript form well after the stigma of print diminished for their male counterparts. The use of the commonplace book as "a statement of personal experience," as Julie Sanders has argued, remained, until the seventeenth century and beyond, an accessible means for women to solidify allegiances as well as to acquire "authorial strength, confidence and aesthetic identity" through identification with a group.[61] Sanders' recent study of the early seventeenth century Aston-Thimelby or Tixall group miscellany certainly helps to demystify the image of the early modern woman writer as an isolated individual separate or separated from society. Sanders' findings support Ezell's contention that texts by women include also those works circulated and compiled

---

[60] Marotti, *Manuscript*, 54.
[61] Julie Sanders, "Tixall Revisited: The Coterie Writings of the Astons and the Thimelbys in Seventeenth-Century Staffordshire," in *Women Writing, 1550–1750*, ed. Jo Wallwork and Paul Salzman, special issue of *Meridian* 18.1 (2001): 41–57, at 52, 50.

by women, preserved and transmitted by "interweav[ing] their voices with the voices of others."[62]

One important aspect of the exchanges in the Devonshire Manuscript is that women felt comfortable to express themselves alongside men and to interweave their voices throughout the miscellany. Coterie circulation usually did not attribute verse to specific authors, which, as Helen Hackett has noted, makes the task of distinguishing between "reading a man using a female voice" and "a woman's own composition" especially difficult.[63] The Devonshire Manuscript, however, contains many attributions using initials and even full names, making the identification of women authors less problematic in those cases. But these initials and full names are more than just helpful bibliographic details; though the compilers and authors felt they were part of a coterie — a network engaged in writing, responding and correcting one another — they still maintained their individuality by leaving distinct personal markings on the pages of the manuscript, validating their individual efforts, experiences, and sentiments, and those of the other contributors.

The most significant of these marks are by Mary Shelton, Margaret Douglas, and Mary Howard. As mentioned above, the first page of the manuscript features Mary Shelton's full name as well as "margayg," and "garet how," which could represent Margaret Howard (Douglas). Mary Shelton's full name also appears after a poem in her hand (22v), and the acrostic poem in H1, "Suffryng in sorow in hope to attain" (7r), where the first letter of the first word of every stanza ("Suffryng," "Hope," "Encrease," "Love," "Then," "Vntrew," "Neu[er]") taken together forms the name "SHELTVN." The notation found on 68r reads, "Madame / Madame d / Madame margeret / et madame de Richemont," reflecting a certain experimentation with personal identity. Mary Howard is identified as Duchess of Richmond, whereas Margaret Douglas is given no patriarchal association by H7.

These seemingly idle notations in fact make these women leap out of the manuscript page. In a culture in which the practice of authorial attribution was still emerging and compilation and editorial duty were still mostly anonymous, the intermingled voices of women are often difficult to differentiate from those of men. The indistinctness of voices to those outside the coterie was not usually a concern in commonplace books. The recording of the identities of these women is therefore a fascinating aspect of the Devonshire Manuscript. However, as the sixteenth century progressed, the manuscript text (especially the courtly lyric) moved from manuscript compilation to print miscellany, and, as Elizabeth Heale

---

[62] Ezell, *Social Authorship*, 79.

[63] Helen Hackett, "Cortly Writing by Women," in *Women and Literature in Britain, 1500–1700*, ed. Helen Wilcox (Cambridge: Cambridge Univ. Press, 1996), 169–89, at 172.

has shown, the early Tudor courtly balet "became an almost exclusively male-voiced genre with the female-voiced poems of passion and retaliation largely silenced." The move from manuscript to print, Heale contends, saw "the role of women as crucial to the culture and the production of courtly verse disappeared from sight."[64] Tottel's Miscellany and later anthologies of Wyatt's works completely eclipse these marks of self-validation by women in the Devonshire Manuscript. As our experiments have shown, approaching early modern manuscript texts with new digital tools allows those aspects that have disappeared from the original — such as the contributions of women — to resurface.

4. Conclusion

Margaret Ezell argues that until recently, "little effort has been made to catalogue and reconstruct patterns in women's manuscript texts to provide an inclusive overview of literary activities rather than isolated, individual authors."[65] The use of visual representation tools allows us to draw out a more encompassing view of early modern writing; one, as Rabb explains, that does not depend so much on a linear progression along a continuum, but which attempts to capture a more circular, back and forth movement "along the interconnecting threads of a fabric of words."[66] Of course, each line, dot, or position of a word produced with these digital tools reflects an editorial decision made in the process of encoding the manuscript. There was also the assumption that the order of the manuscript materials, foliation by foliation, bore some relationship to the order of their entry into the manuscript — something that our own work and that of others draws into question. This research model, however, has a flexibility that will allow the opportunity for more accurate representation as a greater understanding about the composition of this particular manuscript text becomes available. Though the nature of the networks of interaction documented via these methods would not necessarily be altered, new information regarding the order of entries could impact the way we understand instances of successive layering within the exchanges of the manuscript.

The kinds of observations that can be investigated with these visualization tools are tentative; even so, they can be revealing inasmuch as they offer the ability to expose areas of investigation by giving new perspectives and highlighting problems. Many issues illuminated by these tools would be difficult to identify

---

[64] Heale, "'Desiring Women Writing'," 26.
[65] Ezell, *Social Authorship*, 23.
[66] Rabb, "Work of Women," 354.

and examine when looking at the flat manuscript page: the centrality of Margaret Douglas's interactions, for instance, or the emergence of certain words such as "women" and "foe," which demonstrate the conspicuousness and importance of certain themes and how they relate to the social networks in specific sections of the manuscript. The applications described here are but a small indication of the technology available, and yet they demonstrate the potential of visualization tools for textual analysis in the humanities.

Appendix 1

A. Hands in the Devonshire Manuscript (following Baron)

Named hands
  HS — Henry Stuart (Lord Darnley)
  MD — Margaret Douglas
  MF — Mary (Howard) Fitzroy
  MS — Mary Shelton
  TH1 and TH2 — Scribes associated with Thomas Howard (Lord Surrey)
Unidentified hands
  H1 — Hand 1
  H1.1 or H1? — Hand 1? or Hand 1.1
  H2 — Hand 2
  H3 — Hand 3
  H4 — Hand 4
  H5 — Hand 5
  H6 — Hand 6
  H7 — Hand 7
  H7.1 or H7? — Hand 7? or Hand 7.1
  H8 — Hand 8
  H9 — Hand 9
  H10 — Hand 10
  H11 — Hand 11
  H12 — Hand 12
  H13 — Hand 13

B. Selected Indications of Non-Professional Scribal Presence

6r — H1 gets larger and sloppier over the course of the page

15r–16v — H2 gives capital "B" in correct and incorrect manner

16v — H2 copies beginning of next line continuous with present line, cancels it

17v — H2 has filled "w," leaning "l," obscured "u" and obscured minim on "m" in "In feythe welcum to me myselffe" (l. 15)

19r — H2 sketches a little heart

27v — TH2 begins indenting every second line but with inconsistent execution

29r — TH2 uses a terminal "s" in the initial position

40v — MD's hand gets larger, sloppier, and fainter over course of page

41r — MD fails to provide macron for "n" in "miyd" (mind) (l. 1)

43r — MD begins following line continuous with current line, realizes her mistake, and cancels (l. 8)

43r — MD fails to provide macron for "n" in "myd" (mind) (l. 30)

43r — MD begins a poem, crosses out the first line, and starts again on the next page

43v — MD appears to have retroactively linked two previously separate words ("be" and "ffor" as "be-ffor") in "by prowff I se beffor myne neyne" (l. 5)

44v — MD's hand greatly enlarges over the course of the page; two big smudges

46r — TH1 squeezes a virgule in between two words so that it becomes a vertical bar

47v — H11's lines cross the page boundary

58r — MD incorrectly spells "Ioy" (joy) as "yoI" (l. 3)

65v — MS, where one word appears on the facing page ("beste")

65r — MD's hand becomes larger and sloppier over course of three stanzas, with many smudges

The following errors made by H8 may be the result of haste, not lack of training:

70v — one word ("of") added in margin, possibly as an afterthought (l. 4)

76r — terminal "s" in initial position (l. 6)

77r — combines two lines and omits a line in "What shulde I saye"

77v — carries over from previous line "for love to finde suche crueltye /" and "for hertye love to finde such crueltie"

78v — retroactively separates two words in "that bothe / we might be well contente" (l. 30)

79v — scribe makes an abbreviation for "ra" and writes out "a" in "Wherefor I praye you forget not" (l. 9)

81r — three instances where a single metrical line is combined with two graphical lines in "now all of chaunge"

83v — starts to write, realizes error, cancels and starts again

84r — writes first line in large letters, then reverts to usual size

85v-87r — inconsistencies with indentation and capitalization over the course of a 100-line poem that omits three lines

88r — MD's (emotional?) "testament Intyer" blotches, smudges, large untidy writing

91v — TH2 uses terminal "s" in initial position in "so cesseth loue / and forth to loue a newe"

Smudges, blotches, ink spills, incomplete erasures, cross-outs (e.g. 39v, 58v)

Stanzas that span pages/columns (e.g. 71r, 79v, 80r)

Poems that break off short (review — possible additions):

22v — "the knot which fyrst my hart dyd strayn"

22v — "He Robyn gentyll robyn"

62r — "fancy framed my hart ffrust"

66r — "Myght I as well within my songe"

87v — "My mothers maides"

Omitted lines:

17v — last stanza (H2)

74v — stanza 3 (H8)

75v — l.11 of sonnet (H8)

77r — l. 18 (H8)

80r — l.31 (H8)

85v — ll. 28–30 (H8)

Overwriting/Scribal Corrections/Scribal Errors:

16v — H2 overwrites "d" with "c" in "& yf suche chance do chawnce" (l. 30)

17r — H2 overwrites "s" with "w" in "And wylt thow leve me thus" (l. 17)

18v — H2 overwrites "y" with "r" in "truly . therfore they be to blame" (l. 16)

40r — MD overwrites "t" with "p" in "my ffathffulnes with sech despyt" (l. 6)

A full list of examples is available from the encoded text by searching on "orig/reg" and "sic/corr" pairs, as well as on "overwritten" and "overwrites".

C. Originals

H1

    58v — "Sum sum*m* say I love sum say I moke"

H2

    7v — "My ferefull hope from me ys fledd"

    8r — "Yowre ferefull hope cannot p*r*evayle"

    8v-9r — "Bownd am I now & shall be styll"

    10v — Anthony Lee's "May not thys hate from *thee* estarte"

    18v — Rychard Hattfeld's "All women have vertues noble & excelent"

    21v-22r — Anthony Lee's "In faythe methynks yt ys no Ryght"

H7

    59v — Edmund Knyvett's "Wyly no dought ye be a wry"

    59v — "To dere is bowght the doblenes"

    60v — "Myn vnhappy chaunce / to home shall I playn"

    62v — "In plac*es* Wher that I company"

    63v — Edmund Knyvett's "If *that* I cowlde in versis close"

    68r — "Madame"

H12

    62r — "fancy framed my hart ffrust"

H13

    66r — "The pleasaunt beat of swet delyte dothe blynd"

HS

    57r — "My hope is yow for to obtaine"

MD

    41r — "ther ys no cure ffor care σ off miyd"

    41r-41v — "as ffor my part I know no thyng"

    43v-44r — "what nedythe lyff when I requyer"

    44r — "and thys be thys ye may"

    58r — "when I bethynk my wontet ways"

    58v-59r — "my hart ys set not to remove"

    59r — "lo in thy hat thow hast be gone"

    61v-62r — "ffanecy fframed my hart ffurst"

    65r — "my hart ys set nat to remowe"

    67v — "the sueden ghance ded mak me mves"

    88r — "now that ye be assemblled heer"

MS

    22v — "A wel I have at other lost"

    59r — "wan I be thyng my wontyd was"

60r — "to men that knows ye not"
65r — "I ame not she be prowess off syt"
65v — "to cowntarffete a mery mode"
68r-68v — "my ywtheffol days ar past" *

TH1

44v — "Too yoye In payne my will"
45r-46r — "T Hou"'s "Yff reason govern fantasye"
46v-47r — "What helpythe hope of happy hape"
47v — "This rotyd greff will not but grow"

TH2

26r — "Now may I morne as one off late"
26v — "mar h"'s "Wyth sorowful syghes and wondes smart"
27r — "What thyng shold cawse me to be sad"
27v — "Alas that men be so vngent"
28r — "Who hath more cawse for to complayne"
28v — "I may well say *with* Ioyfull hart"
29r — "T. h."'s "To yowr gentyll letters an answere to resyte"
67v — "am el mem"

D. Further Examples of Personal Interaction via Scribal Annotation

02v — MD inserts "that I hawe lost" into H1's poem
03r — MD adds lines to H1's poem
15r — (possibly H1) inserts change into H2's poem "haue now"
22v — H10 declares "finis" to H3's part-poem
23r — (possibly) MD inserts "ffytt" into H3's poem
24v — (possibly) unknown hand writes "s a i r" after "ffynys q*uod*" by H3
47v — a hand not unlike H5 continues a poem by H11 and breaks off ("o hart aprest")
55v — MD inserts "he cum" into MF's poem
61v-62r — unknown hand "corrects" MD's poem
69r — TH2 adds three words to H8's poem "as semyth me"

Appendix 2

A. Using IRC Analysis Tools on an Encoded Text

The supportive technical structure which was employed in undertaking the analysis is composed of three overarching components — a transcript of the manuscript's content derived from the XML-encoded source, a local Internet Relay Chat (IRC) server, and a collection of small programs known as IRC bots. The roles of each of these, and the methods by which they are combined together to generate the output used in the analysis, are discussed below.

We have the ability to manipulate an XML-encoded text in a variety of ways depending on the needs of our analysis. For example, XML may be transformed through XSLT into a different XML file, a PDF file, an HTML web page, a delimited text file for importation into a spreadsheet application such as Calc or Excel, or any other appropriate format. In the case of the analysis being discussed here, the encoded text was transformed into a basic text file comprising of a transcript of the manuscript's contents, broken down into individual lines. The transformation stripped away the components of the encoding that are not a part of the original manuscript, including all tags, notations on physical bibliography, and comments made by the encoders. What results is a text file with one line of text for each line in the original manuscript. This file becomes the source from which we can undertake further aspects of the analysis. The contents of the transcript file are used to reproduce the conditions of concurrent interaction between users.

A further component of the analysis toolkit is an IRC server itself, which in this case is a very simple IRC server application written in Python and running under Linux.[67] The IRC server provides the operating environment under which analysis procedures can be executed. Once the server is up and running, we create a channel on the server in which to execute the analysis. An IRC channel is essentially an Internet chat room in which participants log in and converse with one another by sending text messages to the room. The analysis strategy is to simulate the conditions of a real-time chat room by injecting the text of the manuscript from the transcript file, line by line, into the IRC channel, with each hand of the manuscript seeming to "speak" to the rest of the group.

This brings us to the third component of the analysis toolkit, a collection of scripts which instantiate what are known in IRC parlance as "bots."[68] In the case

---

[67] For our experiment, we used miniircd: http://freshmeat.net/projects/miniircd.

[68] Bots are automated software applications that perform simple and repetitive tasks. Bots can be written in a variety of programming languages and programmed to perform a wide array of different jobs.

of this analysis, we are using bots written in Perl to interact with an IRC channel and respond in a controlled manner to conversational events taking place therein. Given that there are roughly 20 hands at work in the manuscript, and the total number of lines of text runs into the thousands, it would be highly impractical to attempt to reproduce the contents of the manuscript manually. Bots provide a means of automating the simulation of a conversation. For each hand present in the manuscript, one individual bot is instantiated — we will call these the hand bots. Upon instantiation, each hand bot logs into the IRC server as though it were a real user. The bot's user name in the IRC channel corresponds to the name of the hand it represents, e.g., the bot representing Henry Stuart's hand is assigned the user name Henry Stuart in the channel. Instantiating one bot per manuscript hand populates the IRC channel with users. However, these users do not actually perform any actions on their own — the hand bots which control these users are programmed to respond to specific instructions, and in the absence of such instructions they do nothing. This arrangement allows for the manuscript transcript to be output in a controlled and ordered fashion.

What remains, then, is inducing the hand bots (and thus the IRC channel users) to output those lines of the manuscript for which they are responsible and no others. This is accomplished by the use of another bot that is programmed to output a series of instructions, one by one, into the IRC channel — we'll call this the controller bot. The instructions contain two pieces of information: the name of the hand bot that is to respond, and the line number of the transcript that the hand bot should output. When the controller bot outputs an instruction, all hand bots observe and evaluate the instruction. However, the instructions apply to only one hand bot, and only one will ultimately respond. When a hand bot determines that it is the target of an instruction, it retrieves the line of text indicated by the instructions from the manuscript transcript and outputs it to the channel. There is therefore a call-and-response behavior between the controller bot and the hand bots. The controller bot calls a hand bot, and a hand bot responds with a line of manuscript text. This process repeats itself for each line in the manuscript, and in so doing simulates the actual occurrence of a real chat room session. The entire process takes about eight hours to complete.

While all this is transpiring, PieSpy, another type of IRC bot, is operating in the background, observing the ongoing conversation and responding to changes in the channel wrought by the interactions between its users.[69] The PieSpy analysis tool was originally designed to be deployed on an active IRC channel in which a real-time conversation is taking place between channel users. The use of bots,

---

[69] See also Mutton, 35–43.

as described above, allows us to simulate these conditions. Within the PieSpy configuration file are directives that can be set to specify which IRC server and channel the tool should monitor. When launched, PieSpy logs in to the designated server, joins a channel, and begins to monitor the conversational activity taking place.

PieSpy operates by interpolating channel activity into diagrams designed to reflect the strength of relationship between each user in the channel. The generated diagrams contain clusters of nodes joined together with lines, with each node corresponding to a user active within the channel. The connections between the nodes, and the position of each node relative to the others, form the crux of the analysis. Those users who seem to be addressing one another are shown to have a stronger connection to each other than to others in the channel, indicated by the proximity of their respective nodes and the thickness of the line joining them together. Similarly, those users who participate more in the conversation are given a more dominant role in the channel than those users who say relatively little, and are shown to be nearer the centre of the cluster of user nodes. The end result of using PieSpy to analyze the manuscript transcript is a collection of about 200 diagrams. These can be strung together into an animation that shows the evolution of the ongoing conversation.

PieSpy offers some capacity for fine-tuning its interpretation of activity on the channel. The configuration file allows for the specification of a temporal decay value, which is used by PieSpy in quantifying the degree to which a channel user can be considered active within the conversation. A higher setting for temporal decay causes those channel users who have not output anything recently to be dropped from the analysis more quickly, removing them from any subsequent channel activity diagrams until they are observed to be speaking again. The exact method by which this figure is interpreted by PieSpy is not documented, but some experiments demonstrated its potential utility in generating a variety of different views of the source data. The default setting of 0.02 produced diagrams in which users persist for a relatively long time beyond their final output to the channel. Although their diminishing roles in the channel are more or less accurately described by the diagrams, the resultant user node clusters tend to be more cluttered when using the default temporal decay setting. User nodes are present which, strictly speaking, should be interpreted as inactive. Therefore, it is instructive to run the complete simulation through multiple times, altering the temporal decay setting slightly with each iteration to influence the weighting PieSpy imparts upon the channel users. This produces diagrams that achieve a visual representation of the channel activity that is both informative and accurate.

UNIVERSITY OF VICTORIA

Paratext and Pointy Brackets: How Early Modern Archives Can Inform Digital Collections[1]

ERIKA FARR

GIVEN MY CURRENT RESPONSIBILITIES TO LEAD BORN-DIGITAL INITIATIVES at Emory University Libraries, it may seem surprising to hear me speak about the production of electronic editions of early modern texts. After all, the prophetic writings of Lady Eleanor or the political texts of Queen Elizabeth were certainly not born digital; they did not come into being through digital media. Instead, such documents emerged from another, earlier media transformation. While the source text of these electronic editions is decidedly born-analog, the apparatus that transforms them into electronic editions is by necessity digital. Contributing to this digital migration are various technologies, standards, and languages such as the Text Encoding Initiative (TEI) guidelines for developing and exchanging electronic texts, the XSLT stylesheets that transform the TEI XML into XHTML, and the Cascading Style Sheets (CSS) that determine how content appears on the web. The TEI elements, the XSLT and the CSS are exemplary in their status as digital natives and effect great change on their print-born source texts. This relationship between the digital and the analog, the paratext and the main text, and new methodologies and old will be the focus of my paper as I discuss how decisions about a collection of early modern electronic editions can influence digital collection building.

---

[1] The author is Head of Digital Archives, Emory University's Manuscript, Archives, and Rare Book Library (MARBL). This paper was first delivered at the 2009 Congress of Medieval Studies, Kalamazoo, MI, at a panel entitled "Electronic Editing of Medieval and Renaissance Texts: The Emory Women Writers Research Project," Sheila T. Cavanagh presiding.

First, I will share a bit more background about the project that is the focus of my remarks today, the Emory Women Writers Resource Project (EWWRP). Second, I will discuss how encoding a text generates a digital paratext for the electronic edition, by considering arguments made by Julia Flanders and Domenico Fiormonte about "Markup and Digital Paratext." I will next turn to issues around encoding and scholarly editing. Concluding thoughts will offer some insights I have gained from my experience with the EWWRP.

The EWWRP is a collaborative venture between Professor Sheila Cavanagh of Emory's English Department and the Lewis H. Beck Center for Electronic Collections housed in the Emory University Libraries. When first created in the mid-nineteen-nineties, the program was one of the first digital collections published by Emory and established a model that would be replicated at our institution of bringing field expertise, pedagogical vision, information science, and technical acumen together through faculty-library partnerships. The initial objectives of this program included offering open-access electronic editions of often difficult-to-find texts by early modern women writers and providing opportunities for pedagogical exercises involving scholarly editing and early texts.

Over the past 14 years, the EWWRP has been witness to significant developments in technology, encoding practice, and collection development strategies. On the technological front, the EWWRP has employed TEI standards for text encoding and, in keeping with these evolving standards, has moved from an earlier version of the standard such as P3 to the subsequent versions of P4 and soon P5, the latest release of the guidelines. I mention these encoding milestones not because they are unique to the EWWRP; quite the contrary, any humanities project engaged in text encoding that as been in production for a decade or more has likely undergone similar changes, at roughly the same times, with comparable results. Rather, I highlight these updates because they demonstrate how disciplined (or mostly disciplined) use of standards equates to sustainability and because they are evidence of how the paratextual elements ferry the "main text" through turbulence and change.

In addition to these technical and encoding shifts, the types of documents collected in this digital library have become varied in historical period and genre. With the core set of texts that launched the program comprised largely of seventeenth-century texts written by (or about) English women, the site initially had a strong English Renaissance focus. Fairly early in the program's collecting life, however, we began publishing texts from later time periods and from across the Atlantic, enough to begin creating some classifications around date, geography, and genre. The pedagogical and scholarly interests of project partners and project managers led to a rather organic approach to collection development for several years. Upon receiving a National Endowment for the Humanities grant to produce some 250 electronic editions of women's genre fiction, one collection of the EWWRP promised to consume all others, with the child far surpassing the parent in collection size. It was during this grant period that the EWWRP reconsidered its titles, developing collecting areas and reshaping the interfaces and encoding to enact changes in policy. I will return to this evolution of collection development and library building in my discussion of how early editorial decisions about the early modern texts enabled a relatively painless shift in policy and encoding later.

With this context in place for the EWWRP, I now turn to how our TEI encoding of EWWRP editions produces a digital paratext that influences reception on behalf of a "main text." Gerard Genette's concept of paratext is likely a familiar one to my readers. In his study *Paratexts: Thresholds of Interpretation*, Genette defines and illustrates this concept, explaining its relationship to the main text. Paratextual elements, Genette explains, "surround [the text] and extend it, precisely in order to *present* it, in the usual sense of this verb but also in its strongest sense: to *make present*, to ensure the text's presence in the world, its 'reception' and consumption in the form (nowadays, at least) of the book" (*Paratexts*, 1). In his study, Genette is focused on this function and form in printed books, but as he himself claims, "in principle, every context serves as a paratext" (8). Therefore, when texts move from bindings, typesettings, and paper to bits and pointy brackets, one should not be surprised to find paratext manipulating these new digital works.

My first thoughts about digital paratext actually had little do with the EWWRP, but instead involved the digital environs and contexts of born-digital archives, such as the personal computers used by Salman Rushdie recently acquired by Emory. It is with this notion of digital paratext floating about in my head that I attended a talk by Flanders and Fiormonte at Digital Humanities 2007 in Illinois. Digital paratext, it seemed, circulated around far more of my work than I had begun to imagine. To quote Genette himself, "Watch out for the paratext!" (410). In Flanders and Fiormonte's talk, "Markup and the Digital Paratext," they convincingly argued that encoding (TEI, XSLT, and CSS, among others) produces digital paratext that functions much like the paratext described by Genette for print books. They observe, that according to Genette, "any transcription, including the written transcription of an oral speech, is a form of paratext, and we can usefully extend this idea to digital forms by observing that any encoding—in effect, any transmediation—constitutes a form of paratext as well" ("Markup," 60). The enabling apparatus that heralds in a text from print to bits functions much like its analog counterparts and carries equal worth and importance to consumption and use. Within Genette's own text, he acknowledges other media (such as music and the plastic arts) that likely exhibit unique paratext/text relationships, and he speaks to the dynamic and productive relationship between technology and paratext, seemingly holding a theoretical space for explorations of digital paratext like the one undertaken by Flanders and Fiormonte.

Any discussion of a digital paratext understandably necessitates some reformulation or re-conceptualization of Genette's print-based concept. Flanders and Fiormonte undertake such work, in particular addressing the physicality of paratextual elements like title pages and prefaces, by commenting that elements of digital paratexts

> are not always literally visible as part of the legible textual surface: their "strategy" and "pragmatics" operate through the representational and performative mechanisms of the digital interface. [. . .] Their separateness is demarcated through markup, which not only creates a boundary between text and paratext but also makes the paratext into a space of function and behavior: of meaning instantiated through action rather than simply through textual signification. ("Markup," 60)

This focus on performative aspects of paratext and its functionality highlight the ways in which digital paratext is in accordance with Genette's definitions of the print phenomena while at the same time transforming it for a new medium.

Genette argues that studying and understanding paratext is important because its effect "lies very often in the realm of influence — indeed, manipulation — experienced subconsciously" (409). In order to avoid being unknowingly played or manipulated, then, readers must understand the form and function of paratext, just as authors or other creators (such as editors or publishers) must understand the capabilities of such devices. This need to understand and acknowledge paratext becomes especially important in digital media, since, as Flanders and Fiormonte rightly point out, the paratext is often invisible to users, working its manipulative magic behind the web interface in the form of XSLT or CSS.[2]

In keeping with Genette's systematic approach, Flanders and Fiormonte helpfully identify three categories of digital paratext:

1.   descriptive (syntagmatic and paradigmatic axes): those paratexts which contain information about a text, including various kinds of metadata;

---

[2] As mentioned earlier, CSS is a language used to style encoded web content for presentation, usually through web interfaces. XSLT is a language that can transform documents encoded in Extensible Markup Language (XML) into other formats or XML documents.

2.   normative: those which constrain the behavior of the text (for instance, schemas);

3.   pragmatic: those which mediate or represent the text as a discursive object, and which produce its digital phenomenology. ("Markup," 60)

Because I am interested in how TEI encoding produces digital paratext that, in Genette's terms, surrounds and presents the electronic edition, I will largely focus on this first category, that of descriptive digital paratext. A component of TEI that immediately comes to mind when thinking about digital paratext is the TEI header, which is a required element of any TEI encoded text. After all, the TEI itself defines this mandatory feature as a set of "descriptions and declarations" that "provide an electronic analogue to the title page attached to a printed work" ("The TEI Header"). The necessity of the TEI header within the text encoding guidelines nicely demonstrates Genette's argument about the importance of paratext. He claims "a text without a paratext does not exist and never has existed" (3). The same is true in the digital realm, and is codified in the TEI guidelines, purposefully or not.

TEI headers may include up to four parts: one, the file description, which is a bibliographic description of the digital text, including details such as a source description; two, the encoding description, which documents the production practices and standards; three, the profile description, which provides contextual and content-based information about a document; and four, the revision description, which records changes made to the file over time. Together these components comprise a digital title page and represent one form of digital paratext. It consists of many of the characteristics included in Genette's account of a title page such as the title, the name of the author, and publisher details and then extends beyond by divulging production details of digitization and encoding, as well as detailing revisions over time.

As an illustration, I would like to talk through a TEI header, one for Anne Kemp's "A Contemplation on Bassetts-down-Hill," a seventeenth-century country house poem. First, I'll consider the illocutionary force of this paratextual component, using Genette's illocutionary categories as guides: information, interpretation, commitment, advice or command, and performative. Kemp's header is largely informative in its illocutionary force, providing such basic information as author, title, publisher, and details about the source file. While such informative work may seem transparent or objective in its purpose, the story this information tells stands to influence readers, such as the gender of the author and the date of publication. In addition to information, this header also imparts interpretation on the main text, largely through classification and representation of subject analysis. In the profile description, the encoder has specified genre ("Poetry") and keywords ("English Poetry," "Women Authors," and "17th Century"). As Genette argues, such articulations do not act as mere "assertions" but rather mark a "decision" made and an insistence that the reader approach a text within a given framework. In his formulation, not "This text is a poem" but "Please read this text as a poem." These keywords are used to influence reader reception by creating a particular context, be it generic, historical, or social, and, by so doing, behave interpretively as well as informatively. This paratext also makes a certain kind of commitment to the reader about the text to follow. If we look again at the title statement, we notice a descriptor following the title, "an electronic edition." Again, this phrase could be understood as "purely" informative, but it also carries with it a promise from the creator to the reader that what follows is not strictly a facsimile but instead a transmediation of the source text that carries with it new form, function, and/or interpretation.

Because the TEI header, for the EWWRP anyway, is visible to the reader, it is a natural jump to understand this element of the text and its functions as fundamentally paratextual in nature. When in partnership with XSLT and CSS, however, this descriptive function of the header's encoding can migrate into normative and pragmatic modes. For instance, the Kemp header includes classification information for its text, including ethnicity, geography, and date. Reliable use of TEI elements in this document and across the collection allows for certain functionality within the user interface. In this case, paratextual influence makes a secondhand impact on the reader's experience, but a real one nonetheless, with similar illocutionary force as discussed with the header itself, though especially interpretive and in some ways performative here.

Key decisions and implementation of TEI with the early modern texts enabled the easy integration and development of additional EWWRP collections, which, in turn, transformed and multiplied the paratext for individual texts, early modern and beyond. The power of standards, such as XML and TEI, when appropriately used and documented, is that one can enhance and develop a publication, produce new collections, and, all the while, keep early texts current and seamlessly integrated. The descriptive and interpretive elements in Kemp's poem became the best practice that evolved into collection tagging within the EWWRP digital library. As new materials were added, collections were formed and encoding (and its paratextual influence) enabled us to sort the texts into like groups. The TEI encoding, plus the software, queries, and website design that comprise the EWWRP, enact an interpretive illocutionary moment that functions on multiple levels: one, this text belongs to this collection, and two, this collection is a part of this larger electronic archive. Such an understanding of paratext is arguably more expansive than Genette's own view since components such as website design and query structures exist discretely from the text file itself, but these broadly conceived paratextual elements enable the consumption and interpretation of the main text.

My analysis of the digital paratext circulating around a TEI encoded text has highlighted the influence TEI elements and metadata can have on the presentation and reception of an early modern poem. One important part of Genette's conception of paratext that I have not addressed is authorial agency. Genette argues for the importance of "authorial point of view" in studying and understanding paratext. I am not suggesting that Anne Kemp has a "point of view" on TEI headers or Library of Congress Subject Heading classification. I am suggesting, however, that producers of the electronic edition do hold opinions on such matters. And, using Genette's own turn of phrase, this authorial perspective is relevant for both "the author and his allies" (or in this case, her) (*Paratexts*, 2). If one views a producer of electronic editions as an authorial ally rather than an encoder or programmer, then the contributions and output shift from pointy brackets and code to paratext and influence. A shift that leads me to my next, and final, thought about encoding and digital collections.

I hope that my discussion of paratext has demonstrated the important work of markup in an electronic edition. Ultimately, we decided that the categories of "Edited Texts" and "Unedited Texts" we created in earlier versions of the EWWRP were false ones. We transformed this presentation of scholarly editions within our site from the misleading dichotomy of edited/unedited to a sub-collection of Critical Editions. As has been observed by others, the very process of encoding a text is itself editing, even if one does not add traditional editorial apparatus like an introduction or annotations. One must make decisions about a text that impact its representation and its consumption: decisions about the fundamental structure of text, the level of encoding (e.g., down to the paragraph, the word, or the character; or how its divisions will relate to each other and the text as a whole). How one makes these decisions, documents them, and implements them determines how accessible the digital text will be and in what context it will reside. In J. Stephen Murphy's article "The Death of the Editor," he laments the degraded role of scholarly editors in academic publishing and argues that the production of electronic editions is no friend to editorial practice. Murphy identifies weaknesses of certain electronic editions — those that offer a proliferation of versions without identifying an authoritative text — especially for certain users, such as undergraduates. But in the process of making his argument he seems to miss the rich opportunity that awaits us. Worrying about junior scholars and the tenure review process, Murphy wonders: "If you are a young scholar trying to write a dissertation or publish a monograph (or two) in order to secure tenure, how likely are you to take the time to learn the craft of both editing and digital mark-up?" In this question, he unnecessarily separates the "crafts" of scholarly editing and text encoding. Instead, innovations in scholarly communication and digital publishing suggest that we should capitalize on the established practices of scholarly editing while developing a new set of methodologies that engage with emerging technologies such as TEI and XML. Projects such as the EWWRP, where collection development, scholarly engagement, and technical education merge, promise to be the training bed for these new forms of editing.

Perhaps my title for this paper should be not plural but rather singular: how *an* early modern archive informed *a* digital collection. Encoding practices and policy development for one small digital archive of texts by early modern women have shaped the ongoing development of a broader digital library and influenced how those collections are accessed through the Web. The production of high-quality digital texts is an intellectual, scholarly process that requires numerous editorial interventions and a seemingly unending series of decisions about textual representation, all of which produce unique manifestations of a given work. And that work includes both a rich digital paratext and a "main" text. As the EWWRP's transformation from text lists to a series of collections demonstrates, this paratext is surprisingly adaptive, while the texts themselves remain constant. Just as Genette would have it: "Being immutable, the text itself is incapable of changes in its public in space and over time. The paratext—more flexible, more versatile, always transitory because transitive—is as it were, an instrument of adaptation" (*Paratexts*, 408). Adaptation and transformation—not death and burial—should be the hallmark of 21st-century editorial theory and practice.

Works Cited

Emory Women Writers Resource Project. 2006. The Lewis H. Beck Center for Electronic Editions. 30 August 2010 http://womenwriters.library.emory.edu/.

Flanders, Julia, and Domenico Fiormonte. "Markup and the Digital Paratext." Address at Digital Humanities 2007 (The 19th Joint International Conference of the Association for Computers and the Humanities, and the Association for Literary and Liguistic Computing, University of Illinois, Urbana-Champaign, June 4–9, 2007; *Digital Humanities 2007 Conference Abstracts* (Graduate School of Library and Information Science, University of Illinois at Urbana-Champaign, 2007), 60–61.

Genette, Gérard. *Paratexts: Thresholds of Interpretation*. Cambridge: Cambridge
    Univ. Press, 1997.
Kemp, Anne. TEI Header. "A Contemplation on Bassets-down-Hill, an electron-
    ic edition." Emory Women Writers Resource Project, 2006. 30 August 2010
    http://womenwriters.library.emory.edu/teiheader.php?id=kemp.
Murphy, J. Stephen. "The Death of the Editor." *Essays in Criticism* 58.4 (2008):
    289–310. 30 August 2010 doi: 10.1093/escrit/cgn020.
TEI: Text Encoding Initiative. 2007. TEI Consortium. 30 August 2010
    http://www.tei-c.org/index.xml.
"The TEI Header." *P5: Guidelines for Electronic Text Encoding and Guidelines*.
    2007. TEI Consortium. 31 August 2010 http://www.tei-c.org/release/doc/tei-
    p5-doc/en/html/HD.html.

EMORY UNIVERSITY

Textual Criticism

The Sense of a Letter:
Brilliana Harley's Advice Manuscript
(BL MS. Add. 70118)[1]

JOHANNA HARRIS

L ATE IN 1638, THE PURITAN LADY BRILLIANA HARLEY (C.1598–1643) WROTE
an unusual letter to her eldest son, Edward (1624–1700).[2] 'Ned', as she called
him, was fourteen and had recently departed the family home, Brampton
Bryan, in northwest Herefordshire, for the first time, and was newly arrived as
an undergraduate at Magdalen Hall, Oxford. In its content, the letter was not unusual in early modern terms; it proffered advice on matters of civic and spiritual
guidance relevant to Ned's university context and life beyond. It clarified, from
Harley's perspective, the most important precepts for Ned to remember, revealing a wide array of intellectual and literary influences that synthesised with her

---

[1] This paper was first delivered at the 2010 International Congress on Medieval Studies,
Kalamazoo, MI, at a panel entitled Early Modern Women's Manuscripts, Margaret P. Hannay
presiding.

[2] Lady Brilliana Harley's 'Letter of Advice' to Edward (c.1638), British Library MS. Add.
70118. The transcription of this text is my own. Harley's wider corpus of letters, of which four
hundred are extent, are BL Add MSS 70001–70004, 70105, 70110. Where Harley's letters have
been published, quotations derive from T. T. Lewis, ed., *Letters of the Lady Brilliana Harley*
(London: Camden Society, 1853), hitherto referred to as *Letters*. Harley's unpublished letters
appear in my own transcriptions, and are referenced according to their manuscript location,
as per the Portland Collection in the British Library, with folio and date where given. For the
major historical account of the Harley family, see Jacqueline Eales, *Puritans and Roundheads:
The Harleys of Brampton Bryan and the outbreak of the English Civil War* (Cambridge: Cambridge Univ. Press, 1990).

puritan outlook — described here as a Protestant humanism.[3] It is more unusual in the way it demonstrates an early modern woman writer following a tradition of advice writing more closely aligned with fathers' advice to sons than to mothers' advice books and legacies, and especially in the ways these are characterised in modern literary criticism. Discussions of mothers' advice writing regularly emphasize patriarchal restrictions on acceptable femininity and maternal roles, albeit with an allegedly liberating rhetoric of biological and textual reproduction.[4] The usual emphases most frequently employed are not particularly useful for describing Harley's style or content.

This text, BL MS. Add. 70118, is discovered in a repository separated from the rest of Harley's extensive corpus of letters. Those responsible for the cataloguing of the Harley family papers probably viewed the text as somewhat different from her epistolary manuscripts, and kept the texts distinct.[5] Setting speculation aside, what is certain is that Ned preserved this text with great care, ensuring it remained for future generations of the Harley family. It is most remarkable for its material design and formal character. It does not concur materially or formally with her usual letter writing style, but provides a sense, for her, of the way formal tradition blended with textual innovation, and the way she conceived of women's writing responsibilities as little different from men's. With this text, we are challenged to perceive it as much more than a manuscript work by an early modern woman. Harley wrote with a larger and more

---

[3] On the use of this term for moderate puritans such as Sir Robert and Lady Brilliana Harley, see Margo Todd, *Christian Humanism and the Puritan Social Order* (Cambridge: Cambridge Univ. Press, 1987, 2002).

[4] This is the perspective suggested in a recent comprehensive survey of the state of the field in early modern women's writing: Mihoko Suzuki, ed., *The History of British Women's Writing, 1610–1690*, Vol. 3 (Basingstoke: Palgrave Macmillan, 2011), 3. See also Jennifer Louise Heller, *The Mother's Legacy in Early Modern England* (Aldershot: Ashgate, 2011) and Betty S. Travitsky, ed., *Mothers' Advice Books* (Aldershot: Ashgate, 2001). The most common subjects of study are those advice works produced in print, including Elizabeth Grymeston, *Miscelanea* (1604), Dorothy Leigh, *The Mother's Blessing* (1616), Elizabeth Clinton, *The Countess of Lincolnes Nurserie* (1622), and Elizabeth Jocelin, *The Mother's Legacie for Her Unborne Childe* (1624).

[5] The largest proportion of the Harley family papers are found in the Portland Collection of the British Library. Others are scattered in repositories across the UK. For an account of the provenance of these papers, see Clyve Jones, "The Harley Family and the Harley Family Papers," *British Library Journal* 15.2 (1989): 122–33. It is plausible that even Harley's own children or grandchildren were the first to set the text aside. The meticulous archival habits of the Verney family towards correspondence offer a helpful example of the length to which ancestors went to preserve the written documents of the family's past: see Adrian Tinniswood, *The Verneys: A True Story of Love, War and Madness in Seventeenth-Century England* (London: Jonathan Cape, 2007).

important tradition in mind: the writing of parental advice and particularly fathers to sons (from classical times to her present moment), and the maintenance of a strong Protestant humanist character and community within the rapidly changing world of early seventeenth-century England.

When Harley wrote letters to her son, her habit was to write upon one folded folio sheet, taking three quarto sides to write, and leaving the final side to enfold the rest and to bear the superscription and her seal. She was usually concerned with space, cramming words to fit into a page rather than taking a new sheet. In this letter of advice, however, no economy of paper was demonstrated. BL MS. 70118 consists of six folded folio-size sheets, bound in the center fold with thread, forming a booklet of twelve quarto-sized pages, each carefully spaced. The front sheet appears like a title page, with "For my Deare sonne, <u>Edward Harley</u>" neatly scripted and justified in the centre. Unusually (for this writer), her handwriting has very few corrections or revisions, and is accompanied by biblical references in the margins. We can surmise, then, that unlike her other letters, this manuscript was carefully drafted before being copied into a fair presentation text in which she seeks, in some ways, to imitate the appearance of printed text. Research on the significance of manuscript space in letters encourages the view that the blank pages at the end of Harley's text suggest greater liberality with her use of paper than was usual in other letters.[6] This possibly indicated a more heightened degree of deference than usual to Ned as recipient or, more likely, suggests she viewed this composition as having the potential to reach an audience beyond her son. The lack of any evidence of a covering sheet in which the letter was 'sent' to Ned, or a seal, creates further interesting possibilities, drawing Harley's deliberate styling of the text as a 'letter' into fascinating perspective: if it was given by Harley to Ned in person, and took the physical form of a booklet, then why style it as a 'letter'? The text's appearance and construction also confirm that this was a text designed to be easily transportable for Ned; she encouraged him that it be "some times" consulted, paralleling its purpose with other printed texts of advice on conduct and virtue characteristically designed for "ready use," multiple readings and reference, and affirming that its material aspects were far from ancillary to its content.[7]

---

[6] On manuscript space in letters, see Jonathan Gibson, "Significant Space in Manuscript Letters," *The Seventeenth Century* 12 (2002): 1–9; and on the issues this raises for editors, see A. R. Braunmuller, "Accounting for Absence: The Transcription of Space," in W. Speed Hill, ed., *New Ways of Looking at Old Texts* 1 (Binghamton, NY: RETS, 1993), 47–56.

[7] The area of material studies with regard to early modern letters is rapidly expanding, propelled in large part by the work of James Daybell, most recently in *The Material Letter*

On the first page inside the booklet, Harley begins with an opening saluta-
tion, 'My Deare, / and Most Dearely beloued sonne', repeatedly using the phrase,
"my deare Sonne" throughout the work. She closes with her own name — claiming sole authorship — but never uses personal names in the body of the work,
including Ned's. Neither does the manuscript bear any localising details of date,
place, or other relationships, and there are only abstract references to 'home',
'the university', 'father' and 'mother', 'your parents', and 'my Deare Sonne'. In
terms of its formal characteristics, the work blends a variety of generic influences. Inside the booklet, Harley's words are laid out as though she is writing
verse, but without metre or rhyme. Many of the lines do not fill the width of
the page and the first word of most lines is capitalised. This draws the eye to
notice several half-length and even one-word lines, and to her capitalisation of
several key words. Intriguingly, Harley's final lines resemble a benediction, and
conclude with "A Men." All these features radically distinguish this composition from Harley's other letters, offering an opportunity to challenge and extend
the way we currently think about early modern women's manuscripts, women's
contributions to the culture of advice writing, and the boundaries, fluidity, and
scope of early modern genre, more broadly.

This is a distinctive and fascinating text which requires consideration of the
literary and intellectual culture to which Harley believed she was contributing,
regard for the material and ideological implications of literary form as essentially
entwined, and engagement with the question of why she gave the text its overarching epistolary character. The focus of this essay, therefore, builds on Harley's exercise of a generic flexibility, and the way she weaves her purpose into its
material and literary character, to contrast with the characteristics usually applied to the subgenre of mothers' advice for children, such as the desire to write
advice in only the most extreme conditions which threatened death (pregnancy
or terminal illness), or in the absence of an alternative male voice of wisdom
(widowhood).[8] For Harley, these conditions did not apply. Her impulse instead

---

*in Early Modern England: Manuscript Letters and the Culture and Practice of Letter Writing,
1512–1635* (Basingstoke: Palgrave Macmillan, 2012).

[8] In addition to the scholarship on early modern women's advice writing noted above, see
also Ulrike Tancke, *'Bethinke Thy Self' in Early Modern England: Women's Writing Identities*
(Amsterdam: Rodopi, 2010); Edith Snook, *Women, Reading, and the Cultural Politics of Early
Modern England* (Aldershot: Ashgate, 2005); eadem, "'His open side our book': Meditation
and Education in Elizabeth Grymeston's *Miscelanea, Meditations, Memoratives*," in Naomi J.
Miller and Naomi Yavneh, eds., *Maternal Measures: Figuring Care-giving in the Early Modern
Period* (Aldershot: Ashgate, 2000), 163–75.

drew from a long history of letter writing to justify participation in the parental tradition of scripting sound humanist and Christian moral advice.

Systems of formal classification inevitably encounter exceptions or examples which test the boundaries, and these often serve to reveal the inadequacies in our quest for a taxonomy of early modern form. BL MS. 70118 is just such an example. The few historians and literary critics aware of this manuscript have tended to overlook its formal complexities, under-representing the significance of Harley's contribution to early modern literary and intellectual culture, or to what we know of early modern attitudes to the formal qualities of advice writing. In these assessments, the material and ideological implications of literary form need to be more closely examined. The text has been described as "a memorandum of advice in which [Harley] counselled him [Ned] to live a holy life,"[9] as "a small booklet summarizing her most treasured teachings," composed for her "own sense of mission and identity," and, that for "godly matrons" such as Harley it was the experience of faith that gave her "the confidence and credentials to exhort her son."[10] One further discussion of the work refers to it as mother's advice in an epistolary form, but the account suffers from extensive errors in both material description and quotation of the text.[11] Such portrayals of the text omit to comment upon the flexibility with which its overt epistolary characteristics blend with its poetic structure, its carefully crafted booklet form, the internal absences of any personalising references, and the closing frame of Christian benediction and prayer, among other things, as well as the distinctive contribution it makes to the popular early modern genre of advice literature by an early modern woman.[12]

Margaret Ezell has argued that manuscript texts by early modern women do not fit comfortably into the categories currently delineated by editorial theory or material analysis, especially 'socially circulated' texts, such as poems, poetic

---

[9] J. T. Cliffe, *The Puritan Gentry: The Great Puritan Families of Early Stuart England* (London: Routledge, 1984), 89.

[10] Diane Willen, "'Communion of the Saints': Spiritual Reciprocity and the Godly Community in Early Modern England," *Albion* 27 (1995): 19–41, at 31–32.

[11] Kenneth Charlton, *Women, Religion and Education in Early Modern England* (London: Routledge, 1999), 234–35.

[12] Two further works which discuss Harley's letter writing in the context of advice deserve note. Raymond Anselment overlooks the existence of BL MS. 70118, in "Katherine Paston and Brilliana Harley: Maternal Letters and the Genre of Mother's Advice," *Studies in Philology* 101 (2004): 431–53. However (and after this paper was originally delivered in 2010), Edith Snook has published *Women, Beauty and Power in Early Modern England: A Feminist Literary History* (Basingstoke: Palgrave Macmillan, 2011), in which she briefly discusses Harley's 'short advice book', particularly in the light of the book's interest in early modern clothing and cultural identity (see esp. chap. 4).

miscellanies, commonplace books, and recipe books, where several authors can be represented, but which are ultimately cast into obscurity because of their 'messy' nature. Ezell draws on the expanding field of scholarship on early modern women's letters, particularly with regard to manuscript 'space', to show how meaning was implicitly conveyed through aspects such as the placement and size of the signature, the width of the margins, and the seal; all of which extend a text's 'meaning' well beyond the careful selection of words on the page.[13]

Ezell's argument about the material meanings of women's manuscripts can be extended further. D. F. McKenzie's observation that "forms effect meaning"[14] presupposes that an understanding of 'form' pushes beyond the material appearance of a text to the intellectual traditions from which it derived, and to which it contributed. For this to be true in our readings of early modern women's manuscripts, it is essential that we aim to understand how specific forms were understood, what they meant, and how a contemporary awareness of their imperatives and widely read exemplars created possibilities for their shaping and reshaping. For instance, with regard to BL MS. 70118, we are challenged by more than its unique material features. It is an intriguing fusion of epistolary, poetic, and prayer forms in an advice booklet. In its intermixing of these forms, it is not confused; rather, it embodies the intellectual character of the writer herself. Harley was an avid reader who reveals across her works a wide range of classical and theological influences, sermons, political polemic, history, and prose fiction. Understanding this profile, and her intellectual capability, is important when considering what she aimed to achieve in creating this 'letter' of advice. Her composition challenges the boundaries we apply to early modern genres, but it does so through significant stylistic and material influences that have been neglected. The significance of her text, in terms of its materiality, the social and literary conventions it follows or contradicts, and the combination of genres it creatively weaves within the frame of a letter, can be better understood in the light of what she might have thought about her composition in terms of its ideological purpose.

Letters have been an apposite form for the writing of advice since the classical period. With their rhetorical possibilities for artful candour, they convey conventional instruction on virtue in mutually supportive tones of conversation and personalized exhortation. Articulating advice in letters meant that the content was situated in a form that had traditions dating back to the origins of rhetorical

---

[13] Margaret J. M. Ezell, "Editing Early Modern Women's Manuscripts: Theory, Electronic Editions, and the Accidental Copy-Text," *Literature Compass* 7 (2010): 102–9 at 106–7.

[14] D. F. McKenzie, *Bibliography and the Sociology of Texts,* The Panizzi Lectures, 1985, (London: British Library, 1986), 4.

dialogue. In being styled as a letter, a text could gesture at being just one part of a fluid and democratic exchange, of a cultivated relationship of reciprocity, and could therefore imply that the development of character took place as part of a conversation or a broader community of participation. This creates a natural fit with the civic humanism of Harley's England, as well as with the more particular tenets of her radical Protestant convictions. Letter writing enabled a sense of mutual participation integral to the kind of advice that was aimed at enhancing notions of civic duty and virtue that emphasised individual spiritual reformation for wider, corporate benefit.

Attending to the wide range of ideological influences of Harley's manuscript letter of advice is a task beyond the necessary limits of this brief discussion. I will focus on one key characteristic in the rest of the essay that helps to elucidate her intellectual purpose, and the most substantial influence upon her mindset about good conduct and how to write about it: the apostolic letters to the early church communities as recorded in the New Testament. This is not to diminish the influence of a wider array of classical works of advice upon Harley's writing and thought. She demonstrates throughout her letter-writing life an understanding of the classical tradition that mingled the communication of knowledge and experience with the fashioning of character in its letters, and was strongly influenced by Seneca's *Epistulae Morales*, in particular — his stylised and fictional collection of letters to his friend Lucilius, and read extensively in the early modern period for its moral philosophical advice.[15] It is also unthinkable that she had no knowledge of the most influential work of advice in the period, Cicero's *De officiis* (On Duties), which was styled as a letter, and of which the Harleys owned no fewer than three copies by July 1637.[16] About *De officiis*, Patrick Collinson stated, "There was a cracked gramophone record which a certain kind of Elizabethan, patriot and citizen as much as subject, never tired of playing, and the tune had

---

[15] 'Commonplace book of Brilliana Conway, 1622', Portland Papers, Nottingham University Library, Manuscripts Department. Seneca's *Moral Epistles* is heavily referenced in this early record of Harley's reading.

[16] On the early modern publication history of *De Officiis*, see Howard Jones, *Master Tully: Cicero in Tudor England*, Bibliotheca Humanistica & Reformatorica 58 (Nieuwkeep: De Graaf, 1998), esp. 114–52, 191–215. On the place of Cicero in early modern English culture, see for instance Ian M. Green, *Humanism and Protestantism in Early Modern English Education* (Aldershot: Ashgate, 2009). For a record of the three editions of *De officiis* owned by the Harley family, see BL MS. Add. 70001, fols. 328r-335v, 'A Catalogue of Bookes taken the 12th Day of July 1637', Sir Robert Harley's manuscript inventory of the library at Brampton Bryan, Herefordshire. The catalogue keeps no record of precise bibliographic details such as date or place of publication, or size, but records titles of works and a disciplinary categorisation (such as philology and divinity).

been composed by Marcus Tullius Cicero in his *De officiis*."[17] William Cecil reportedly carried a pocket-sized copy of *De officiis* everywhere "to his dying day" (along with his Bible) — a fact advertised in Henry Peacham's own text on conduct, *The Compleat Gentleman* (1622).[18]

It is not new to highlight the classical influence upon early modern sociability, including upon the practices of letter writing. The New Testament epistles are of equal importance within this classical tradition, but tend to receive less attention in the field. Particular corollaries between Harley's use of letters to style advice and the apostolic use of epistolarity can be drawn. In Harley's puritan worldview, the Bible was the primary text guiding spiritual formation, and while often noted as a literary influence, it remains neglected as an important example of how attention to literary form helped to create meaning, particularly in terms of letter writing. The examples presented here attempt to offer some new ways of thinking about this relationship between biblical letters and early modern works of advice styled as letters, and focus upon letter writing's natural prerogative for physical separation, its stance as a paper form of conversation and in upholding principles of dialogue and social interaction, and the role of letters in the shaping and display of Christian character.

In the same way that one of the intentions of the biblical epistles was to unite the dispersed community of believers, Harley's letter of advice capitalized on the imperative of writing to Ned because of their geographical separation. The apostle Paul was conscious that his epistolary 'presence' should be a representation of his real presence: "Let such an one think this, that, such as we are in word by letters when we are absent, such will we be also in deed when we are present" (2 Corinthians 10:11, AV). Like the apostolic imperative of writing to spiritual children, Harley's letter was intended to be a surrogate for the performance of parental duty in person. She described her letter as a visual emissary, enabling her to continue fulfilling her responsibility:

> it was my constant
> practice offten to put you in
> minde of those things which
> tende to your Cheefest good, but
> now distance of place will not
> giue leaue to performe that duty
> so offten as I desire,

---

[17] Patrick Collinson, "Servants and Citizens: Robert Beale and other Elizabethans," *Historical Research* 79 (2006): 488–511, at 493.

[18] Henry Peacham, *The Compleat Gentleman* (London, 1622), 45.

> therefore Deare sonne Let theas
> Linnes some times present to
> Your Eyes, thos things which I
> Would speake to your Eares (fol. 2.3–9)

As a work of advice this letter has an inbuilt durability, which Harley underscores
in the excerpt above. She draws out the message that it is not to be treated in any
ephemeral manner (as of interpersonal communication now — to read, and dis-
card, or at least never look at again), but she expects Ned to refer to it repeatedly:
"Let theas Linnes *some times* present to Your Eyes. . .". Harley also acknowledges
the imperative of speech and of personal presence in letter writing. She anticipates that her letter should prompt the sensory experiences in Ned of seeing and
hearing: her lines, carefully crafted, are to "present to / Your Eyes," and are to be
heard as "thos things which I / Would speake to your Eares"; the letter, then, is a
proxy for her physical presence and her audible voice, and is to be so familiar in
these things as to infer her real presence and thereby the letter's authenticity. This
also allowed Harley, to an extent, to cultivate an impression of surveillance, setting up the idea of her letters acting as her constant 'eye', overcoming her physical absence. The experience of writing the letter, and of Ned's life and activity
beyond home, are drawn into the same moment and place, as she conveys a sense
of her accompanying eye:

> Nowe I looke upon you as
> On Lanceing forth into the seas
> Of this world . . . (fols. 5r.13–6.2)

The material text that Ned held before him bore some essential hallmarks of his
mother's presence in ways that a printed text could not, in the visual appearance
of her "Linnes," and in the expectation that Ned will 'hear' her familiar voice. It
was a text that in its material, manuscript form heightened the responsibility of
the reader (to act in accordance with the principles outlined) and could in effect
be more directive than print. Instructions in the hand of his mother, rather than
in impersonal print, raised the stakes. Harley could have simply given to her son
any number of popular published works of instruction to guide this new phase of
his life — a copy of *De Officiis* (available in multiple bilingual, Latin, and English
editions from 1534 onwards), or of Erasmus' *Enchiridion Militis Christiani* (published in English in 1533), Lord Burghley's *Certaine Preceptes* (1611), Peacham's
Compleat Gentleman (1622), Richard Braithwaite's *The English Gentleman* (1631),
or *Sir Walter Raleigh's Instructions to his Sonne* (1632) — but as far as we know,

Harley did not send any conduct manuals to Ned, despite the vibrant culture of
reading and book exchange between them that is witnessed in her other letters.
Instead, it seems she drew inspiration from these sorts of humanist advice works
in crafting her own text, distinctive in its material presence and voice. Of course,
in styling hers as a letter of advice she capitalized on her authority in the par-
ent-child relationship. The letter begins, "My Deare and Most Dearely beloued
sonne," clarifying that the contents to follow will derive from a deep concern
and love for him as her child; she repeatedly references "Deare sonne" throughout, emphasizing her pre-eminent position. But just as the presence of the letter
highlights her physical absence, Harley subordinates herself and her husband,
Sir Robert Harley, as Ned's earthly parents, to his Heavenly parentage. She refers
to "your / Father on Earth" and "the awe / Of your parents," and offsets these
phrases against "your heauenly Father":

> But doo
> You remember that though your
> Father on Earth see you not
> Yet your heauenly Father dous
> And him learne to feare . . . (fol. 8v.6–10)

Ned is also to be governed by the "watchfulness" of his own conscience. For instance, when she tells him to be wary of "that / Pernicious sinne". . ."Druncken-
ness / It is the sinn of this Agge" (fol. 8r.7–8), she instructs him to "be wacthfull
against it" (fol. 8r.9) and to "Be wacthfull ouer your self that you doo / Not eas-
sely speake Euill of any" (fol. 10v.13–14). Ned's watchfulness over the consistency
of his character was to be his chief guide for principled living. His conscience
was his constant companion, and was God's eye upon (and prompt within) him.
Thus, the peace of his conscience was the marker of heavenly approval and his
constant goal:

> And suppos you could outwardly
> Apear holy yet if your hart
> Be not so you will haue no Comfort
> For if Men Aproufe of you
> And your owne Contience Condeme
> You what peace can you haue (fol. 4r.10–4v.3)

Concern about Ned's circles of acquaintance in Oxford is prominent in BL MS.
70118. She warns Ned against associating with those of weak character, because
it could result in a disappointing self-reflected image, for "They endeuor all they

can to / Make al that keepe Company / With them like themselves" (fols. 6v.12–7r.1). However, her concern is also discussed in terms that would have had, for her recipient, a more vivid epistolary resonance. Harley is very alert to the classical trope of letter writing as conversation, articulated by Cicero, Seneca, Pliny, and many others,[19] and so it is unsurprising to find that she incorporates this into the instructional content of her work and highlights them through the material implications of the form. Ned's discourse and conversation with others now participates in a wider and varied social forum, and so she warns him that the 'company' he kept would be reflected in his conversation:

> be wacthefull
> What Company you most Conuers
> With, It is A true obsaruation
> That men are as apte to take
> Vp the Jestures and fraises
> Of thos with whom they dayly
> Conuers with, As paper is to
> Partake of the perfume with
> which it lyes. (fol. 5r.1–9)

Harley used more than words and images to give the impression that, as Ned's parents, she and her husband remained his watchful observers. Through letter writing, a posture of defiance to physical absence could be portrayed, as the form acted as a surrogate for verbal conversation. Repeatedly throughout her other letters, Harley writes of correspondence as a "paper conuersing" or a "paper discours,"[20] rendering even the actual paper she wrote upon, and which Ned then held, as a symbolically significant presence. In this way the material artefact reinforced the role of the letter as a watchful 'eye' (and 'I'). Her sense of the way character will be shaped by discourse reveals the extent of the influence she identified in all letter writing in the making (or breaking) of character. Language and dialogue revealed the company one kept, the character of those with whom one conversed the most, and if letter writing functioned as conversation, then Harley's role as letter writer was integral to the formation of Ned's character.

Yet her imagery of paper, perfume, and mutual participation in the excerpt above evoked deeper meaning still. The description of Ned's life as 'paper' that

---

[19] A good summary of classical attitudes to letters as 'conversation' is in Bruce Redford, "The Epistolary Tradition," in David Hopkins and Charles Martindale, eds., *The Oxford History of Classical Reception in English Literature* (Oxford: Oxford Univ. Press, 2012), 427–46.

[20] *Letters*, XIII (24 Nov 1638), CLXV (20 June 1642).

could be read for the essence of his character by its 'scent' accords a highly sensory value to letter writing as well as to the experience of a letter's materiality. There was, truly, a 'correspondence' between principles and performance, between language and character. Attempts to obfuscate the truth in letters (to presume that the absence a letter denoted was sufficient cover) is rendered pointless by recognition of another imperative — its dialogic nature, as a "paper discours." This warrants a further speculation: that Harley was also subtly reminding Ned that the true state of his character would be sensed through their ongoing correspondence.

This highly sensory imagery used in relation to the formation of character also evokes an important biblical equivalent. In his second letter to the Christian community at Corinth, the apostle Paul used the same evocative imagery of fragrance in writing to equate the perception of scent with faithful adherence to advice:

> Now thanks be unto God, which always causeth us to triumph in Christ, and maketh manifest the savour of his knowledge by us in every place. For we are unto God a sweet savour of Christ, in them that are saved, and in them that perish: To the one we are the savour of death unto death; and to the other the savour of life unto life . . . (2 Corinthians 2:14–16, AV)

In translations of the New Testament from William Tyndale's 1526 and 1534 texts onwards, "savour" was frequently used to render the Greek and Hebrew 'smell', rather than the now-usual implication of 'taste'.[21] In conveying that the Christian life of faith was to be evident as though an 'aroma', Paul was the 'sweet scent' of Christ, spreading knowledge of God through the impressions he himself made. He rendered his apostolic service as a pleasing sacrifice; its proclamation was an offering to God, and his "sweet savour" would be noticeable. Paul's prepositional structure, Margaret Thrall has argued, gives the sense of expecting either intensification of action or a change of state.[22] This would be a linguistic stance aptly suited to a text promoting particular precepts for godly living in a contesting environment. Harley's use of sensory imagery to imply that true character was as easy to discern as perfume thus furthered the importance of her letter writing, as an ongoing conversation with Ned, and his "Jestures" and "fraises," when

---

[21] See *OED*, 'savour', 1, 2.

[22] Margaret E. Thrall, *A Critical and Exegetical Commentary on the Second Epistle to the Corinthians 1–7*, Vol. 1 (London: Continuum, 1994), 201. It is worth noting that in the Old Testament, 'savour' took the literal meaning of the aroma of incense and sacrifices, seen as pleasing to God. In the New Testament, this relates to spiritual sacrifices. See Susan Ashbrook Harvey, *Scenting Salvation: Ancient Chiristianity and the Olfactory Imagination* (Berkeley: Univ. of California Press, 2006).

pleasing in their fragrance, could be the "sweet savour" for change amongst the company in which he now found himself.

Ned Harley's new and more challenging university context called for an intensified performance of such already-held precepts for living. Harley believed him now to be in a godless environment, where her use of the imagery of savouring and distaste was distinctly applicable: the "ripeness of judgment and holynes" of godly men who left the universities at this time for other positions were symbolically the "ripe grapes" who were "gleaned," while "the spoyleing of the universitys and corrupting of the jentry theare breed" she described as the "sower on[e]s" left behind in "the garden."[23]

Harley's use of the common biblical knowledge she shared with Ned is also evident in the tropes she uses to discuss his virtuous action. Encouraging Ned to exhibit virtue in his wider context, she repeatedly paraphrases scripture. For instance,

> . . . my Deare Sonne as you
> Are Commaunded to keepe your
> Hart, with all the deligence for out
> of it are the *Issues* of Life
> So sheawe the holiness of your
> Hart by a holy life. . . (fol. 5r.4–9)

Here, directly quoting from the advice of King Solomon to his son,[24] she conceptualises godly living as the product of an organic fruitfulness, of duties themselves as functioning like children or offspring, and she depicts Ned, elsewhere in the text, as her produce:

> you knowe in
> frutes it is not the excelency to
> be an Apell, or a plume, but to be
> of such a kinde of Apell or plume
> which is excellent, that gaines the
> Esteme . . . (fol. 3r.5–8)

Ned was encouraged to view the proceeds of his "Hart" (his thoughts, words, and deeds) as his progeny. As parents were motivated to instruct their children in good conduct because of the positive reflection it could cast upon themselves and their fulfilment of duty (a sign of their own excellent "frute" — duties and

---

[23] *Letters*, XVI (20 May 1639).

[24] Proverbs 4:23 (AV).

children), so children were to view their production of virtue in the same terms of parental concern for *their* produce; this created a communal scenario of mutual understanding where civic duty, family, and responsibility were concerned, and both cases would reflect well upon the heart and character of the one producing the good 'fruit'. Additionally, by implying this shared knowledge, she promoted a sense of community within which Ned, despite the absence that a letter signified, could configure himself: a community of people who shared a common awareness of these 'commandments', had a shared purpose in producing virtue, and who were upheld through the circulation of letters. Harley's letter articulated a biblical prescription for both individual and community witness, which also — through framing the performance of duty as the production of good fruit — would create the sense that Ned's good performance would prove her own fulfilment of duty: one which draws on the notion of taking pride in this public witness, as found in the apostolic expressions of pride in the positive performance of Christian duty and character (2 Corinthians 11:2; 3:1–3).

Harley closes her letter of advice in curiously resounding fashion, with a benediction and "A Men." In doing so, she draws her text into a realm where more than just solitary writing, followed by reading, takes place. She creates the sense that through the sharing of letters, there is a communion in which both writer and recipient mutually participate. The writing and the reading of letters may take place at different moments in time, but the letter itself creates a moment and a space of immediacy in which the participants are present with one another. The apostolic epistles frequently close with benedictions and several close with 'Amen,' and thereby testify to the surmounting of geographic separation through letter writing, representing their common bond and sense of unified identity. In closing her letter this way, Harley participates in the epistolary styles of her own puritan culture, as well as in those of the earliest Christian community. The double motion of affirmation that the letter contains in closing, however, is unusual. After "A Men.," Harley adds the signature that is typical to her larger body of letters, "Your affectinat Mother, Brilliana Harley," simultaneously authenticating herself to her son, and boldly confirming her authorship of this literary gift.

Brilliana Harley's letter of advice reveals her participation in the long literary history of classical humanist and Christian morality, demonstrating a carefully constructed synthesis of her puritan faith and classical humanism. Her text imitated the epistolary conventions of the early church community; apostolic epistles were full of advice, and as such were fundamental exemplars for her composition of weighty spiritual direction. They were written to instruct the Christian community in counter-cultural living, and Harley's advice to Ned similarly fixated on the recognition that the principles of their spiritual tradition ran counter to the culture at Oxford he was discovering. But her letters bore the same responsibility of witnessing to Christian virtue as Paul had expected of his letters; he had specifically used the metaphor of the 'epistle' to describe the most incisive evidence possible of true character and belief:

> Do we begin again to commend ourselves? or need we, as some others, epistles of commendation to you, or *letters* of commendation from you? *Ye are our epistle* written in our hearts, known and read of all men: Forasmuch as ye are manifestly declared to be the epistle of Christ ministered by us, written not with ink, but with the Spirit of the living God; not in tables of stone, but in fleshy tables of the heart. (2 Corinthians 3:1–3)

Unlike many examples of 'mothers' advice', this manuscript does not offer any gendered explanation for taking up the pen, and it deserves to be considered in a broader literary context than the suppositions usually made about women's advice writing. In its material and literary attributes, Harley's text is more fruitfully examined in relation to the Christian humanist intellectual culture in which she was an active participant. While there are multiple texts of advice that fall within the literary traditions of this culture — also deserving attention as influences upon Harley — it is the often neglected consideration of the apostolic letters to the early church community which offer an important ideological key to interrogating the formal choices behind her stylization of this creative work of epistolary advice.

Like the Pauline expression that "epistles" witnessed to ideology, Harley's letter of advice demonstrates that she needed to reinforce Ned's understanding of the ideological outlook of his parents, the responsibility they bore to inculcate it in their children, and the origins from which it derived, for his benefit. Yet she also composed it because the fulfilment of their spiritual duty (to those to whom they "ministered") as parents would be evidenced, in return, by the reception of their own "epistle" (Ned), "declared" to a wider audience. Ned's religious steadfastness and particularly, his spiritual 'fruit', would be some measures of this fulfilment; as she wrote in another letter to him, "The Lord in mercy make you grow in the sweet graces of His spirit, and then you will be louely in the eyes of all Gods chillderen."[25] Equally, just as Paul spoke on behalf of others ('we', 'our'), so Harley's epistle signified corporate implications. As Thrall commented, "the Corinthian church [was] known as Paul's foundation, and the more thoroughly people become acquainted with its life, i.e., 'read the letter', the more convincing

---

[25] *Letter* LXXVII (9 May 1640).

the proof of his apostolic effectiveness will become."[26] Ned's performance of his mother's advice would bear witness as much to his own heart as to influence the public reception of the corporate spiritual identity of which they both were representatives. It would also benefit this corporate body; late in 1639, Harley wrote echoing Solomon's advice in Proverbs 4:

> I dout not but that you are deligent in the way in which you are to store yourself with knowledg, for this is your haruest in which you must gather the fruts which beare; after you may bring out to your owne and others profete.[27]

Herein lay a clear connection between the creation of character and its cultivation through letter writing, both materially and metaphorically. Harley was at pains to ensure that Ned viewed his fulfilment of the advice in her letter as proceeding from his heart, "inscribed" by God's work upon his conscience. At the same time, however, it would point towards her own participation in his character 'production', specifically confirming the instrumentality of her letters, and of this composition, BL MS. 70118, as a designedly epistolary work of advice.

UNIVERSITY OF EXETER, UK

---

[26] Thrall, *Commentary on the Second Epistle to the Corinthians*, 222.
[27] *Letter* LIV (4 Nov. 1639).

Reforming Sir Thomas More in the Court of Katherine Parr[1]

SUSAN M. FELCH

ONE OF THE MOST FAMOUS STORIES THAT CIRCULATED IN THE SIXTEENTH century concerning Katherine Parr, the sixth wife of Henry VIII, was first recorded by John Foxe in his 1570 edition of Actes and Monuments.[2] Parr, says Foxe, was an active "gospeller" at the English court. She not only sponsored daily religious services, particularly during Lent, at which one of her chaplains would preach, but she also encouraged conversations about spiritual matters and urged her courtiers to study the scriptures. Although such activities were conducted in her privy chamber, they were "not secretly done," nor did she try to hide her reformist sympathies. In fact, Foxe notes, Parr "frankly" debated the king himself over matters of religion to the point of putting herself in

---

[1] This paper was first delivered at the 2009 Modern Language Association convention, Chicago, IL, at the Josephine Roberts Forum: Early Modern Women's Manuscripts, Elizabeth H. Hageman and Margaret P. Hannay presiding. This paper was originally entitled "'Not Secretly Done': Private Prayer Books in the Court of Katherine Parr."

[2] John Foxe, [T]he ecclesiasticall history contaynyng the actes and monumentes of thynges passed in euery kynges tyme in this realme (London, 1570; STC 11223), 1422. The account of Parr's gospelling activities and subsequent confrontation with Henry VIII is first recorded in the second edition of Actes and Monuments (1570), pages 1422-25, and is repeated in the 1576 (pages 1212-14) and 1583 (pages 1242-44) editions. This narrative is taken from the 1570 edition. Quotations from Foxe are cited from John Foxe. Acts and Monuments [...] . The Variorum Edition. [online]. (hriOnline, Sheffield 2004). Available from: http://www.hrionline. ac.uk/foxe/. [Accessed 09.30.2004]. Although the story is not attested in other contemporary accounts, there is no reason to doubt its essential authenticity, and Foxe retained it in the subsequent editions of 1576 and 1583; see Susan M. Felch, ed., Elizabeth Tyrwhit's Morning and Evening Prayers (Aldershot: Ashgate, 2008), 4-6, and Janel Mueller, ed., Katherine Parr: Complete Works and Correspondence (Chicago: Univ. of Chicago Press, 2011), 21-25.

jeopardy. When Stephen Gardiner, bishop of Winchester, and Thomas Wriothesley, the Lord Chancellor, convinced Henry that Parr's energetic exchanges with
him overstepped the bounds of wifely submission and edged toward treason, the
queen was forced to deftly reconstruct herself as a paragon of loyalty, in a master-
ful speech that Foxe records in its entirety.

The drama of Parr's successful confrontation with Henry makes a great story, but it should not be allowed to overshadow her more substantial accomplishments, particularly her steady and remarkable contribution to the development
of reformation literature in the first half of the sixteenth century. There are many
facets of her work that we could examine—her patronage of writers such as Hugh
Latimer, Miles Coverdale, Nicholas Udall, and Thomas Cranmer; her revision
of the devotional *Imitation of Christ*; her efforts to provide a vernacular biblical
commentary through the translation of Erasmus's *Paraphrases*; or her own confessional writings in *The Lamentation of a Sinner*. In this paper, however, I will
concentrate on the singular transformation of a Roman Catholic martyr into a
spokesperson for reformed religion by tracing the use of Sir Thomas More's Tower Meditations in two manuscripts and a printed book bound in an enameled
gold case. This small archive of prayerbooks demonstrates the Lutheran-inflected
piety of Parr's court, the deeply held conviction of the early reformers that they
were reforming the true church, not creating a new church, and their sense of
continuity with humanist reforms even as they recast traditional materials within an evangelical frame that anchored the emerging Protestant piety which blossomed in Cranmer's *Book of Common Prayer*.

The first manuscript I propose to examine has recently been identified by
Janel Mueller as one written in Katherine Parr's own hand.[3] Previously known as
Lady Jane Grey's prayerbook (BL MS Harley 2342), it has been valued primarily
for its marginalia: a series of poignant farewells written in 1554 by Jane Grey and
her husband Guildford Dudley to her father during the period when they were
imprisoned separately in the Tower of London before their executions. Sir John
Bridges, the lieutenant of the Tower, to whom Jane Grey also inscribed a note encouraging him to live and die as a faithful Christian, apparently facilitated the
exchange of farewells by carrying the prayerbook among the principals. Mueller
argues that the prayerbook itself, however, was written by Parr for her own use.
Later, on her deathbed in 1548, Parr gave it to the young Jane Grey, who was living in her household and who was the chief mourner at her funeral.

---

[3] Details of Parr's prayerbook are taken from *Complete Works*, ed. Mueller, 489-619; my
thanks to Professor Mueller for allowing me access to her manuscript before its publication.

The tiny manuscript prayerbook, approximately 3 x 4 inches in size, is bound inside five modern leaves. Its 143 vellum leaves, the first four damaged in places beyond legibility, are inscribed entirely with Parr's handwriting. Although there are no illuminations, some capital letters are retraced in gold ink on a blue or red background and some lines are completed with a decoration of blue and red rectangles, occasionally ornamented with gold lines. As Mueller notes, "This is exactly the decorative program used by Parr in her incomplete manuscript of *Prayers or Meditations* (the Kendal autograph), reportedly made as a gift for a Mistress Tuke, an attendant at the Henrician court, presumably in or after 1545."[4]

In appearance and in its organization, Parr's manuscript prayerbook follows the traditional form of late medieval devotional miscellanies, many of which were composed for, and probably by, women, both lay and religious.[5] Rather than being organized, as were Books of Hours, into prayers to be said at set times throughout the day, devotional miscellanies contained prayers, meditations, religious explications, and scripture passages that were intended to be read rather than recited.[6] Fifteenth-century miscellanies were particularly associated with the *devotio moderna*, a movement that also produced the *Imitation of Christ*, which Parr chose to revise in her first published book, *Prayers or Meditations*. To the continuity of this devotional tradition, with its Christocentric focus and emphasis on personal piety, Parr brings her own Lutheran-inflected, reformist commitments as well as the decision to write only in English. The first part of her prayerbook includes prayers from printed sources, mainly reformed primers, and from manuscript meditations written in the Tower of London by Sir Thomas More and Bishop John Fisher when both were awaiting execution for refusing to recognize Henry as supreme head of the English church. The second part of the prayerbook consists entirely of biblical passages, mostly psalm verses, many of them arranged in collage fashion. Most poignantly, the final five prayers, the last one incomplete, are written in a larger, looser hand without decoration and are short pleas for aid, copied, with minor revisions, from Wolfgang Capito's paraphrases on the psalms as translated

---

[4] Mueller, *Katherine Parr*, 490.

[5] Mueller, in contrast, identifies the prayerbook as conforming to the genre of Books of Hours or Primers (491), although she does admit that it carries "no trace of the primers' prominent internal structure" (494), that is, the canonical Hours of the Blessed Virgin Mary.

[6] See, for instance, Huntington MS. 142 and Westminster Abbey MS. 39 as well as Jessica Brantley's reading of a Carthusian miscellany, BL MS. Add. 37049 in *Reading in the Wilderness: Private Devotion and Public Performance in Late Medieval England* (Chicago: Univ. of Chicago Press, 2007).

by Richard Taverner.[7] Mueller suggests that they were most likely written "in the late stages of [Parr's] only known pregnancy and [during] the onset of the fever that caused her death at the age of thirty-six."[8]

Parr's choice of genre, the devotional miscellany with its wide-ranging set of eclectic prayers, and her selection of biblically-infused content exemplifies the consensus of the early English reformers, highlighting their sense of continuity with humanist reform movements; their embrace of Lutheran distinctives, including a high view of the vernacular scriptures; and their conviction that they were reforming the true church, not creating a new church.[9]

As has already been noted, many of the newer devotional miscellanies were generated by the reforming *devotio moderna* movement of the fifteenth century, even as that movement continued to use the more traditional Books of Hours. Indeed, individual prayers, such as the "Conditor celi et terre," which Parr includes, circulated freely among Books of Hours and devotional miscellanies. Yet when Parr uses these older prayers, she consistently revises them according to evangelical distinctives: there are no rubrics that promise indulgences; no prayers to the Virgin Mary or to the saints; no prayers to be said during Mass; no remembrances of or for the dead. Nor, most remarkably, are there the entries one might most expect from a woman in her thirties—namely, traditional prayers for childbirth, even among the final five prayers, which may have been written shortly before her own death from childbirth. In other words, Parr's prayerbook joins with other reformation writings of the period to protest, via their exclusion, a standard collocation of practices assumed to be superstitious—in clear contrast, for instance, to the revised but still traditional official prayerbook issued by Henry in 1545 which, while it excluded indulgences, did include prayers to Mary and the saints and for the dead.[10] In addition to what it omits, Parr's prayerbook

---

[7] Richard Taverner, *An epitome of the Psalmes, or briefe meditacions vpon the same, with diuerse other moste christian prayers* (London, 1539; *STC* 2748); translation of Wolfgang Capito, *Precationes Christianae ad imitationem psalmorum compositae* (Strasbourg: Rihel, 1536).

[8] Mueller, *Katherine Parr*, 508.

[9] Mueller positions Parr's prayerbook somewhat differently, highlighting what she sees as Parr's unusual or even exceptional stance of including both conservative and reformed prayers and arguing that the prayerbook is a "proving ground for alternative modes and common expressions of Christian devotion in her day" (494). See also her comment that Parr's personal prayerbook "could take on certain functions that a diary or privately kept journal might serve in our own day. Parr could assemble a set of contents that expressed her own priorities and preferences in devotional utterance without being constrained by institutional or confessional norms" (492).

[10] *The primer, set foorth by the Kynges maiestie and his clergie, to be taught, lerned, [and] read: and none other to be vsed throughout all his dominions* (London, 1545; *STC* 16034).

demonstrates its evangelical distinctives both in its indebtedness to Lutheran-inflected and translated devotional materials and in its insistent recourse to the vernacular Bible. At the same time, the use of traditional materials, side by side with Protestant texts and English scripture, reinforces the reformers' convictions that the true church was to be reformed, not overthrown.

This set of interlocking commitments—to humanist reforms, to Lutheran-inflected theology, and to the continuity of the church—can all be illustrated by looking at how Parr uses and repositions as reformed devotional aids the prayers of two Roman Catholic martyrs, Bishop John Fisher and Sir Thomas More, prayers threaded with doctrines of penance, purgatory, Marian devotion, and transubstantiation. It is important to note that the inclusion of Fisher and More in a Protestant prayerbook may not have required as much explanation in the late 1540s as it does for us today. Both men were recognized and respected humanist scholars, known for their promotion of educational and religious—though not Protestant—reform; their imprisonments induced a great deal of sympathy; and, perhaps most importantly, they could be seen as *English* models of piety. Not until Reginald Cardinal Pole's campaign during the reign of Mary Tudor to champion them as *Roman Catholic* martyrs did they posthumously assume a highly public position antithetical to Protestantism. For instance, when the Protestant human-ist Ralph Robinson translated More's *Utopia* in 1551 and dedicated it to William Cecil, he praised More's "excellent qualities, wherewith the great goodnes of God had plentyfully endowed him" and thought it necessary only to add this caveat: "that it is much to be lamented of al, and not only of us English men, that a man of so incomparable witte, of so profounde knowlege, of so absolute learning, and of so fine eloquence was yet neverthelesse so much blinded, rather with obstina-cie, then with ignoraunce that he could not or rather would not see the shining light of godes holy truthe in certein principal pointes of Christian religion." Hav-ing stated his disapproval of More's theology, however, Robinson then quickly dismissed its significance in light of Utopia's greater claim to teach "good, and holsome lessons, which be there in great plenty, and aboundaunce."[11] Similarly, Katherine Parr could assume that the work of Fisher and More, along with that of Erasmus and Mary Tudor herself who contributed to the translation of the latter's *Paraphrases*, should be incorporated into the true church, providing those texts were sheared of heretical dogma.

---

[11] *A fruteful, and pleasaunt worke of the beste state of a publyque weale, and of the newe yle called Vtopia: written in Latine by Syr Thomas More knyght, and translated into Englyshe by Raphe Robynson citizein and goldsmythe of London, at the procurement, and earnest request of George Tadlowe citezein [and] haberdassher of the same citie* (London, 1551; *STC* 18094), ff. 3v–4r.

It was just such shearing that Parr herself undertook when she included three of Sir Thomas More's Tower prayers in her manuscript. For the most part, the prayers themselves are unimpeachably orthodox, whether one is a Roman Catholic or a Protestant. But in the first and longest prayer, the Trinity Prayer, Parr makes five significant revisions.

First, she omits the rubric for confession that most likely would have been said during penance before the administration of last rites, two ceremonies rejected by Protestants. The opening of More's prayer begins "O Holy Trinitie, the father, the sonne, and the holy ghost, thre egall [sic] and coeternall parsons, and one almightye God, haue mercye on me, vyle, abiecte, abhominable sinnefull wretche: mekely knoweledgyng before thyne hygh maiesty my long continued synnefull life, euen from my very childhed hitherto. In my childhed, in this poynte and that poynte, etc. After my childehed in thys poynte and that point, etc. and so foorth by euery age."[12] Parr follows the text closely, with only minor alterations through the word "hitherto": she then omits the rubric that would direct one through the sacrament of penance, the elucidation of sins committed in childhood and after childhood throughout one's life.

Second, Parr consistently translates More's Latin scriptural quotations into English, signaling her commitment to the vernacular scriptures. For instance, when he cites a composite of Saint Paul's words from Galatians 6:14 and Philippians 1:21, 23, "*Mundus mihi crucifixus est, et ego mundo. Mihi vivere Christus est, et mori lucrum. Cupio dissolui et esse cum Christo*,"[13] Parr gives her own translation: "the worlde ys crusified to me and I to the worlde. Criste is to me life / and to dye ys my gayne and advantage: I desire to be lewsed and to be with Christe."[14]

Third, Parr silently omits a reference to purgatory, another doctrinal sticking point between Roman Catholics and Protestants. More inserts the notion of purgatory into a list that contrasts the benefits of belonging to Christ with a pure love of Christ himself: "Geue me good lord, a longing to be with the, not for thauoiding of the calamyties of this wretched world, nor so much for the auoiding of the paines of purgatory nor of the paines of hel neither, nor so much for the atteining of the joyes of heauen, in respect of mine own commodity, as euen for a very loue to the."[15] Parr retains the sense of longing for Christ out of sheer love for her savior, but dismisses any mention of purgatory from her list: "Gyue me good lorde a longynge to be with the not for the aduoydinge of the aduercyties of this

---

[12] *The vvorkes of Sir Thomas More Knyght, sometyme Lorde Chauncellour of England, wrytten by him in the Englysh tonge*, ed. William Rastall (London, 1557; *STC* 18076), 1417.

[13] *The Workes of Sir Thomas More Knyght*, ed. Rastall, 1417.

[14] All translations taken from Mueller's edition of Katherine Parr, *Works*, 514.

[15] *The vvorkes of Sir Thomas More Knyght*, 1418.

wretched worlde: nor somuch for the aduoidynge of the paynes of helle / nother so muche for the attteynynge [sic] of the Joyes of heuyn in the respecte of myne owene commoditie / as euyn for a very loue to the."[16]

Fourth, Parr omits a long reference to the Mass and its sacramental efficacy. More devotes several lines to detailing Christ's physical presence in the Mass, the pious believer's actual participation in Christ's body through the sacrament, and through the sacrament his membership in the Catholic church:

> And giue me warmeth, delight and quicknes in thinking vpon thee. And giue me thy grace to long for thinc holy sacramentes, and specially to reioise in the presence of thy very blessed boby [body] (swete sauiour christ, in the holy sacrament of thye altare) and duelye to thanke the for the gracious visitacion therewith, and at that high memorial, with tender compassion, to remember and consider thy most bitter passion. Make us al good lorde virtually perticipaunt of that holye sacrament thys day, and euery daye make vs all liuely membres swete sauioure Christe, of thine holy mistical body, thy catholyke church."[17]

Although Parr follows More in his desire to think upon Christ, she substitutes for his short meditation on the sacrament the word "thee," thus turning the prayer's attention from sacramental to devotional union with Christ:

> And geue me warme delyte and quietnes in thinkinge vpon the and gyue me thye grace to longe for the and make vs all lyuely members (o sauyour Christe) of the holy mysticall body the catholike Churche."[18]

Significantly, Parr retains the corporate nature of More's conclusion, aligning herself and her prayers within the tradition of the holy catholic church.

Fifth, Parr translates More's final Latin invocations into English and omits his prayer to the Virgin Mary, concluding with these words: "O lord in the haue I trysted / Lette me neuer be confunded eternally. Amen."[19]

It is in these acts of revision that Parr shows her skill in recasting traditional materials within an evangelical frame and anchoring the emerging Protestant piety that blossomed in Cranmer's *Book of Common Prayer*. These revisions centrally position Parr among the English reformers who were taking upon

---

[16] Mueller, *Katherine Parr*, 514-15.
[17] *The vvorkes of Sir Thomas More Knyght*, 1418.
[18] Mueller, *Katherine Parr*, 515.
[19] Mueller, *Katherine Parr*, 515.

themselves the task of weighing inherited religion against the truth of the Word
of God, a task emblematically represented in the *Actes and Monuments* woodcut
of blind justice at the end of Book 6, which is entitled "A liuely picture describing the weight and substaunce of Gods most blessed word agaynst the doctrines
and vanities of mans traditions."[20] Beyond the excision of problematic content,
however, Parr also recasts traditional material by including the Tower prayers in
a miscellany that is an *aid to* devotion rather than an *artifact of* devotion. This
contrast is more sharply drawn when we compare Parr's prayerbook to a near-
contemporary version of the same Tower prayers, a prayer roll, some 4.4 x 25.2
inches in size, written on two sheets of vellum stitched together, that dates from
approximately 1550 and is now held at the Folger Shakespeare Library.[21] This roll,
the second of the manuscripts that I wish to examine, includes the three Tower
prayers used by Parr plus the prayer for friends that she unaccountably omits.
The Tower Meditations are followed by an exhortation to prayer and good works
often appended to the *Imitation of Christ*, as well as a crude pen and ink drawing
of Christ rising from an empty tomb, and a Latin prayer.

Prayer rolls were fairly common throughout the fifteenth century and into
the sixteenth century. They usually contained traditional prayers, such as the
Arms of Christ, the penitential psalms, or prayers for childbirth, and frequently
were illustrated. The drawing on this prayer roll, for instance, is reminiscent of
one of the illuminations on a long prayer roll owned by Henry VIII and recently
exhibited at the British Library on the 500th anniversary of his birth.[22] Such rolls
might be used as devotional aids, but they were also themselves devotional artifacts, frequently employed as amulets, charms to be worn in order to ward off
illness or disaster, carried in a bag hung around the neck or tucked into a sleeve.
The existence of a prayer roll that is inscribed not with a traditional prayer but
rather with one penned by Sir Thomas More suggests the rapid manuscript circulation and popularity of his Tower Meditations.

While this particular prayer roll amulet may date from the later 1550s
and Cardinal Pole's promotion of the cult of More, the contrast between Parr's

---

[20] This woodcut first appears in the 1576 edition of Actes and Monuments, page 795; it
may be viewed at http://www.johnfoxe.org/woodcuts/f0828w.gif.

[21] Folger MS. X.d.532. The text of this prayer roll is nearly identical to the first printing
of the meditations in 1557. The prayer roll may be viewed at http://www.folger.edu/html/fol-
ger_institute/sacred/image8.html.

[22] BL MS. Additional 88929, formerly Ushaw College, Durham, MA 29; facsimile in *Henry VIII: Man and Monarch*, ed. Susan Doran (London: British Library, 2009), 46. The prayer
roll may also be viewed at http://britishlibrary.typepad.co.uk/digitisedmanuscripts/2011/02/
henry-viii-prayer-roll.html.

incorporation of the prayers within the framework of evangelical piety and the prayer roll's function as a discrete—and possibly superstitious—artifact demonstrates the importance for the reformers of employing a judicious scriptural hermeneutic in the creation of new devotional aids. Note, for instance, the proliferation of religious artifacts hanging from the left scale pan of Justice in the *Actes and Monuments* woodcut as contrasted with the simple "Verbum Dei" resting in the right pan. And consider the material difference between carrying a small prayer roll and reading a devotional codex, no matter how small or decorated that codex might be.

If direct Bible reading was important for both men and women, no less important was the creation of additional religious texts that were both shaped by and would shape the reading of scripture: the daily sermons given by Parr's chaplains; the translation of Erasmus's paraphrases; Parr's redaction of the *Imitation of Christ* and her own confessional meditation; and, of course, the preparation of a devotional miscellany. In other words, Parr's program of publications, including her own private prayerbook, joined with the work of other reformers to create an entirely new body of religious literature. I use the descriptors "entirely new" deliberately, for although, as I have already argued, the reformers had no intention of establishing a new *church* and took considerable pains to incorporate traditional materials into their sermons, commentaries, and devotional aids, the *corpus* of literature they created—whether revised or freshly composed—was itself new, subject always to a critical, scriptural hermeneutic. The emblematic artifact here might be the imagined—though probably never constructed—book wheel that enabled a reader, or a writer, to comb through and select compatible materials from a variety of sources including, for Parr, traditional prayers, scripture passages in English, sixteenth-century humanist meditations, reformed psalm paraphrases, and her own compositions.[23]

To her credit, Parr not only contributed to this growing body of evangelical literature, but also encouraged others in her court to pursue similar projects. The closest analogue to her own prayerbook is that composed by one of her ladies of the privy chamber, Elizabeth Tyrwhit. Tyrwhit's prayerbook, which does not survive in manuscript, draws from the same sources used by Parr: traditional prayers, Lutheran-inflected primers, the Capito-Taverner psalm paraphrases, texts by John Fisher, as well as the Trinity Prayer from Thomas More's Tower Meditations. Unlike Parr, however, Tyrwhit construed her prayerbook not as a devotional miscellany, but rather as a revision of the traditional Books of Hours,

---

[23] A picture of the book wheel imagined by Agostino Ramelli may be viewed at http://www.uoc.edu/humfil/digithum/digithum2/catala/Art_Heras/ramelli_gros_ret.gif.

organizing her material into Morning and Evening Prayers, according to the pattern for lay devotion already customary by the late fifteenth century and later authorized by Cranmer's *Book of Common Prayer*.[24] I think it unlikely that Parr's prayerbook was meant simply as a kind of private journal, as Mueller argues, in which "Parr could assemble a set of contents that expressed her own priorities and preferences in devotional utterance without being constrained by institutional or confessional norms."[25] Parr's compilation is exemplary rather than exceptional among reformist literature of the period, and devotional miscellanies traditionally were composed for use in religious communities or in the domestic worship of large households. If the intended audience for Parr's prayerbook, however, is not specified, Tyrwhit's prayerbook, at least as it comes down to us in printed form, is quite clearly intended for general use, as was a similar prayerbook, printed in 1550 by Robert Toye, which exists now only in a single, incomplete copy.[26] Both the Tyrwhit and Toye prayerbooks explicitly extend Parr's publication program into the domestic worship of private households. Tyrwhit also demonstrates that she had internalized Parr's critical, scriptural hermeneutic.

Her version of More's Tower Meditation follows Parr's redaction—omitting the penitential rubric and the references to purgatory, the Mass, and Mary—but Tyrwhit goes further by substituting a clear-cut statement of reformed soteriology for the traditional plea for justification that More and Parr both retain. Thus towards the conclusion of the Trinity Prayer, Parr requests:

> O glorious trynytie vouchesaue of thie goodnes to wasshe me with that blessed blood that thow O swete sauyour Christe sheddest oute of thy body in the dyuers tormentes of thye moste bitter passyon.[27]

Although Tyrwhit follows Parr's wording—citing the blood that Christ shed rather than using the language of More, "that blessed bloode that issued out of

---

[24] The fifteenth-century cleric Jean Quentin, for instance, recommended in his highly influential "The Preface and Manner to Live Well, Devoutly, and Salutarily Every Day for all Persons of Mean Estate," which first appeared in English in 1529, that Matins, Lauds, and Prime be said by laypeople in the morning, Terce recited at the noontime meal, and the four remaining canonical prayers recited sometime between dinner and supper (*This prymer of Salysbury use is set out a long without ony serchyng* [Paris, 1529; *STC* 15961.3]; see also Susan M. Felch, "The Development of the English Prayer Book," in *Worship in Medieval and Early Modern Europe: Change and Continuity in Religious Practice*, ed. Karin Maag and John D. Witvliet [Notre Dame: Univ. of Notre Dame Press, 2004], 132-61).

[25] Mueller, *Katherine Parr*, 492.

[26] [*The primer in English.*] (London: Toye, 1550; *STC* 16051).

[27] Mueller, *Katherine Parr*, 515.

thy tender bodie"—she adds references to Christ's resurrection and ascension, specifies true believers as those who are chosen and elect, and concludes the prayer as it had begun with a Trinitarian formula (omitting several lines from both Parr and More): [28]

> O glorious Trinitie, vouchsafe of thy goodnesse to wash me, with that blessed bloud that thou my sweet saviour Jesus Christ diddest shed out of thy bodie, in the divers torments of thy most bitter passion, that by that same greevous passion, glorious resurrection and ascension, I may come to that unspeakable joie, the which thou hast prepared for thy chosen and elect, through the same Jesu Christ our saviour, to whome with the Father, and the holie Ghost, three persons and one God be all honour and glorie world without end: So be it.[29]

Here Tyrwhit shows herself to be an apt student of Parr's devotional revisionism, further aligning More's Tower prayers with her own theological agenda. Tyrwhit extends Parr's project even further, not only copying excerpts from the Taverner-Capito psalm paraphrases for her own prayerbook, as had Parr, but also utilizing fragments from various psalms to compose her own inventive psalm collage.[30]

Yet, despite these reformist textual revisions, the single extant copy of the 1574 edition of Tyrwhit's prayerbook is itself enclosed in what we might at first take to be an artifact *for* devotional use—the gold-enameled covers of a tiny girdle book, measuring less than 3 inches square.[31] While we do not know if this girdle book originally held a manuscript version of Tyrwhit's *Morning and Evening Prayers*, tradition says that it did, and that the book was a gift to the Princess Elizabeth from her former governess, Elizabeth Tyrwhit, during the princess' confinement in the Tower of London by her sister, Mary Tudor. The cover itself was probably made around 1540 by the Flemish goldsmith Hans von Antwerpen, who worked in London and for the Tudor court. The front cover is a depiction of the Judgment of Solomon, in which the king threatens to kill an infant and then awards the baby to the mother who is unwilling to see the child murdered. The back cover shows the scene of Moses raising up a brass serpent to stem

---

[28] Mueller calls it a "Cranmerian distillation" (personal communication).

[29] Felch, *Elizabeth Tyrwhit's Morning and Evening Prayers*, 84.

[30] For an analysis of this particular psalm collage, see Susan M. Felch, "'Halff a Scripture Woman': Heteroglossia and Female Authorial Agency in Prayers by Lady Elizabeth Tyrwhit, Anne Lock, and Anne Wheathill," in *English Women, Religion, and Textual Production, 1500-1625*, ed. Micheline White (Burlington, VT: Ashgate, 2011), 147-66.

[31] BM M&ME 1894, 7-29, 1.

the plague sent by God as a judgment against the unbelieving Israelites as they wandered in the wilderness (Numbers 21: 6-9). Within the tradition of biblical images, this scene is sometimes paired with a crucifix, the raising up of the serpent being explicitly described as Christological in the gospel of John (3:14). The conjunction of Brass Serpent and Judgment of Solomon, however, is uncommon either in texts or in visual media. Although here it is the *text* of *Morning and Evening Prayers* that is meant to be used, if Elizabeth Tyrwhit, or Elizabeth Tudor, did contemplate these covers as a devotional artifact, what might she have seen?[32]

Two types of Christ, to be sure: the crucified Lord and the true judge of all hearts. But for the reader whose eyes had been clarified by a critical scriptural hermeneutic, the pairing might well have prefigured the emblematic figure of justice in *Actes and Monuments*, representing the need to weigh rightly the claims of idolatrous superstition and true religion. The Solomonic reformer, able to distinguish the lies of the false mother from true maternal love, would also discern when the salvific force of the brass serpent had become an empty object of idolatry, serpent and pole both later destroyed by the godly king Hezekiah.[33] Opening the covers, the discerning reader would then be prepared to bring heart and lips together in confession and praise, to say with Thomas More, and Katherine Parr, and Elizabeth Tyrwhit in the words of the Tower Meditation: "Give me good Lord a full faith, a firme hope, a fervent charitie, [and] a love to thee, good Lord."[34]

CALVIN COLLEGE

---

[32] Alexandra Walsham argues that Protestant women might have used such visual aids in "Jewels for Gentlewomen: Religious Books as Artefacts in Late Medieval and Early Modern England," in *The Church and the Book*, ed. R. N. Swanson, Studies in Church History 38 (Woodbridge: Boydell Press for the Ecclesiastical History Society, 2004), 123-42.

[33] 2 Kings 18:4.

[34] Felch, *Elizabeth Tyrwhit's Morning and Evening Prayers*, 84.

Monastic Authorship, Protestant Poetry, and the Psalms Attributed to Dame Clementia Cary[1]

JAIME GOODRICH

IN 1793, FRENCH SOLDIERS BURST INTO THE ENGLISH BENEDICTINE CONVENT in Cambrai and loaded the surprised nuns into carts without giving them time to collect their belongings. While the leaders of the French Revolution eventually sent the nuns back to England, many of this convent's voluminous writings still remain on the Continent. This paper considers the larger scholarly implications of one such manuscript: a fragmentary set of Psalm paraphrases previously ascribed to Dame Clementia (Anne) Cary (1615–1671). This text, referred to hereafter as the Cambrai Psalter, is part of MS 20H39 in the Archives Départementales du Nord, Lille, France. Dame Clementia was the daughter of Elizabeth Cary, the first Englishwoman to write an original play. On the basis of the Cambrai Psalter alone, Dame Clementia has joined her mother in the canon of early modern women writers. Feminist scholars have favorably compared the Cambrai Psalter with the metaphysical poems of John Donne and George Herbert, and Jane Stevenson and Peter Davidson published part of Psalm 148 in their groundbreaking anthology *Early Modern Women Poets*.[2] The warm reception of the Cambrai Psalter might therefore seem to mark the triumphant success of

---

[1] This paper was first delivered at the 2009 MLA convention, Philadelphia, PA, Josephine A. Roberts Forum: "Early Modern Women's Manuscripts," Elizabeth H. Hageman and Margaret P. Hannay presiding. Its original title was "Who Is Mrs. M. B.? Monastic Authorship and Dame Clementia Cary's Psalms."

[2] *Early Modern Women Poets: An Anthology*, ed. Jane Stevenson and Peter Davidson (Oxford: Oxford Univ. Press, 2001), 247–48.

recent efforts to add women writers and Catholic authors to the literary canon. Yet Dame Clementia was not the author of these Psalm paraphrases, which are in fact a manuscript copy of a work written by the Protestant poet Samuel Woodford. First published in 1667, Woodford's *A Paraphrase upon the Psalms of David* was popular enough to see two reprints (1668 and 1670) and a revised edition (1678). Despite Woodford's contemporary popularity, critics have been unaware of his role in the Cambrai Psalter for several reasons. Although the Cambrai Psalter was originally nine quires in total, only three are extant and none of them identify the text's author. In addition, Woodford's paraphrases have not been reprinted in their entirety since the 17th century and remain virtually unstudied today. Indeed, the marvels of modern technology played a pivotal role in determining Woodford's authorship: a Google search of one line pointed to an opensource edition of John Holland's *Psalmists of Britain* (1843), which reprinted several of Woodford's paraphrases.

Yet while new digital technologies made this identification possible, or at least easier, the manuscript itself and its conflicting signals regarding authorship always indicated that the text's attribution to Dame Clementia was not as straightforward as previous scholarly accounts have suggested. Indeed, Heather Wolfe has already noted that the text's hand bears a strong similarity to that of Dame Mary Cary (1621–1693), another of Elizabeth Cary's daughters.[3] While a consideration of the striking differences between the hands of Dame Clementia and Dame Mary is outside the scope of this essay, I accept Wolfe's attribution and will consequently treat Dame Mary as the copyist.[4] The reception history and authorship of the Cambrai Psalter (c. 1667–1693) make this text a useful means of considering both scholarly interest in the writings of early modern women writers, particularly nuns, and the role of writing in the Cambrai convent.[5] Out of a laudable desire to reclaim the works of a group marginalized by earlier literary critics and historians, previous scholars have ignored the contradictory nature of

---

[3] Heather Wolfe, "The Scribal Hands and Dating of *Lady Falkland: Her Life*," *English Manuscript Studies 1100–1700* 9 (2000): 187–217, esp. 193.

[4] The dating of the work (after 1667) also slightly favors Dame Mary, who died at Cambrai in 1693, while Dame Clementia died in 1671 at the Paris foundation that she had established in 1650.

[5] Internal evidence in the Psalms indicates that the copyist worked from the first edition rather than the second. The 1667, 1668, and 1670 printings of the first edition contained a list of errata that were corrected only in the second edition of 1678. The Cambrai Psalter's copy of Psalm 147 contains two of these errata, suggesting that the copyist used an edition prior to the 1678 revision. However, it does appear that she revised one error in Psalm 75 ("o're" instead of "e're"), indicating that the copyist may have been paying attention to Woodford's list of errata.

this manuscript and based their attribution on circumstantial evidence outside the confines of the text. This mistaken attribution offers a cautionary tale about working with manuscripts from the Continental convents for Englishwomen, works that are frequently unsigned and fragmentary. While a text may have been written in a so-called "feminine" hand, that apparent fact does not mean that a woman was the work's author.[6] The Cambrai Psalter is also valuable for what it can tell us about the unusual circumstances of authorship within the Cambrai convent. The copyist adapts Woodford's Psalms into a text suitable for convent life, transforming a work with Protestant undertones into an articulation of a feminine perspective based on the mysticism practiced at Cambrai. As a result, the Cambrai house's copy of Woodford's Psalms provides an important glimpse into how Catholic convents received and adapted popular devotional literature even across confessional lines.

Between 1638 and 1639, four of Elizabeth Cary's daughters joined the English Benedictine convent at Cambrai, all professing in 1640.[7] This convent was only one of many founded by Catholic Englishwomen who were eager to pursue a religious profession then illegal in their own country. The Cambrai house, however, was especially appropriate for the daughters of a woman known for her writing, for it had an unusual dedication to learning. Father Augustine Baker, its unofficial spiritual leader, had instructed the nuns to use reading and writing as an initial stage in their progress toward mystical union with God, which he and his followers called "the way of love."[8] Dame Gertrude More, Baker's most

---

[6] Although scholars often describe hands as "feminine," no clear-cut criteria have been established for what this term might mean. For a useful critical debate over women's handwriting and Mary Shelton's potential role as copyist of "O Happy Dames" in the Devonshire MS (BL MS Add. 174892), see Jonathan Goldberg, *Sodometries: Renaissance Texts, Modern Sexualities* (Stanford: Stanford Univ. Press, 1992), 59–60; Jonathan Goldberg, *Desiring Women Writing: English Renaissance Examples* (Stanford: Stanford Univ. Press, 1997), 144–63; Elizabeth Heale, "'Desiring Women Writing': Female Voices and Courtly 'Balets' in some Early Tudor Manuscript Albums," in *Early Modern Women's Manuscript Writing: Selected Papers from the Trinity/Trent Colloquium*, ed. Victoria E. Burke and Jonathan Gibson (Aldershot: Ashgate, 2004), 9–31; and R. Siemens et al., "Drawing Networks in the Devonshire Manuscript," above in this volume, 125–63.

[7] For information on their professions, see "Records of the English Benedictine Nuns at Cambrai (now Stanbrook), 1620–1793," ed. Joseph Gillow, in *Miscellanea VIII* (London: Catholic Record Society, 1913), 44–45. Claire Walker provides a seminal overview of these convents: *Gender and Politics in Early Modern Europe: English Convents in France and the Low Countries* (New York: Palgrave Macmillan, 2003).

[8] Helpful introductions to Baker's method include James Gaffney, *Augustine Baker's Inner Light: A Study in English Recusant Spirituality* (Scranton: Univ. of Scranton Press, 1989) and Anthony Low, *Augustine Baker* (New York: Twayne, 1970), 53–74. Baker's own most thor-

famous disciple, describes the "way of love" as solely dependent on loving God: "to loue God, & seeke after him alone was a most happy thing, and that . . . alone was able to make me truly happy."[9] Instead of prescribing rigid devotional practices, Baker encouraged the nuns to read and write spiritual texts in order to determine an entry point to the "way of love" that best suited their own personality. Due to this emphasis on learned piety, Baker's method resulted in a rich tradition of copying, translating, and composing devotional texts.[10] Three of the Cary sisters — Dame Clementia, Dame Mary, and Dame Magdalene (Lucy) — participated in the spiritual and scholarly labor that became the hallmark of the Cambrai convent. While Dame Magdalene probably composed a biography of their mother and Dame Mary transcribed devotional works, Dame Clementia copied Julian of Norwich's *Revelations* and wrote religious poetry.[11] A catalogue of the convent's library mentions "The Spirituall Songs of our V[ery]. R[everend]. Dame Mothere Clementia Carys in 3 parts."[12] In addition, her obituary refers to the "spirituall soungs wch she composed for ye solace of ye sicke & infirme."[13]

The arguments for Dame Clementia's authorship of the Cambrai Psalter depend largely on these "spirituall soungs." Dorothy Latz first discovered the Psalter, and her pioneering 1989 work *"Glow-Worm Light": Writings of 17th Century English Recusant Women from Original Manuscripts* tentatively identified the text, which she titled *Songs from the Psalms*, as Dame Clementia's: "There is . . . a strong possibility that these are the songs written by Dame Clementina [sic] for we

---

ough explanation of his method occurs in his biography of Dame Gertrude More: Augustine Baker, *The Life and Death of Dame Gertrude More*, ed. Ben Wekking (Salzburg: Institut für Anglistik und Amerikanistik, 2002), 61–85.

[9] Gertrude More, *The Spiritual Exercises* (Paris, 1658), 31.

[10] For a useful introduction to this tradition, see Heather Wolfe, "Reading Bells and Loose Papers: Reading and Writing Practices of the English Benedictine Nuns of Cambrai and Paris," in *Early Modern Women's Manuscript Writing*, 135–56.

[11] Edmund Colledge and James Walsh state that Sloane 2499 "closely resembles" the hand of Dame Clementia: Edmund Colledge and James Walsh, "Introduction," in *A Book of Showings to the Anchoress Julian of Norwich*, ed. Edmund Colledge and James Walsh, vol. 1 (Toronto: Pontifical Institute of Mediaeval Studies, 1978), 8. The attribution of the *Life* of Elizabeth Cary is still debated, though Heather Wolfe has made a persuasive case for Dame Magdalene's authorship: Wolfe, "The Scribal Hands and Dating of *Lady Falkland: Her Life*," and "Introduction" in *Elizabeth Cary, Lady Falkland: Life and Letters*, ed. Heather Wolfe (Cambridge, MA and Tempe: ACMRS, 2001), 59–64.

[12] Dorothy L. Latz, *"Glow-Worm Light": Writings of 17th Century English Recusant Women from Original Manuscripts* (Salzburg: Institut für Anglistik und Amerikanistik, 1989), 18.

[13] "The English Benedictine Nuns of Our Blessed Lady of Good Hope in Paris, Now at St. Benedict's Priory, Colwich, Staffordshire: Notes and Obituaries," ed. Joseph S. Hansom, in *Miscellanea VII* (London: Catholic Record Society, 1911), 342.

know she wrote spiritual poetry for the encouragement of those who were ill."[14] Latz's statement reveals the interpretive leaps necessary to all previous identifications of the paraphrases as Dame Clementia's. First, the manuscript has no evident link to illness. More seriously, this argument problematically views Psalms and spiritual songs as interchangeable, even though contemporaries generally used "spiritual song" to denote a category of ecclesiastical music separate from Psalms and hymns. In 1653, for instance, Cuthbert Sydenham summarized the prevailing definition of spiritual songs as "such as contain not only praises, but exhortations, prophesies, thanksgiving; and these only sung with the voyce and tongue."[15] The term's application to songs of thanksgiving and praise is evident in spiritual songs written to address contemporary events, such as a 1644 broadside ballad on the Civil Wars, *A Spirituall Song of Comfort or Incouragement to the Souldiers that Now Are Gone Forth in the Cause of Christ* (Wing S269A). Latz also noted that the Psalms employ a female speaker and that Dom Justin McCann did not attribute them to Baker in his definitive listing of Baker's works. In 1997 Latz repeated her claim more definitively, stating, "records show that [Dame Clementia] wrote 'Songs from the Psalms' for the entertainment and encouragement of the nuns."[16] Latz's footnote, however, provides only the same information supplied in *"Glow-Worm Light"*: namely, Dame Clementia's obituary as well as McCann's list of Baker's manuscripts.[17] In 2001 Heather Wolfe interjected a more cautious note by stating that the Cambrai Psalter was "possibly" the collection of songs mentioned in the convent's catalogue.[18] Nevertheless, Latz's attribution remained generally accepted. In 2003, Marion Wynne-Davies characterized the Cambrai Psalter as "the clearest example of Anne/Clementia's style and interests," and her later publications continued to argue that Dame Clementia was the author of the Psalter.[19] For example, in her 2007 monograph *Women Writers and Familial Discourse in the English Renaissance: Relative Values*, Wynne-Davies

---

[14] Latz, *"Glow-Worm Light,"* 78.

[15] Cuthbert Sydenham, *A Christian, Sober, and Plain Exercitation* (London, 1653), 172. The allusion is to Ephesians 5:19 and Colossians 3:16.

[16] Dorothy L. Latz, "Neglected Writings by Recusant Women, Part I – Poetry: 17th Century English Metaphysical Poetesses Gertrude More, Clementia Cary, Gertrude Aston Thimelby and Katherine Thimelby Aston," in *Neglected English Literature: Recusant Writings of the 16th-17th Centuries* (Salzburg: Institut für Anglistik und Amerikanistik, 1997), 11–48, at 14.

[17] Latz, "Neglected Writings," 41, n. 6.

[18] Wolfe, "Introduction," in *Life*, 46, n. 93.

[19] Marion Wynne-Davies, "Suicide at the Elephant and Castle, or Did the Lady Vanish? Alternative Endings for Early Modern Women Writers," in *Region, Religion, and Patronage: Lancastrian Shakespeare*, ed. Richard Dutton, Alison Findlay, and Richard Wilson (Manchester: Manchester Univ. Press, 2003), 121–42, at 137.

identifies the "spiritual songs" of Dame Clementia as "almost certainly translations of the psalms, since the Archives Départementales du Nord, Lille retains
three loose quires of psalm translations in Anne's handwriting."[20] Most recently,
I also accepted Latz's attribution in my dissertation (2008), where I treated the
Cambrai Psalter as the work of Clementia Cary while nonetheless providing a
caveat in a footnote: "the authorship of this work is uncertain."[21]

This footnote acknowledged an unease over the mixed signals sent by
the manuscript itself about its authorship and state of revision. MS 20H39 is a
cache of diverse fragmentary documents of roughly octavo size. Like the rest
of the documents in MS. 20H39, the Psalter is partial. Out of an original nine
quires, only three remain: quire two (containing the end of Psalms 69, 70–71,
and 73–78), quire eight (containing 120–123, 126–132, 134–136, 138, and half
of 139), and quire nine (containing 139–150). The most obvious clue that the
text's authorship was more complicated than previously recognized is that the
Cambrai Psalter contains variants of Psalms 70 and 130 which are attributed
to "Mrs. M. B." (Woodford's friend Mary Beale). Another troubling fact was
that the Cambrai Psalter numbers the Psalms in accordance with Protestant
tradition, an odd choice for a Catholic nun who would presumably follow the
numbering of the Vulgate and Douai-Rheims Bible. Similarly, the Psalms often
used the language of the Geneva and King James Bibles rather than the Douai-
Rheims. The Cambrai Psalter also appeared to be a strange combination of fair
and foul copy. All three quires are numbered and frequently use catchwords,
suggesting that the copy was meant to be a finished project. In addition, the
transcriber clearly and frequently indicates that she eliminates sections of the
original text by using a dash to mark elisions, suggesting that she was working from a complete copy. At the same time, as Latz herself notes, "some of
the poems are obviously in rough draft, with words and lines crossed out and
others written above them or at the sides"[22] (Figure 1). Strangely, the majority
of these variants appear to be made in the same ink as the original line, as if
these alternate readings were written at the time of copying. At several points,
dashes have been turned into crosses as extra material has been added, as in

---

[20] Marion Wynne-Davies, *Women Writers and Familial Discourse in the English Renaissance: Relative Values* (New York: Palgrave Macmillan, 2007), 120. Also see Marion Wynne-
Davies, "'To have her children with her': Elizabeth Cary and Familial Influence," in *The Literary Career and Legacy of Elizabeth Cary, 1613–1680*, ed. Heather Wolfe (New York: Palgrave
Macmillan, 2006), 223–41, at 226.

[21] Jaime Goodrich, "Early Modern Englishwomen as Translators of Religious and Political Literature, 1500–1641" (Ph.D. diss., Boston College, 2008), 528, n. 3.

[22] Latz, *"Glow-Worm Light,"* 80.

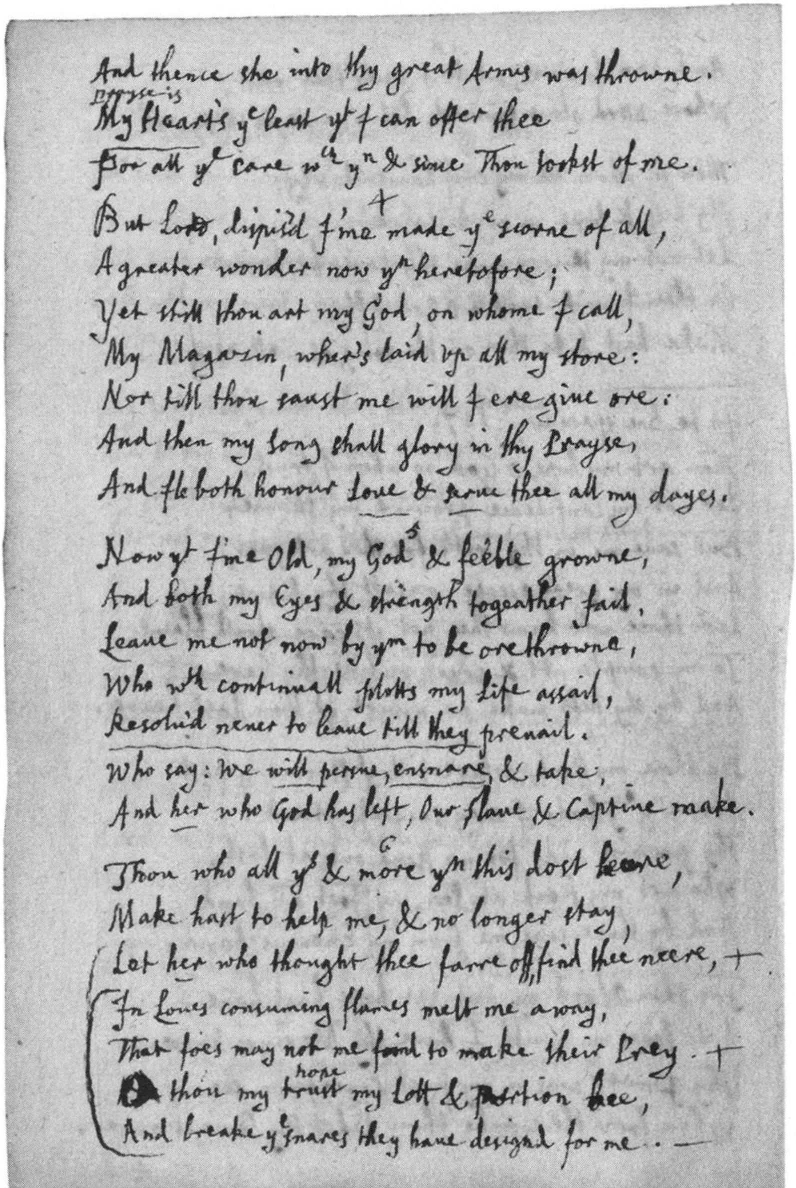

And thence she into thy great Armes was throwne.
My Heart's ye least yt f can offer thee
For all yt care wth yn & since Thou tookst of me.

But Lord, despis'd f'me made ye scorne of all,
A greater wonder now yn heretofore;
Yet still thou art my God, on whome f call,
My Magazin, wher's laid vp all my store:
Nor till thou canst me will f ere giue ore:
And then my song shall glory in thy Prayse,
And fle both honour loue & serue thee all my dayes.

Now yt f'me Old, my God & feeble growne,
And both my Eyes & strength togeather fail,
Leaue me not now by ym to be orethrowne,
Who wth continuall plotts my life assail,
Resolu'd neuer to leaue till they preuail.
Who say: we will persue, ensnare, & take;
And her who God has left, Our slaue & Captiue make.

Thou who all yt & more yn this dost knowe,
Make hast to help me, & no longer stay,
Let her who thought thee farre off find thee neere, +
In loues consuming flames melt me away,
That foes may not me find to make their Prey. +
O thou my trust my lott & portion bee,
And breake ye snares they haue design'd for me. —

Figure 1. Lille, Archives Départementales du Nord, MS 20H39. Reproduced by permission of Archives Départementales du Nord. Photo: Virginie Huleux.

the cases of Psalms 73 and 135. Such alterations suggest that the copyist had either altered her original as she went (and was therefore editing the text) or was purposely making a memorial copy of a draft that included variant readings. These contradictory signals are easily explained once the manuscript is compared with Woodford's text, for it is evident that these alternative lines and underlinings mark the copyist's alteration of the text. The Cambrai Psalter is therefore a fair copy of selections from Woodford in which the scribe made on-the-spot alterations and deletions as necessary.

The ascription of the Cambrai Psalter to Dame Clementia Cary may have flown in the face of physical evidence from the manuscript itself, but it nevertheless fulfilled a larger goal of bringing critical attention to early modern women and Catholics. Scholars had neglected 17th-century English nuns partly because their works remained in Continental or monastic archives and were therefore unknown to a wide audience. In addition, the nuns' confinement to the cloister appeared to indicate a removal from contemporary events and culture as well as a sublimation of their individual voices and agencies. The nuns, then, fell into the category of women writers whose works did not agree with the feminist project of finding proto-feminist foremothers.[23] Those critics who attributed the Cambrai Psalter to Dame Clementia sought to fit the text within this feminist framework, presenting the Psalms as evidence of Dame Clementia's agency as well as her situation within broader historical, political, and literary contexts. Latz, for example, presents the Cambrai Psalter as a counterpart to larger trends in 17th-century literature by describing it as containing examples of "true metaphysical poetry."[24] Wynne-Davies highlights the "marked authorial independence" and "Donne-like" nature of Dame Clementia's writings even as she contextualizes the Cambrai Psalter as a response to "the political concerns of her period."[25] I myself previously viewed the Cambrai Psalter as evidence of Dame Clementia's "emotional" reaction to the fact that England remained unconverted to Catholicism.[26] This common interest in the originality of Dame Clementia's text responded to feminist imperatives to recover identifiably female voices. My discovery that the Cambrai Psalter is primarily the work of Samuel Woodford may

---

[23] Margaret Ezell, "Re-Visioning the Restoration: Or, How to Stop Obscuring Early Women Writers," in *New Historical Literary Study: Essays on Reproducing Texts, Representing History*, ed. Jeffrey N. Cox and Larry J. Reynolds (Princeton: Princeton Univ. Press, 1993), 136–50.

[24] Latz, *"Glow-Worm Light,"* 10.

[25] Wynne-Davies, "Suicide at the Elephant and Castle," 137.

[26] Goodrich, *Early Modern Englishwomen as Translators*, 528.

therefore be disappointing. Yet this new attribution reveals exactly what Latz and Wynne-Davies claimed all along: the Cambrai Psalter contains a female voice that responds to 17th-century Protestant poetry.

The remainder of this essay explores the nuances and ramifications of a voice that is so dependent on another's words that a symbiotic authorial relationship develops between the original writer and his female copyist. The following examination of the relationship between Woodford and Dame Mary has larger implications for our understanding of authorial roles in the early modern period. While the feminist recovery of early modern women writers has been author-driven, the early modern era had much looser conceptions of intellectual property than our own models and therefore did not necessarily foreground the author.[27] Although print was already linked with literary authorship by the late seventeenth century, author-centric models do not reflect the unique forms of authorship that emerged out of the convent as a literary space. Indeed, Claire Walker and Heather Wolfe have already published several important studies of the Cambrai nuns' attitudes of collaboration, humility, and self-correction.[28] At Cambrai, the nuns themselves could not own property, including books, as their Constitutions reveal: "All yᵉ bookes must belong to yᵉ common librarie . . . and be common to all indiffirentlie; and let none say yˢ belongeth to me; I bought it or brought it."[29] As a result, Dame Mary's fair copy of Woodford was probably meant as a communal document to be read and shared by other nuns at Cambrai. Dame Mary clearly felt a need to rewrite Woodford in order to make his text appropriate for this audience. Though only part of Dame Mary's transcription is

---

[27] For a trenchant discussion of author-centered approaches, see Jerome J. McGann, *A Critique of Modern Textual Criticism* (Charlottesville, VA: Univ. of Virginia Press, 1983, repr. 1992), ch. 7. Influential considerations of collaborative authorship in the early modern period include Stephen B. Dobranski, *Readers and Authorship in Early Modern England* (Cambridge: Cambridge Univ. Press, 2005); idem, *Social Authorship and the Advent of Print* (Baltimore: Johns Hopkins Univ. Press, 1999); Arthur F. Marotti, *Manuscript, Print, and the English Renaissance Lyric* (Ithaca, NY: Cornell Univ. Press, 1995); Jeffrey Masten, *Textual Intercourse: Collaboration, Authorship, and Sexualities in Renaissance Drama* (Cambridge: Cambridge Univ. Press, 1997); and Wendy Wall, *The Imprint of Gender: Authorship and Publication in the English Renaissance* (Ithaca, NY: Cornell Univ. Press, 1993).

[28] Claire Walker, "Spiritual Property: The English Benedictine Nuns of Cambrai and the Dispute over the Baker Manuscripts," in *Women, Property, and the Letters of the Law in Early Modern England*, ed. Nancy E. Wright, Margaret Ferguson, and A. R. Buck (Toronto: Univ. of Toronto Press, 2004), 236–55; Wolfe, "Introduction," in *Life*, 45–54; and Heather Wolfe, "Dame Barbara Constable: Catholic Antiquarian, Advisor, and Closet Missionary," in *Catholic Culture in Early Modern England*, ed. Ronald Corthell, Frances E. Dolan, Christopher Highley, and Arthur F. Marotti (Notre Dame, IN: Univ. of Notre Dame Press, 2007), 158–88.

[29] Lille MS 20H1, 32.

extant, her copy of Woodford omits at least five psalms: 72, 124, 125, 133, and 137. In addition, only three of the psalms have been copied without any alterations to content: 77, 126, and Mary Beale's version of 130. Significantly, the Constitutions specify that the monastery's confessor must "haue a special care that no bookes, written or printed (euen papers of instruction or deuotion) that sauour not of a religious Monastical spirit, or that tend not vnto it, be kept in the Monasterie: and therefore let the catalogue be examined at euerie Visit and at such time as the Ordinarie shall iudge fit."[30] Without Dame Mary's revisions, Woodford's Psalms would not have met this stricture, indicating that her connection with Woodford's text was symbiotic rather than parasitic. By extensively excising and altering Woodford's text for her monastic audience, Dame Mary took on an editorial role that allowed the paraphrases to survive within the religious life of her community. In doing so, she transformed a text belonging to the dominant culture of Protestant England into an endorsement of the mysticism integral to the Cambrai convent's spiritual practice.

While the Cambrai Psalter does speak of exile in moving terms, Dame Mary nevertheless disengages with current political events by focusing her copy on the relationship between the speaker and God rather than external circumstances. This inward turn erases the political nuances of Woodford's version in order to create a Psalter ideal for sparking the mysticism of the Cambrai community. Woodford's preface states that he has written his paraphrase of the Psalms partly for "the glory of God, and service of his Church."[31] By "Church," Woodford alludes to the Anglican Church, and his interest in ecclesiastical structure is further apparent in his dedication of the text to George Morley, bishop of Winchester and a pillar of the Restoration church. Morley's staunch Royalist stance and his own exile during the Civil Wars may have made him a figure sympathetic to the nuns at Cambrai, who had their own connections to the Caroline court through Queen Henrietta Maria. Nonetheless, Woodford's preface also links his text to contemporary political events, explicitly framing Psalm 72 as a reflection of Charles II by comparing "the Happiness and Glory of his Kingdom with that of Solomon" (C2v). Of course, Charles had failed the hopes of English Catholics by not enacting religious tolerance upon his accession. Perhaps it is no wonder, then, that Dame Mary omits a Psalm explicitly linked to Charles and one that might be read as unqualified praise for the king's mercy: "Th'Opprest He with

---

[30] Lille MS 20H1, 5.
[31] Samuel Woodford, *A Paraphrase upon the Psalms of David* (London, 1667), (a)1v. All further references to Woodford's text will be given parenthetically, according to stanza and line numbers as well as page numbers.

His Arms shall save, / And with the Needy His Old League renew" (10.3–4; 198). In addition, Dame Mary omits several Psalms that expressly foreground warfare. Psalms 124, 125, and 137 all contain graphic descriptions of God's just avengement of Israel's enemies. This excision of military material made Woodford's *Paraphrase* more suitable for the nuns at Cambrai, whose emphasis on divine love clashed with martial ideals.[32]

Yet these omissions of warfare have another, more subtle effect: they center the Psalms on the relationship between God and the speaker, rather than triangulating God, the speaker, and his enemies. At several moments, Dame Mary rewrites Woodford in order to replace references to war with new material centered on the speaker's soul. Her version of Psalm 71 is particularly intriguing for the ways in which it transforms God's wrath into a purifying fire of love, analogous to the "way of love" sought by the Cambrai nuns. Woodford's version of stanza six conveys the Psalm's interest in punishing enemies:

> Let those, who thought Thee farr off, find Thee near,
> When in consuming flames they melt away,
> And to Eternal Wrath are made a prey!
> Let shame, Reproach and Scorn their Portion be,
> And all the snares their malice had design'd for me! (6.3–7; 194)

In Dame Mary's hands, however, this verse becomes a call for the speaker's immersion in God's purifying flame:

> Let <u>her</u> who thought thee farre off, find thee neere, +
> In Loues consuming flames melt me away,
> That foes may not me find to make their Prey. +
> O thou my trust [hope] my Lott & Portion bee,
> And breake yᵉ snares they haue designd for me.[33]

In the manuscript, this section is encased in a bracket, which apparently serves a similar purpose as underlining: it indicates Dame Mary's alterations of the orig-

---

[32] Of course, as Claire Walker has made clear, the nuns did involve themselves in worldly matters such as the Civil War by providing spiritual and material resources for the Royalist cause: Claire Walker, "Loyal and Dutiful Subjects: English Nuns and Stuart Politics," in *Women and Politics in Early Modern England, 1450–1700* (Aldershot: Ashgate, 2004), 228–42, and eadem, *Gender and Politics*, 102–29.

[33] All citations of the text are rendered as closely as possible to the original copy in terms of layout, underlining, and other markings. All words placed in brackets are superscripts in the manuscript.

inal. We might first note that Dame Mary has astonishingly turned the male enemy into a female believer: "those" become "her." In addition, God's "consuming flames" are no longer those of "Wrath," but rather of "Loue." It is this "Loue" that protects the believer, allowing her to avoid "foes" and their "snares." Instead of cursing these enemies with "shame, Reproach, and Scorn," Dame Mary interjects an interest in the speaker's "trust" or "hope" in God. Besides refocusing the Psalm on the dynamic between the speaker and God, this move envisions a kinder God than the vengeful deity of Woodford's poem. Significantly, Dame Mary also augments "Portion"—a word evocative of the dowries brought by the nuns to their convents—with "Lott," suggesting the relationship between the nuns' monastic "Portion" and their heavenly "Lott." While this version still mentions the speaker's "enemies," their "snares" are merely a catalyst for a closer union between God and the monastic female speaker.

As these changes reveal, Dame Mary translates Woodford's Psalter into an interior discourse with God, crafting an internalized spirituality more usually associated with Protestantism but yet also typical of devotional practices at Cambrai. In fact, Protestantism's reliance on such interiority may have made Woodford's text of special interest to the nuns. For example, Dame Mary chooses to rewrite Woodward's version of Psalm 149's exhortation for temple services in God's honor:

> In the High Dance His great Name let them praise,
> And that it may approach His Throne above,
> The service with shrill Trumpets raise,
> And send up Theirs, as He showers down His Love:
> They are His Pleasure, and His chiefest Prize,
> And though in others mean, yet beauteous in His eyes. (2.1–6; 434)

Dame Mary transforms Woodford's text by casting these lines into a direct call from God:

> — Thy faithfull seruice yield to me aboue,
> And send vp thine as I shower downe my Loue:
> Thou art my Pleasure, & my chiefest Prize,
> And tho in others mean, yet beauteous in my Eyes. —

As the dashes indicate, Dame Mary has omitted line 1 of stanza 2 as well as stanzas three through five. Yet it is her substitutions, which are marked by underlining, that are most interesting. Dame Mary replaces references to the "High Dance" and "shrill Trumpets" with a more generalized call for "faithfull seruice," more appropriate for nuns whose worship certainly did not include dancing. Furthermore, she rewrites this piece so that it is in the voice of God, altering the third-person pronoun to a first-person pronoun. This small change creates a reciprocal intimacy between God and the reader, suggesting that God calls the reader to "faithfull seruice" because of his loving "Pleasure" in the reader, who in turn responds by sending her "Loue" "vp" to heaven. This immediacy mimics the one-on-one discourse nuns at Cambrai were encouraged to have with God, in which their written or mental addresses to God would eventually be met with direct heavenly guidance. A similar moment occurs in Dame Mary's version of Psalm 128, where she changes the original reference to the blessed man's wife into an address from God to the speaker: "<u>Thou shallt</u>, like to a Fruitfull Vine, / Both into breadth, & clusters run; / To <u>me</u> shallt look, as to thy Sun, / And still haue fruit, on wch y^t Sun may shine. — " Here she replaces "Thy wife" with "Thou shalt," also changing "To him" and "to her" into "To me" and "to thy." As a result, the stanza substitutes a God/speaker relationship for the wife/husband dynamic, perhaps responding to the traditional idea that nuns were the brides of Christ. At the same time, Dame Mary models a tender relationship between God and the female speaker correlating with the ultimate goal of the "way of love": the experience of a reciprocal love between the nun and the Lord.

Dame Mary also alters Woodford's *Paraphrase* in order to make it consonant with the Benedictine Rule's emphasis on humility. Noting that "by [our] humilitie of hart, god lifteth [us] vpp to heauen," the Rule lays out twelve degrees of humility that move from an internal submission to God's will toward public displays of humility shown by the nun "in her worke in the Church, Monastery or Garden or in the way abroude in the Feilds, or in what Place soeuer shee sitt, stand, or walke."[34] Since writing was an important form of "worke" at Cambrai, it is understandable that such an emphasis on humbleness would also carry over to this form of labor. Dame Mary often appears to have revised Woodford so as to introduce an aspect of humility. For example, she rewrites stanza eight of in Psalm 71 in order to displace the speaker's agency onto God [Figure 1]:

Thou from my Infancy hast made me see
Thy wondrous Works, w^{ch} <u>thou</u> [I] ~~abroad~~ [for me] <u>hast</u> [~~haue~~] shewen.
Now y^t I'me Old continue y^m to me,

---

[34] Saint Benedict, *The Rule of the Most Blissed Father Saint Benedict*, trans. Alexia Grey, in *Recusant Translators: Elizabeth Cary, Alexia Grey*, ed. Frances E. Dolan, The Early Modern Englishwoman: A Facsimile Library of Essential Works, series I, part 2, vol. 13 (Aldershot, UK: Ashgate, 2000), 31, 39.

That <u>thou</u> [I] mayst perfect w^t thou [I] hast [~~may~~] begun,
And <u>shew</u> [~~tell~~] Posterity w^t thou hast done!

In this case, the words that have been stricken are, in fact, Woodford's original version: "which I abroad have shown / . . . / That I may perfect what I have
begun / And tell Posterity" (8.2, 8.4–5; 194). While Dame Mary originally included Woodford's wording as an alternate version, her deletions indicate a complete rejection of Woodford's phrasing. This adaptation removes the focus from
Woodford's insistent "I" to God, who becomes the agent of his own "wondrous
Works." Rather than stressing the speaker's ability to "beg[i]n," "show," "perfect,"
and "tell," Dame Mary places that authority in God's hands. Another intriguing
elision of the speaker's agency occurs in the first stanza of Psalm 131. Woodford's
text asserts the speaker's innocence: "Alike before Thee open ly / My Innocent
heart, and humble eye, / Which have no pride, but from the malice of my Foe"
(1.3–5). Dame Mary converts this declaration of innocence into an acknowl-
edgment of the speaker's sorrowful guilt: "Alike before thee often ly / My <u>guilty</u>
heart, & <u>weeping</u> eye." This new focus on "guilt" reinforces the speaker's subordinate status to God, a motif of dutiful subjection that continues in her three
versions of line five. In order, they are "W^ch humbled are & far cast downe below"
(a marginal note); "<u>Thou knowst I now seek</u> [I now seek only thee] <u>But</u> [only]
<u>thee; & vnto thee to go</u>,"; and "W^ch haue no prid, but from ye malice of my foe"
(Woodford's original line). While the first version — and probably the last composed, due to its marginal placement — turns Woodford's mention of the "eye"
into evidence of the speaker's humble abasement, the other renditions insert a
completely new idea: the hope of union with God. Humility therefore becomes
a necessary preparation for the speaker's goal of completely submerging herself
within God, the goal of the "way of love." Dame Mary herself performs this extreme modesty by scrupulously noting her relationship to Woodford's original.
Not only does she generally mark her alterations of the paraphrases, but she also
excises Woodford's version in a manner that leaves it legible and therefore allows
for the possibility of comparison between her work and the original. As a result,
Dame Mary participates in a symbiotic form of authorship, basing her work on
Woodford's text without attempting to eclipse it entirely and, in the process, allowing the work to endure within the context of the Cambrai house.

To modern eyes, Dame Mary's transcription of Woodford's Psalter is perhaps not as exciting a document as Dame Clementia's metaphysical Psalms. Yet
this text is important in its own right as evidence of the literary practices of a
convent more typically known for its encouragement of independent writers such

as Dame Magdalene Cary and Dame Gertrude More. By focusing solely on nuns whose works agree with modern conceptions of literary agency, critics have ignored the larger implications of the wealth of archival material indicating that the Cambrai nuns enthusiastically participated in so-called "secondary" genres such as compilation, transcription, and translation. As this essay has sought to demonstrate, these genres could serve as a space for nuns to negotiate a form of authorship that met the demands of their profession. Dame Mary revised the Psalter to fit her vocation and her context: that of a Benedictine nun whose severe humility was paired with the mystic flights of Augustine Baker's way. By paying attention to how Dame Mary makes Woodford's text serve her own purposes, we can extricate her particular voice. Nevertheless, this voice is ultimately self-effacing, a gesture shown by her careful notation of almost every change she makes to Woodford. These notations do not show a slavish regard for Woodford's original text, but instead offer an example of the unusual authorial positions taken by early modern English nuns. Although we may wish that nuns had written more creative texts, attention to the genres which they *did* utilize can only further enrich our understanding of women writers and authorial roles in the period. After all, without Dame Mary's alterations, Woodford's *Paraphrase* would have been inappropriate for the convent's library and might not have passed the confessor's inspection. Dame Mary was not the only nun at Cambrai to appropriate Protestant material for the convent's devotional life, for the archives at Lille also contain a fragmentary copy of selections from James Merrick's 1678 publication *Annotations on the Psalms* (MS 20H21). The Cambrai convent's ownership and modification of Woodford's and Merrick's texts suggests that the nuns were not necessarily sequestered from mainstream English culture. Indeed, the house clearly found Protestant works useful for spurring their own devotions, as long as these texts could be made compatible with Catholic piety and monastic life. It was this need to rewrite Protestant works that informed the unusual circumstances of authorship evident in the Cambrai Psalter. As a copyist, editor, and collaborative author, Dame Mary undertook several interlocking authorial roles, all of which were equally important in crafting a copy of Woodford's text that suited her house's spiritual purposes.

WAYNE STATE UNIVERSITY

"Who Am I?": Exploring Questions of Authorship Using Digital Texts[1]

IRENE J. MIDDLETON

T HIS PAPER DELVES INTO THE MANY POSSIBILITIES THAT FIRST-PERSON passages offer to explore with undergraduates early modern conceptions of authorship. Digital editions of early modern texts are a particularly fruitful ground for this exploration due to their layers of "authorship" in collaborations and translations. The title might well have been "what's the use of a digital edition?" or "how do we read digital editions?" I present here a case study of how one work from the Emory Women Writers Research Project (EWWRP) might be used in a variety of classroom settings to introduce students to this current critical interest.[2]

The Mirrour of Princely Deedes and Knighthood (*The Mirrour*) is the first known chivalric romance to appear in English and one of the few translated directly from the Spanish without an intermediary French edition.[3] Not coincidentally, it is also one of the digital critical editions I created for the EWWRP. Although *The Mirrour* is a printed text from the late sixteenth century, the approaches I discuss here could be easily adapted for other eras. *The Mirrour* was translated circa 1578 by Margaret Tyler from the 1562 Spanish original *Espejo de*

---

[1] This paper was first presented at the 2009 International Congress on Medieval Studies, Kalamazoo, MI, at a panel entitled "Electronic Editing of Medieval and Renaissance Texts: The Emory Women Writers Research Project," Sheila T. Cavanagh presiding.

[2] Scholars currently concerned with these questions include Margaret Ferguson, Suzanne Hull, Cecile Jagodzinski, Arthur Marotti, Jeffrey Masten, Lori Newcomb, James Raven, J. W. Saunders, Helen Small, Naomi Tadmor, Wendy Wall, and Ramona Wray, among many others.

[3] Diego Ortúñez de Calahorra, *Espejo de principes y cavalleros* (1562). Rptd. as *The Mirrour of Princely Deedes and Knighthood*, trans. Margaret Tyler (London: Thomas East, 1580). Rptd. as digital critical edition, *The Mirrour of Princely Deedes and Knighthood*, ed. Irene Middleton. Emory Women Writers Resource Project. Atlanta: Emory Univ., forthcoming.

principes y cavalleros by Diego Ortúñez de Calahorra. It has already proven of interest for authorship studies, primarily as a piece of female writing, as a translation, as a collaborative work, and as an early romance. Tyler translated only the first book of the romance, through volumes and editions appeared in England from circa 1580 to 1601. The translation's influence on English literature was widespread, as searches of Early English Books Online (EEBO) for "mirrour of knighthood" and the names of the main characters aptly demonstrate (though the references are usually mocking after the publication of the English edition of *Don Quixote*.)[4]

The Mirrour is now best known for Tyler's address to the reader defending women reading and writing secular material, but the romance itself is a thrilling tale of two generations of a European family. Ortúñez de Calahorra follows, as Daniel Eisenberg describes it, the "unanimous pretense that the works were true histories, only rescued from oblivion and modernized by a sixteenth-century contemporary."[5] Tyler retains this fiction while also acknowledging Ortúñez de Calahorra's role, setting up three layers of authorship for the English edition.

Thus far, it is primarily the last layer of authorship — Tyler's — that has elicited interest from English-language scholars. Because *The Mirrour* has primarily drawn attention as women's writing (see for example the facsimile edition published by Ashgate as part of the Early Modern Englishwoman series), her identity and her prefatory argument for a woman's right to write have been the focus of most critical work.[6] What Tyler *doesn't* do in that argument is as compelling as what she does. She does not use the rhetoric of erotic friendship that Jeffrey Masten argues is the basis of male-male co-authorship.[7] Instead of rewriting this *topos* to fit her situation, Tyler chose a more careful and, I would suggest, more radical rhetorical stance. She claims to have transliterated the text and yet also claims to be a co-author, distancing herself from the content of the romance while

---

[4] Henry Thomas in his work *Spanish and Portuguese Romances of Chivalry: The Revival of the Romance of Chivalry in the Spanish Peninsula, and its Extension and Influence Abroad* (Cambridge: Cambridge Univ. Press, 1920) began to trace *The Mirrour*'s influence (272–75, 298–99).

[5] Daniel Eisenberg, *Romances of Chivalry in the Spanish Golden Age* (Newark, DE: Juan de la Cuesta, 1982), 43.

[6] See, e.g., Catherine Gallagher, "A History of Precedent: Rhetorics of Legitimation in Women's Writing," *Critical Inquiry* 26.2 (Winter 2000): 309–27; Kathryn Coad's "Introductory Note," in *Margaret Tyler*, The Early Modern Englishwoman: A Facsimile Library of Essential Works. Part 1: Printed Writings, 1500–1640, Vol. 8 (Aldershot: Scolar Press, 1996, ix–xi; Louise Schleiner, "Margaret Tyler, Translator and Waiting Woman," *ELN* 29.3 (March 1992): 1–8; and the inclusion of Tyler's address to the reader in several anthologies.

[7] Jeffrey Masten addresses this in *Textual Intercourse: Collaboration, Authorship, and Sexualities in Renaissance Drama* (Cambridge: Cambridge Univ. Press, 1997).

arguing for her right to read and write secular prose. She refuses the dangerously erotic example of male-male collaboration and instead argues from a more acceptable female-male Petrarchan relationship, one that sets her in the position of the untouchable, chaste beloved. From within this conservative heterosexual framework, Tyler evolves a radical argument that women should be allowed to write. Women, she argues, need to protect their reputations and therefore must be allowed to read works dedicated to them to insure their names are not attached to scandalous material. From this she derives, "it is all one for a woman to pen a story, as for a man to address his story to a woman" (digital [vi]).

The choice to focus on Tyler's admittedly compelling argument has left the bulk of her work under-examined. We have focused on the writing that is solely hers, falling into an anachronistic single-author trap. I too should be so accused in adding Tyler's work to a women-writers archive. Dealing with knights, ladies, giants, monsters, illicit sex, travel, and the occasional moral, the book's content offers much to engage the current reader as well as the early modern one.

One of the few academic works to discuss both the prefatory material and the novel's content is the compelling and well-argued "Translation as Collaborative Authorship: Margaret Tyler's *The Mirrour of Princely Deedes and Knighthood*" by Deborah Uman and Belén Bistué.[8] Their work examines how Tyler changed the text in her translation and the impact of those changes on the early modern reading experience. Uman and Bistué argue that, because of these changes, Tyler should be considered a co-author. However, they read the textual examples as though Tyler fully supplanted in the early modern English reader's mind both the Spanish author — Ortúñez de Calahorra — and the fictional author(s) mentioned in the narrative. When they examine the replacement of Ortúñez de Calahorra's initials on the title page with "M. T.," Uman and Bistué argue that "[b]ecause she is the only 'translator' in the English version, the English reader can easily hear the 'I' of the fictional translator that appears in the first and last lines of the text as Tyler's voice" (303).

I disagree with this last claim — that "the English reader can easily hear the 'I' of the fictional translator . . . as Tyler's voice" (303). Although Tyler's is the only name that appears on the English version, the work is acknowledged as a translation and references a fictional ancient authority as its origin. Early modern readers may not have heard Tyler's voice or may have shifted among voices based on

---

[8] Uman and Bistue, "Translation as Collaborative Authorship: Margaret Tyler's *The Mirrour of Princely Deedes and Knighthood*," *Comparative Literature Studies* 44 (207): 298-323. Tina Krontiris in her book *Oppositional Voices: Women as Writers and Translators of Literature in the English Renaissance* (New York: Routledge, 1992) is one of the few others who address the content of *The Mirrour*. See n. 9 below.

their assumptions of gendered authorship. It is this layering of authorship that makes this work especially compelling for the classroom, as I hope the following will demonstrate.

The Mirrour is a particularly fecund place for examining layers of authorship beginning with the shifting conception of gendered authorship in Tyler's prefatory address to the reader. As Uman and Bistué point out, Tyler spends time distancing herself from her Spanish co-author — crediting him with the content of the romance — rather than working in the intimate partnership Masten finds among male co-authors:

> Thou hast heere, gentle Reader, the historie of **Trebatio** an Emperour in **Greece**: whether a true storie of him in déede, or a fained fable, I wot not, neither dyd I greatly seeke after it in yᵉ translation, but by me it is done into English for thy profit & delight. . . . The first tongue wherein it was penned was the **Spanish**, in which nation by common report, the inheritance of all warlike commendation hath to this day rested. . . . For I take the grace thereoff to be rather in the reporters deuice then in the truth of this report, as I would that I could so well impart with thée yᵉ delight which my selfe findeth in reading the **Spanish**: but seldome is the tale carried cleane from an others mouth. . . . The inuention, dispositiō, trimming, & what els in this story, is wholy an other mans, my part none therein but the translation, as it were onely in giuing entertainment to a stranger, before this time vnacquainted with our coūtry guise. (digital [iii-iv])

If male co-authors present theirs as an erotic relationship, then a female co-author, facing even stronger prohibitions against public authorship and its associations with illicit and copious sexuality, would need to firmly separate her creative process from her male co-author's as part of her modesty *topos*. To put it colloquially, she needs the early modern reader to "blame" Ortúñez de Calahorra for the scandalous parts.

Paradoxically, Tyler also includes an argument for the propriety of women writing secular material. Tyler abuts and even intersects the two seemingly contrary positions — she asserts her right to write secular material yet states she did not actually do so. In other words, she draws attention to both her authorship and Ortúñez de Calahorra's. Tyler is allowing the early modern reader to read the romance as the work of a woman or a man or both, simultaneously or in sequence as the subject matter changes.

This free-flowing conception of authorship is especially compelling in the first-person passages of the romance. Like early modern readers, students must decide who "delivers" each passage — the fictional ancient author, Ortúñez de Calahorra, Margaret Tyler, or one or both of the authorial *personae*. Most often, the brief first-person passages are ambiguously gendered and full of possibilities for discussion. Immediately following Tyler's "To the Reader" the narrator states, "I will report here" the "worthy deedes" of Trebatio "according as Artimidoro the Grecian hath left them written in the great volumes of his Chronicle" (digital 1). Coming on the heels of Tyler's argument for women writing, it is tempting to read the genderless "I" as Tyler's voice. Only if one recalls that she translated the work from Spanish does it become clear that Artimidoro must be the fictional original author, not the unnamed Spanish one. It is only on reflection, then, that one realizes that "I" must be Ortúñez de Calahorra.

Sometimes, the first-person passages seem to fall into "appropriate" genders, though there lurks a danger of sinking into gendered stereotypes in presuming to know how an early modern reader might perceive these passages. When the narrator admits uncertainty — "I dare not say" — over whether Princess Briana's joy at seeing her sons grow up outweighs her sorrow over her missing husband, the temptation is to read the genderless first person as female because of the context of female interiority (digital 50). At another moment, the universal masculine so common to moral comments "reads" as male:

> But of this manner and condition are we mortall men, that for our pleasures we sometimes forget our spouses the one halfe of our selues: sometimes neglect our children the more halfe of our selues: (as in whom the hope of posteritie resteth) and lastly sometimes we ouertourne our countrey which ought to be déerer to vs then our selues. . . . (digital 291)

Some of the language might be masculine — "we mortal men" and the talk of treason — and if read as such, would mean a male narrator is addressing a male audience with that first person plural, which could open up discussions about the audiences for romances in England and Spain. Yet, on the whole, the language is rather carefully gender-neutral: "we mortal men" might easily refer to "mankind" rather than *men* per se, especially since the passage then mentions "spouses," not "wives."

There is only one instance in the romance when the narrator clearly speaks with a male voice. An injured giant calls on the knight Rosicleer to put him out of his misery, which Rosicleer refuses to do. The narrator comments, "But truly, if I had bene in **Rosicleers** case, I should not haue bene so straunge: seing, that bothe it shoulde haue bene the Gyants last request and so little encombraunce towardes me" (digital 189). While modern readers of either gender might identify with the speaker's attitude, the straightforward offer of physical violence would appear decidedly masculine for an early modern reader.

However, the gendering of authorship does not end here. The text also gives the reader an active role in the creation of meaning that recalls Tyler's initial claim (that it is "all one" to read and to write) and opens up further questions about early modern conceptions of author and readership. After commenting on seeing God's hand in the saving of the Knight of the Sun from certain death as a child, the narrator directly addresses the reader: "And you which reade this history, may be brought by good reason to giue credit to this my report, sith you your selues are witnesses of the euident presence of the Almightie in so certeine a daunger" (digital 50). The reader is brought *into* the story as a witness who must confirm the truth of the narrator's moral. One sentence later, the reader seems to be more involved in the creation of meaning than the narrator, who mentions again his/her distance from the events: "But mine Author willing to entreate somewhat of him, setteth it downe thus" (digital 50–51). The layers of responsibility for the narrative are extended outwards to define an active reader, one who must assist in the creation of the story. If the reader is co-creator, then the gender of the reader becomes a further layer of authorship to be navigated.

The final instance of first-person narration continues the active role for the reader and looks forward to the next volume. It states:

> So vp to the house they goe, and héere breaketh of the first booke, what happened by the way the seconde booke declareth. Now lette vs remember by the way where we lefte our worthy Princes, what when we haue néede of them we may there finde them. (digital 357)

There is then a list of where each character has been left, ending with "the princesse **Clarindiana** a womā knight, of whom this whole story specially entreateth, but more at large héereafter. And thus endeth the first booke" (digital 357). According to Uman and Bistué, "This final summary reintroduces the romance's narrator, whom Tyler has already established as the female translator. In doing so, this unassuming report again makes visible Tyler's strategy of self-promotion and collaboration" (307). However, it is important that Tyler does *not* explicitly reintroduce the narrator. By breaking away from the singular-author reading, it is possible to note that the passage actually uses the first person plural: "us" and "we." The narrator addresses the reader as though the reader is a part of a collaborative storytelling. Although the narrator has a unique foreknowledge, the reader is called upon to be active — to "remember" and to "finde." The conclusion is a mnemonic device, but one that again makes the reader an active participant in constructing meaning.[9]

However, these readings do not address the use of a *digital* edition in the classroom. The EWWRP critical edition offers the same reliability, usability, and scholarly content as a print edition while also presenting additional tools and contexts for scholarship and teaching. This edition is accompanied by an introduction to Tyler's biography, to printer Thomas East, to the audience for romances in England, and to the cultural status of romances and *The Mirrour* in particular. The digital edition is also heavily annotated with hyperlinks to additional primary and secondary materials, encouraging students to hopscotch easily to further learning using a familiar method. This exploration duplicates the active reader role that *The Mirrour* hints at by asking the student reader to bring in other contexts to create meaning.

Accessibility was central to the creation of digital edition of *The Mirrour*. All texts in the EWWRP are available free thanks to support from Emory University and the National Endowment for the Humanities, unlike prohibitively expensive facsimile editions.[10] The EWWRP edition was created to increase the accessibility of the text while retaining accuracy. The blurred Blackletter font of the original has been replaced by a more approachable Roman font using optical recognition software and extensive proofreading. To partly replicate the reading experience of the original, the digital edition retains the original spellings, contractions, and unusual printing choices. The printer Thomas East used a Roman font for proper names; to create a similar eye-catching "pop," we render these in bold type. Some of the uncertainty of reading the original has been lost, as the abbreviations for "the," "that," "thou," etc. have been, wherever possible, rendered according to the sense of the passage, reducing the detective work necessary for an early modern reader.

Students reading the digital edition will also be able to explore conceptions of Tyler's authorship in new ways. While there is not yet a full-text digital edition of Ortúñez de Calahorra's work, bilingual readers might be able to read the

---

[9] This author-reader collaboration could also been analyzed in light of the likelihood that Tyler was accustomed to reading aloud and may have expected her work to be so. On Tyler reading aloud, see Louise Schleiner, *Tudor and Stuart Women Writers* (Bloomington: Indiana Univ. Press, 1994).

[10] Currently, *EEBO*, free to students whose school subscribes, has an incomplete, image-only edition of *The Mirrour*.

modern printed edition alongside the accessible *Mirrour* to discover ways Tyler influenced the work.[11] This kind of edition would be prohibitively expensive to print and have such a small potential audience that it would be unlikely to find a publisher.

Word-count programs also yield interesting results. Tyler's word use suggests she considers herself a co-author. According to Brown University's Women Writers Online version of Tyler's "To the Reader," Tyler uses "I," "my," and "selfe" more than 100 times in these four pages. This is more often than she uses "the," "of," or "to." This might suggest that Tyler actually felt some ownership over the material, but certainly puts herself forward in the mind more than the "author" (used three times), "Spanish" or "Spaniard" (used 7 times), or the "history," the narrative's usual term for the supposed Ur-text (used once). We hope that full text searching may develop new arguments about Tyler's authorship.

Although it is perhaps lamentable, students today are more likely to click between windows than to go find a book. An online edition may encourage more use of online resources like the OED or searches for contextual material than if they had to make a trip to the library (though I realize these are potential, perhaps even ideal, student behaviors). *EEBO* might provide students with new insights into the relationship between authors and printers, for example. There often appears in *The Mirrour* an acute accent over the first of a double "ee". These seem to have been a particular trait of publisher Thomas East's treatment of Blackletter works, rather than authorial. A brief *EEBO* search of East's works would lead students to *The Shepheard's Calendar*, where these marks appear in East's 1581 edition but not in the earlier edition.

The digital edition of *The Mirrour* would be useful for at least three advanced English courses — early modern women's writing, romances, and early modern prose. Translation and readership would be key concepts for all three courses, though a full analysis of both gender and authorship issues would be more likely to appear in the class on early modern prose. The context of each course would also likely guide students to focus on different layers of the narrative voice.

Although the course on early modern women's writing would likely include translations of men's writing by women or vice versa, the very focus on *women's* writing would likely preempt questions of the meanings and reception of "cross-gendered" authorship for many students during their readings. The basic assumption would be that because it is a course on women's writing, cross-gendered translations must be women's writing. The article by Uman and Bistué

---

[11] Uman and Bistué have begun this work in their article "Translation as Collaborative Authorship: Margaret Tyler's *The Mirrour of Princely Deedes and Knighthood*."

mentioned above demonstrates this approach, as does Tina Krontiris's insightful analysis of Tyler's address to the reader and the romance.[12] In keeping with her book's overall premise, Krontiris presents the female figures of the romance as though they were wholly Tyler's creation to analyze their relation to patriarchal norms as well as Tyler's. This is not to suggest that these are poor readings by any means, merely that they examine *only* how Tyler might have affected *The Mirrour* and how only her sex affects a reader's experience. Students in the women's writing course are also those likely to be able to address complex questions about gendered authorship, such as whether trying to identify "male" or "female" aspects of a work reinforces gender stereotypes or essentializes gendered writing attributes.[13]

For the course on romances, *The Mirrour* would likely be the only female-authored work. While Tyler's role might be discussed, it would potentially be a student's only exposure to "early modern women's writing" and most discussion would have a genre context rather than a gender one. Students in this course, for example, might be (or become) aware that Ortúñez de Calahorra's claim to have discovered and translated the text was a trope of romances and would perhaps be able to talk about its parallels to Tyler's claim in the preface. Indeed, given that her name replaces Ortúñez de Calahorra's on the title page, her claim to be merely a translator *with* an argument for authorship might have suggested to early modern readers familiar with Spanish and French romances that she was merely setting up a false claim of translation and was in fact the author. Genre-focused students might replicate this experience, as they would not have discussed the restrictions on women's writing (though they are mentioned in the prefatory material) and would be more likely to associate her modesty *topos* with those of men. These students could investigate the changing cultural capital of *The Mirrour* through EEBO searches and put Tyler's claim that chivalric romance is a useful tool for teaching morality into its proper generic context.

Surprisingly, it seems a prose fiction course might be most likely to address cross-gendered authorship and early-modern reader response. Likely dealing with multiple works of translation and multiple works by both genders, questions of gender and authorship seem most likely to come up in these contexts. Putting *The Mirrour* alongside *Urania, Don Quixote,* and — most compellingly for its possible conversations about co-authorship — *Arcadia* would provide

---

[12] Krontiris, *Oppositional Voices: Women as Writers and Translators of Literature in the English Renaissance.*

[13] Pilar Godayol Nogue's article "Living on the Border: Feminine Subjectivity in Translation," in *Investigating Translation*, ed. Allison Beeby, Doris Ensinger, and Marisa Presas (Philadelphia: John Benjamins, 2000), 37–42, examines this issue in relation to translation.

undergraduates with the context necessary for conversations about both gendered authorship and genre. This class might be able to investigate broad questions, such as when or if women's translation of secular prose works was accepted and how that compares to the reception of women's authorship. These students might address why translations were appealing to readers: Were translations popular because they appealed as "new" things? As "foreign" things? Students could discuss the differences in cultural perceptions between romances and other pieces of prose and whether these shift across the period.

These possibilities are centered on potential English classes. Other departments might address the question of the translation's methods or its cultural meanings, attempt a bilingual comparative study, or have students work on creating their own digital editions. Of course, much of what I have proposed here is also predicated on my fantasy that students would read Tyler's prefatory material rather than jumping straight to the "good stuff." That second choice is made all the easier by the structure of the EWWRP website, which drops you at the table of contents, rather than at the first page of text. There is no need for students to flip through an introduction and perhaps have their eyes caught by an illustration. No, here you can just as easily click on "Chapter 1" as on the far less tempting "critical introduction" or "M.T. to her Reader," but I hope that these possibilities might encourage you to "further wade," as Tyler puts it, into this work.

MANCHESTER METROPOLITAN UNIVERSITY

The Woman in Black: The Patron of Antoine Vérard's Edition of the Horloge de Sapience (PML 17591)[1]

CAROLYN DISKANT MUIR

AMONG THE RICH HOLDINGS OF THE PIERPONT MORGAN LIBRARY IN NEW York is an incunabulum from 1493/94. Entitled the *Horloge de Sapience* or *Clock of Wisdom*, this work is one of a set of six luxury copies of this book produced by the Parisian publisher and bookseller Antoine Vérard. One of its most intriguing features is the appearance in a number of miniatures of a heretofore-unidentified woman dressed in black (Figure 1). This article will propose an identity for this woman, the original owner of the book.

Antoine Vérard dominated French publishing from 1485 to 1512. Besides producing books printed on paper illustrated with woodcuts, Vérard had a sideline business in luxury book production. Most of these works were printed on vellum and contain hand-painted miniatures. As a publisher, Vérard kept exceptional control over all details of his creations. Two points in particular stand out about his books. First, Vérard is included in numerous presentation miniatures giving a book to a princely patron, replacing the author commonly depicted in such scenes.[2] And second, Vérard wrote prologues dedicating books to specific

---

[1] This paper was first presented at the 2010 Renaissance Society of America Annual Meeting, Venice, Italy, at a panel entitled "Early Modern Women's Manuscripts (3)," Margaret Hannay presiding.

[2] The most complete study of Vérard's career and works is Mary Beth Winn, *Anthoine Vérard, Parisian Publisher 1485–1512: Prologues, Poems, and Presentations* (Geneva: Librairie Droz, 1997). This information on Vérard's activities is taken from Winn (15–38) who says that no other publisher of the time included himself as the donor in presentation scenes (69).

Figure 1. Presentation to the patron. *Horloge de Sapience*, 1493/94. New York, Pierpont Morgan Library, 17591, fol. a1r.

individuals. Most were addressed to Charles VIII, king of France from 1483 to 1498 and Vérard's primary patron during the 1490s.[3] Vérard then presented copies of these same luxury editions to other patrons, differentiating each book by its unique hand-painted pictures.

One such edition was the *Horloge de Sapience*, a French translation of the *Horologium Sapientiae*, written in 1334 by the Dominican mystic Henry Suso.[4] One of the most widely read books of its time, this work formed part of a wider devotional movement that preached interior change as essential for the devout Christian.[5] The book's content takes the form of a dialogue on the Passion, with ardent declarations of love and finally marriage to Eternal Wisdom, the alter ego of Christ. The book's impact was spread by its translations into numerous languages and printed editions.[6]

The six luxury copies of Vérard's edition all contain the same text and a prologue to Charles VIII. Yet, though the text is the same, the pictures are not. While three copies contain only three miniatures each, the other three are much more lavishly illustrated. The king's copy (Paris, BnF, vélins 359) contains twenty-five miniatures; a second copy for his cousin, Charles d'Angoulême (Paris, BnF, vélins 360), has twenty-one; and the copy in the Pierpont Morgan Library contains sixteen miniatures, thirteen of which are original to the book.

It must be acknowledged at the outset that no conclusive proof of this woman's identity has been found. In identifying book owners, scholars typically put forward two types of evidence: records of ownership such as inventories or wills and identifying marks such as coats of arms or inscriptions. Neither exists in this case.

The absence of written records is of course disappointing, but given the vicissitudes of history not surprising. The lack of identifying marks such as coats of arms is more unusual, although such marks cannot always be found even for

---

[3] Winn, *Anthoine Vérard*, 52, 55, 104.

[4] The book was translated into French in 1389 by Jean du Neufchâteau, a Franciscan monk: Geneviève Hasenohr, "Aperçu sur la diffusion et la réception de la littérature de spiritualité en langue française au dernier siècle du Moyen Age," in *Wissensorganisierende und wissensvermittelnde Literatur im Mittelalter: Perspektiven ihrer Erforschung*, ed. Norbert Richard Wolf (Wiesbaden: L. Reichert, 1987), 57–90, at 73 n. 63.

[5] Barbara Newman, "Henry Suso and the Medieval Devotion to Christ the Goddess," *Spiritus* 2 (2002): 1–14, at 9.

[6] It was translated into Middle French, Middle Dutch, Italian, Middle English, Bohemian, Swedish, Danish, and Hungarian. Pius Künzle, ed., *Heinrich Seuses Horologium Sapientiae: Erste kritische Ausgabe unter Benützung der Vorarbeiten* (Freiburg: Universitätsverlag Freiburg Schweiz, 1977), 250–76.

books belonging to highborn patrons.[7] In this case, the treatment of the borders may explain the absence of any heraldic device. The elaborate wide borders in the other copies of this edition contain numerous decorative motifs such as flowers and animals, as well as coats of arms. The king's copy, for instance, is dotted with fleurs-de-lys and floral patterns (Figure 2).

The contrast between these carefully painted, brightly colored, and profusely decorated borders and those of the Pierpont Morgan copy is striking. Its borders are narrow, with a pattern of leaves, flowers, and birds. Only red and blue are used. Not only are the colors and patterns much simpler than those in the other copies, but the borders look roughly painted, lacking the quality of the main miniatures.

These borders, in fact, are almost identical to those of the original woodcuts beneath which were simply painted over (Figure 3). There are thus no motifs or identifying marks particular to this book or its owner. The artist probably did not paint these borders himself, but delegated them to someone else, a common workshop practice. As to why the high standard of the miniatures was not applied to the borders, time pressure or cost may have driven the artist to take a shortcut for a less important part of the book's decorative scheme.

We must therefore turn to other means to consider who the patron might have been. We know that the *Horloge de Sapience* was one of the most widely read books in France in the fourteenth and fifteenth centuries.[8] We also know that it was read by women as well as men.[9] But what will really help to solve this puzzle are the miniatures, which will lead to a number of conclusions about the woman

---

[7] For example, Anne-Marie Legaré, "Charlotte de Savoie's Library and Illuminators," *Journal of the Early Book Society for the Study of Manuscripts and Printing History* 4 (2001): 32–87, at 35, in proposing that some of Charlotte's books ended up in the library of her daughter Anne de Beaujeu, acknowledges that "It is worth noting that none of these works contains a mark of ownership and that only a few bear traces of their passage through the Bourbon Library." Winn, *Anthoine Vérard*, observes that even books made for Charles d'Angoulême have no coats of arms (199).

[8] Hasenohr counts fifty extant manuscripts of the work, rising to seventy-five if one also counts extracts ("Aperçu," 70). Moreover, Hasenohr's chart (90) makes clear that the laity owned copies of the *Horloge* more frequently than any other religious text, with twenty-four extant copies.

[9] One prominent instance of a woman owning this book is Charlotte de Savoie, whose ownership is discussed by Geneviève Hasenohr, "L'essor des bibliothèques privées aux XIVe et XV siècles," in *Histoires des Bibliothèques Françaises*, vol. 1: *Les Bibliothèques médiévales du VIe siècle à 1530*, ed. André Vernet (Paris: Promodis/Cercle de la Librairie, 1989), 214–63, at 252, and Anne-Marie Legaré, *Le Pèlerinage de Vie Humaine en prose de la Reine Charlotte de Savoie* (Ramsen, Schweiz: Heribert Tenschert, 2004), 187. This book (BnF, ms. fr. 445) was then passed on to Charlotte's daughter Anne.

Figure 2. Presentation to the king. *Horloge de Sapience*, 1493/94. Paris, BnF, vélins 359, fol. 1r.

Figure 3. Presentation of a book. *Horloge de Sapience*, 1493/94. Paris, BnF, Res D. 2526, fol. a1r.

in black. Painted by the Master of the Chronique scandaleuse,[10] these miniatures include eight depicting this woman. One large miniature immediately follows the table of contents, and the rest, small in size, are scattered throughout the work.

The first miniature in particular provides us with numerous clues about the woman, for it is a presentation scene (Figure 1). A kneeling woman wearing a black dress with fur-trimmed cuffs, white lace collar, and a shoulder-length headdress prays in her private oratory. Kneeling before her is a man who presents her with a book. Based on other presentation miniatures in Vérard's books, there is no doubt that this is Vérard himself.[11]

Presentation scenes in Verard's work are reserved for his most important patrons. The only other copy of this edition to include one is the volume made for the king. Within Vérard's work overall, thirty-eight scenes depict him offering a book to a patron. Most are men, with Charles VIII predominating.[12] Only ten presentation scenes portray women, and eight of these depict two of the most important women in France of that time — Anne de Bretagne, Charles' wife and queen; and Louise de Savoie, mother of the future Francis I, in whose company she is always shown. Anne too is usually shown with her husband Charles. In fact, there are only four instances of a woman alone in a presentation miniature in all of Vérard's books: two depict Anne de Bretagne, one is a generalized, non-specific woman, and the fourth is the woman in black shown here.[13] Clearly, this woman must have been someone of very high rank and importance.

The inclusion of this woman as protagonist in seven small scenes is also rare. While such occur in the case of the other two copies of the *Horloge* with

---

[10] The Master of the Chronique scandaleuse, active from 1493 to ca. 1510, is considered to have been a less conservative, more novel artist than others of his circle. See François Avril and Nicole Reynaud, *Les Manuscrits à peintures en France, 1440-1520* (Paris: Flammarion, 1993), 255, 276–77. He worked on seven books for Vérard and had a clientele of very high rank.

[11] Winn, *Anthoine Vérard*, reproduces numerous other miniatures that depict Vérard presenting his book to a patron, e.g. figs. 4.3, 4.5, and 4.6 to Charles VIII, 5.14 to Louis XII, and 5.8a to Henry VII of England.

[12] Winn, *Anthoine Vérard*, whose data I have used here, cautions (69 n. 33) that she has not been able to examine all the extant vellum copies of Vérard's works. Her lists (474–83) show the result of her work up to that point. The breakdown is Charles VIII (18); Louise de Savoie and Francis I (5); Charles d'Angoulême (2); Louis XII (2); Henry VII (2); Jean d'Albret (1); Anne de Bretagne (3, one of which is in combination with Charles VIII); prince (3); king (1); lady (2).

[13] Mary Beth Winn, "Treasures for the Queen: Anne de Bretagne's Books from Anthoine Vérard," *Bibliothèque d'Humanisme et Renaissance* 68 (1996): 667–80; Winn, *Anthoine Vérard*, 482–83.

numerous pictures,[14] an examination of Vérard's work reveals how rare this is. While a few works include the patron in more than one miniature, none have the patron inserted in so many scenes as these three copies of the *Horloge*: further evidence of the importance of these particular patrons including the woman in black.

A second clue to her identity can be found in the women accompanying her in the presentation scene. The kneeling two in front are extremely well dressed: one in a gold-laced dress with ermine cuffs, the other in a dress with ermine cuffs and trim. In fifteenth-century France, fur was a sign of luxury worn by royalty and nobility, and a hierarchy of types developed based on rarity and price. The rarest and most expensive fur was ermine, and its presence on the dresses of these women indicates their high status.[15] In other words, the patron of this book had a court of noble ladies, implying that her status was even higher than theirs: that she was, in short, a member of the royal family.

But what can we conclude from the patron's own dress: why is she not wearing ermine-trimmed garments? Instead she is dressed almost entirely in black. The color and simplicity of her clothing provides our next clue. Her dress suggests several possibilities: that she was a widow, that she favored simplicity in her dress, and/or that she was extremely pious. Widowhood may or may not be the case, as black was certainly not confined to mourning clothes, but was a common and fashionable color by this time.[16] In the small scenes the woman also wears black; however, her mantle is lengthened to resemble a nun's garb. The stress throughout the miniatures on her devotion is enhanced by the portrayal of Eternal Wisdom in the guise of a nun, albeit a very elegant one (Figure 4), whereas her standard iconography is a well-dressed laywoman.[17] Moreover,

---

[14] In BnF vélins 359, the king is presented as the protagonist in nineteen small scenes. In BnF vélins 360, Charles d'Angoulême fulfills this role in seventeen small scenes.

[15] Françoise Piponnier and Perrine Mane, *Se vêtir au Moyen Age* (Paris: Société nouvelle Adam Biro, 1995), 34. The exorbitant price of ermine certainly restricted its use. Inventories often listed the amount of ermine used in items of clothing, further testimony to its adding of value to garments.

[16] Black as a fashionable color can be found solidly established in France by the 1440s and by the end of the century became the dominant color for both male and female clothing. See Margaret Scott, *Late Gothic Europe, 1400–1500* (London: Mills & Boon, 1980), 171.

[17] To anyone accustomed to the visual portrayal of Eternal Wisdom elsewhere, her appearance here is surprising, for she is normally presented as a well-dressed lady wearing a crown or halo or both. Certainly that is how she is portrayed in the other vellum copies of Vérard's *Horloge*. Given that Eternal Wisdom was considered to be the alter ego of Christ, a portrayal of her as a nun is really quite odd in theological terms, presenting the viewer with a strange paradox. As the disciple marries Eternal Wisdom (i.e. Christ), and nuns are also brides

Figure 4. Disciple with Eternal Wisdom. Horloge de Sapience, 1493/94. New York. Pierpont Morgan Library, 17591, fol. c4r.

in the presentation scene the woman is praying. This is decidedly rare as compared to other presentation scenes by this artist and others in which the patron routinely reaches for the book (Figure 2). [18] Whoever she was, this woman was unusually devout.

When we also consider what we know about Vérard himself, we find a final clue to her identity, for we know that in the 1490s Vérard aimed above all to please his foremost patron, Charles VIII, in the books that he produced.[19] It has been suggested that at least one book was given to someone precisely because of her relationship to the king.[20] This leads to the inference that the woman in black was someone within the court with whom Vérard hoped to win favor.

---

of Christ, this association would seem to be impossible. In the case of the PML *Horloge*, it may be that the artist decided that this more humble and devout portrayal of Christ's alter ego would better suit a book whose patron was a woman of great piety herself.

[18] See for example the presentation miniatures of Anne de Bretagne (Winn, *Anthoine Vérard*, figs. 3.4, 4.8, 5.13) in which Anne reaches for the book. This common action can be found in the presentation miniatures of Charles VIII, Louis XII and Henry VII referred to in note 11.

[19] Vérard's choice of which books to publish during these years was largely determined by the king's taste: Winn, *Anthoine Vérard*, 52, 55, 104.

[20] Winn, *Anthoine Vérard*, 75, in discussing Vérard's 1504 edition of the *Temple d'Honneur* by Jean Lemaire de Belges, with a dedication to Anne de Beaujeu, suggests the following reason as to why the work was produced: "If anything prompted Vérard to publish this text, aside perhaps from Lemaire's financing, it was probably the fact that Anne de France was the sister of Charles VIII, Vérard's first and foremost patron." Vérard often gave unsolic-

Combining all of these points leads us to surmise that this woman was un-usually devout, of royal status, and living at the court of Charles VIII. Three of the prominent women at the court may be eliminated: Anne de Bretagne (Charles' wife and queen), Anne de Beaujeu (Charles' eldest sister), and Louise de Savoie (Charles d'Angoulême's wife). From evidence in books and inventories, the book collections of these women are by now well known. The fact that this book has never appeared in the records of any princely collection, including those of these three families, makes it unlikely that it belonged to one of them.

Yet one other woman was very much a part of that court circle in 1493/94: Jeanne de France, also known as Jeanne de Valois, the other sister of Charles VIII and the wife of Louis d'Orléans. A deeply pious woman, known to be much loved by her brother the king, whose later circumstances removed her personal posses-sions from the royal collections, Jeanne de France emerges as a serious contender to be the woman in black.

Born in 1464 to Louis XI and Charlotte de Savoie, Jeanne was the middle child between Anne and Charles.[21] As she suffered from a deformity, her father the king could not bear the sight of her and sent her at age five to Lignières to be raised.[22] Jeanne was betrothed as a baby to her cousin Louis d'Orléans, and the

---

ited books to members of the aristocracy and royalty in the hope of gaining commissions. See Winn, *Anthoine Vérard*, 123, 129, 399–400 for examples.

[21] Françoise Guyard, *Chronique de l'Annonciade: Vies de la Bienheureuse Jeanne de France et du Bienheureux Gabriel-Maria*, ed. Jean-Fr. Bonnefoy (Paris: Editions Franciscans, 1937), the earliest extant life of Jeanne, dates from 1561 and was written by a fellow member of the Annonciade; however, its focus is on Jeanne's later life and the founding of the order. Moreover, as it may have been written with the hope of Jeanne's beatification, its historical accuracy cannot be assumed, as historians have noted various errors. Louis Doni-d'Attichy, *Tableau de la Sainte vie et mort de Jeanne de Valois, fille de Louis XI, épouse de Louis XII, fondatrice de l'ordre de l'Annonciade* (Paris: Cramoisy, 1625), though later, is more complete in its telling of Jeanne's entire life history. Numerous biographies exist from the nineteenth and twentieth centuries. Among the most useful and relevant are Claude-Charles Pierquin de Gembloux, *Histoire de Jeanne de Valois, duchesse d'Orléans et de Berry, reine de France, fonda-trice de l'ordre des Annonciades* (Paris: Gaume frères, 1840); René de Maulde, *Jeanne de France, Duchesse d'Orleans et de Berry (1464–1505)* (Paris: H. Champion, 1883); Ann M.C. Forster, *The Good Duchess: Joan of France, 1464–1505* (London: Burns, Oates & Washbourne, 1950); Jean-François Drèze, *Raison d'Etat, Raison de Dieu: Politique et Mystique chez Jeanne de France* (Pa-ris: Beauchesne, 1991); *Jeanne de France (1464–1505), duchesse de Berry, fondatrice de l'ordre de l'Annonciade* (Bourges: Bibliotheque Municipale de Bourges, 2002); Dominique Dinet, Pierre Moracchini, and Marie-Emmanuel Portebos, eds., *Jeanne de France et l'Annonciade: actes du colloque international de l'Institut Catholique de Paris* (Paris: Editions du Cerf, 2004).

[22] Forster, *The Good Duchess*, 12.

marriage took place in 1476. With the groom detesting the marriage, the two did not live together afterwards, but Jeanne continued to reside at Lignières.[23]

Her life changed in August of 1483 with the death of her father, whereupon Jeanne returned to Amboise, home of her mother, Charlotte, who unfortunately also died in December of that year. Her sister Anne, officially regent until Charles came of age, arranged for Jeanne to have an allowance and house in Amboise, although her husband Louis was rarely there.[24] Louis, in fact, launched a series of rebellions against the throne, for which he was imprisoned from 1488 to 1491,[25] only being released due to Jeanne's petitions to her brother the king. With Charles' unexpected death in 1498 and his son having died in 1495, the crown passed out of his direct line to Louis, who became Louis XII. Upon ascending to the throne, Louis promptly and successfully instituted annulment proceedings against Jeanne in order to marry his brother's widow, Anne de Bretagne.[26] Jeanne was given the duchy of Berry and moved to Bourges in 1499 where she spent the rest of her life.[27] In 1501 she founded an order of nuns dedicated to the Virgin Mary, the Order of the Annonciade. She herself was professed in 1504,[28] died in 1505, was beatified in 1742 and canonized in 1950.

In considering whether Jeanne de France could have been the patron for Vérard's book, the following information is pertinent:

First of all, Jeanne had throughout her life a reputation for deep religiosity, far exceeding the usual levels of her day. At age five, she heard the voice of the Virgin Mary telling her to found a religious order in her honor.[29] It was this wish

---

[23] Drèze, *Raison*, 51–71.

[24] According to Maulde, *Jeanne*, 145, one of Anne's first acts as regent was to have her superintendent of finances advise on Jeanne's situation. With Louis unwilling to provide anything for his wife, Anne initially had Jeanne stay with her, and then authorized Jeanne to have a pension of 10,000 livres, the same as her own, plus a house to live in: Maulde, *Jeanne*, 146, 149.

[25] This was known as the "Guerre Folle" or "Mad War" and lasted from 1485 to 1488.

[26] The proceedings can be found in René de Maulde, *Procédures politiques du règne de Louis XII* (Paris: Impr. nationale, 1885). Louis claimed that he was unable to have sexual relations with Jeanne because of her deformity, although Jeanne provided evidence to the contrary.

[27] For details of the generous settlement that Louis gave her, see Simone Bertière, *Les Reines de France au Temps des Valois: Le beau XVIe siècle* (Paris: Editions de Fallois, 1994), 122; Forster, *The Good Duchess*, 81.

[28] Jeanne took vows of poverty, chastity, and obedience, as well as a vow of enclosure in mitigated form (not to leave town without permission). As she relied on her income as a duchess to aid the people of her duchy and the nuns under her care, she could not totally abandon the world: Forster, *The Good Duchess*, 132–34.

[29] Guyard, *Vies*, 76, describes the event as taking place while Jeanne was praying in church, whereupon she felt that Mary said in her heart: "Avant ta mor, tu fond[e]ras une religion en l'honneur de moy. Et en ce faisant, me fairas un grand plaisir et service" (Before your

that Jeanne later fulfilled by establishing the Annonciade. According to contemporaries and her earliest biographers, Jeanne was known for her spirituality and would have preferred not to marry, but to dedicate her life to God.[30] While living in Bourges, Jeanne engaged in acts of self-punishment and deprivation.[31] She was also believed to have united her heart with Christ's in a mystic marriage.[32] Certainly, more than many women, Jeanne would have appreciated the religious messages of the *Horloge*, encouraging her towards understanding of and union with Christ.

A second point to consider is whether Jeanne owned books. Given her status and background, this is a certainty.[33] Descriptions of her life at Lignières indicate that she read books, especially religious books.[34] Unfortunately, the only book ever linked to Jeanne is a book of hours allegedly made during her time in Bourges, but this attribution is not certain.[35] Surprisingly, scholars have completely overlooked Jeanne as a book owner. Though many books belonging to her

death, you will found a religion in my honor. And in so doing, you will do me a great pleasure and service). All biographers repeat this, e.g. Doni-d'Attichy, *Tableau*, 56; Drèze, *Raison*, 137.

[30] Guyard, *Vies*, 240. Doni-d'Attichy notes that the king was annoyed by Jeanne's greater inclination towards the monastic and religious life rather than one secular and worldly (*Tableau*, 42).

[31] See Guyard, *Vies*, 84, who describes how Jeanne wore not only a hairshirt, but also a piece of wood with silver nails pricking her stomach, and how at night when alone she disciplined herself until she bled. She also deprived herself of certain foods for austerity's sake. Doni-d'Attichy, *Tableau*, 197–99, recounts the same story with slight embellishments.

[32] Guyard, *Vies*, 181–84, tells this story.

[33] Hasenohr, "L'essor," 248, in discussing the rise of private libraries in France in the fourteenth and fifteenth centuries says that all queens owned beautiful books, with certain princesses also owning many, giving as examples from the late fifteenth century Charlotte de Savoie, Anne of Beaujeu, and Anne de Bretagne. Legaré, "Reassessing Women's Libraries," 209, also states that queens, noblewomen, even ladies of the bourgeoisie owned manuscripts or printed books, basing this statement on having studied libraries in France and Burgundy from 1300 to 1500.

[34] Drèze, *Raison*, 138, 140.

[35] Louis de Lacger, "Les Masques de la Bienheureuse Jeanne de France, Fondatrice de l'Ordre de l'Annonciade," *Revue d'histoire franciscaine* 8.1 (1931): 56–74, at 57–59, discusses the book (Arsenal, ms. 644) and the miniature on folio 26v, believing the work to depict Jeanne on account of the escutcheon of France and the initials IM standing for Jeanne-Marianne, although her physical appearance is quite generalized. He suggests that the miniature was painted between her arrival in Bourges and her death. Elodie Lequain, "Anne de France et les livres: la tradition et le pouvoir," in *Patronnes et mécènes en France à la Renaissance*, ed. Kathleen Wilson-Chevalier (Saint-Etienne: Publications de l'université de Saint-Etienne, 2007), 155–68, at 157, is more cautious, suggesting that the book belonged to a royal princess, perhaps Anne de Beaujeu or her sister Jeanne.

mother Charlotte have not been traced to Charles or Anne, no one has suggested that Jeanne too would have inherited part of her mother's collection.[36] But Charlotte in her will left a provision for Jeanne, the only provision explicitly made to any of her children.[37] It is most probable, therefore, that Jeanne too inherited some of her mother's books and added to that collection after Charlotte died.

Where then are her books? Why is there no record of them? The answer lies in the fact that in 1499 Jeanne left the court, never to return. She certainly would have taken her personal property with her. Unfortunately, no records exist in Bourges of Jeanne's possessions. Her will was simple and contains nothing about her personal effects.[38] The Bourges archival records mainly concern the Annonciade rather than Jeanne herself.[39]

The most important evidence to consider therefore in determining whether Jeanne might have been the intended owner of this book is her life and activities during the time when it was created.

Would she have been present at court so that Vérard would have been aware of her and might have considered her a likely client? Yes indeed. Jeanne in those years was visibly present at court, and had been so since 1483. She resided mainly

---

[36] Ursula Baurmeister and Marie-Pierre Laffitte, *Des Livres et des Rois: La Bibliothèque Royale de Blois* (Paris: Bibliothèque Nationale, 1992), 71, referring to an inventory made after Charlotte's death listing 160 volumes as hers, opine that these volumes were divided among her children, without however mentioning Jeanne's name. Legaré, *Le Pèlerinage* notes that over forty books once belonging to Charlotte have not been traced, speculating that Anne may have disposed of many of these missing books before her own death in 1522 (192). She too does not raise the possibility that some may have gone to Jeanne.

[37] Théodore Godefroy, ed., *Histoire de Charles VIII, roi de France, et des choses mémorables advenues de son règne, depuis l'an 1483 jusques à 1498* (Paris: Impr. Royale, 1684), 364: "Item. Donnons à nostre fille d'Orleans la somme de deux cents marcs d'argent de nostre vaisselle, pour luy aider à soy emmenager" (Item. We give to our daughter of Orleans the sum of two hundred silver marks of our plate, to help her to fit herself out). The will was written at Amboise on December 1, 1483.

[38] See Guyard, *Vies*, 282–88 for details.

[39] Drèze, *Raison*, 31, tells us that Jeanne left only about a dozen letters that mainly relate to the captivity of Louis in 1488–89; to the annulment process in the autumn of 1498; and to the taking possession of her property of Berry in 1498–99. Maulde, *Jeanne*, 378, says that there is no trace of Jeanne's short administration in Berry and no registers of her treasury in the Archives de Cher. Unfortunately, fires and civil wars destroyed much evidence of her time there, with the city archives lost as well as the church itself. With the 1562 Wars of Religion, troops wrecked the church in Bourges and defamed Jeanne's remains: Forster, *The Good Duschess*, 84, 86, 170. Correspondence with Xavier Truffaut (Archives départmentales du Cher) and Marie-Jeanne Boistart (Réseau des bibliothèques municipales de Bourges) confirms the lack of any inventory of Jeanne's personal possessions made during her years at Bourges or upon her death.

at Amboise and participated in important state events. For example, the list of attendees at the baptism of Charles' son, Charles Orland, in 1492 includes Jeanne and her husband.[40] During the 1490s, Jeanne traveled to various chateaux as was the custom,[41] and was recorded as present at a grand dinner at Blois in 1495 attended by all three siblings and their spouses.[42]

We can also assume that she would have had her own court of ladies, based on evidence from her years at Bourges. Several highly born women were part of her entourage there, including duchesses and queens.[43] This court was an echo of an earlier one that she had at Lignières.[44] It is reasonable to assume that, while married to Louis and living in and around Amboise between 1483 and 1498, Jeanne also had her own court, the one that may be visually referred to in the presentation miniature here.

Events surrounding Jeanne's unhappy marriage to Louis indicate that she had a close relationship with the king, her brother. Despite Louis' rejection of her, Jeanne remained loyal to him and worked tirelessly for his release from prison. She took her case to Charles whom she begged to free Louis, with Charles finally agreeing out of love for his sister.[45] Throughout the period of Louis'

---

[40] Hilarion de la Coste, *Les Eloges de nos Rois et des Enfans de France* (Paris: Cramoisy, 1643), 62–63, describes the baptism held on October 13 at Plessis. Louisa Stuart Costello, *Memoirs of Anne, Duchess of Brittany, twice Queen of France* (London: W. & F.G. Cash, 1855), 195, comments that after Louis was freed, Jeanne lived separately from him "in pious seclusion, seldom appearing at Court on festive occasions, but only on those of State."

[41] According to Maulde, *Jeanne* (229) and Drèze (*Raison*, 84), during the period after Louis' release from prison, the two were seen together at Tours, Amboise, Blois and Madeleine near Orleans, and at Chateauneuf-sur-Loire. Bertière (*Reines*, 103) and Forster (*The Good Duchess*, 56) add other chateaux to this list. Such traveling was common for the court. See Robert J. Knecht, *The French Renaissance Court, 1483–1589* (New Haven: Yale Univ. Press, 2008), 40, for details of Charles VIII's travels.

[42] Maulde, *Jeanne*, 241.

[43] Doni-d'Attichy, *Tableau*, 198, refers to her "Dames et Damoiselles" leaving her room at night. This reference indicates ladies of quality, not servants. Maulde, *Jeanne de France*, 392–400, confirms this in describing the little court that formed around Jeanne as suitable to her rank and state. He names her closest advisors, as well as the small circle of women, all of whom were very highborn, giving details of their affiliations.

[44] Drèze says that Anne de Culan, her guardian, grouped around her young women of honor (*Raison*, 137).

[45] Maulde, *Jeanne* (224–25) quotes both Jeanne's plea and her brother's reply. Louis was released in May 1491 and had his goods restored to him a month later. In telling this story, Doni-d'Attichy notes (*Tableau*, 115) that some had noted that the king was resolute because Louis had badly treated "Madame Jeanne his sister, whom he loved particularly, because they were both born under the crown" ("Madame Ieane sa soeur, laquelle il aymoit particulierement, à cause qu'ils estoient tous deux nez sous la Couronne").

imprisonment, many observed Charles' affection for Jeanne.[46] She also received extra funds from the royal chancellery during this period due to her close relationship to Charles.[47]

This evidence of Charles' close and affectionate bond with his sister is further seen in his repeated efforts in later years to pressure Louis to fulfill his husbandly duties. While Louis did live with Jeanne immediately after his release, afterwards Charles noticed discord between them and often urged Louis to visit Jeanne.[48] Charles also increased Jeanne's pension in 1495. This concern for Jeanne's welfare and happiness lasted until Charles' death in 1498. Certainly their close relationship was well known, and one can assume that Vérard, well versed in court goings-on, might have concluded that Jeanne was someone to favor in order to win approval from the king.

One final piece of evidence relates to Jeanne's clothing. Numerous accounts note Jeanne's simple dress and modest lifestyle during her years at court. Moreover, during Louis' imprisonment, this lifestyle was enforced by the confiscation of his possessions. As he was absent, Jeanne was considered to be like a widow.[49] She was even recorded as dressing like a widow, and was said to have worn mourning clothes when she pleaded with Charles to release Louis.[50] Although there is no record of her dress in the following years, her deep religiosity and simplicity of lifestyle along with her wearing widow's weeds for three years might well have caused Vérard (and/or his artist) to decide to portray her all in black.

It is true that there is no conclusive proof linking Jeanne de France to this book; yet there is an abundance of circumstantial evidence pointing in that direction. In the many recent studies of women's book patronage in fifteenth century France, Jeanne de France is never even mentioned. Yet it cannot be doubted that she too, like her mother, her sister, her cousins, and her friends would have read, enjoyed, and owned books. The Pierpont Morgan Library *Horloge* is a likely candidate to have been one of them.

UNIVERSITY OF HONG KONG

---

[46] Maulde, *Jeanne*, 213–14.

[47] Drèze, *Raison*, 82.

[48] Maulde, *Jeanne*, 241–42; Drèze, *Raison*, 92–93.

[49] Maulde, *Jeanne*, 177, 217; Drèze, *Raison*, 82.

[50] Maulde, *Jeanne*, 224; Françoise Bouchard, *Sainte Jeanne de France: La Reine servante de Marie* (Montsûrs: Editions Résiac, 1999), 41.

"All the Adulteries of Art": The Dramatic Excerpts of Margaret Bellasys's BL MS. Add. 10309[1]

LAURA ESTILL

ARGARET BELLASYS'S VERSE MISCELLANY, BL MS. ADD. 10309, CONTAINS three dramatic extracts from Renaissance plays. First let me introduce you to the manuscript: BL MS. Add. 10309 is a more than 300-page-long duodecimo manuscript that was written in the late 1620s and early 1630s.[2] The first seventy-five pages are filled by "The Characterismes of Vices," a moralizing tract based on works by the Puritan preacher Thomas Adams and Bishop Joseph Hall.[3] The rest of the miscellany includes poetry by Donne, Carew, Jonson, Herbert, and others.

We do not know much for certain about Margaret Bellasys's identity. There were at least five women named Margaret Bellasys from roughly the time period this manuscript was compiled.[4] What we do know is that Margaret signed her

---

[1] This paper was first delivered at the 2010 International Congress of Medieval Studies, Kalamazoo, MI, at a panel entitled "Early Modern Women's Manuscripts," Margaret P. Hannay presiding.

[2] Peter Beal, comp., *Index of English Literary Manuscripts*, Vols. 1 & 2 (London & New York: Mansell, 1980 & 1993); *Catalogue of English Literary Manuscripts*, https://celm2.dighum.kcl.ac.uk.

[3] Lambert Ennis argues that Bellasys wrote the opening tract and altered the source-texts enough to make it an original work. See "Margaret Bellasys' 'Characterismes of Vices'," *PMLA* 56.1 (1941): 141–50.

[4] Most scholarship accepts Peter Beal's and the British Library catalogue's identification of Margaret as the daughter of Thomas Belasyse (1577–1652), first Viscount Fauconberg of Henknowle, a royalist who eventually embraced Cromwell and who converted to Catholicism

name on the last page of the manuscript. Bellasys's miscellany differs from other better-known women's manuscript miscellanies, such as those by Anne Southwell (Folger MS. V.b.198), Ann Bowyer (Bodleian MS. Ashmole 51), or Constance Aston Fowler (Huntington MS. HM 904)[5] because Margaret Bellasys may not have actually written this manuscript. BL MS. Add. 10309, however, deserves consideration because it was owned by a woman.

Ian Moulton suggests that this collection was written by a professional scribe, because of the neat hand and use of catchphrases, though Ilona Bell and Margaret Hannay point out that neither of these elements rule out a woman compiler.[6] The question remains, however, about Bellasys's involvement in the creation of this manuscript. Did she select the poems and songs? Without assuming that Bellasys had the agency of a compiler, I follow Sasha Roberts and Bruce R. Smith in considering Bellasys the primary reader of these texts (even if the compilation was created by a scribe).[7]

Bellasys's manuscript contains three extracts from drama. "I keep my horse, I keep my whore," from Middleton's *The Widow*, comments directly on systems of gender and ownership (f. 96). Jonson's "Still to be neat" from *Epicoene* is an anti-cosmetic diatribe about women and falseness (f. 100v). Jonson's "Come sweet Celia, let us prove" from *Volpone* is a carpe diem song that Volpone uses to woo the married Celia (f. 117). These selections share three traits: they are all taken from plays, they are all songs, and they all comment on ideas of gender.

---

later in his life. As Ian Frederick Moulton points out, however, this Margaret died in 1624: see *Before Pornography: Erotic Writing in Early Modern England* (Oxford: Oxford Univ. Press, 2000), 230, n. 71. Gary Taylor suggests that another Margaret (d. 1671, daughter of Sir George Selby and wife of William Bellasys) might have written the manuscript: see "Some Manuscripts of Shakespeare's Sonnets," *Bulletin of the John Rylands Library* 68 (1985–86): 210–46.

[5] For a general discussion of women's manuscript miscellanies, see Elizabeth Clarke, "Women's Manuscript Miscellanies in Early Modern England," in *Teaching Tudor and Stuart Women Writers*, ed. Susanne Woods and Margaret P. Hannay (New York: MLA, 2000), 52–60; and Victoria E. Burke, "Manuscript Miscellanies," in *The Cambridge Companion to Early Modern Women's Writing*, ed. Laura Lunger Knoppers (Cambridge: Cambridge Univ. Press, 2009), 54–67. See *The Southwell-Sibthorpe Commonplace Book*, ed. J. Klene, MRTS 147 (Tempe: ACMRS, 1997), and *The Verse Miscellany of Constance Aston Fowler,* ed. D. Aldrich-Watson, MRTS 210 (Tempe: ACMRS, 2000).

[6] Moulton, *Before Pornography*, 58. Bell and Hannay made these comments at the International Congress on Medieval Studies in Kalamazoo, Michigan, 2010 in the question and answer period for the Renaissance English Texts Society panel.

[7] Sasha Roberts, *Reading Shakespeare's Poems in Early Modern England* (London and New York: Palgrave Macmillan, 2003), esp. 179–83; Bruce R. Smith, *Homosexual Desire in Shakespeare's England: A Cultural Poetics* (Chicago: Univ. of Chicago Press, 1994), 239. Though Taylor suggests that there might have been two main contributors to this manuscript ("Some MSS"), I concur with Roberts who identifies only one hand throughout the manuscript.

Dramatic excerpting (or extracting) is the practice of copying selections from a play, either at a performance or from a printed playbook. In the early 1610s, Edward Pudsey transcribed some of the actors' lines while attending a performance of *Othello*.[8] In *Volpone*, Ben Jonson dramatizes a foolish character, Sir Politic Would-be, who collects "notes / Drawn out of playbooks." Many dramatic "extracts" (particularly songs), as this paper discusses, may not have been copied from the play itself, but rather taken from an intermediate source. The print *Index of English Literary Manuscripts* lists more than two hundred manuscripts that contain dramatic extracts from early modern plays written before the closure of the theatres in 1642 — and the forthcoming online *Catalogue* will list even more. Even so, many dramatic extracts have not been thoroughly examined or, in some cases, even catalogued. Recently, scholars have turned to women manuscript compilers as well as women play readers and playgoers. Examining how playgoers and play readers adapt, respond to, and recontextualize dramatic material adds to our knowledge of print and manuscript circulation as well as early modern reading and writing habits. Here, I analyze three dramatic songs in order to discuss one woman's engagement with the ideas of gender presented in early modern theatre as registered in her verse miscellany.

The first dramatic extract found in Bellasys's manuscript is a song from Middleton's play *The Widow*. The main plot of this play revolves around numerous suitors seeking to marry Valeria, who, like all the most attractive widows in Renaissance plays, has a lot of money. The song comes at the beginning of the third act, when Ansaldo, a handsome youth, meets Latrocinio, who is singing. In this context, Middleton could have chosen almost any song to entertain his audience.[9] Middleton's thief, Latrocinio, however, sings "I keep my horse, I keep my whore," which, as the title in Bellasys's manuscript reminds us, is about a cut-purse. The speaker in the song (just like the singer in the play) is a thief. With the last line of the song, "Deliver your purse, Sir," Latrocinio draws his weapon and attempts to attack Ansaldo. Ansaldo pulls out his gun and orders the thief to sing a new song as punishment. In the end, though, Latrocinio is as triumphant as the thief in the song who has his choice of women and gets the money: Latrocinio's

---

[8] Pudsey's commonplace book is in two parts: Bodleian MS. Eng. poet. d. 3 and Shakespeare Birthplace Trust office ER 82. See Juliet Gowan, "An Edition of Edward Pudsey's Commonplace Book (c. 1600–1615) from the Manuscript in the Bodleian Library" (MPhil thesis, Univ. of London, 1967), the only edition of Pudsey's manuscript, though it remains unpublished.

[9] Latrocinio's first song, "Kuck before and Kuck behind" (3.1.6), is now lost, which attests to how it circulated independently from the play. For a discussion of the separate circulation of songs from plays, see Tiffany Stern, *Documents of Performance in Early Modern England* (Cambridge: Cambridge Univ. Press, 2009), esp. ch. 5.

friends arrive and they steal everything from Ansaldo, including the shirt from his back. To celebrate, the thieves sing yet another song.

"I keep my horse" is appropriate for the play not only because of the parallels the song's speaker has with Latrocinio, but also because it comments on the themes in the play. The opening line, "I keep my horse, I keep my whore" is about gender and ownership, just like the main plot of the play. The singer calls the unnamed whore 'mine,' claiming ownership over her, which contrasts with Valeria's position as a widow, who is not a woman owned, but a woman able to own property. The song jokingly suggests the possibility of rape; "the cook maid has no mind to sin" but feels forced to please the thief. As Latrocinio threatens Martia-as-Ansaldo with a weapon and takes something against her will, this scene also brings up the potential of rape, particularly for audience members and readers familiar with the play, who know that Ansaldo will later be revealed to be a woman. Latrocinio's theft, then, takes on sexual overtones when he and his companions rob and partially strip Ansaldo/Martia.

While Middleton's song can be read as a microcosm of the different themes in the play, in Bellasys's manuscript "I keep my horse" is entirely recontextualized. The compiler of BL MS. Add. 10309 did not copy the song from a print edition of the play: although the play was probably written around 1616, it was not published until 1652, well after this manuscript was compiled. The version of the song in BL MS. Add. 10309 differs from the 1652 quarto, though the differences could be explained by reconstruction from memory.[10]

As "I keep my horse" demonstrates, dramatic extracts are not always taken directly from the play. Songs in particular circulated separately from the plays: songs are easier to memorize than speeches and function as a self-contained artistic unit, unlike some other dramatic extracts where readers and playgoers

---

[10] In Gary Taylor's textual notes to *The Widow*, he notes that Bellasys's manuscript is the furthest from the printed 1652 quarto of all extant versions of the songs (*Middleton and Early Modern Textual Culture*, 1087). Taylor claims the variants "either represent an authorially variant version of the song or a very corrupt transcription" (1087) and does not consider the possibility of memorial reconstruction. See *Thomas Middleton: The Collected Works* and *Thomas Middleton and Early Modern Textual Culture*, ed. Gary Taylor, John Lavagnino, et al. (Oxford: Oxford Univ. Press, 2007). This song is also found in Bodleian MS. Ashmole 38 (where it is attributed to the play), which suggests that the play was revived around 1636–1638. The generally accepted dates of manuscript compilation for BL MS. Add. 10309 run from the 1620s to the early 1630s, though this manuscript might have been written during a 1630s revival of the play. See Gary Taylor and Andrew J. Sabol, "Middleton, Music, and Dance," in *Thomas Middleton and Early Modern Textual Culture*, 119–81, esp. 152. In the preface to *The Collected Works*, Taylor suggests that this song was recycled in two later Restoration plays, but I have been unable to find corroborating evidence.

copied dialogue or selections from speeches. There are roughly twice as many manuscripts that contain songs from plays (with or without music) than non-sung dramatic excerpts. The wider circulation of songs from plays (as well as the after-life of this song in the late seventeenth century) attest to songs' ability to exist as separate pieces of artwork from their plays.[11]

The second dramatic extract in BL MS. Add. 10309 is the anti-cosmetic diatribe, "Still to be neat," from Jonson's *Epicoene* (see Figure 1). *Epicoene* shares a major plot point with *The Widow*, cross-dressed marriages. In the secondary plot of *The Widow*, the character of Martia/Ansaldo assumes multiple gender roles: a male actor performs a female character (Martia), who spends most of the play disguised as Ansaldo, the handsome young man. In the last act, Ansaldo dresses as a woman, and Francisco falls in love with her, much to the amusement of the other women who erroneously believe that Ansaldo is a man. At the end of the play Ansaldo is revealed to be Martia and her marriage to Francisco is saved.

The better-known cross-dressing in *Epicoene*, however, functions in the opposite way: it dissolves a marriage. Dauphine, intent on earning his inheritance early, convinces his rich uncle Morose to marry Epicoene, who is a boy dressed as a woman. At first, Epicoene seems like the perfect and quiet wife, but after they are married, she becomes a loud shrew. Finally, Morose offers Dauphine 500 pounds a year to end the marriage, whereupon Dauphine reveals that Epicoene was never a woman so his uncle can have a divorce. In a play about performing (false) gender, "Still to be neat" comments on the inherent falseness of cosmetics and fashion, the external markers typically associated with femininity. Clerimont, a friend of Dauphine who sings the song, rejects "powder'd" and "perfum'd" exteriors, claiming that they do not reflect interior beauty.[12] As a dramatic extract, "Still to be neat" encapsulates the idea of gender as performance on which Jonson bases his cross-dressing plot.

Like "I keep my horse" and the other extracts in this manuscript, this song can be read without the context of the play, however thematically linked to the rest of the play it may be. "Still to be neat" appears in six other manuscripts that

---

[11] *The Widow* was revived in the Restoration and William Lawes composed new music for "I keep my horse." In 1686, John Playford printed a version of Lawes' music and claimed the song was taken from Shakespeare's *1 Henry IV* in his *The second book of the Pleasant musical companion* . . . (London, 1686).

[12] For a further analysis of the significance of "Still to be neat" in relation to the events of the play see Mary Chan, *Music in the Theatre of Ben Jonson* (Oxford: Oxford Univ. Press, 1980), 70–72. Chan argues that the song "stands on its own, as an ideal never achieved" in the play (72); this paper further shows how the song stands on its own in manuscript circulation.

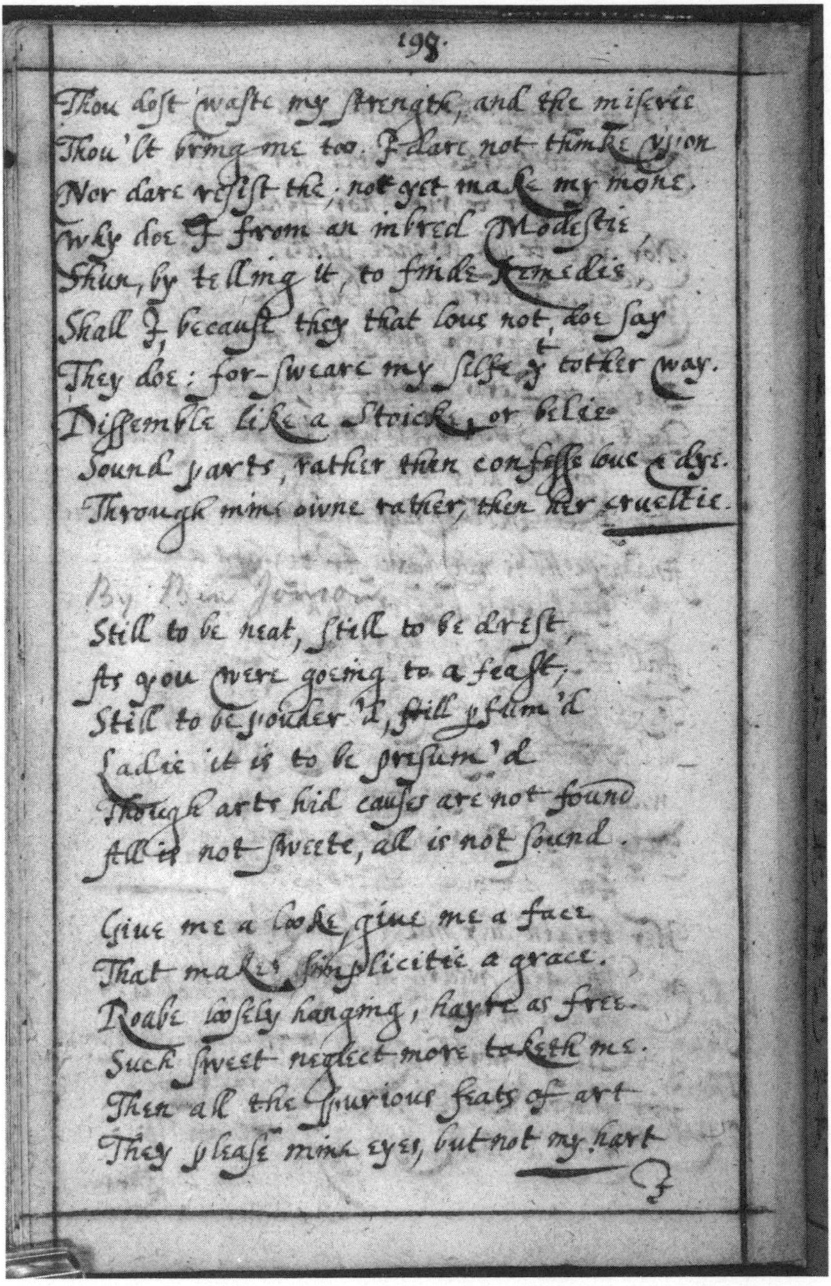

·198·

Thou dost waste my strength, and the miserie
Thou'lt bring me too, I dare not thinke vp'on
Nor dare resist thé, not yet make my mone,
Why doe I from an inbred Modestie
Shun, by telling it, to finde remedies,
Shall I, because they that loue not, doe say
They doe: for-sweare my selfe y'other way.
Dissemble like a Stoick, or belie
Sound parts, rather then confesse loue & dye.
Through mine oivne rather, then her crueltie.

By Ben: Jonson

Still to be neat, still to be drest,
As you were goeing to a feast;
Still to be pouder'd, still p'fum'd
Ladie it is to be presum'd
Though arts hid causes are not found
All is not sweete, all is not sound.

Giue me a looke, giue me a face
That makes simplicitie a grace.
Robe loosely hanging, hayre as free,
Such sweet neglect more taketh me.
Then all the curious feats of art
They please mine eyes, but not my hart

Figure 1. © British Library Board (BL MS. Add. 10309, f. 100v)

can be dated to the 1620–1630 period.[13] These other manuscript versions of "Still to be neat" suggest that this song may not have been copied from a print version of the play; it could have been copied from another manuscript, or, like "I keep my horse," it could have been written from memory. After its initial 1609 performance, *Epicoene* was revived twice before the Restoration: the first time, in 1619/20, and the second time, at court, in 1636.[14] When BL MS. Add. 10309 was being compiled, "Still to be neat" and other songs from *Epicoene* were not dated poems fading from memory, but rather songs that were performed and sung.[15]

As we reach the third dramatic extract in this manuscript, the category of dramatic extracts itself has to be called into question. Jonson's song, "Come sweet Celia, let us prove"[16] (see Figure 2) was initially written for *Volpone* (performed 1605–1606, printed 1607), but was also included in Jonson's collections of poems, *The Forest* (1616, as poem V). In the folio of Jonson's works (1616), which contains both *Volpone* and *The Forest*, this song appears twice. Generically, this piece is both a dramatic extract, that is, a section taken from the play, and also a self-contained piece that exists outside the play and circulates alone. The generic boundaries of this piece are further blurred when we consider the musical factor. When the lyrics are printed or copied by hand, this 'song' appears to be simply a poem, even if (as in *The Forest* and *Volpone*), it is given the title "Song." Even when it is printed with music, as in Alfonso Ferrabosco's *Ayres* (1609), the 'song' on the page is not the same as a performed song. Both versions of the song on the page (with and without music) can conjure mental performances of the song and the title reminds us of the insistent orality of theatre, music, and yes, even poetry. "Come sweet Celia" is simultaneously a song and a poem, simultaneously

---

[13] The *CELM* dates Bodleian MSS. Malone 19, Rawl. poet. 31, and Rawl. poet. 199 to the 1620s-1630s. Bodleian MSS. Ashmole 38, Eng. poet. e. 14, and BL MS. Egerton 2230 were probably compiled in the 1630s. Folger MS. V.a.162 and Bodleian MS. Don. d. 58 were written in the mid-seventeenth century and also contain this poem. I do not know the date of Yale MS. fc. 132/1.

[14] Richard Dutton, ed., *Epicene, or, the Silent Woman*, by Ben Jonson (Manchester: Manchester Univ. Press, 2003), 76.

[15] Like "I keep my horse," "Still to be neat" continued to circulate in the mid- to late seventeenth century. New York Public Library MSS. Drexel 4041 (ca. 1630–1650) and 4257 (ca. 1630–1659) both contain "Still to be neat" with musical notation. *Epicoene* was one of the first plays revived after the Restoration. The song was printed with music in Playford's *Select Ayres and Dialogues* (1669), and without music in the print verse miscellany, *Westminster Drollery* (1671).

[16] This song is more commonly written as "Come my Celia, let us prove," but I follow Bellasys's manuscript by saying "sweet." Bodleian MS. Malone 31 (according to the *Union First Line Index of Manuscript Poetry*) similarly begins "Come sweet Celia."

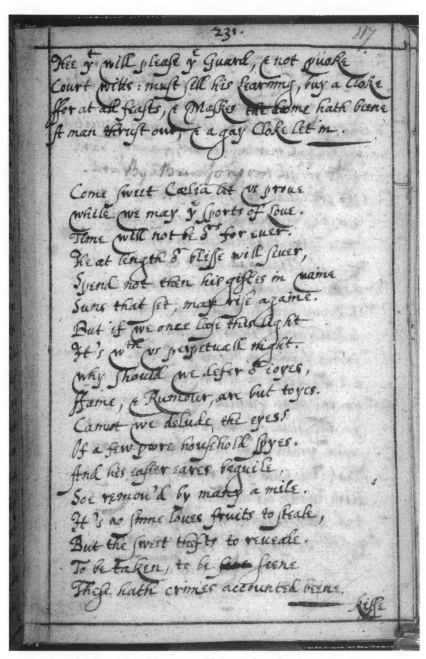

Figure 2. © British Library Board (BL MS. Add. 10309, f. 117r)

part of *Volpone* and separate from *Volpone*.[17] In Bellasys's manuscript, the poem is followed by "Kiss me, sweet, the wary lover" (f. 117v), which is published as a companion piece to "Come my Celia" in *The Forest*.[18]

Before concluding this discussion of the dramatic extracts in BL MS Add. 10309, there is one final selection to discuss: a piece titled "Verses before a masque" (f. 140v). This piece begins "Gentlemen, y'are welcome, but not from me" and is possibly unique in manuscript poetry.[19] This piece might be a prologue to a lost masque, or perhaps a prologue that we have not yet associated with a masque. Although it is unclear which masque this prologue prefaced, its presence in the manuscript perhaps points to the compiler's interest in drama in a way that my previous discussion of the multiple (and non-theatrical) possible sources of the other songs has belied. As a female, Bellasys is excluded from the anticipated male audience of the performance ("Gentlemen"). This prologue is an example of a dramatic extract whose dramatic origins are now lost: now it can only function as a self-contained piece without referring to its larger work.

When I began this paper, I had expected to discuss the gendered contents of this manuscript at more length (the poems directed at a specifically female readership, or ostensibly written for one particular woman; the poems in women's voices; the poems about women's bodies and sexuality). For instance, in Bellasys's manuscript, "I keep my horse" follows "Why should passion lead thee blind" (ff. 95v–96), a poem about loving a girl who is "too young to know delight," but when Cupid brings his fire to her, he will "mak[e] her taste and colour sweeter." Both of these poems focus on women's bodies as sexual objects to be enjoyed by a male at his leisure: when she "tastes" best or, in Middleton's song, even against her will.

---

[17] For a reading of the significance of "Come my Celia" in relation to the events of the play and Ferrabosco's music, see Chan, *Music,* 89–98.

[18] These pieces also appear together in Bodleian MS. Malone 31. "Come, my Celia" and "Kiss me, sweet," however, are more frequently found separately in manuscript. Bodleian MS. Rawl. poet. 172, Folger MSS. V.a. 262 and V.a. 339, and Yale B. 356 contain only "Come, my Celia," whereas Bodleian MSS. Eng. poet. e. 14, Firth e. 4, and Folger MS V.a. 345 contain only "Kiss me, sweet."

[19] This piece is not found in any other manuscripts according to the *Union First Line Index of English Verse* (http://firstlines.folger.edu), which includes the first line indices of the British Library, the Bodleian Library, the Huntington Library, the Folger Library, the Houghton Library, Leeds University Brotherton Collection, the Yale Beinecke Library, and some print sources. Furthermore, I have not been able to locate a print version of this speech in *Literature Online* or *Early English Books Online*.

Moulton concluded that the poems in this manuscript express "arguments for and against women," spoken by a variety of speakers.[20] Looking at some of these poems as dramatic extracts recontextualized in manuscripts shows that one individual poem can contain multiple and opposing views: the poems surrounding "I keep my horse" can emphasize the themes of sexual dominance over women, yet a reader familiar with the play might find the song a reminder of Middleton's strong female protagonist, Valeria, the titular Widow. Roberts argues that "these multiple perspectives add up to something more than the proliferation of points of view as *neither* poem emerges with an authentic, authoritative, or dominant voice on the position of women."[21] Roberts points out that all miscellanies foster "intertextual scepticism" in readers by juxtaposing different voices and points of views, while also creating an awareness of different forms, genres, and generic conventions.

This brings me to my conclusion, which is to ask: what are the generic conventions of dramatic extracts? To begin to answer this larger question, I turn back to Bellasys's text and the title of my presentation, taken from Jonson's "Still to be neat": "all the adulteries of art." In this case, adultery means, according to the *OED*, "adulteration, debasement, corruption."[22] Adulteration is "corruption by spurious admixture."[23] I believe the notion of adulterous art plays out in two different levels (beyond Jonson's original meaning) with regards to BL MS. Add. 10309. As a miscellany, this manuscript can be seen as being filled with "spurious admixture": it contains poems, songs, and selections from plays regardless of their literary lineage. The dramatic extracts in this manuscript, furthermore, are also adulterated because each one embodies a mixture of drama, song, and poetry.

Perhaps looking at the dramatic extracts in any given manuscript is an artificial heuristic; however, it is no more artificial than the other critical lenses we often use. Examining dramatic extracts follows Leah Marcus's call to "unedit the Renaissance": extracts allow us to find polysemous and variable meanings instead of narrowing the text to one possible reading.[24] While we will probably never ascertain Margaret Bellasys's opinions, analyzing dramatic extracts can help us understand

---

[20] Moulton, *Before Pornography,* 62.
[21] Sasha Roberts, "Women's Literary Capital in Early Modern England: Formal Composition and Rhetorical Display in Manuscript and Print," *Women's Writing* 14.2 (2007): 246–69.
[22] *Oxford English Dictionary,* "adultery," n. 2. http://dictionary.oed.com. The *OED* cites this particular example for proof of the meaning.
[23] *OED,* "adulteration," n. 1.
[24] Leah Marcus, *Unediting the Renaissance: Shakespeare, Marlowe, Milton* (London and New York: Routledge, 1996). See also Marcus, "Afterword: Confessions of a Reformed Uneditor," in *The Renaissance Text: Theory, Editing, Textuality,* ed. Andrew Murphy (Manchester: Manchester Univ. Press, 2000), 211–16.

the cultural and literary context in which her miscellany was compiled. Furthermore, dramatic extracts themselves remind us that the smallest part of a play can contain the meaning of that play, can stand alone with its own significance, and can gain new implications in different print and manuscript contexts.

TEXAS A&M UNIVERSITY

The Autograph Manuscript of Mary's *Wroth's* Pamphilia to Amphilanthus[1]

ILONA BELL

WROTH'S *PAMPHILIA TO AMPHILANTHUS* IS THE FIRST SEQUENCE OF love sonnets and the first substantial collection of original, secular lyrics written and published by an Englishwoman. It exists in two distinct versions: the printed sequence that appears at the end of the 1621 *Urania* and Folger Shakespeare Library manuscript V.a. 104, a fair copy written in Wroth's own italic hand with numerous corrections and multi-stage revisions.[2] Although the majority of the poems appear in both sequences, the differences are far more significant than scholars and editors have realized. The manuscript is clearly earlier since its revisions are incorporated into the printed sequence.[3] Gavin Alexander and Heather Dubrow have described the material makeup of the Folger manuscript, but the complete Folger sequence has never appeared in print.[4] All modern printed editions of *Pamphilia to Amphilanthus* reproduce the

---

[1] This paper was presented at the Sidney Society session on Mary Wroth at the 2010 Renaissance Society of America Conference in Venice, Italy, and the Renaissance English Text Society panel on Early Modern Women's Manuscripts at the International Congress on Medieval Studies in Kalamazoo, Michigan, 2010. Both panels were organized by Margaret Hannay.

[2] The poems were printed in Lady Mary Wroth, *The Countesse of Montgomeries Urania* (London: Prtd. for John Marriott and John Grismond, 1621).

[3] Mark Bland, *A Guide to Early Printed Books and Manuscripts* (Chichester, UK, and Malden, MA: Wiley-Blackwell, 2010), 93, comments that Mary Wroth has been "justly appreciated for [her] disciplined and elegant script."

[4] Gavin Alexander, "Constant Works: A Framework for Reading Mary Wroth," *Sidney Journal* 14 (2000): 5–32, and Heather Dubrow, "'And Thus Leave off': Reevaluating Mary Wroth's Folger Manuscript, V.a.104," *Tulsa Studies in Women's Literature* 22 (2003): 273–91, both provide insightful descriptions of the manuscript's material makeup. Tom W. N. Parker,

1621 sequence of poems, and virtually all critical analyses of Wroth's poetry are based on this well-known, readily available collection.

Steven May and I are working on an edition of *Pamphilia to Amphilanthus,* to be published in print and online that will include both the manuscript and the printed sequences.[5] The intellectual justification for our edition is based on the following claims: (1) The Folger sequence is a suspenseful, passionate collection of poems that is substantially different from and superior to the received 1621 text and that deserves to be published, analyzed, and taught in its own right. (2) By printing MS. V.a.104 for the first time, our edition will enable scholars, teachers, and students to recognize and study its boldly unconventional female lyric voice — a voice that is of great consequence for the history of English poetry from the Renaissance to the present day. (3) *Pamphilia to Amphilanthus* warrants a new, thoroughly annotated scholarly edition, since existing modern editions are sparsely annotated. By inviting readers to compare the manuscript and the printed text, our edition will show that Wroth's poems are far more enigmatic and complex than scholars have realized. (4) Wroth's intimate manuscript poems challenge current scholarly paradigms of English Renaissance women, bringing them into consonance with their continental contemporaries.

Our edition will supersede the most authoritative and widely cited modern edition, Josephine Roberts' *The Poems of Lady Mary Wroth,* which no longer meets current editorial procedures.[6] Wherever the two sequences differ in substance, Roberts argued in favor of the printed version because in 1983 it was standard practice to honor the author's final revisions. Roberts incorporated the revisions written above the line in MS. V.a.104, relegated the original altered wording to a list of variants, and failed to note many places where Wroth changed words by writing over individual letters. Most importantly, she reproduced the 1621 sequence on the grounds that it represented "the author's final intentions regarding

---

Proportional Form in the Sonnets of the Sidney Circle (Oxford: Clarendon Press, 1998), comments briefly on how the changes affect the formal pattern of songs and sonnets, but does not consider how Wroth's rearrangement altered the meaning of the poems.

[5] The Other Voice in Early Modern Europe: the Toronto Series, English Texts, Elizabeth H. Hageman (Toronto: Centre for Reformation and Renaissance Studies). Since this essay was written, *Mary Wroth's Poetry: An Electronic Edition,* ed. Paul Salzman, has become available online at http://wroth.latrobe.edu.au/

[6] Josephine A. Roberts, ed., *The Poems of Lady Mary Wroth* (Baton Rouge: Louisiana State Univ. Press, 1983; repr. 1992). Other modern editions include Gary F. Waller, ed., *Pamphilia to Amphilanthus* (Salzburg: Institut für Englische Sprache und Literatur, Univ. Salzburg, 1977); R. E. Pritchard, ed., *Poems: A Modernized Edition / Lady Mary Wroth* (Keele: Keele Univ. Press, 1996); Stephanie Hodgson-Wright, ed., *Women's Writing of the Early Modern Period, 1588–1688: An Anthology* (New York: Columbia Univ. Press, 2002); Lady Mary Wroth, *Pamphilia to Amphilanthus* (Oxford: Benediction Classics, 2007).

the order of the poems."[7] Roberts thought the printed sequence more polished and artful since many of 1621's revisions make minor improvements (regularize meter, correct scribal slips, fix subject/verb agreement). Yet, even though she reproduced the 1621 selection and order of poems, Roberts used Folger MS. V.a.104 as the copy text for what she thought of as accidentals (spelling, punctuation, capitalization, and some but not all verbal variants) on the grounds that Wroth's autograph manuscript reflects her own authorial preferences, whereas (Roberts posited) the printed text reflects the compositor's interpolations.[8]

Roberts' composite text has proven problematic on theoretical as well as practical grounds. To begin with, as recent bibliographical studies demonstrate, the loose spelling and punctuation of the Folger manuscript is less indicative of Wroth's own distinctive writing style than it is typical of manuscripts intended for private use. Importing the spelling, punctuation, and some of the wording from the Folger manuscript distorts the way Wroth would have expected and wanted her poems to appear in print. Moreover, as the textual analysis of Donne's manuscript variants has demonstrated in the years since 1983, the unitary theory of a single definitive text that seeks to recuperate and instantiate the author's "final" intentions fails to acknowledge the highly fluid nature of writing during this period when authors regularly prepared different versions for different audiences and different occasions.[9] Roberts imported individual readings from the manuscript because she did not realize that the 1621 first edition was a systematically revised, expurgated text. She failed to recognize that many of Wroth's changes are calculated evasions that cloud the diction, twist the syntax, and alter the context in order to obscure the meaning. Roberts' editorial decisions along with her introduction to "The Nature of the Poetry" have made it virtually impossible for readers to discern the dramatic development, psychological complexity, and originality of Wroth's earlier manuscript poetry.

---

[7] Roberts, *Poems* 74. Pritchard, *Poems,* 14, concurs that "[t]he ordering of *Pamphilia to Amphilanthus* for the 1621 printing must be Wroth's."

[8] Pritchard writes (*Poems,* 14–15), "it seems probable that someone else made [the 1621] edition more orthodox as regards spelling and punctuation, without solving all the problems, and it should not be thought of as having determining authority in every respect."

[9] For a powerful account of the phenomenon, see Mark Bland, "Making Variants," in *A Guide to Early Printed Books and Manuscripts,* 149–59. In *The Sidney Family Romance: Mary Wroth, William Herbert, and the Early Modern Construction of Gender* (Detroit: Wayne State Univ. Press, 1993), 194, Gary Waller comments that neither his use of 1621 as the copy text nor Roberts' use of the Folger manuscript as her copy text "is entirely satisfactory" since "*Pamphilia to Amphilanthus* might be best seen as a continuous text, unraveling as it is put together, never resting in a final form."

It is easy to understand why modern editors and scholars focused their attention on the printed version of *Pamphilia to Amphilanthus* since poets often polish earlier drafts and cull less successful poems when printing their collected works. Yet, during the early modern period, texts were commonly revised for print, not for esthetic reasons but for strategic or ideological purposes. For example, when government censors objected to the presumed allusions to actual extramarital lovers in "The Adventures of Master F. J.," George Gascoigne published an expurgated edition that obscured the plot and weakened the poetry, which is why G. W. Pigman chose the earlier, unrevised version as the copy text for his Oxford edition.[10]

The 1591 "pirated" edition of Samuel Daniel's poems was revised for analogous reasons.[11] As Daniel insisted in the preface to the 1592 authorized edition, the earlier text contained "private passions" and "secrets" "never meant" for the public.[12] Even if Daniel facilitated the 1591 publication, as some scholars have argued, his authorized edition omitted the most erotic and irate poems, shuffled the remaining poems, and interspersed numerous eternizing poems in order to transform his earlier impassioned lover's persuasion, written for a private manuscript audience, into conventional Petrarchan love poetry. Daniel's revisions and reorganization along with the new title *Delia*, an anagram for ideal, made the entire sequence seem abstract and universal.[13]

Wroth would almost certainly have known about Daniel's stratagem since his private manuscript poems were printed along with the pirated text of *Astrophil and Stella*, the sonnet sequence written by Wroth's uncle Sir Philip Sidney and subsequently edited by her aunt Mary Sidney Herbert, Countess of Pembroke, after whom Wroth was named. The two women were very close. Wroth

---

[10] George Gascoigne, *A Hundreth Sundrie Flowres*, ed. G. W. Pigman III (Oxford: Clarendon Press; New York: Oxford Univ. Press, 2000).

[11] *Syr P.S. His Astrophel and Stella. Wherein the excellence of sweete poesie is concluded. To the end of which are added, sundry other rare sonnets of diuers noble men and gentlemen*, At London for Thomas Newman (ESTC 22536).

[12] Cecile M. Jagodzinski, *Privacy and Print: Reading and Writing in Seventeenth-Century England* (Charlottesville and London: Univ. of Virginia Press, 1999), 11, examines the ways in which the "personal contact that once existed between poet and listener or author and reader" is transformed by subsequent generations who were writing for print: "As the manuscript era slowly ends, authors only attain the writer's crown by permitting readers to sit in as members of a gigantic coterie."

[13] For a more detailed account of Daniel's pirated text, see Ilona Bell, *Elizabethan Women and the Poetry of Courtship* (Cambridge: Cambridge Univ. Press, 1998, repr. 2010), 126–51.

spent a lot of time at Wilton, her aunt's country estate.[14] And so did Samuel Daniel.[15] The countess was Daniel's patron, and Daniel was the tutor of her son William Herbert, Mary Wroth's first cousin and the love of her life.[16] Although we do not know when their love affair began, we do know that William Herbert was the father of Wroth's illegitimate children Katherine and Will.[17]

Wroth's excisions and concealments resemble Gascoigne's and especially Daniel's. Her case is even more instructive because it enables us to compare her self-bowdlerized printed text to a prior autograph manuscript rather than an earlier printed text. Many of Wroth's revisions were designed not to make the poetry better, but to make the content more acceptable to the reading public and the censors.[18] Her autograph manuscript contains 117 poems, ranging from 14-line sonnets to a 312-line song. Wroth substantially transformed the sequence for print. She cut the most transgressive poems, which were not printed until the twentieth century,[19] and moved nine poems to *Urania*. She also cut or revised key words or phrases in many of the remaining poems. By then repositioning numerous poems, she destroyed the dramatic development and altered the meaning of the sequence as a whole. Finally, she added a new overarching poem towards the beginning to steer readers' expectations of what was to come. The resulting 1621 sonnet sequence seems static, abstract, and deeply conventional.

Because virtually all scholarship to date has been based on the printed sequence, most critics have willingly accepted Roberts' repeatedly cited assertions

---

[14] See Margaret P. Hannay, *Mary Sidney, Lady Wroth* (Farnham and Burlington, VT: Ashgate, 2010), 4–5.

[15] On Daniel's connection to the Sidneys, see Michael Brennan, *Literary Patronage in the English Renaissance: The Pembroke Family* (London and New York: Routledge, 1988), ch. 6, and Gavin Alexander, *Writing after Sidney: the Literary Response to Sir Philip Sidney, 1586–1640* (Oxford: Oxford Univ. Press, 2006).

[16] See Margaret P. Hannay, "'Your Vertuous and Learned Aunt': The Countess of Pembroke as a Mentor to Mary Wroth," in *Reading Mary Wroth: Representing Alternatives in Early Modern England*, ed. Naomi J. Miller and Gary Waller (Knoxville: Univ. of Tennessee Press, 1991), 15–34, and Hannay, *Mary Sidney, Lady Wroth*, 92 and 229 ff.

[17] Hannay presents valuable new information about the children in *Mary Sidney, Lady Wroth*. See esp. 107–8, 161–62, 193–96, and 251–54.

[18] As H. R. Woudhuysen writes in *Sir Philip Sidney and the Circulation of Manuscripts, 1558–1640* (Oxford: Clarendon Press, 1996), 15, "The attraction of manuscript circulation lay in the medium's social status, its personal appeal, relative privacy, freedom from government control, its cheapness, and its ability to make works quickly available to a select audience."

[19] Pritchard includes the 103 poems from the 1621 sequence of *Pamphilia to Amphilanthus* as well as the poems from both the 1621 *Urania* and the Newberry manuscript of *Urania*, but he neither mentions nor includes the six Folger poems omitted from 1621 which contravene his view of Wroth's "old fashioned and belated" Petrarchism.

that "the rhetoric of wooing or courtship is largely absent from her collection," that Amphilanthus is barely discernible in the poems, and that except for their female speaker Wroth's lyrics "adhere closely to the well-defined Petrarchan mode."[20] Yet in the Folger sequence Pamphilia actively woos Amphilanthus. Particularly in the excised poems, she takes the initiative, urging him to act on their mutual "desire." Her persuasive purpose is most notable in the aubade which has escaped the attention of modern scholars because it was cut from 1621, relegated to a separate section at the back of Roberts' edition, and omitted altogether from other modern editions. The dramatic situation, the conventions of the genre, and the simple intimate language make it clear that Pamphilia and Amphilanthus have spent the night together. Wroth removed the aubade from the printed text because it leaves no doubt that their love affair was consummated. Indeed, Pamphilia eagerly urges Amphilanthus to awaken so that they can continue their lovemaking.

Modern annotations make Donne's and Shakespeare's elusive complexities comprehensible. Donne's poems, for example, would be seriously depleted if editors had not recovered his much-used pun on the word "die," meaning to reach sexual climax. When we compare the manuscript of *Pamphilia to Amphilanthus* to the printed text, Wroth's diction becomes as cryptic, opaque, and veiled and her syntax as knotty and ambiguous as Donne's or Shakespeare's. Yet modern editions of *Pamphilia to Amphilanthus* provide only minimal glosses. The lack of annotations often makes Wroth's language seem either misleadingly transparent or inept and impenetrable.[21] By using one comparatively clear usage to unpack more coded innuendoes, my annotations will reconstruct Wroth's lexicon and unpack her patterns of imagery, giving readers access to the ways in which her poems acquire multiple, distinct meanings in the private manuscript and the printed text. For example, the aubade imbues the word "ioye" with both heavenly bliss and erotic pleasure. The word not only retains both meanings in the surrounding Folger poems, but it also alerts us to the erotic subtext of poems that appear earlier in the manuscript.

---

[20] Quoted from *Poems*, 48, 59. Pritchard's introduction (12) reiterates Roberts' view that "the man is silenced, removed from sight (no blazonings for him) and, apart from a few sonnets to his eyes, not even addressed . . . the focus is entirely on the solitary, withdrawn speaker and her obsessions and anxieties."

[21] Pritchard (*Poems*, 12) praises Wroth's plain style: "there is an effective plainness of diction, graceful flow, and use of relatively straightforward 'conceits' or analogies, suggesting the general influence of Jonson." He then proceeds to criticize her for failing to live up to this view of her poetry: "Wroth's grammar, sentence construction and punctuation were relatively loose frequently producing obscurity and uncertainty in interpretation (without this necessarily being intended or advantageous)" (4). No modern editor would venture to judge Shakespeare or Donne in this way.

Even poems that remain much the same in both sequences acquire very different meanings where Wroth changed the surrounding poems. In the Folger manuscript "crowne of Sonetts," Pamphilia pleads with Amphilanthus to honor their extramarital love, endorse her pregnancy, and acknowledge their illegitimate child. Although the fourteen-poem sequence of interlocking sonnets remains intact in 1621 since it would have been extremely difficult to alter the intricate rhyme scheme, the context significantly alters the meaning. By removing the aubade which appears just a few poems earlier and the song which follows, Wroth made "a crowne of Sonetts" look like a paean to transcendent Neoplatonic love. "A crowne" is just one of many, many places where Wroth's multivalent diction, ambiguous syntax, and loose punctuation enable the 1621 poems to look very different, thereby obscuring the lovers' sexual intimacy from the uninitiated public.

Pamphilia to Amphilanthus was printed in 1621 at the end of *The Countesse of Mountgomery's Urania*. Because *Urania*'s central characters are named Pamphilia and Amphilanthus and because the sonnet sequence is entitled *Pamphilia to Amphilanthus*, the joint publication invited seventeenth-century readers to envision the sonnets and romance as interlocking texts. Wroth even signed Pamphilia's name after discrete groups of poems. The prose narrative further links the poems to the romance by describing how Pamphilia wooed Amphilanthus in encoded poetry. In *Urania* (1621) Pamphilia's carefully veiled poems address Amphilanthus both directly and indirectly, through apostrophe, metaphor, and myth. The poems neither name names nor mention identifying physical features or specific events so that Pamphilia can deny their private meaning if anyone disapproves or tries to interfere. But Amphilanthus gets it right away. To him, Pamphilia affirms her coded subtext by welcoming the physical intimacy her poems precipitate.

Wroth's account of how private lyric dialogues work in *Urania* helps explain how her own manuscript poems were written, read, and circulated. In her pioneering study *Gender and Authorship in the Sidney Circle*, Mary Ellen Lamb analyzed relationships between poets and their audiences in *Urania*.[22] Yet neither Wroth's commentary nor Lamb's illuminating analysis have been adequately applied to Wroth's songs and sonnets. Indeed, the connection between the poems and the romance is less visible to modern readers of Roberts' scholarly editions than it was to seventeenth-century readers because, having already published

---

[22] Mary Ellen Lamb, *Gender and Authorship in the Sidney Circle* (Madison: Univ. of Wisconsin Press, 1990), 142–93.

Pamphilia to Amphilanthus in her 1983 *Poems of Lady Mary Wroth*, Roberts omitted the sonnet sequence from her 1995 edition of *Urania, Part 1*.[23]

Even when the much-trumpeted "death of the author" killed biographical criticism, theoretically sophisticated Wroth scholars continued to explore parallels between Wroth's life and writing. *The Countess of Montgomery's Urania* is widely seen as a *roman à clef* that shadows Wroth's life and the lives of those she knew by fragmenting actual characters and events into multiple characters and overlapping plots.[24] Family members and friends, including her husband Robert Wroth, her lover William Herbert, her aunt Mary Sidney Herbert, and her cousin-by-marriage Susan Herbert, the eponymous Countess of Montgomery, play fictionalized yet identifiable roles.[25] Much as the printed sonnet sequence parallels the 1621 published romance more closely than scholars have recognized, so too the unprinted Folger manuscript version of *Pamphilia to Amphilanthus* parallels the manuscript continuation of *Urania* (unpublished until 1999) more closely than scholars have recognized. The unexpurgated sonnet sequence contains numerous hints of a broken, secret marriage contract, clandestine trysts, and children born out of wedlock — concerns that propel the manuscript continuation of *Urania* even as they haunted Wroth's own clandestine love affair with Herbert, which yielded two out-of-wedlock children.[26]

The two versions of *Pamphilia to Amphilanthus* epitomize the transition from private manuscript to print. Wroth is the scion of a preeminent literary family. *Pamphilia to Amphilanthus* alludes to poems by her father Robert Sidney; her uncle Philip Sidney; her aunt Mary Sidney Herbert; and her lover William Herbert.[27] Wroth carried on a private lyric dialogue with members of her

---

[23] *The First Part of The Countess of Montgomery's Urania*, ed. Josephine A. Roberts (Binghamton, NY: Medieval and Renaissance Texts and Studies, 1995).

[24] As Hannay explains, "Wroth's tales often begin with an event or situation that happened to her or to someone else she knew, but then they tend to veer off into fantasy." Readers must beware: "Wroth often added details that seem intensely autobiographical but are factually untrue" (*Mary Sidney, Lady Wroth*, xii).

[25] For an imaginative psychological study of Wroth's romance, see Waller, *The Sidney Family Romance*.

[26] As Hannay astutely remarks (*Mary Sidney, Lady Wroth*, xiv), "What makes Wroth unusual is not her love for her inconstant cousin, William Herbert, but her transformation of that love into art."

[27] Roberts' edition cites some of the allusions to poems by Wroth's uncle Philip Sidney and her father Robert Sidney, as well as the poem by her lover William Herbert that Wroth included in *Urania*. In "William Herbert and the Hell of Deceit," presented at the Renaissance Society of America Conference (Chicago, 2008), Mary Ellen Lamb began to explore the exchange of lyrics between Wroth and Herbert.

exceedingly literary family through this network of allusions; however, the original meaning of these allusions is largely concealed in the expurgated, seemingly conventional sequence of poems printed in 1621.[28]

Folger MS. V.a.104 shows Wroth to be a better, more exciting and original poet than scholars have recognized. Yet quite apart from any intrinsic merit, the manuscript of Wroth's poems comprises a valuable resource for students and scholars of poetry, Renaissance literature, and the history of the book because autograph texts of Renaissance sonnet sequences are so rare; there are none for Sidney's, Spenser's, or Shakespeare's sonnets, or Donne's *Songs and Sonets*. As Germaine Warkentin's informative analysis of Wroth's father's manuscript poems demonstrates, the few surviving holograph manuscripts provide invaluable information about the ways in which sonnet sequences were constructed.[29] Wroth's poetry provides an even more instructive case study because, unlike manuscript poems by Wroth's father or printed poems by their more celebrated contemporaries, *Pamphilia to Amphilanthus* survives both in Wroth's own handwriting and in books printed during her lifetime. Indeed, the annotated copy of the printed text with corrections in Wroth's own handwriting shows her continuing engagement with the poems even after they were published.[30]

My coeditor Steven May and I spent a month studying the Folger manuscript.[31] Wroth's revisions are far more pervasive and extensive than Roberts' list of variants acknowledges. We found many places where Wroth changed particular words by writing over individual letters. Some revisions seem to be scribal corrections or minor improvements made by Wroth as she went along, but changes in pen and ink suggest that others were introduced at a later time, most likely when Wroth was beginning to revise the manuscript for print.

Roberts dated the manuscript sometime between 1615 and 1620 on the assumption that the poems were transcribed during a single period in Wroth's life.

---

[28] As Woudhuysen observes (*Circulation*, 12), "Manuscripts had the added advantage of allowing authors and scribes to reach precisely the audience they wanted to address."

[29] See Germaine Warkentin, "Robert Sidney's 'Darcke Offerings': The Making of a Late Tudor Manuscript *Canzoniere*," *Spenser Studies* 12 (1998): 37–74.

[30] For a reproduction of this "unique copy" of the 1621 text with corrections in Wroth's own handwriting, see *Mary Wroth*, The Early Modern Englishwoman: A Facsimile Library of Essential Works, Part 1, Printed Writings, 1500–1640 (Aldershot: Ashgate, 1996), ed. Betty Travitsky and Josephine A. Roberts, selected and introduced by Josephine A. Roberts. Roberts apparently did not know about this copy when she edited *The Poems*. She added some of Wroth's corrections to the list of variants in her paperback edition, but did not seriously consider the challenge it poses to her decision to use the Folger manuscript as copy text.

[31] I am deeply indebted to Steven May whose contribution to my understanding of Wroth's manuscript is incalculable.

However, the poems were most likely copied onto unbound gatherings of paper, since different parts of the manuscript were transcribed at different periods in Wroth's writing career. By identifying and dating three related but distinct watermarks and connecting them to changes in handwriting, ink, visual markings, numbers, and layout, we determined that Wroth transcribed the manuscript in three distinct sections at three different times. The online Gravell Watermark Collection (which did not exist when Roberts dated the manuscript) suggests that Wroth could have begun to transcribe the first, elaborately patterned group of fifty-five songs and sonnets a decade earlier than Roberts thought, when English sonneteering was still in vogue — not long after Mary Sidney's arranged marriage to Robert Wroth in 1604. If, as our examination of the manuscript provisionally suggests, Wroth was writing about Pamphilia's clandestine love affair with Amphilanthus when she was herself engaged and then unhappily married to Robert Wroth but in love with William Herbert, that would further explain the opacities and ambiguities of *Pamphilia to Amphilanthus*.

Folger MS. V.a.104 is the *sole* extant manuscript of *Pamphilia to Amphilanthus*. Even though Donne's love poems did not circulate until more than a decade after they were written, over 5,000 manuscript copies of his poems survive from the decades before and after his death.[32] Even a poem by the relatively unknown writer Anne Vavasour exists in multiple manuscript copies.[33] By contrast, there are no copies of Wroth's manuscripts. We can infer, therefore, that she either shared her private poems orally by reading or reciting them to her immediate coterie, or showed the poems to a select, extremely restricted audience of trustworthy family and friends while safeguarding the originals.[34] Wroth's title *Pamphilia to Amphilanthus* makes it clear that Amphilanthus is Pamphilia's intended and most important lyric audience. If Amphilanthus was modeled on William Herbert, as scholars believe and Wroth's pointed puns on the name Will hint, it seems likely that William Herbert was Wroth's own original and most important private lyric audience.

Wroth's handwritten manuscript provides valuable information about the ways in which private poetry invited dialogue, established intimacy, and protected itself from misprision and misuse. The revised, expurgated 1621 sequence transformed Pamphilia's passionate, private lover's persuasion into a conventional, generalized meditation on love that would have been appropriate for a public

---

[32] See Gary A. Stringer, gen. ed., *The Variorum Edition of the Poetry of John Donne*, vol. 2, *The Elegies* (Bloomington and Indianapolis: Indiana Univ. Press, 2000), XLIX–LIII.

[33] See Bell, *Elizabethan Women*, 75–99.

[34] As Woudhuysen observes (*Circulation*, 154), "once a poet's verse began to circulate in manuscript, it tended to continue to do so."

lyric audience. Together, the new retrospective poem, the omitted poems, the targeted, strategic revisions, and the reshuffled order disembody Amphilanthus and conceal Pamphilia's persuasive purpose. Wroth *needed* to remove, recast, or obscure her more erotic poems to present Pamphilia as an honorable Renaissance woman — and to present herself as a proper lady-poet.

Roberts privileged the printed sequence over the earlier Folger collection of poems because, at the time, it was standard editorial practice to honor the author's final revisions. In the last decade or two, scholars have begun to recognize that manuscript texts have their own distinctive merits. Jill Seal Millman's and Gillian Wright's 2005 anthology *Early Modern Women's Manuscript Poetry* includes a selection of seventeen poems from the Folger manuscript.[35] The Brown Women Writers' Project is planning to begin publishing women's manuscripts. Recent scholarly studies such as Margaret Ezell's *Social Authorship and the Advent of Print* argue that manuscript texts challenge paradigms derived from printed texts.[36] Shifting scholarly attention from print to manuscript will drastically alter our understanding of early modern women and women writers.[37]

Wroth's autograph poems epitomize the challenge that manuscript texts pose to current presumptions about early modern women writers, presumptions derived heretofore primarily from print. The normative constraints of chastity, silence, and obedience dominate published texts.[38] Yet prescriptive writing intensifies its dictates whenever social practice challenges established ethical codes. When Josephine Roberts published her 1983 edition, continental Renaissance women such as Louise Labé and Veronica Franco were known to have written amorous poetry, but it was thought that English women writers were restricted to translations and religious subjects.[39] By relegating Wroth's most daring and erotic poems to the back of her edition, Roberts reproduced and perpetuated the

---

[35] Jill Seal Millman and Gillian Wright, eds., *Early Modern Women's Manuscript Poetry* (Manchester and New York: Manchester Univ. Press, 2005).

[36] Margaret J. M. Ezell, *Social Authorship and the Advent of Print* (Baltimore: Johns Hopkins Univ. Press, 1999).

[37] Ezell makes the argument compellingly in "The Laughing Tortoise: Speculations on Manuscript Sources and Women's Book History," *ELR* 38 (2008): 331–55.

[38] See the following classic studies: Suzanne W. Hull, *Chaste, Silent & Obedient: English Books for Women, 1475–1640* (San Marino: Huntington Library, 1982); Elaine V. Beilin, *Redeeming Eve: Women Writers of the English Renaissance* (Princeton: Princeton Univ. Press, 1987); Margaret Patterson Hannay, ed., *Silent But For The Word: Tudor Women As Patrons, Translators, and Writers of Religious Works* (Kent, OH: Kent State Univ. Press, 1985).

[39] I am grateful to Anne Lake Prescott for suggesting the parallel between Wroth and her continental peers. For some links between Wroth and Labé, see Prescott's essay, "Mary Wroth, Louise Labé, and Cupid," *Sidney Journal* 15 (1997): 37–40. For an illuminating study of Mary

ideological constraints that purified Pamphilia and disembodied Amphilanthus in the 1621 printed text. By omitting these poems altogether, subsequent editors silenced them even further. The public proscriptions Wroth faced in 1621 will continue to cloud and constrain her poetry and its representation of women as long as V.a.104 remains unprinted and unread.

To conclude, the 1621 version of *Pamphilia to Amphilanthus* is a self-bowd-lerized text that is widely seen as a skillful but derivative collection of lyrics lack-ing any narrative development. Admirers generally describe Wroth's poems as "conventional," "abstract," "universal," and "outmoded"; they have also been called "boring" and "unspectacular but competent." By comparison, the earlier, unpublished sonnet sequence preserved in the Folger manuscript is individuated, suspenseful, and at times even joyous — the opposite of how Wroth's poems are typically seen today. Its ongoing, evolving lyric dialogue of clandestine love is unprecedented for an early modern English woman writer. Comparing the two sequences shows Wroth to be a far more versatile, psychologically complex, mul-tifaceted, and original poet than scholars and critics have realized.

WILLIAMS COLLEGE

Wroth and European women writers, see Ann Rosalind Jones, *The Currency Of Eros: Women's Love Lyric In Europe, 1540–1620* (Bloomington: Indiana Univ. Press, 1990).

Sixteenth-Century Artisanal Practices and Baconian Prose[1]

KEN HILTNER

E MPLOYING A CLEVER RHETORICAL DEVICE, FRANCIS BACON OPENS HIS *Novum Organon* with a question not only unanswered, but unasked. "On the state of the sciences, [we must admit] that it is neither prosperous nor far advanced; and that quite a different way must be opened up for the human intellect than men have known in the past. . . ."[2] Although this sentence is a declaration, it is difficult to even finish it without having a question take shape in the reader's mind: is an altogether new path "for the human intellect" actually going to be proposed here by Bacon? Not only keeping us in suspense, but deliberately building on it by deferring this question, Bacon skips to a second: "One must also speak plainly about usefulness, and say that the wisdom which we have drawn in particular from the Greeks seems to be a kind of childish stage of science, and to have the child's characteristic of being all too ready to talk, but too weak and immature to produce anything" (6). Fifteen years earlier Bacon had made similar charges in *The Advancement of Learning,* even naming these puerile Greek philosophers of nature ("Aristotle, Plato, Democritus, Hippocrates, Euclides, Archimedes"),[3] but these allegations had been buttressed by pages of

---

[1] This paper was first presented at the 2010 Modern Language Association convention, Los Angeles, CA, at the Josephine Roberts Forum: "Bacon in the Twenty-First Century," Arthur F. Marotti presiding.

[2] Francis Bacon, *The New Organon,* ed. Lisa Jardine and Michael Silverthorne (Cambridge: Cambridge Univ. Press, 2000). All references to *The New Organon* are to this edition (cited as *NO*).

[3] Francis Bacon, *The Advancement of Learning,* in *Francis Bacon: The Major Works,* ed. Brian Vickers (Oxford: Oxford Univ. Press, 2009), 144. Hereafter *AL*.

argument; here, instead, the author speaks with such confident condescension that we wonder for a second time just what sort of breakthrough could justify such unabashed arrogance.

In *The Advancement of Learning* the unexpected answer did not appear until two dozen pages into the text. But following this dramatic lead-in (altogether absent in the earlier work), in the *Novum Organon,* in phrases drawn almost verbatim from the *AL,* Bacon answers our question early in the opening paragraph of the Preface. Having taken such pains to refashion his prior thinking for a powerful rhetorical delivery, one might compare Bacon here with Plato in his *Republic.* As the story goes, like Bacon, Plato continued reworking his introductory passage so that it rhetorically would better frame what was to follow, with Socrates descending through an obsolete goddess' festival in order to deliver his own new articles of truth to humanity. And yet, both writers, on more than one occasion in these respective texts, famously penned scathing attacks on rhetoric, leaving us with the daunting task of sifting through not only what they had to say damning rhetoric, but also how they persuasively employed rhetoric to say it.

As to the still-unanswered question of what Bacon proposed as an alternative to classical science, until recently many scholars responded to this query with some reading of Bacon's own innovations, his celebrated "method," largely ignoring the aforementioned newly-placed emphasis in the opening lines of the *NO* on a separate, inchoate tradition, which, quietly moving alongside of classical learning, had recently far outstripped its accomplishments. It is from this tradition, and its parishioners, on which Bacon will build his new method by standing on their shoulders.

> If you look closely at the wide range of books which are the boast of the arts and sciences, you will frequently find repetitions of the same thing, different in manner of treatment but anticipated in content, so that things which at first glance seem to be numerous are found on examination to be few. . . . [However] . . . in the mechanical arts [of the artisan] we see the opposite situation. They grow and improve each day as if they breathed some vital breeze. In their first authors they usually appear crude, clumsy almost, and ungainly, but later they acquire new powers and a kind of eloquence. . . . By contrast, philosophy and the intellectual sciences are, like statues, admired and venerated but not much improved. (*NO,* 7)

In spite of its glorious beginning, for two thousand years classical science had stagnated, yet in a mere two hundred years (by Bacon's reckoning), largely uneducated artisans, who could read neither Greek nor Latin, nor understand formal mathematics, had unleashed a tidal wave of progress — a wave which the arts and sciences of the universities had simply missed.

To Bacon, science had simply been misguided: "anyone who has turned his attention from workshops to libraries . . . will pass from admiration of variety to amazement at the poverty and paucity of the things which until now have held and occupied the minds of men" (*NO*, 79). Accordingly, because "science is to be sought from the light of nature, not from the darkness of antiquity," "what is absolutely needed is to do a thorough survey and examination of all the mechanical arts [of the artisan] . . . and then to make a compilation or particular history of the great accomplishments, the magisterial achievements and finished works, in each art, together with their modes of working or operation" (*NO*, 151). This is an astonishing statement, as Bacon intends to largely turn his back on the orthodox, classical science taught in universities to study instead "the magisterial achievements," the literal masterpieces, of largely uneducated artisans.

In this paper, I would like to focus on the question of early-modern authorship by considering how artisanal practices, which were of singular importance to Bacon's new approach to science and the world, also profoundly shaped his writing and understanding of rhetoric. Following Owen Hannaway, Ann Blair, Anthony Grafton and others,[4] I proceed from the position that the disciplinary divide we often perceive between the sciences and the humanities is in part the lasting legacy of the nineteenth-century European educational system. As the body of his own work repeatedly proves, there is no clear line between Bacon the scientist and Bacon the writer — a fact that presents us with a unique opportunity, as the windfall of recent work arguing for an artisanal influence on Bacon's science will also throw considerable light on his writing practices. In short, as we shall see, Bacon's prose owes an enormous debt to the writings of sixteenth-century artisans.

Though the debt that Bacon owes to the artisan is written large, not only in the *Novum Organon* but throughout his writings, scholars of science have been slow to acknowledge it. This in spite of the fact that sixty years ago Edgar Zilsel for the most part saw the same story, written not only in Bacon's writing, but in the history of science itself:

> In the period from 1300 to 1600 . . . Both professor and humanist literati distinguished liberal from mechanical arts and despised mechanical

---

[4] Owen Hannaway, "Georgius Agricola as Humanist," *Journal of the History of Ideas* 53, no. 4 (1992): 553–60. See also especially Ann Blair, "Reassessing Humanism and Science," *Journal of the History of Ideas* 53 (1992): 535–40, and Anthony Grafton, *Defending the Test* (Cambridge, MA: Harvard Univ. Press, 1991).

labor . . . [yet] . . . Craftsmen were the pioneers of casual thinking in this period . . . Thus the two components of the scientific method were separated
by a social barrier: logical training was reserved for upper-class scholars;
experimentation, casual interest, and quantitative method were left to more
or less plebeian artisans. Science was born when, with the progress of [arti-
san-created] technology, the experimental method eventually overcame the
social prejudice against manual labor and was adopted by rationally trained
scholars. This was accomplished about 1600 (Gilbert, Galileo, Bacon).[5]

However, the strongest support for the notion that Bacon, and modern science itself, owes a massive debt to artisans came with the 1957 publication of Paolo Rossi's *Francis Bacon: From Magic to Science*. Rossi boldly opened by relating how in
1531 Juan Luis Vives "makes the statement that scholars would be well advised to
study the technical methods of such trades as building, navigation, and weaving;
they should, besides, observe the artisan at work and question him on the secrets
of his craft."[6] Taking this prescription, a generation later "Bacon, Galileo, and
Harvey, among others, explicitly acknowledged their debt to the artisan."[7] However, for these thinkers to study and observe artisans, let alone to subsequently
acknowledge a debt to them, required the overturning of two thousand years of
prejudice. As Rossi notes, not only did Plato and Aristotle deny full citizenship
to artisans, but Aristotle distinguished the artisan from the slave only in that he
cares for the needs of more people. "For Aristotle the aims of the artisans . . . are
degrading because their occupations are base and require no special skill [as defined by Aristotle]. Thus the contrast between slave and free citizen, artisan and
scientist, practical and theoretical knowledge became merged during the classical and medieval eras for most of civilized Europe."[8]

---

[5] Edgar Zilsel, "The Sociological Roots of Science," *American Journal of Sociology* 47. 4
(Jan. 1942): 544.

[6] P. Rossi, *Francis Bacon; From Magic to Science* (London: Routledge, 1968): 1.

[7] Rossi, *Bacon*, 2.

[8] Rossi, *Bacon*, 26. With Plato these beliefs become more specific. Plato asks, "Who is
likely to know whether the proper form of a shuttle is embodied in any piece of wood? The
carpenter who made it (ὁ ποιήσας), or the weaver, who is to use it?" Plato, *Cratylus*, trans. H.
N. Fowler, Loeb (Cambridge, MA: Harvard Univ. Press, 1967), 29. Plato answers: certainly the
weaver. As Plato refines the notion in Book X of the Republic, "The user of anything is the one
who knows most of it by experience, and he reports to the maker the good or bad effects in use
of the thing he uses . . . the maker will have right belief (πίστιν ὀρθήν) . . . but the user will have
true knowledge (ἐπιστήμην)." Plato, *Republic*, trans. P. Shorey, Loeb (Cambridge, MA: Harvard Univ. Press, 1963), 601e–602a.

As Rossi would note in a later work, this antithesis "between technics and science . . . was born of the very economic structure of a slave society . . . in which contempt felt for the slave (or anyone engaged in manual activities) is extended to that activity itself."[9] Consequently, Benjamin Farrington rightly argues that, although an unlikely apologist, we nonetheless "find Bacon fighting for the idea that the philosopher, if he is to create a science fruitful in works, must overcome his contempt for the craftsman."[10]

It is in some sense the continued existence of this prejudice into our own era that caused certain writers, such as Rupert Hall, to counter Zilsel, Farrington, and especially Rossi by arguing that "modern studies combine in revealing that the empirical element in the scientific revolution, taking the word in its crudest, least philosophical and most craftsmanlike sense, has been greatly exaggerated; correspondingly we are learning to attach more and more significance to its conceptual and intellectual aspects."[11] (In some sense Hall's is an understandable response in that prior to Thomas Kuhn's important *The Essential Tension* it was unclear why certain fields of early-modern science did not show direct artisanal influence.)[12] Yet Bacon himself directly addressed this already long-standing prejudice against artisanal practices in the close of his *New Organon*: regarding the recent history of the mechanical arts, "we must put aside our arrogance and

---

[9] Paolo Rossi, *Philosophy, Technology, and the Arts in the Early Modern Era*, trans. Salvator Attanasio (New York: Harper and Row, 1970), 147.

[10] Benjamin Farrington, *Francis Bacon: Philosopher of Industrial Science* (New York: Henry Schuman, 1949), 15.

[11] Rupert Hall, "The Scholar and the Craftsman," in *Critical Problems in the History of Science,* ed. Marshall Clagett (Madison: Univ. of Wisconsin Press, 1959), 3–23, at 18.

[12] The influence of artisans on early modern science was legitimately questioned because certain fields, astronomy for example, owed little to the mechanical arts. Kuhn (perhaps best remembered for introducing the notion of "paradigm shifts") offered a provocative solution to this quandary by asking, "Among the large number of topics now included in the physical sciences, which ones were in antiquity foci for the continuing activity of specialists?" His answer? Astronomy, statics, optics, mathematics, and harmonics. These "classical sciences" formed the basis of science as it was still taught in universities in the seventeenth century. Clearly these disciplines necessitated certain esoteric skills — not the least of which being a working knowledge of classical and mathematical languages beyond the scope of the artisan. Newton's *Principia*, which had little to do with artisanal discoveries, was perhaps the crowning early modern triumph of classical science. On the other hand, Kuhn notes that something startling and new emerges on the scene in the sixteenth and seventeenth centuries which he dubs "Baconian after its principal publicist." In contrast to the well-entrenched, well-regarded classical sciences, the gains of the artisans were certainly perceived as the low road of inquiry, but they nonetheless represented a breathtaking new avenue for science to take: Thomas S. Kuhn, *The Essential Tension: Selected Studies in Scientific Tradition and Change.* (Chicago: Univ. of Chicago Press, 1977), 35–36, 42.

scorn, and give our full attention to this history, despite that it is a mechanics'
art (as it may seem), illiberal and mean. The preferable arts are . . . agriculture,
cookery, chemistry, dyeing, the manufacture of glass, enamel, sugar, gunpowder,
fireworks, paper and suchlike" (*NO* 228).

Drawing attention to this prejudice is important. As Bacon speaks vexingly
little about his own writing practices, and there was such strong early-modern
bias against all practices artisanal, few authors prior to Bacon directly acknowledged their debt to the artisan. (Although, as we shall see, Montaigne, as well as
many of those who followed Bacon, clearly did.) In order to see this artisanal influence on Bacon's writing, it will be helpful to draw parallels to his science.

Through the work of Husserl, Heidegger, Horkheimer, Adorno, and others,[13]
the first half of the twentieth century witnessed a radical change in how we viewed
the relation of Baconian science to the rise of technological modernity. No longer was this shift to technology taken to be a phenomenon of the eighteenth and
nineteenth centuries. In a view seconded by historians,[14] Bacon in particular was

---

[13] For how these thinkers contributed to the understanding of Bacon as generating the
rhetoric which brought about the change of practices that led to the Industrial Revolution, see
Paolo Rossi, "Bacon's Idea of Science," in *The Cambridge Companion to Bacon*, ed. Markku
Peltonen (Cambridge: Cambridge Univ. Press, 1993), 25–46, at 43–45.

[14] In the last seventy or eighty years certain historians have also shifted their focus to the
practices which contributed to the Industrial Revolution. As L. C. Knights declared over fifty
years ago: "The last twenty or thirty years have seen a revolution in our attitudes towards the
seventeenth century . . . [as historians] . . . have pushed back the beginnings of the Industrial
Revolution and demonstrated a direct line of connection between the commercial and industrial enterprises of the Elizabethans and early Stuart times and the greater changes of the eighteenth century": *Explorations: Essays in Criticism, Mainly on the Literature of the Seventeenth
Century* (New York: George W. Stewart, 1947), 108. However, it was perhaps E. P. Thompson's
enormously influential *The Making of the English Working Class* which most compellingly
argued for shifts in proto-industrial practices as the origin of the Industrial Revolution: E.
P. Thompson, *The Making of the English Working Class* (London: Camelot, 1963). More recent work by Franklin F. Mendels and H. Medick, in introducing the distinction between the
proto-industrial *Kaufsystem* and the *Verlagsystem*, holds that the former, an early organization of artisanal practices, greatly predates the Industrial Revolution — by centuries. See F. F.
Mendels, "Proto-industrialization: The First Phase of the Industrialization Process," *Journal
of Economic History* 32.1 (1972): 241–61, and H. Medick, "Proto-Industrialization on Test with
the Guild of Historians: Response to Some Critics," *Economy and Society* 15.2 (1986): 251–72.

Bacon's texts themselves, as Marxist historiographers and R. K. Merton noticed before
both Zilsel and Rossi, certainly reveal that the Industrial Revolution had its roots in artisanal
practices emerging long before the seventeenth and eighteenth centuries. Marxist historiography in particular has looked at the manner by which early capitalism spawned the growth
of profitable artisanal activities which fueled the scientific revolution, though Bacon himself
rejected this view. (Bacon held that economic concerns did not fuel the scientific revolution

held to have laid down the rhetoric that profoundly influenced human practices for centuries. It is certainly true that Bacon was pivotal in generating the rhetoric which changed the manner by which human beings relate to the world in practice; however, implied in the work of Zilsel, Rossi, and Kuhn (as well as in that of William Eamon, Steven Shapin, and Pamela Smith)[15] is the notion that it is simply putting the cart before the horse to assume that rhetoric predates practice. To the contrary, in so far as Bacon clearly acknowledges that his science owes much to artisanal practices, it is these proto-industrial practices which are found to be, if not generative of, at least a prime influence on, the rhetoric. As we shall see, not only Bacon's writings, but his very writing style, owe a massive debt to artisanal practices.

Building on the work of Rossi and Kuhn, in 1988 Antonio Pérez-Ramos championed the late sixteenth-century belief of artisans that their work was (as Rossi had intimated) "a form of cognition."[16] Pérez-Ramos introduced the idea of

---

because artisans, "concerned only with wages and professional matters," were not able to advance science, except when "some unusually intelligent craftsman, seeking to achieve a reputation, devotes himself to making some new invention, usually at his own expense" [*NO*, 66].) A. R. Hall, for example, accepts a "Marxist proposition that the development of commerce and industry in the Renaissance, and perhaps particularly its global extent, stimulated a certain kind of intellectual activity in Europe": *The Revolution in Science, 1500–1750* (London: Longman, 1983), 23. Separate from the Marxist approach, in 1938 R. K. Merton, following Max Weber's scorching indictment linking the rise of capitalism with Protestantism, argued that the emergence of the new science was associated with the high value given to work, especially manual and artisanal work, by Protestants: *Science, Technology and Society in Seventeenth-Century England* (New York: Howard Fertig, 1970). Though a highly sophisticated artisanal guild system in England certainly predates the rise of Protestantism, these studies, which argue for an artisanal component to the scientific revolution, rightfully take a close look at the involvement of the artisan.

[15] William Eamon, for example, in looking at "artisanal recipes from a broad range of crafts, from metallurgy and 'practical alchemy' to dyeing textiles and preparing drugs," argues that published collections of these works not only "played an instrumental role in disseminating craft information to the virtuosi," but, more than just "passive vehicles for the transmission of 'raw data' to natural philosophers," these works "were bearers of attitudes and values that proved instrumental in shaping scientific culture in the early modern era": *Science and the Secrets of Nature* (Princeton: Princeton Univ. Press, 1994), 8–9. Even more recent works by Steven Shapin and Pamela H. Smith have developed similar themes. See Steven Shapin, *The Scientific Revolution* (Chicago: Univ. of Chicago Press, 1996) and Pamela H. Smith, "Vital Spirits: Redemption, Artisanship, and the New Philosophy in Early Modern Europe," in *Rethinking the Scientific Revolution*, ed. Margaret J. Osler (Cambridge: Cambridge Univ. Press, 2000), 119–36.

[16] A. Pérez-Ramos, *Francis Bacon's Idea of Science and the Maker's Knowledge Tradition* (Oxford: Clarendon Press, 1988), x.

"maker's knowledge . . . a tradition . . . which postulates an intimate relationship between objects of cognition and objects of construction, and regards knowledge as a kind of making or as a capacity to make (*verum factum*)."[17] Bacon developed a "conception of science as predominantly bent on the active engagement of man in Nature's processes over and above the intellectual apprehension of them in the old demonstrative fashion . . . [which] . . . sends us back to Bacon's appreciation of the mechanical arts as an epistemological alternative, enshrined in the realm of the *doable*, the *makeable*, the *constructable*" (emphasis Pérez-Ramos's).[18] Precisely because they were making something through a cognitive practice which engaged their entire bodies, artisans laboring over furnaces were learning far more about thermodynamic processes than had millennia of thinkers contemplating the nature of fire. Not surprisingly then, observing smiths working at

---

[17]   A. Pérez-Ramos, *Bacon's Idea*, 48.

[18]   A. Pérez-Ramos, *Bacon's Idea*, 143. Though Pérez-Ramos does not make the connection, the fact that Greek knowledge was largely ocular in nature bolsters his argument. Long before Plato's theory of forms/ideas, εἶδος had its root in a verb for seeing, which in the perfect tense (οἶδα) means not only "I have seen," but at the same time, "I know." (It is for this reason that εἶδος is alternately translated as "form" or "idea," because it is either a form one has seen or an idea one now knows.) Because to both Plato and the presocratics "to have seen" was "to know," there was this thoroughly ocular element to much of the Greek science which endured into Bacon's era (what Kuhn dubbed "classical science"). The seventeenth-century triumph of this tradition must certainly have been the *Principia*, as Newton, having no way to get into outer space, merely used what he had *seen*, as well as what others had *observed*, to think through the motions of the heavens. On the other hand, natural philosophers had learned very little by observing fire. Because smiths working at their forges were engaging thermodynamic processes in a way which went beyond the Greek ocular tradition, their work represented not only the basis for a new science, but an entirely new form of embodied cognition.

       Though Plato's (and subsequently Aristotle's; see for example Aristotle's *Politica*, 1282ff.) view of maker's knowledge as inferior to user's knowledge would be enormously influential throughout Western history, Pérez-Ramos also brings attention to Judaeo-Christian counters to the notion. In the words of Philo of Alexandria: "No one [except of course the Greeks] doubts that the parent must have knowledge (ἐπιστημόνα) of his offspring, the craftsman of his handiwork . . . God is in very truth the father, craftsman, and steward of the heaven and the universe and all that is therein": Philo of Alexandria, *Complete Works*, trans. F. H. Colson and G. H. Whittaker, Loeb (Cambridge, MA: Harvard Univ. Press, 1963) 2: 22–23. However, it is not until the sixteenth and seventeenth centuries that the question of Plato's view of maker's knowledge comes under siege. As it became apparent that through the process of making objects artisans gained real knowledge, it became increasingly difficult to dismiss such knowledge as being of an inferior sort. As Pérez-Ramos notes, Aristotle had denigrated the artisan's arts by emphasizing "their stagnation since they were first discovered or divinely granted to man," but the centuries immediately before Bacon had seen quite the opposite situation: *Bacon's Idea*, 144.

their forges, Bacon intends to forsake the Greeks and their "Muses as barren virgins . . . [and to instead] . . . rely upon Vulcan" (4. 393).[19]

In order to communicate such practical knowledge, we find Bacon hoping that one day language might be dispensed with altogether. As Brian Vickers rightly notes, Bacon "never looked forward to the marriage of words and things. Rather, at the millennial point [the completion of Bacon's proposed thousand-year human quest for knowledge], the mind of man should be able to commune directly with . . . 'natural and material things.'"[20] Until then, Bacon considered, but never significantly developed, the creation of an entirely new language; indeed, a new type of hieroglyphics.[21] Short of this, and working within the boundaries of existing language, Bacon proposed that instead of using language to freely and arbitrarily mimic things (res) with words (verba), we keep language's mimetic aspect seriously in check. Wildly and illiberally using metaphors and tropes to represent a thing (let alone a process) of which we did not yet have a maker's knowledge — which indeed is largely the vocation of writers — simply would not do. In fact, it would do nothing but confuse. What Bacon proposed still had a mimetic element to it, but there was the hope that if the entire process of a thing being brought forth into being could be reflected in language, it would be far better mirrored. In something of a paradox then, Bacon provisionally saw the maker's knowledge of the artisan (which deconstructed the artificial/natural binary and brought into question mimesis) bringing about an improvement in mimesis itself — a very optimistic thought, so much so that Michael McCanles has suggested that because Bacon made such unique claims regarding words (verba) mimicking things (res), at root "Derrida's pessimism is the result of Bacon's aspiring

---

[19] In some sense, Amos Funkenstein had suggested this same notion two years before Pérez-Ramos: "The study of Nature in the seventeenth century was neither predominantly idealistic nor empirical. It was first and foremost *constructive*, pragmatic in the radical sense. It would lead to the conviction that the doable — at least in principle — is also understandable" (emphasis Funkenstein's): *Theology and the Scientific Imagination from the Middle Ages to the Seventeenth Century* (Princeton: Princeton Univ. Press, 1986), 78. But Pérez-Ramos's presentation of "maker's knowledge," in addition to being exhaustive and tremendously influential, is significant in that, as an historical analysis, it argues that maker's knowledge "cannot be easily accommodated within the general matrix of Western philosophical discourse": "Bacon's Forms and the Maker's Knowledge Tradition," in *The Cambridge Companion to Bacon,* ed. Peltonen, 99–120, at 104.

[20] Brian Vickers, "Bacon and Rhetoric," in *The Cambridge Companion to Bacon,* ed. Peltonen, 200–31, at 227.

[21] See especially Paolo Rossi, *Logic and the Art of Memory: The Quest for Universal Language,* trans. Stephen Clucas (London: Athlone Press, 2000).

optimism."[22] At the very least, insofar as Bacon seriously brought mimesis into question for writers like Locke and Hobbes, he accordingly opened it up for the post-structural response.

As to how Bacon implemented his new understanding in practice, in order to insure that we are not misguided by specious tropes, metaphors, analogies, or even words born of irresponsible *mimesis,* Bacon proposed that "for all that concerns ornaments of speech, similitudes, treasury of eloquence and like such emptiness, let it be utterly dismissed. Also let those things which are admitted be themselves set down briefly and concisely" (4. 254). Bacon, then, embarking upon a "plain style" of expression in an attempt to check arbitrary *mimesis,* was attempting to use language in something of a new way. This is not to say, however, that he was the first to undertake this project.

The question of just what literary forms influenced Bacon is certainly not new. Fifty years ago Morris Croll, in boldly arguing that modern English prose began with Bacon, dubbed this new approach "anti-Ciceronian" or "Attic" to reflect Bacon's (along with Montaigne's) introduction of an Attic-influenced plain style of writing which would "dictate the prevailing form of prose style in all the countries of Europe."[23] There is much to support this view as Bacon himself acknowledged his debt to the "Attic" aphorism: "The earliest and most ancient investigators of truth, with better credit and success, used to cast the knowledge which they set themselves to gather from the contemplation of things and to store for use in the form of *aphorisms,* or short, unconnected sentences, not methodically arranged; and did not pretend or profess a universal art" (*NO,* 71, Bacon's emphasis). Bacon's frustration with the writing of just a few generations before him, which had been influenced by the "Ciceronian" model, also bolsters Croll's claim. This approach to writing "hunted more after words than matter; more after the choiceness of phrases, and the round clean composition of the sentence, and the sweet falling of the clauses, and the varying and illustration of their works with tropes and figures, then after the weight of the matter, worth of subject, soundness of argument, life of invention, or depth of judgment . . . . In

---

[22] Michael McCanles, "From Derrida to Bacon and Beyond," in *Francis Bacon's Legacy of Texts: The Art of Discovery Grows with Discovery,* ed. William Sessions (New York: AMS Press, 1990), 25–41, at 41.

[23] See Morris W. Croll, *Style. Rhetoric and Rhyme: Essays by Morris W. Croll,* ed. J. Max Patrick and Robert O. Evans (Princeton: Princeton Univ. Press, 1966). For a more recent account of how Bacon's writing style owes a large debt to classical aphorisms, especially Hippocrates's *Aphorisms,* see Stephen Clucas, "A Knowledge Broken," in *English Renaissance Prose: History, Language, and Politics,* ed. Neil Rhodes (Tempe: Medieval and Renaissance Texts and Studies, 1997), 147–72.

sum, the whole inclination and bent of those times was rather towards copia than matter" (3. 283–84). Croll's view, however, was quickly challenged by R. F. Jones, who, acknowledging that Bacon's plain style was a paradigm for modern prose, nonetheless argued that it was Bacon's scientific project itself that provided the greatest influence on his writing.[24] While this view was qualified and expanded by Lisa Jardine in the mid-1970s, it too was amended, this time by Brian Vickers, who compellingly argued that although Bacon was clearly anti-Ciceronian, this hardly made him a hard-edged *anti-rhetorical* writer.[25] As I hope to have shown in my opening paragraphs, Bacon's writing certainly shows the signs of carefully crafted rhetoric. Bacon saw a role for rhetoric, but only if it was checked in scientific writing.

Bacon, however, was influenced by more than the Attic aphorism. Consider Montaigne as a source. It has been argued not only that Bacon's writing was influenced by Montaigne's *Essays,* but also that Montaigne also preferred the Attic "directness and sharpness of Plutarch, Tacitus, and Seneca."[26] But it is also true that in at least three of the forms he undertakes, Montaigne — who thankfully never misses the chance to make a statement of authorial intent — clearly references a non-Attic source. As early as 1580 he was beginning essays by noting that "master-craftsmen" speak better and "with more authority" than Montaigne himself did.[27] While this has simply been dismissed as false humility on the part of the writer, rather than as a sincere authorial statement, he further notes in his autobiography that he intends to write in a "low style," patterned on the "simple language . . . of soldiers."[28] Again this could just be a turn of speech, but it is a striking coincidence that actual soldiers of the time, in writing their own biographies, were declaring that they intended to write "without rhetoric or fancy turns of phrase," instead

---

[24] R. F. Jones et al., *The Seventeenth Century: Studies in the History of English Thought and Literature from Bacon to Pope* (Stanford: Stanford Univ. Press, 1951).

[25] See Lisa Jardine, *Discovery and the Art of Discourse* (Cambridge: Cambridge Univ. Press, 1974), and Brian Vickers, "The Royal Society and English Prose Style: A Reassessment," in *Rhetoric and the Pursuit of Truth: Language Changes in the Seventeenth and Eighteenth Centuries,* ed. Brian Vickers and N. S. Struever (Los Angeles: William Andrews Clark Library, 1985), 1–76.

[26] Floyd Gray, "The Essay as Criticism," in *The Cambridge History of Literary Criticism*: Volume Three, *The Renaissance,* ed. Glyn P. Norton (Cambridge: Cambridge Univ. Press, 1999), 271–77, at 271.

[27] Michel de Montaigne, *The Complete Michel de Montaigne,* trans. and ed. M. A. Screech (London: Penguin, 1993), 457.

[28] *The Autobiography of Michel de Montaigne,* trans. and ed. Marvin Lowenthal (New York: Houghton Mifflin Co., 1956), 58, 60.

relating "sincere, plain and uninvented truth" in a "not polished style."[29] Indeed, having recently completed a book-length study of early-modern artisan autobiography, James Amelang notes that "virtually all autobiographical writing by craftsmen insisted on being one thing: plain. Plain style meant simplicity, and simplicity meant the absence of its opposites: artifice, decoration, adornment, even literary effort itself."[30] (This style of writing was not, however, limited to craftsmen. In her 1609 diary, the midwife Louise Bourgeois, for example, clearly declares how "little artifice" there will be in her "discourse.")[31]

When Montaigne moved to the subject of travel writing, he came to similar conclusions: "A plain ignorant Fellow is more likely to tell the Truth," for the educated "cannot forbear to alter the Story; they never represent things to you simply as they are, but rather as they appeared to them."[32] This is clearly not humility on Montaigne's part, but rather an awareness that a new kind of writing, hoping for greater fidelity to facts, was arriving on the early-modern scene. Prior to Bacon's *The Advancement of Learning* in 1605, artisans were — not only in essays, autobiographies, and travel writing, but in a variety of additional genres — repeatedly making the claim that they intended a new, simple style as backlash to what Croll called the "Ciceronian" influence.

While the former apprentice Richard Johnson prefaced his 1599 novel *Tom a Lincolne* by apologizing that "my skill in penning it is very simple . . . presenting so rude a work,"[33] other novelists, like the silk-weaver Thomas Deloney, opened his 1597 *The Gentle Craft, Part 1* with a simple, confident statement of what he intended: "Gentle reader, you that vouchsafe to cast curteous lookes into this rude Pamphlet: expect not herein to find any matter . . . curiously pen'd with pickt words, or choice phrases, but a quaint and plaine discourse."[34] As he states it even more plainly in the preface of his *Jack of Newbury* published in the same year, "this [is] my rude worke . . . briefly written, and in a plain and humble manner."[35] It could be argued that this is less a choice than a necessity, as artisans

---

[29] The soldiers Alonso de Contreras, Diego Dunque, and Pedro de Castaneda are quoted by James S. Amelang in his *The Flight of Icarus: Artisan Autobiography in Early Modern Europe.* (Stanford: Stanford Univ. Press, 1998), 156–57.

[30] Amelang, *The Flight of Icarus,* 155.

[31] Louise Bourgeois, *Observations diverses.* quoted and translated by Amelang in *The Flight of Icarus,* 156.

[32] Michel de Montaigne, *The Complete Michel de Montaigne,* 364–65.

[33] Richard Johnson, R. I., *The Most Pleasant History of Tom a Lincolne,* ed. Richard S. M. Hirsh (Columbia, SC: Univ. of South Carolina Press, 1978), 3.

[34] Thomas Deloney, *The Gentle Craft, Part 1* in *The Novels of Thomas Deloney,* ed. Merritt E. Lewis (Bloomington: Indiana Univ. Press, 1961), 174.

[35] Thomas Deloney, *Jack of Newbury* in *The Novels of Thomas Deloney,* 3.

would have largely lacked the education to make any attempt at a high style. But we know that Deloney, for example, was well educated, beginning his publishing career fifteen years earlier with at least three translations from Latin to English.[36] (Moreover, although more the exception than the rule, certain artisan/ writers, such as Thomas Tusser, favored—and mastered rather well—a more ornate prose.)[37] As becomes apparent when we consider the form of writing (the craft manual) that is the obvious artisanal predecessor of Baconian writing, there were well-founded reasons for inaugurating this new approach.

In 1572 Thomas Hill prefaced his enormously popular (it was repeatedly reprinted for over a century) *The Profitable Arte of Gardeninge* with a declaration of "simplenes of stile, and the want of eloquence," a promise to write "a simple and rude worke."[38] An overwhelming number of such works that contain prefatory remarks (like Walter Bailey in 1588), make similar opening pledges to provide only "simple discourse."[39] Those that dispense with the preface (like the anonymous *The Orchard and the Garden* of 1594) nonetheless nearly always follow the plain plan.[40] Many, like Gervase Markham, made quite clear that this new writing was not even intended for an audience expecting embellishment: "I have adventured to thrust into the world this booke, which nothing at all belongeth to the silken corner but to the plaine russet honest Husbandman."[41] The reason for preferring the plain style becomes obvious when we consider amateur gardener Sir Hugh Plat, who wrote extensive gardening manuals in the artisanal style from the 1590s to 1608. In Plat's rather extensive preface to one of the late works, he declares that the manual is "not written at adventure, or by an imaginary conceit in a Schollers private studie, but wrong out of the earth, by the painfull hand of experience."[42]

---

[36] See Lewis's comments in *The Novels of Thomas Deloney*, xxiv.

[37] Thomas Tusser, *Five Hundred Points of Good Husbandry* (London, 1573).

[38] Thomas Hill, *The Profitable Arte of Gardeninge* (London: Prtd. by Thomas Marshe, 1572), 8.

[39] Walter Bailey, *A Short Discourse of The Three Kindes of Peppers in Common Vse, and Certaine Special Medicines Made of the Same, Tending to the Preseruation of Health* ([Eliot's Court Press?], 1588), 1.

[40] *The Orchard, and the Garden Taining Cerne Necessarie, Secret, and Ordinarie Knowledges in Grafting and Gardening. Wherein are Described Sundrie Waies to Graffe, and Diuerse Proper New Plots for the Garden. Gathered from the Dutch and French. Also to Know the Time and Season, When It is Good to Sow and Replant all Manner of Seedes* (Prtd. by Adam Islip, 1594).

[41] Gervase Markham, *The English Husbandman* (London: Printed by Thomas Snodham for John Browne, 1613), 1.

[42] Sir Hugh Plat, *Floraes Paradise Beautified and Adorned with Sundry Sorts of Delicate Fruites and Flovvers* (London: Printed by H. L. for William Leake, 1608), 11.

This appeal to experience and practice itself is common in the genre, often connected with the declaration of plain style, as in Richard Gardiner's manual of 1599: "... accept of this my short and simple pennings of this my practice and experience in Gardening."[43] However, Plat makes especially clear that there is a reason for not only appealing directly to experience, but rejecting traditional prose as well:

> I leave method at this time to Schoolemen, who have already written many large and methodical volumes of this subject (whose labours have greatly furnished our studies and libraries, but little or nothing altered or graced our Gardens and Orchards) that you will accept my skill, in such a habit and forme as I shalle think most fit and appropriate for it, & and give me lease rather to write briefly & confusedly, with those that seeke out the practicall, and operative part of Nature.[44]

The work having been published three years after Bacon's *Advancement of Learning,* there remains a question if Plat here has been influenced by Bacon, or Bacon through similar statements made by Plat a decade earlier.[45] In any event, both are clearly writing in the artisanal tradition. And just as Bacon felt free to stray

---

[43] Richard Gardiner, *Profitable Instructions for the Manuring, Sowing, and Planting of Kitchin Gardens Very Profitable for the Commonwealth and Greatly for the Helpe and Comfort of Poore People. Gathered by Richard Gardner of Shrewsburie* (London: Printed by Edward Allde for Edward White, 1599), 1.

[44] Plat, *Floraes Paradise*, 3.

[45] Consider Plat's 1594 statement: "you have read that Art doth perfect Nature, which can never be more profitably understood than in this sense; for although Nature appears a most fair and fruitful Body, and as admirable in her variety as abundance, yet the Art, here mentioned, is as a Soul to inform that Body to examine and to refine her actions, and to teach her to understand these abilities of her own, which before lay undiscovered to her." While there are clearly differences here with Bacon's most mature thought (Plat's soul/body metaphor for example), there are also striking similarities with ideas which do not appear until ten years later in Bacon's writing: Sir Hugh Plat, *The Jewel House of Art and Nature Containing Divers Rare and Profitable Inventions, Together with Sundry New Experiments in the Art of Husbandry: With Divers Chimical Conclusions Concerning the Art of Distillation, and the Rare Practises and Uses Thereof, Faithfully and Familiarly Set Down, According to the Authours Own Experience* (London: Printed by Bernard Alsop, 1653), 3. First published in 1594.
     While Bacon believed that the future would best be served by rationalizing artisanal practices through his own proposed method, a decade before *The Advancement of Learning* Plat felt that artisans could do the job alone, if only supported: "Now therefore I see it is time, and high time to let the world, and all posterity to understand, that ... our english Artists ... [would be able] ... if the stipend of honor and merit were now propounded, fully to discover a world of new inventions, whereof no *Polidore* hath as yet taken any note or notice": Sir Hugh

from the plain style for rhetorical presentation (as in the opening of the *Novum Organon),* so does Plat, although the latter nicely makes clear that he, like Bacon, is merely provisionally using rhetoric: "And let not the concealing, or rather the figurative describing of my first & principal secret, withdraw your good and thankful acceptation, from all that are subsequent; on which, I have bestowed the plainest and most familiar phrase that I can."[46] While the best argument for Bacon the rhetorician may well come from his success in allowing posterity to conclude that the artisanal plain style of writing was *his* innovation, even near-contemporaries who had enormous respect for Bacon, like Thomas Sprat, knew where the style originated. In his *History of the Royal Society,* Sprat made clear that members of the Society, following Bacon, attempted to "reject all the amplifications, digressions, and swellings of style: to return back to the primitive purity, and shortness, when men delivered to many *things,* almost in an equal number of *words.* They have extracted from all their members a close, naked, natural way of speaking; positive expressions; clear senses; a native easiness . . . preferring the language of Artisans, Countrymen, and Merchants, before that, of Wits, or Scholars."[47] To Sprat, echoing the artisanal call to return to experience, it is artisans and scientist "who bring *Knowledge* back to our very senses, from whence it was at first deriv'd to our understandings . . . who can behold, without indignation, how many . . . uncertainties . . . specious *Tropes* and *Figures* have brought to our knowledge?"[48]

Sprat here directly addresses one of the central linguistic issues for the artisans (and later Bacon). As has been argued by Pierre Bourdieu, "the essential part of the *modus operandi* which defines practical mastery is transmitted in practice, in its practical state, without attaining the level of discourse."[49] Through their remarkable achievements artisans brought home the fact—obscured by two thousand years of Plato's influence—that it was possible for human beings to encounter their world collectively, and make their way in it quite well, without language being there ahead of us as some sort of fixed and immutable (as Plato argued) medium of understanding. Not only does language not precede a

---

Plat, *A Discouerie of Certaine English Wants, Which Are Royally Supplyed in this Treatise* (London: Prtd. by P. S. for William Ponsonby, 1595), 3.

[46] Plat, *Discouerie,* 4.

[47] Thomas Sprat, *History of the Royal Society,* ed. Jackson I. Cope and Harold Whitmore Jones (London: Routledge, 1959), 113.

[48] Sprat, *History of the Royal Society,* 112. This all goes back to the characterization of the Bible as being written in *stilus humilis.*

[49] Pierre Bourdieu, *Outline of a Theory of Practice* (Cambridge: Cambridge Univ. Press, 1977), 87–94.

variety of non-discursive practices, as Bourdieu argued, perhaps it is the other way around. As Nietzsche noted, because a people are held together not only by language, but by a wide variety of practices they share (existing only in a practical state), we can "think, feel, will, and remember, and we could also 'act' in every sense of the word . . . [indeed] . . . The whole of our life would be possible, without, as it were, seeing itself [mimetically] in a mirror."[50]

Rediscovering the importance of non-discursive practices, the artisans realized that now it was linguistic practices that needed to play catch-up if they were to more widely communicate their discoveries. Words needed to simply and accurately reflect the remarkable new things they brought into world. In order to take advantage of the printing technology they created, and realizing that the wildly fanciful language of high culture was far too removed from the new reality they were literally forging, sixteenth-century artisans accordingly stripped language bare. Not surprisingly, they also began adapting the new plain style for their biographies, travel writings, novels, and so forth.

As to these far-reaching implications of the plain style, they were probably best first understood by John Locke. In chapter ten of the third book of *An Essay Concerning Human Understanding*, Locke, beginning with a veiled nod to Bacon, suggests that that "men are guilty of . . . [rendering] . . . signs less clear and distinct in their signification that naturally they need to be."[51] The closest thing to a solution to what Locke perceived as a fundamental problem of signification (and epistemology) was the artisanal plain style Bacon appropriated:

> I confess, in discourses where we seek rather pleasure and delight than information . . . such ornaments . . . can scarce pass for faults. But . . . we must allow that all the art of rhetoric . . . all the artificial and figurative application of words eloquence hath invented, are for nothing else but to insinuate wrong ideas, move the passions, and thereby mislead judgment; and so indeed are perfect cheats . . . in all discourses . . . where truth and knowledge are concerned, [such figures] cannot but be thought a great fault.[52]

Not surprisingly, post-structuralists have repeatedly and mercilessly returned to Locke's suggestion that, even with a plain style, reality can be mimicked (indeed re-presented) truthfully in language. Most, however, have ignored that the suggestion comes to Locke from Bacon — and, of course, to Bacon from artisans.

---

[50] Friedrich Nietzsche, *The Gay Science,* trans. Walter Kaufmann (New York: Random House, 1974), 354.

[51] John Locke, *An Essay Concerning Human Understanding* (Chicago: Britannica, 1952), 291.

[52] Locke, *An Essay Concerning Human Understanding,* 299.

Although obviously philosophically influential in its own right, in a now-classic reading of the rise of the novel, Ian Watt noted how Locke came to influence English prose itself as the "chapters at the end of the third Book of the *Essay Concerning Human Understanding* . . . [began] . . . to be reflected in literary theory" and the plain-style writing of Defoe and Richardson.[53] This, of course, echoes Morris Croll's statements regarding the enormous influence of the plain style on English prose, although Watt (perhaps correctly) saw Locke as a major force in popularizing the approach. However, because Watt failed to recognize not only Bacon's influence on Locke, but an artisanal influence on Bacon, he took this new style to be largely an eighteenth-century innovation.

In propounding the importance of the artisanal plain style of writing on Bacon I do not mean to suggest that this was his only model. Certainly Bacon's aphorisms owe much to their Attic predecessors. Furthermore, there remains the question of how Bacon's "plain artisan style" relates to the equally plain Puritan approach to writing. However, as I hope to have shown in this essay, the plain style of the artisan dovetails so seamlessly with the ideological underpinnings of Bacon's overall project that its influence cannot easily be dismissed.

UNIVERSITY OF CALIFORNIA, SANTA BARBARA

---

[53] Ian Watt, *The Rise of the Novel: Studies in Defoe, Richardson, and Fielding* (Berkeley: Univ. of California Press, 1965).

Francis Bacon in Collaboration[1]

ALAN STEWART

Francis Bacon opens his 1608 *Redargutio philosophiarum* (*Refutation of philosophies*) with the statement "I am preparing a refutation of philosophies but know not how to begin."[2] Or so reads Benjamin Farrington's translation. Bacon's Latin, however, gives "paramus" (we are preparing) and "nescimus" (we do not know), and indeed much of the first-person narrative is rendered in the first person plural. But at times Bacon's narrative dramatizes this confusion between the singular and the plural, the *I* and the *we*. A friend returns from France, and asks what the narrator is doing.

> 'Your enquiry is timely', said I, 'for, just in case you think I have nothing on hand, I am planning an Instauration of Philosophy, containing nothing empty or abstract, but designed to improve the conditions of human life.' 'A noble task,' said he. 'Who is helping you?' 'You must understand,' I replied, 'that I am working in complete isolation.' 'That is a hard lot,' said he, and

---

[1] This paper was first presented at the 2001 Modern Language Association Convention, Los Angeles, CA, at the Josephine A. Roberts Forum, Arthur F. Marotti presiding. It was then entitled "Editing Somebody, Possibly Francis Bacon". Later versions were delivered at the Five Colleges Seminar, Amherst; the Univ. of Chicago; Sussex Univ.; and University College London. I am grateful for the invitations to speak, and for the helpful responses at each venue.

[2] "Atque in redargutione ipsa philosophiarum quam paramus, nescimus fere quo nos vertamus": Francis Bacon, *Redargutio Philosophiarum*, in *Works*, ed. James Spedding, Robert Leslie Ellis, and Douglas Denon Heath, 7 vols. (London: Longman, 1857–1859) [hereafter *SEH*], 3: 557; trans. Benjamin Farrington, *The Philosophy of Francis Bacon: An Essay on its Development from 1603 to 1609 with New Translations of Fundamental Texts* (1964; Chicago: Univ. of Chicago Press [Phoenix Books], 1966) [hereafter Farrington], 103.

immediately added, 'But take it from me that there are others who have the matter at heart'.[3]

The friend then goes on to relate what happened to him in France. In Paris, a friend introduced him to a gathering which he describes as 'the happiest experience of my life'.[4]

> There were some fifty men there, all of mature years, not a young man among them, all bearing the stamp of dignity and probity. . . . they were chatting easily among themselves but sitting in rows as if expecting somebody. Not long after there entered to them a man of peaceful and serene air, save that his face had become habituated to the expression of pity. They all stood up in his honour.[5]

The new arrival asks the men how they could all afford to be there, and they tell him "we all put what you have to tell us above any other business."[6] The "man of peaceful and serene air" then takes his seat, and delivers an address, which is the "refutation of philosophies."

It's a curious framing device that moves from Bacon's claim to be working on a refutation "in complete isolation" to a scene in which the refutation-deliverer is accorded massive respect by a group of fifty like-minded high-ranking men. The move plays on ideas of singular versus plural, isolation versus collectivity, that I shall argue in this chapter are not only integral to Bacon's philosophy, and a reflection of the collaborative nature of his scientific work,[7] but also a result — or at least a philosophical reworking of — the material conditions of Bacon's writing.

---

[3] "Opportune, inquam; nam ne nihil me agere existimes, meditor Instaurationem Philosophiæ, quæ nihil inanis aut abstracti habeat, quæque vitæ humanæ conditiones in melius provehat. Honestum profecto opus, inquit: et quos socios habes? Ego certe, inquam, in summa solitudine versor. Duræ inquit, partes tuæ sunt; et statim addidit; Atque tamen scito hæc aliis curæ esse": *SEH* 3: 559; Farrington, 104.

[4] "nihil in vita mihi accidit jucundius": *SEH* 3: 559; Farrington, 104.

[5] "Erant autem circiter quinquaginta viri, neque ex iis quisquam adolescens, sed omnes ætate provectiores . . . invenisse eos familiariter inter se colloquentes; sedebant tamen ordine sedilibus dispositis, ac veluti adventum alicujus expectantes. Neque ita multo post ingressum ad eos virum quondam, aspectus (ut ei videbatur) admodum placidi et sereni; nisi quod oris compositio erat tanquam miserantis; cui cum omnes assurrexissent": *SEH* 3: 559; Farrington, 104.

[6] "Cumque unus ex cœtu respondisset, eum ipsum hoc otium illis fecisse, cum quæ ab ipso exspectarent illi ducerent omni negotio potiora": *SEH* 3: 560; Farrington, 104–5.

[7] As explored, for example, in Rose-Mary Sargent, "Bacon as an Advocate for Cooperative Scientific Research," in *The Cambridge Companion to Bacon*, ed. Markku Peltonen (Cambridge: Cambridge Univ. Press, 1996), 146–71; and Cesare Pastorino, "The Mine and the

This last aspect is hinted at in the final sentence before the address: "My friend gave me a record of [the address] which he made at the time. It was the best he could do, but he had to admit that when he went over it at home with the friend who had introduced him they found it very inferior to the original."[8]

The tortured story of this text — delivered orally, taken down by a listener, reconstructed by him, edited by him and another, and *still* considered "very inferior to the original" — sounds very familiar to me, as someone who has spent years dealing with the fragmentary traces of the early writings of Bacon. The processes of early modern composition — especially collaborative composition — and the mechanics of the period's scribal publication combine to render our modern notions of authorship extremely crude. This chapter outlines the rationale by which various texts of the 1580s and 1590s have been claimed as Bacon's — even though they were circulating under the name of his friend and patron, the earl of Essex.[9] It then goes on to question what it would mean if the same rationale were to be applied to Bacon's later works — works that we know to have been written to some degree in collaboration with others.

The Oxford Francis Bacon is a sixteen-volume edition that aims to supplant the standard Victorian edition by James Spedding, Robert Leslie Ellis, and Douglas Denon Heath.[10] Like most authorial editions, *The Oxford Francis Bacon* is a venture in which the concept of Bacon as sole "author" is valorized, and certain assumptions concerning authorship are made integral to the editorial process, and most crucially in the choice of "source-text," the basis for the edited text. The methodology of the edition was first outlined by the founding co-general editor Graham Rees in 1986:

Furnace: Francis Bacon, Thomas Russell, and Early Stuart Mining Culture," *Early Science and Medicine* 14 (2009): 630–60.

   [8] "Nam aiebat qui hæc narrabat, se illa tum excepisse ut potuit; licet cum apud se una cum illo amico suo, qui eum introduxerat, ea recognosceret, fateretur ea longe inferior iis quæ tum dicta essent visa esse. Exemplum autem orationis, quod circa se habebat, proferebat": *SEH* 3: 560; Farrington, 105.

   [9] For a fuller treatment of this question, on which this chapter draws, see Alan Stewart, "The Making of Writing in Renaissance England: Re-thinking Authorship Through Collaboration," in *Renaissance Tranformations: The Making of English Writing (1500–1650)*, ed. Margaret Healy and Thomas Healy (Edinburgh: Edinburgh Univ. Press, 2009), 81–96.

   [10] *The Oxford Francis Bacon*, 16 vols. (Oxford: Oxford Univ. Press, 1996 and ongoing) [hereafter *OFB*]: to date, seven volumes (1, 4, 6, 11, 12, 13, 15) have been published. Spedding's edition comprises the *Works* [*SEH*], and the companion volumes *Letters and the Life*, ed. James Spedding, 7 vols. (London: Longman et al., 1861–1874) [hereafter *LL*].

A source-text is any text (be it a manuscript or printed book) which has some claim to authority. In the present case there are are four categories of source-text:
1. Editions printed in Bacon's lifetime with his authority.
2. First editions printed by later editors (Rawley, Gruter, Tenison etc.) from authoritative manuscripts now no longer extant. To the same category belong later editions of the same printed texts (provided that they were published with the authority of those same editors).
3. Manuscripts prepared by Bacon or his amanuenses.
4. Later manuscript copies of Bacon MSS (where no other authoritative sources are extant).
Nothing else is truly authoritative . . .[11]

In this formulation, material evidence on which the edition is based is selected (or rejected) according to the criterion of the personal involvement of the author Bacon in the production of those materials. In the case of my volume, comprising Bacon's early writings (from 1584–1596), this means in the production of *manuscript* materials.[12] These manuscripts are frequently not autograph, not "prepared by Bacon or his amanuenses" but scribal copies. Moreover, they do not bear his name. In some cases, this is because they are texts Bacon intended to circulate anonymously; other texts, however, do make an authorial claim, but the author is not Bacon. These were designed to circulate under the name of Bacon's patron and friend Robert Devereux, second earl of Essex; Bacon later described how for some years "I did nothing but deuise and ruminate with my selfe to the best of my vnderstanding, propositions & memorials, of any thing that might concerne his Lordships honor, fortune, or seruice."[13] Some of this labour took the form of explicit counsel to the earl, such as letters of advice from Bacon to Essex. But it seems that much of what Bacon undertook for the earl was not in his own voice. He planned, drafted, and composed letters that were signed by the earl, and contributed to entertainments that were publicly associated with the earl. It was only in subsequent centuries that these texts would be claimed as Bacon's. An entertainment written for the 1595 Accession Day celebrations was first claimed

---

[11] Graham Rees, "*Instauratio instaurationis*: Towards a New Edition of the Works of Francis Bacon," *Nouvelles de la république des lettres* 7 (1987): 37–48 at 45–46.

[12] Alan Stewart with Harriet Knight, eds., *Early Writings, 1584–1596*, OFB 1 (Oxford: Oxford Univ. Press, 2012).

[13] *Sir Francis Bacon his apologie, in certaine imputations concerning the late Earle of Essex Written to the right Honorable his very good Lord, the Earle of Deuonshire, Lord Lieutenant of Ireland* (London: [Richard Field] for Felix Norton, 1604), A5ᵛ-A6ʳ.

for Bacon by editor Thomas Birch in the mid-eighteenth century, while letters written ostensibly by Essex to Fulke Greville and to Roger Manners, earl of Rutland, were claimed as Bacon's by editor James Spedding a century later. Since the ascriptions to Bacon were made, scholars have been largely content to accept these works as his, and have deployed them extensively in their analyses of Bacon's relationships with Essex and Elizabeth, and his treatment of learning in the years before the publication of *The Advancement of Learning.*

In the past two decades, however, the debate over the authorship of some these works has been reignited. Paul Hammer has taken issue with the attribution of these pieces to Bacon,[14] pointing out that Essex was building a team of secretaries (augmented by scholarly friends including Bacon). He sees these writings as "the product of a cooperative effort between Essex, his secretaries and, perhaps, Francis Bacon," with Essex at the helm: "Essex himself *had a major part* in composing these productions but he also *used the assistance of* his secretariat and possibly also of Francis Bacon."[15] Brian Vickers, however, sees these "Essex" pieces as "interlinked in many ways, mirroring the development of Bacon's thought in the 1590s, and reflecting characteristic methods of composition,"[16] and suggests that "Essex seems to have called on [Bacon's] help when he needed some particularly delicate piece of writing, such as an eloquent or tactful composition involving the queen." He points out that there is plenty of evidence that Bacon acted "as go-between and ghost-writer for Essex," and sees "Bacon, already an experienced lawyer and politician, expending much energy between 1595 and 1600 as a private counselor" to Essex.[17]

My own edition takes seriously Vickers's notion of Bacon as a "counselor" (although it backdates the beginning of the Bacon-Essex relationship to 1588).[18] Even though it was Essex who 'authorised' a piece and under whose name it would circulate, the writers he employed were keen that their own ideas should come through. In this way, Bacon's "counsel" to Essex should be seen as more wide-ranging than the explicit letters of advice that he wrote to the earl between 1596 and 1600. Essex deliberately chose high-ranking academics and top intelligence

---

[14] Paul E. J. Hammer, "The Uses of Scholarship: The Secretariat of Robert Devereux, Second Earl of Essex, c. 1585–1601," *English Historical Review* 109 (1994): 26–51; idem, "The Earl of Essex, Fulke Greville, and the Employment of Scholars," *Studies in Philology* 91 (1994): 167–80.

[15] Hammer, "Essex, Greville, and the Employment of Scholars," 172; italics added.

[16] Brian Vickers, "The Authenticity of Bacon's Earliest Writings," *Studies in Philology* 94 (1997): 248–96.

[17] Vickers, "Authenticity," 257–58, 263.

[18] The following discussion draws on my "Introduction" to Bacon, *Early Writings, OFB* 1, xxxiii–xxxv.

gatherers not because he needed mechanical scribes or administrators, but because of what they could offer intellectually. It is a fair assumption that Francis Bacon was called on initially for his legal expertise. But certainly by 1593, he was providing 'counsel' in a larger sense.

The nature of Bacon's counsel can be indicated through a couple of examples. The Gibson papers at Lambeth Palace Library hold a tract that is docketed in Bacon's hand, "A letter framed for my Lord of Essex to the Queen." Here Bacon does not take on the earl's own voice, but walks him sentence by sentence through a letter Essex should write: "That you desire her Majesty to believe . . . that [it] is not conscience to yourself of any advantage . . . that moveth you to send her these lines of your own mind . . ." and so on.[19] This is no more than a plan; it would be possible for Essex to compose and pen the letter, and for Bacon's input to be undetectable, were it not for this chance survival. Another example is found in an undated letter (probably 1593) from Essex to Bacon, now in the Anthony Bacon papers at Lambeth.[20] Essex explains that he is under pressure from the queen to produce, at short notice, "a draft of an Instruction" on intelligence concerning Rheims and Rome, home to two English seminaries. Although the premise of this demand is that Elizabeth intends to send one of her Privy Council on a mission, Essex doubts this is the case: instead, the queen "doth it rather to try my judgement in it." In other words, the writing produced is a test of the capabilities of the earl. Faced with this challenge, however, Essex does not sit down and pen a tract himself. Instead, he seeks out the expertise of two men: Thomas Phelippes, the noted cryptographer who worked closely with the late Secretary of State, Francis Walsingham, and Francis Bacon:

> Master Phellipes hath known Master Secretary's courses in such matters; so as I may have counsel from you [Bacon] and precedents from him [Phelippes]. I pray you, as your leisure will serve, send me your conceipt as soon as you can; for I know not how soon I shall be called on. I will draw some notes of mine own which I will reform and enlarge by yours.

Phelippes will provide "precedents"; Bacon will supply "counsel" in the form of written "notes"; Essex will then "reform and enlarge" his own draft incorporating anything useful from Bacon's. The work will clearly stand as Essex's: the earl here commissions the piece, suggests the mechanism for its composition, perhaps — although this is not clear — polishes the final product himself, presents it

---

[19] LPL MS. 941, art. 139 (*LL*, 2: 194–96).
[20] Essex to Francis Bacon, [after 25 February 1593]. LPL MS. 653 art. 2, holograph. Modernized transcription by Spedding: *LL*, 1: 251.

to the queen himself, and takes credit for it. This is the kind of arrangement that Hammer envisions, with Bacon providing only part of the process, and Essex in control as author, the hierarchy of master and scribal servants playing itself out. But even within that process Bacon is providing advice: indeed, Essex specifically requests "counsel" of his friend. It is a symbiotic relationship at play, in which Essex uses Bacon's expertise, and Bacon guides the activities of the earl. In short, the Essex profile and image of 1592–1596 is inseparable from Bacon's intellectual agenda. This does not make Essex a cipher, however — by the end of this period, late 1596, we can see divisions emerging as Essex fails to follow Bacon's advice, provoking the first of several clear-eyed and disapproving letters of advice from Bacon to the earl.

This understanding allows the Bacon edition to claim certain "Essex" texts — but such a strategy inevitably has other ramifications. In particular, what might it mean to apply our understanding of Bacon's methods of writing in the 1590s to a period later in his career, when he occupies the position of authority and authorship that Essex had occupied earlier? In the final decade of his life, Bacon was an author *par excellence*: a writer who thought of himself as an author, who spoke of himself in terms of Demosthenes, Seneca, and Cicero,[21] and who executed the print publication of his books for which he would be remembered, starting with 1620's *Novum Organum*, and continuing through the various parts of the unfinished *Instauratio magna*, the 1625 revision of the *Essayes*, and the posthumously published *Sylva sylvarum* and *New Atlantis*. My editorial work on Bacon's writings from 1584 to 1596 relies on the notion that there is a kind of "pure" Bacon in the later work against which we can identify the ideas and style of these earlier, less obviously Bacon-authored works. But if Bacon is writing as Essex in the 1590s, is it possible that someone else might be writing as Bacon in the 1620s?

An obvious starting point for such an inquiry would be in the realm of translation. It is well known that Bacon commissioned the translation of several of his works. His 1609 *De sapientia veterum* was translated by Arthur Gorges into English as *The wisdom of the ancients*. *De sapientia veterum*, *Essayes*, and *The Advancement of Learning* were translated into French during Bacon's lifetime by Jean Baudouin and others; the *Essays* became the Italian *Saggi morali* by means of various individuals perhaps including Charles Cavendish, going through eleven editions by Bacon's death in 1626. But those acts of translation are familiar to us: the text appears in print in an "original" language as penned by the author (English or Latin), and then moves into other languages with the help of intermediaries.

---

[21] See Bacon to Lancelot Andrewes, [1622?]. *LL* 7: 371–74 at 373; also Bacon to James, 16 July 1621, *LL* 7: 297.

A more complicated picture emerges in the production of Bacon's Latin writings. Sometime after *The Advancement of Learning* was published in November 1605, Bacon contacted Dr Thomas Playfere, the Lady Margaret Professor of Divinity at Cambridge, a renowned preacher and distinguished Latinist, asking him to help in giving a 'second birth' to the *Advancement*, "if it might be translated into Latin, without manifest loss of the sense and matter." Aware of "the worth of your labours, whether such as your place and profession imposeth on you, or such as your own virtue may, upon your voluntary election, take in hand," Bacon could offer "no other persuasions" to take on the translation "than either the work itself may affect you with, or the honour of his Majesty, to whom it is dedicated, or your particular inclination to myself."[22] But Playfere took the bait — Bacon's late seventeenth-century editor Thomas Tenison recorded that "The Doctor was willing to serve so Excellent a Person, and so worthy a Design"[23] — and committed himself to translating the *Advancement*, but as early as the summer of 1608, there were signs that all was not well. In a notebook Bacon wrote on 25 July his plan for "Proceeding with the translation of my book of Advancement of Learning: hearkening to some other, if Playfere should fail."[24] Indeed Playfere did fail. Tenison wrote that Playfere "within a while, sent him a Specimen of a *Latine* Translation. But Men, generally, come short of themselves when they strive to out-doe themselves. They put a force upon their Natural Genius, and, by straining of it, crack and disable it. And so, it seems, it happened to that Worthy and Elegant Man. Upon this great Occasion, he would be over-accurate; and he sent a Specimen of such superfine Latinity, that the Lord *Bacon* did not encourage him to labour further in that Work, in the penning of which, he desired not so much neat and polite, as clear Masculine, and apt Expression."[25] Playfere apparently lost his mind, and then died on 1 February 1609.[26]

The planned translation was laid to one side, only to be revived in the early 1620s. In a letter to the bishop of Winchester, Lancelot Andrewes, probably dating to the summer of 1622, Bacon complained that, despite some positive comment from European intellectuals, the first published installment of the *Instauratio magna*, the *Novum Organum* (1620), "flies too high over men's heads." He

---

[22] Bacon to Playfere, *LL*, 3.

[23] Thomas Tenison, "An account of all the Lord Bacon's works," in Tenison, ed., *Baconiana, or, Certain genuine remains of Sr. Francis Bacon, Baron of Verulam, and Viscount of St. Albans in arguments civil and moral, natural, medical, theological, and bibliographical* (London: J.D. for Richard Chiswell, 1679), b2r–h4v, at c5r.

[24] BL Additional MS. 27278.

[25] Tenison, "Account," c5r–v.

[26] P. E. McCullough, "Playfere, Thomas," *ODNB* 44: 567–68.

therefore intended "to draw it down to the sense, by some patterns of a *Natural Story* or *Inquisition*," and had found in his past writings a handy expedient:

> for that my book of Advancement of Learning may be some preparative, or key, for the better opening of the Instauration; because it exhibits a mixture of new conceits and old; whereas the Instauration gives the new unmixed, otherwise than with some little aspersion of the old for taste's sake; I have thought good to procure a translation of that book into the general language, not without great and ample additions, and enrichment thereof; especially in the second book, which handleth the Partition of Sciences; in such sort, as I hold it may serve for the first part of the Instauration, and acquit my promise in that part.[27]

Another letter of June 1622 (to Redemptus Baranzano) confirms that Bacon had commissioned another translation of *The Advancement of Learning*, and that he expected it by the end of the summer.[28] While Bacon does not mention the identity of his translators, Thomas Tenison in 1679 goes further:

> knowing that this Work was desired beyond the Seas, and being also aware, that Books written in a modern Language, which receiveth much change in a few Years, were out of use; he caus'd that part of it which he had written in *English*, to be translated into the *Latine* Tongue, by Mr. *Herbert*, and some others, who were esteemed Masters in the *Roman* Eloquence.[29]

It would seem that this "Mr. *Herbert*" was the poet George Herbert, then orator at Cambridge University. Izaak Walton relates that Herbert met Bacon during one of King James's visits to Cambridge:

> The year following, the King appointed to end His progress at *Cambridge*, and to stay there certain dayes; at which time, he was attended by the great Secretary of Nature, and all Learning, Sir *Francis Bacon* (Lord *Virulam*) and by the ever memorable and learned Dr. [Lancelot] *Andrews* Bishop of *Winchester*, both which did at that time begin a desir'd friendship with our *Orator*. Upon whom the first put such a value on his judgement, that he

---

[27] Bacon to Lancelot Andrewes, [1622?]. *LL*, 7: 371–74 at 373.

[28] "Librum meum de progressu Scientiarum traducendum commisi; Illa translatio, volente Deo, sub finem Aestatis perficietur; Eam ad te mittam": Bacon to Redemptus Baranzanus, 30 June 1622, London. Folger Shakespeare Library, Washington, DC, MS. X.d.174; trans. Spedding, *LL* 7: 377. See below, n. 46.

[29] Tenison, "Account," c4ᵛ.

usually desir'd his approbation, before he would expose any of his Books
to be printed; and thought him so worthy of his friendship, that having
translated many of the Prophet *Davids* Psalms into English Verse, he made
George Herbert his Patron of them, by a publick dedication of them to him,
as the best Judge of *Divine Poetry*.[30]

In fact, when Bacon dedicated his *The translation of certaine psalmes into English verse* to "To his very good friend, Mr. George Herbert" in 1625, he opened by
mentioning "The paines, that it pleased you to take, about some of my Writings,
I cannot forget: which did put mee in minde, to dedicate to you, this poore Exercise of my sicknesse."[31] It would seem, then, that Bacon dedicated his translation
to Herbert in return for Herbert's translation of Bacon;[32] it has been argued that
Herbert's Latin poem "Aethiopissa ambit Cestum" was sent to Bacon in return
for a copy of the *Instauratio magna* (as suggested in his lines "A diamond to mee
you sent, / And I to you a Blackamore present.")[33]

Herbert was not alone in providing Bacon with Latin texts. In 1623, Bacon
told his friend Tobie Matthew that the *Essayes* were being translated into Latin
"by the help of some good pens which forsake me not,"[34] presumably a reference
to some friends or followers who had remained loyal since his fall from grace in
the spring of 1621. His editor Tenison reveals that "The Latine translation" of Bacon's *Essayes* "was a Work performed by divers Hands; by those of Doctor *Hacket*
(late Bishop of *Lichfield*) Mr. *Benjamin Iohnson* [sic] (the learned and judicious
Poet) and some others, whose Names I once heard from Dr. *Rawley*; but I cannot

---

[30] Izaak Walton, *The life of Mr. George Herbert* in *The lives of Dr. John Donne, Sir Henry
Wotton, Mr. Richard Hooker, Mr. George Herbert written by Izaak Walton; to which are added
some letters written by Mr. George Herbert, at his being in Cambridge: with others to his mother,
the Lady Magdalen Herbert; written by John Donne, afterwards dean of St. Pauls* (London: Tho.
Newcomb for Richard Marriott, 1670), B5^r.

[31] Bacon, *The translation of certaine psalmes into English verse* (London: Hanna Barret
and Richard Whitaker, 1625), A3^r. William A. Sessions points out that "in one version of Bacon's will, Herbert (along with John Selden) is made executor of his literary works," while
Herbert "wrote three official Latin letters to Bacon, four Latin poems in his honor, an English poem prefacing a fifth Latin poem": W. A. Sessions, "Bacon and Herbert and an Image of
Chalk," in *Too rich to clothe the sunne: Essays on George Herbert,* ed. Claude J. Summers and
Ted-Larry Pebworth (Pittsburgh: Univ. of Pittsburgh Press, 1980), 165–78, at 167 and passim.

[32] See *The Works of George Herbert*, ed. F. E. Hutchinson (Oxford: Clarendon Press,
1941), xxxix–xl.

[33] Sessions, "Bacon and Herbert," 169; Herbert, "To the Right Hon. the L. Chancellor (Bacon)" in *Works,* ed. Hutchinson, 209; see Hutchinson's comment on 551.

[34] Bacon to Matthew, *LL,* 7:429.

now recal them."[35] John Hacket (1592–1670) was a product of Westminster School and Trinity College, Cambridge (Bacon's alma mater), and in 1621 was appointed household chaplain to John Williams, when he was appointed Lord Keeper; a fluent Latinist, Hacket later authored the Latin play *Loyola*, and eventually advanced to become bishop of Coventry and Lichfield. Ben Jonson (1572–1637) was also a Westminster boy, albeit twenty years before Hacket; as is well known, he cast himself as an accomplished classicist, and, Ian Donaldson notes, "[h]is name was reportedly listed among the eighty-four 'Essentials' or founding members of an 'Academ Royal', first proposed to the crown in 1617 by his friend Edmund Bolton";[36] his *Discoveries* contains a lengthy appreciation of Bacon. John Aubrey adds that Thomas Hobbes "assisted his lordship in translating severall of his *Essayes* into Latin, one, I well remember, is that *Of the Greatnes of Cities*: the rest I have forgott."[37] Although Bacon commissioned these translations, it would seem that he had the last word: Tenison noted that Bacon "so suted the Style [of his translators] to his Conceptions, by a strict Castigation of the whole Work, that it may deservedly seem his own."[38] I shall return to this question of style versus conception later.

Aubrey's mention of Hobbes brings us to my second area where Bacon seems to have worked collaboratively — his own household. At its height, Bacon's household numbered over one hundred male servants; among the men who worked with him in his latter years were the mineralogist Thomas Bushell, the chaplain William Rawley, the diplomat-to-be William Boswell, as well as the young Hobbes. One Bacon household member, the Dutch apothecary Peter Boener, recalled that he "seldom saw him take up a book: he only ordered his chaplain and me to look in such and such an author for a certain place and then he dictated to us early in the morning what he had invented and composed during the night."[39] William Rawley, who took upon himself to edit Bacon's unpublished works, claimed that he was "employed, as an *Amanuensis*, or dayly instrument, to this *Honourable Authour*; And acquainted with his *Lordships* Conceits, in the composing, of his *Works*, for many years together; Especially, in his writing Time."[40]

---

[35] Tenison, "Account," e7ᵛ.

[36] Ian Donaldson, "Jonson, Benjamin [Ben] (1572–1637)," *ODNB* 30: 681–94.

[37] John Aubrey, *Brief Lives*, ed. Oliver Lawson Dick (1949; Ann Arbor: Univ. of Michigan Press, 1962), 149–50.

[38] Tenison, "Account," c4ᵛ–c5ʳ.

[39] Peter Boener, in A.C. Loffelt, "A Notice of Bacon," *The Athenaeum*, pt. 522, no. 2276 (10 June 1871): 720–21.

[40] William Rawley, "To the Reader," in Bacon, *Resuscitatio*, ed. Rawley (London: Sarah Griffin, for William Lee, 1657), (a)4ʳ–b(1)ᵛ, at (a)4ʳ.

Rawley also claimed to be able to approximate Bacon's English style when translating his Latin tract *In felicem memoriam Elizabethae* into the vernacular: "I
was induced, many years agoe, to put the same, into the *English Tongue*; Not, *Ad
Verbum*; For that had been but Flat, and Injudicious; But, (as far, as my slender
Ability could reach,) according to the *Expressions*, which, I conceived; his *Lordship* would have rendred it in, if he had written the same in *English*."[41] In these accounts, Boener and Rawley write, in Boener's case, from dictation; Rawley, claiming a closer relationship, knew Bacon's "Conceits."

John Aubrey wrote of Hobbes's working relationship with Bacon — and
while Aubrey's anecdotes are best taken with a ton of salt, there may be something useful here:

> His Lordship was a very Contemplative person, and was wont to contem-
> plate in his delicious walks at Gorhambury, and dictate to Mr. Thomas
> Bushell, or some other of his Gentlemen, that attended him with inke and
> paper ready to sett downe presently his Thoughts. His Lordship would of-
> ten say that he better liked Mr. Hobbes's taking his thoughts, then any of
> the other, because he understood what he wrote, which the others not un-
> derstanding, my Lord would many times have a harde taske to make sense
> of what they writt.[42]

At first sight, this might appear to be a case of Bacon dictating to amanuenses.
But the passage does not bear this out. Among the mess of pronouns, it seems
that Hobbes is the man best charged with "taking his [Bacon]'s thoughts" because whereas Bacon would "have a hard taske to make sense of what they [other
scribes] wrote," "he [Bacon?] understood what he [Hobbes] wrote." None of the
writing here is Bacon's. The writing is done by Hobbes, or "some other of his
Gentlemen" — and Bacon then has to interpret what they have written, a process whose difficulty lies not in undecipherable handwriting, but in undecipherable versions of Bacon's "Thoughts." This fits with another statement of Aubrey's
about Hobbes: "The Lord Chancellor Bacon loved to converse with him." The
process here is less verbatim dictation, and more a conversation leading to writing; yes, Bacon speaks, but it is the role of his gentlemen to *draft*.

We should perhaps not be surprised by this model of authorship, since Bacon describes it in minute detail in one of his own works. This kind of household
academy was explored by Bacon imaginatively in *New Atlantis*, a text that he is
thought to have written around 1623. *New Atlantis* describes a fictional land,

---

[41] Rawley, "To the Reader," (b)1ʳ.
[42] Aubrey, *Brief Lives*, 149–50.

Bensalem, on which a European ship is washed ashore. The narrator's description of this realm culminates in the institution known as Salomon's House, which was understood to forward Bacon's notion of a collaborative academic institution: Rawley wrote that Salomon's House should be seen as "a Modell or Description of a Colledge, instituted for the Interpreting of Nature, and the Producing of Great and Marueilous Works for the Benefit of Men."[43] Salomon's House famously contains a division of intellectual labor. Twelve fellows known as the *"Merchants of Light"* "Sayle into *Forraine Countries"* to bring back "the *Bookes,* and *Abstracts,* and *Patternes* of *Experiments* of all other *Parts."* Three *"Mystery-Men" "Collect* the *Experiments* of all *Mechanicall Arts;* And also of *Liberall Sciences;* And also of *Practises* which are not *Brought into Arts."* Three *"Pioners* or *Miners"* "try *New Experiments,* such as themselues thinke good." Three *"Depredatours" "Collect* the *Experiments* which are in all *Bookes."* With these four groups doing the groundwork, three *"Compilers" "Drawe* [their] *Experiments . . .* into *Titles,* and *Tables,* to giue the better light, for the drawing of *Obseruations* and *Axiomes* out of them." There is a then a further set of three *"Dowry-men* or *Benefactours"* who look for practical applications for the experiments: they "bend themselues, *Looking* into the *Experiments* of their *Fellowes,* and cast about how to draw out of them *Things* of *Vse,* and *Practise* for *Mans life,* and *Knowledge* as well for *Workes,* as for *Plaine Demonstration* of *Causes, Meanes* of *Naturall Diuinations,* and the easie and cleare *Discouery,* of the *Vertues* and *Parts* of *Bodies."* Following meetings of all the fellows, three *"Lamps"* take responsibility "to *Direct New Experiments,* of a Higher *Light,* more *Penetrating* into *Nature* then the *Former";* three Inoculatours *"Execute* the *Experiments* so *Directed,* and *Report* them"; and three *"Interpreters of Nature"* "raise the former *Discoueries* by *Experiments,* into *Greater Obseruations, Axiomes,* and *Aphorismes."*[44] This is precisely the kind of research institution that could produce the massive collections of knowledge called for in Bacon's grand project, the *Instauratio magna.*

But where is the author in this institution? And who is doing the writing? The account of Salomon's House is given by one of the "fathers" of the house. At his entrance, he is described as "a man of middle stature and age, comely of person, and had an aspect as if he pitied men," a description that relates him to the man in the *Redargutio philosophiarum* who addresses the audience in Paris, and whose "face had become habituated to the expression of pity." John Guillory has recently shown how this Father, who enters in elaborate pomp, seems to be a

---

[43] William Rawley, "To the Reader," in Francis Bacon, *Sylua syluarum: or A naturall historie In ten centuries,* ed. William Rawley (London: William Lee, 1626 [i.e. 1627]), a2r.

[44] Bacon, *New Atlantis* in *Sylua syluarum,* f4r–g1r.

portrayal of Bacon.[45] But this father does not identify himself as any of the thirty-three *"Merchants of Light," "Depredatours," "Mystery-Men," "Pioners," "Compilers," "Dowry-men," "Lamps," "Inoculators,"* and *"Interpreters of Nature."* In Bacon's fantasy academic world, all the work is delegated, *including* the writing. And this should not be surprising. The world in which he moves is a culture in which leading politicians, courtiers, and administrators routinely use a cadre of secretaries, clients, friends, and scribes not simply to advise them on their writings, or research their writings, or copy out their writings, but also to draft their writings. This is a form of collaborative writing in which the head of the household takes responsibility, credit or blame for the work of his household — Bacon's *New Atlantis* image is of perfect control by the father, but in reality, subordinate household members might have a real involvement in molding the writing of the father.

But the household model fails to account for the most surprising form of Bacon's collaborative writing practices. My third scenario is inspired by a letter written by Bacon on 30 June 1622, a year after his fall from grace, to Redemptus Baranzanus (né Jean-Antoine Baranzano),[46] professor of philosophy and mathematics at Anneci, who by 1622 had published three major works: *Uranoscopia, seu universa doctrina de coelo* ([Geneva], 1617), *Novae opiniones physicæ* (Lyons, 1617) and *Campus philosophicus* (Lyons, 1620). Bacon's letter, written in answer to one from Baranzano in which he apparently quizzed Bacon about his attitude to syllogistic reasoning, ends with an invitation:

> Before anything else, I desire a Natural Philosophy out of which philosophy may be built; nor shall I be wanting to the work, so far as in me lies. I wish I may have suitable assistants [Adiutores idoneos]. Nor in this respect can anything fall out more happily than that you, being the man you are, should contribute the first part of the work, by writing [conscribendo] a history of the Heavens, in which only the phenomena themselves, and the different astronomical instruments, with their uses, and then the principal and most celebrated hypotheses, both ancient and modern, and at the same time the

---

[45] John Guillory, "The Bachelor State: Philosophy and Sovereignty in Bacon's *New Atlantis*," in *Politics and the Passions, 1500–1800*, ed. Victoria Kahn, Neil Saccamano, and Daniela Coli (Princeton: Princeton Univ. Press, 2006), 49–74.

[46] Bacon to Baranzano, 20 June 1622, London. This letter was first printed (with a few inaccuracies) in [J.-P. Niceron], *Memoires pour servir à l'histoire des hommes illustres dans la république des lettres*, vol. 3 (Paris: Briasson, 1729), 43–47; Spedding reprints it from Niceron's edition in *Letters and the life*, 7:375–77, with English translation, 377–78 n. 1. The original letter itself was believed by Spedding to be lost, but has now resurfaced, written in a secretary's hand with Bacon's signature, in the Folger Shakespeare Library, Washington, DC, MS. X.d.174.

exact calculations of the periodic returns, and other things of that kind, shall be set forth plainly and simply, without any doctrine or theory whatever. And if to this history of the Heavens you would add a history of Comets (concerning the composition of which I send herewith certain articles and as it were particular topics), you will have erected a truly magnificent frontispiece for Natural History, and done the greatest service to the Instauration of the Sciences, and a very great favour to myself.[47]

So here we have Bacon attempting to persuade Baranzano, whom he has never met, to contribute to his Great Instauration. What he wants from him is not notes or information or references or documents, but a fully-fledged "history of the Heavens" followed by "a history of Comets," histories with no "doctrine or theory," no agenda, and no ax to grind. And he wants Baranzano to *write* these histories. This is a wholesale commission of the text of two sections of the *Instauratio magna*. As it happened, Bacon was no more successful with Baranzano than he was with Thomas Playfere: Baranzano died on 23 December 1622, aged just thirty-three, less than six months after Bacon wrote to him.[48]

So in the final years of his life, Bacon does not produce the Latin version of an English work, but commissions others to do it. Bacon chooses Hobbes over other men of his household, because he could make sense of what Hobbes was writing — and what Hobbes was writing was a draft of Bacon's composition. Bacon commissions Redemptus Baranzano to write part of the Great Instauration that would be published under Bacon's name. Or put another way, multiple aspects of Bacon's writing seem to have been *written* by somebody else.

---

[47] "Historiam naturalem ad condendam Philosophiam (vt et tu mones) ante omnia præopto; neque huic rei deero quantum in me est; vtinam habeam Adiutores idoneos: Neque in hac parte, mihi quippiam accidere possit fœlicius, quam si tu talis Vir, primitias huic operi præbeas, conscribendo Historiam Cœlestium, in quâ, ipsa tantum Phænomena, atque vnà Instrumenta Astronomica, eorumque genera et vsum; dein hypotheses præcipuas et maximè illustres, tam antiquas quam modernas; atque simul exactas restitutionum Calculationes, et alia huiusmodi sincerè proponas, absque omni Dogmate et Themate. Quod si huic Cœlestium Historiæ, Historiam Cometarum adieceris (de quâ conficiendâ, ecce tibi Articulos quosdam, et quasi Topica particularia) magnificum prorsus frontispicium Historiæ naturali Extruxeris; et optime de Scientiarum Instauratione Merueris; mihique gratissimum feceris. Librum meum de progressu Scientiarum traducendum commisi; Illa translatio, volente Deo, sub finem Aestatis perficietur; Eam ad te mittam." Bacon to Baranzano, 30 June 1622, London. Folger MS. X.d.174. For the final sentences see above, n. 28.

[48] Niceron, *Memoires*, 3: 43.

This proposition would seem to be supported by the surviving material evidence, as catalogued by Peter Beal.[49] The surviving autograph drafts by Bacon — that is, pieces written in his handwriting — are scant indeed, and most of them are very brief pieces in little more than note form. His 1594 collection of proverbs, the *Promus*, also contains notes which are a draft of the *Colours of Good and Evill*, and notes on what becomes *De spe terrestri*.[50] The 1608–09 notebook *Commentarius solutus* contains a sketch, *Inquisitio legitima de motu*.[51] A legal commonplace book in Law French contains an unpublished piece *On the King's Prerogative*.[52] Beyond these, all we have are two fragments of rough drafts for a *Memorandum on the Queen's Safety*,[53] a rough (and superseded) draft for a speech for the 1595 Accession Day device,[54] a dozen aphorisms and anecdotes entitled "Elegancies miscellany. Apr. 22. 1601,"[55] a single leaf containing drafts of parts 4 and 12 of "Natura durabilis," part of the *Historia vitae et mortis*,[56] and a draft entitled "Sequela cartarum sive Inquisitio Legitima de calore et frigore."[57] But these are the exceptions.

The norm for Bacon manuscripts lies elsewhere. The norm is a draft in the hand of somebody else (usually presumed by editors to be one of Bacon's secretaries or amanuenses), with Bacon's autograph comments, which are often quite extensive emendations. This is the case with a substantial tranche of Bacon's extant tracts from *A Brief Discourse touching the Happy Union of the Kingdom of England and Scotland* to *The History of the Reign of King Henry VII*.[58] These

---

[49] Peter Beal, *Index of English Literary Manuscripts*, vol. 1: *1450–1625* (London: Mansell, 1980), 17–52. Beal designates each witness with a 'BcF' code.

[50] British Library, London [hereafter BL] Harley MS. 7017, fols. 83ʳ-129ᵛ (BcF 269); ibid., fols. 128ʳ–129ᵛ (BcF 230); ibid., fol. 118 (BcF 305).

[51] BL Additional MS. 27278, fols. 17ᵛ–22ᵛ (BcF 303).

[52] BL Harley MS. 7017, fols. 179ʳ–206ᵛ (BcF 233).

[53] Lambeth Palace Library [hereafter LPL] MS. 936, arts. 1 and 2 (BcF 199).

[54] LPL MS. 936, art. 274 (BcF 309).

[55] Princeton AM 21463 (BcF 85).

[56] BL Additional MS. 38693, fol. 49.

[57] BL Harley MS. 6855, vol. I, fols. 52–60 (BF 111).

[58] The full list is: *A Brief Discourse touching the Happy Union of the Kingdom of England and Scotland* (1603, BL Harley MS. 532, fols. 61ʳ–64ᵛ, Bc 107); *A Preparation for the Union of Laws* (1603, BL Harley MS. 6797, fols. 20ʳ–46ᵛ, BcF 261); *Certain Considerations touching the Better Pacification and Edification of the Church of England* (1603, The National Archives, State Papers 14/5, art. 51, BcF 121); *Valerius terminus* (1603–8, BL Harley MS. 6463, pp. 1–70, BcF 285); *Cogitata et visa de interpretatione naturae* (1607, Queen's College, Oxford, MS. 280, fols. 205–233); *Temporis partus masculus* (1608, BL Harley MS. 6463, pp. 70–73, BcF 307); *Redargutio philosophiarum* (1608, BL Harley MS. 6855, vol. 1, fols. 4ʳ–31ᵛ, BcF 306); *Of the True Greatness of the Kingdom of Britain* (1608, BL Harley MS. 7021, fols. 25ʳ–42ᵛ, BcF 232); *Argument in*

writings include both English and Latin works, occasional political pieces and natural philosophical works, ranging in date from 1603 to 1621: the consistency of this evidence strongly suggests that Bacon's preferred form of writing may always have been collaborative, in the multiple forms I've outlined above.

Where does this leave those attempting to produce an authorial, authoritative edition? The logic that allows me to appropriate Essex's works as Bacon's could equally allow another editor to appropriate Bacon's works for, say, Hobbes or even Herbert. And it may well be that these writers had real intellectual input into the work published as Bacon's. To acknowledge this situation, what we need is an appreciation of the many and different ways that an author produces writing — or, put another way, an appreciation that an author's works may indeed include pieces she or he, in the strict sense of the word, did not *write*. This did not worry Francis Bacon, nor did it worry his editor William Rawley, or any of the seventeenth-century commentators who all recount Bacon's collaborations with other writers with a sense of pride. Putting together the 1657 *Resuscitatio*, Rawley admitted that "in the *Collection* of *Letters* . . . there are inserted some few, which were written, by other *Pennes*, and not by his *Lordships* own: Like as we find, in the *Epistolar Authours; Cicero, Plinius secundus*, and the rest: which because I found them immixed, amongst his *Lordships Papers*; And that they are written, with some similitude of *Stile*; I was loath, they should be left, to a Grave, at that time, when his *Lordships* own *Conceptions*, were brought to life."[59] Rawley knows full well that these letters, signed by Bacon, were the work of "other *Pennes*" but he sees them as importantly similar in "*Stile*" and ultimately deriving from "his *Lordships* own *Conceptions*." Rawley, himself an amanuensis to Bacon, is able to subjugate the labour of writing, of penning, to the more important work of "conception." Tenison used the same language in describing how Bacon castigated the Latin translations and thus "so suted the Style to the Conceptions." It is not what Bacon wrote that is part of his works, it is what he conceived.

But perhaps this reification of "conceptions" from "style" is too easy a way out for Rawley and Tenison, who after all are heavily invested — as Bacon editors — in producing Bacon as an author. I'd prefer to go back to the *Redargutio*

---

the *Case of the Post-Nati of Scotland* (1608, BL Royal MS. 17 A. LVI, fols. 1ʳ–61ᵛ, BcF 99); *Certain Considerations touching the Plantation in Ireland* (1608/9, BL Harley MS 6797, fols. 122ʳ–127ᵛ, BcF 132); *De vijs mortis* (1612–1619, Chatsworth House, Hardwick MS. 72A, fols. 1ᵛ–8ʳ, BcF 294); *Aphorismi de dissolutione rerum* (1612–1619, Chatsworth House, Hardwick MS. 72A, fols. 8ᵛ–30ᵛ); *Filum labyrinthi, sive formula inquisitionis* (BL Harley MS 6797, fols. 139ʳ–146ᵛ, BcF 214); *Arguments of* Law (1615–16, BL Additional MS. 4263, fols. 56ʳ–101ᵛ, BcF 87); and *The History of the Reign of King Henry VII* (1621, BL Additional MS. 7084, BcF 215).

[59] Rawley, "To the Reader," (b)1ʳ.

philosophiarum, to that mangled, "inferior" version of the speech given by the pitiful-looking man in Paris. Yes, it seems that the man gives the speech, and the problems of the text lie in its reconstruction: his "conceptions" should shine through even the compromised "style." But we should remember that the *Redargutio* starts with the Bacon-narrator saying that *he* alone is "preparing a refutation of philosophies." That he is forced to portray his own refutation as a second-hand account of a speech by a man in a different city in a foreign country — and that he talks about himself in the first person plural — suggests a more complex relation between an author and his writing than we are usually willing to admit. And the fact that our only text of the *Redargutio* is a manuscript in the hand of an amanuensis, with Bacon's presence felt only in autograph revisions, hammers the point home.[60]

COLUMBIA UNIVERSITY

---

[60] BL Harley MS. 6855, vol. 1, fols. 4ʳ–31ᵛ.

Editing the Early Modern Text

Editing Richard Tottel's Songes and Sonettes[1]

PAUL A. MARQUIS

I N THE SPRING OF 1996, I ATTENDED A CONFERENCE OF THE RENAISSANCE Society of America in Vancouver, Canada, where I presented a paper on the second edition of Richard Tottel's *Songes and Sonettes*, Q2, published 31 July 1557. In the paper I argued that modern readers could not be fully aware of the extent to which *Songes and Sonettes* influenced the development of 16th-century English poetry because we did not have ready access to Tottel's Q2. We had only Hyder E. Rollins's 1928/29 edition of *Tottel's Miscellany*, based on Q1, published eight weeks prior to Q2, on 5 June 1557. Q2, however, contains many new poems in an arrangement unlike that of Q1. Without a critical edition of Q2, we could not appreciate the manner in which the arrangement had been thoroughly revised in the eight weeks since the book's first edition or ponder the cultural and aesthetic significance of the changes. Indeed, Q2, and not Q1, had become the standard arrangement for no fewer than ten subsequent Elizabethan editions of *Songes and Sonettes* and was more likely the text that had been read by Elizabethan editors, authors, and printers who in the tradition of Tottel treated verse compilations as a viable literary genre. A critical edition of Q2 would allow modern readers to consider the cultural and aesthetic influence of that text on the works of Googe, Robinson, Turberville, Howell, Gascoigne, Edwards, Whetstone, Proctor, Spenser, Gifford, Bodenham, Jaggard, Chester, and Shakespeare.

Encouraged by the interest my argument had received at the conference I submitted a proposal to edit the second edition of Tottel's text to Arthur Kinney

---

[1] This paper was first delivered at the 2007 RETS Open Business Meeting, held at the MLA convention, Chicago, IL, Arthur F. Kinney presiding.

in his capacity as President of the Renaissance English Text Society. The Society met at the MLA in Chicago in 1996, accepted my proposal, and established an editorial board to oversee the editing and publication of the edition. Four scholars and editors were appointed to the editorial subcommittee by the RETS council: George W. Williams, Professor Emeritus, Duke University would chair the committee which had as its members the late W. Speed Hill, Lehman College, City University of New York; Elizabeth H. Hageman, University of New Hampshire; and the late David Freeman, Memorial University, NFLD. In the next four years I communicated mostly with George Williams, though at different points in the project I worked closely with each member of the subcommittee. Indeed, I had the good fortune to participate in Speed Hill's seminar at the Folger Library on "The Theory and Practice of Scholarly Editing" in the fall of 2001. On several occasions I met David Freeman in Nova Scotia as he was passing through to points west. Betty Hageman I met after the completion of the project at the Folger Library, though we had communicated extensively by e-mail and telephone. I could not imagine better treatment by these seasoned scholars and editors, gentle and patient as they were, who provided an invaluable service to their profession by teaching a novice the tricks of the trade. If this new edition of Tottel's *Songes and Sonettes* is useful to scholars and students in the field of Renaissance literature, the credit must go to the editorial team overseeing its production.[2]

My first task was to typescript 280 poems exactly as they had been printed in Q2. We had decided to reprint the second edition as we had found it, except for silent emendations. White letter text was used instead of Tottel's black letter; all other distinguishing type was signified by italics, and modern forms of 's' were used, as were the i/j and the u/v doublets. When I could consult Q2, housed in the British Library, I did so, but I had acquired photo-reprints of this edition, along with Q1 housed in the Bodleian Library, and the various copies of a third edition, Q3, with texts in various states of completion in the Wren Library, Trinity College, Cambridge, the Huntington Library, San Marino, California, and the Harry Ransom Library at the University of Texas at Austin, Texas. By January 1998, I sent my completed typescript to the subcommittee for approval. Each member then corrected my typescript, as far as could be determined by the photocopies of the original text with which they compared my work. The final step in the process was then to read the typescript backwards, letter by letter, compared to the original. At the end of this onerous task, May 1998, we were satisfied that my typescript was as exact a transcription of the original as could be provided.

---

[2] *Richard Tottel's Songes and Sonettes: The Elizabethan Version*, ed. Paul A. Marquis, MRTS 338 (Tempe: ACMRS, 2007).

Next I began work on the Textual Apparatus which involved compiling lists of the substantive and accidental differences between Q1 and Q2, and substantive differences in Q3, published between Q2 and before Q4, which appeared in 1559. Substantives include differences in spellings of words in Q1, Q2, and Q3, where those differences lead to the formation of new words with new meanings. Accidentals involve changes in the punctuation of lines or in the spelling of words in which the meaning is not changed. The most obvious instance of substantive differences between Q1 and Q2 involve the rearrangement of poems by the various poets. Q1 contains 271 poems, numbered 1 to 271 in Rollins's edition. The poems are divided into four large sections and two smaller sections. Poems by Henry Howard, the Earl of Surrey, begin the compilation (1–36); followed by poems by Thomas Wyatt, the Elder (37–127); then poems by Nicholas Grimald (128–167); and the Uncertain Auctours (168–261); before two short clusters of poems by Surrey and Wyatt are found (262–265 and 266–271).

In Q2, published eight weeks later, on 31 July 1557, the order of poems is altered significantly. Six sections of poems are reduced to four. Thirty-nine new poems by Uncertain Auctours are added, and the entire section moved to the penultimate position in the text. Thirty poems by Nicholas Grimald included in Q1 are omitted in Q2, while his ten remaining poems are transferred to the end of the text and his initials are substituted for his name at the beginning of the group. Four poems by Surrey and six by Wyatt placed at the end of Q1 are rearranged and incorporated into the main body of poems by their respective authors. Each change in Q2 involves two alterations — taking the poem or cluster of poems out of the place it occupies in Q1 and inserting it into a new position in Q2 — amounting to 54 changes in the sequence of the poems. Finally, over 400 substantive emendations of words and phrases in the poems are found in Q2. As Hyder Rollins points out, in the eight short weeks between the printing of Q1 to Q2, *Songes and Sonettes* is "completely changed" and "thoroughly revised."[3]

In the substantive changes, much attention is given to Surrey: of his 40 poems, seven receive a total of 40 substantive variants. Wyatt receives the least attention: of his 96 poems, 13 receive three or more substantive revisions, for a total of 55 variants. Of the 94 poems by Uncertain Auctours in Q1, 29 poems receive three or more substantive revisions in Q2, for a total of 145 emendations. Of the 22 emendations in Grimald, the final two poems, both elegies in unrhymed iambic pentameter, receive 20 substantive emendations. Moreover, though variants in punctuation are usually considered accidental — the work of compositors and

³ Hyder E. Rollins, *Tottel's Miscellany 1557–1587* (Cambridge, MA: Harvard Univ. Press, 1928–1929; rev. ed. 1965), 2: 10, 13.

not the work of authors or editors — patterns in the emended punctuation of Q2 parallel the patterns in the substantive emendations. Q2's editor apparently conducts his revisions of the punctuation as an author might prepare his revisions for the press. For example, there are more than 650 changes in punctuation from Q1 to Q2. Where Surrey's 40 poems are altered in 127 places, Wyatt's 96 poems have a mere 119 changes. Punctuation in the Uncertain Auctours section is vigorously emended: 134 poems receive 409 changes in punctuation. Grimald's 10 poems in Q2 are not without emended punctuation, though the final two elegies receive most attention.

Analysis of the substantive and accidental variants between Q1 and Q2 indicates that the editor did not engage in full-scale revisions of each poem. He emended words, phrases, and punctuation as seemed appropriate to his ear in his attempt to produce a strong iambic line and still remain committed to the issues addressed by the speaker of each poem. While specific poems may have ideological significance, one cannot conclude that Q2 is pro-Marian, for example, since certain lines in the 39 new poems by Uncertain Auctours can be considered indirect criticism of Mary's policies. In poem 229, we hear that the "hidden harme" has "broken out" in "our time" (37–38), and in poem 234, "the whole world is set on mischief," "measure and mean" are absent, "trouth is folly" and "mens harts are burnde with sundry sectes" (30–32, 55–56). These statements, combined with the claim by the persona in poem 218 that in this age "such troubles still apperes, | Which never were before this time, no not this in thousand yeres" (23–25), suggest that at least some of the poems by the Uncertain Auctours are critical of Mary's reign. But Tottel was a political survivor. His ability to maintain his monopoly as a printer of law books during the time of Edward VI and Mary Tudor, and later during much of Elizabeth's reign, meant that he was not likely to forfeit his flourishing career in 1557 by publishing an anthology of poems that could be censored, or for which he would be prosecuted and sent to prison, if not worse. Tottel's book sold in 1557, and continued selling through the Elizabethan period, most likely because it included a large number of poems reflecting a breadth of private and public perspectives on the individual and the community in the mid-Tudor world.

The editor of Q3, using Q2 as a copy text, reveals a similar interest in providing a text accessible to readers. This is evident in the impression of the first few leaves. In contrast to Q2, which provides the title page and the preface *To the Reder*, crowded to the left and right margin respectively, Q3's type is recast to compose pages that are centered and more graphically shaped. Compared to the elongated rectangular shape of the preface in Q1 and Q2, the editorial design of the opening leaves of Q3 is strong and impressive. The change in format projects the book as a monument of literary significance.[4] An analysis of the substantive variants of Q3 suggests that this concern for the book as a literary monument is also present in the emendations of specific poems. In Q3, Surrey's poems 7, 8, and 13 are revised significantly; in every instance, Q2's reading is replaced by Q1's. These popular poems receive more attention in Q3 than any others in the collection. Versions of them can be found in the Arundel Harington MS, for example, but no attempt is made in Q3 to return the poems to the readings in that manuscript. Why would the editor emend the revisions of these poems provided by the editor of Q2 back to the readings in Q1? As William Sessions points out, the "ghostly food" in poem 8 may be a synecdoche for the Holy Eucharist that recalls Mary Tudor's religious education and instruction in the Roman Church.[5] If this were so, one might argue that Q3's emendation of the text to its Q1 reading of "costly food" eliminates the subtle allusion to the Catholicism of both Mary and Henry Howard, the Earl of Surrey, the author of the poem. Was Q3 edited in anticipation of the death of Mary and the ascension of Elizabeth, or in the early years of Elizabeth's reign, during a time when it was thought wise to eliminate such allusions? A marshalling of evidence in the revisions to Q3 might provide a sound basis for dating that text, but such evidence must be based as much on bibliographical analysis as on the presence or absence of literary devices such as synecdoche. Indeed, why the editor of Q3 made substantive changes to Q2 that recalled the readings of Q1 is a question that Hyder Rollins concluded was a "mystery" that he was "incompetent to solve" (2: 99). Since then, no one has been more competent.

What can be inferred generally from the variants in Q3 in relation to those in Q2? First, that the variants in Q3 do not radically alter the text of Q2. The editor clearly accepted the most significant changes in Q2, that is, the revised arrangement of authors, the exclusion of Grimald's 30 poems, the inclusion of 39 new poems by the Uncertain Auctours, and the shuffling of poems from one position to another, especially in the Uncertain Auctours section. Moreover, Q3 differs from Q2 substantively in approximately 140 instances: Surrey's poems receive 37 substantive variants; Wyatt's poems, 17 variants; the Uncertain Auc-

---

[4] Wendy Wall has argued that the presentation of title pages and prefaces authorizes the legitimacy of the contents of books. Her comments on the first few leaves of the 1598 *Arcadia* are relevant to Tottel's Q3: "The trappings of the 1598 *Arcadia* — the title page and the two prefaces — helped to create and monumentalize the literary reputation that the combined works established" (*The Imprint of Gender: Authorship and Publication in the English Renaissance* [London and Ithaca: Cornell University Press, 1993], 151).

[5] W. A. Sessions, *Henry Howard: The Poet Earl of Surrey: A Life* (Oxford and New York: Oxford Univ. Press, 1999), 192–93.

tours, 79 variants (with one-third of the changes occurring in the 39 new poems); while the remaining 10 poems by Grimald have 7 substantive variants. Fewer than one-third of the total substantive changes in Q3 revert to Q1. Thus, though Q3's editor respected the readings of Q1, he was motivated less by a need to restore that text than by a desire to continue the initiative, evident from the beginning of the project, to provide a consistent tone to individual poems and a uniform iambic measure to the verses as a whole, that is, to create a text more accessible to the reader.

The relation between the colophon of Q3, which identifies 31 July 1557 as its date of publication, and the text of Q3 requires explanation.[6] From an analysis of entries in the *STC*, it is clear that Tottel's standard practice was to reprint books, especially calendars of English common law, yearbooks, statutes, and books of tenures, using the colophons of those titles printed at earlier dates. At least two of the books by Tottel, the colophons of which claim 1557 as the date of publication, were printed in later years, but impressed with colophons of the original 1557 date.[7] This practice continued throughout Tottel's career, for, as the listings in the *STC* reveal, forty-four texts were reprinted using colophons from earlier editions, twenty of which were published initially in 1556.[8] These were small books of a few pages, but essential reading for those employed in the law profession or simply curious about the constantly changing legal environment in Tudor

---

[6] W. W. Greg suggests that as far as Q2 and Q3 are concerned there are either "two successive editions, one a close reprint of the other, or else a work set up in duplicate" ("Tottel's Miscellany," *The Library*, 2nd ser. 5 [1904]: 113–32, at 120–23. If the editions are "successive," then, as Rollins points out, the colophon of Q3 "may possibly be only a mechanical reproduction of the colophon" of Q2 (2: 13, 19). Indeed, it is difficult to see how Q3 could be a "duplicate" of Q2, given that many readings in Q2 are discarded in Q3 in favor of the old readings of Q1.

[7] I wish to acknowledge with thanks the assistance of Dr. Peter Blayney in calling to my attention Tottel's practice of reprinting the dates of earlier colophons in later editions. The two texts printed after 1557, but employing colophons of books published in 1557, are *STC* 9809 and *STC* 9863, both printed first in 1557 and again in 1566.

[8] These forty-four texts are interspersed between *STC* numbers 9582 to 9967, the entries of which record the publication of yearbooks, and *STC* 15737 and 15774, where the record of translations of French law books by Sir Thomas Littleton, published by Tottel and various other printers, is recorded. These entries by no means exhaust Tottel's record in the *STC*. For a complete list, see the *STC*, Vol. 3, Index 1: "Printers and Publishers," under Richard Tottell (169–70), where no fewer than 719 entries are recorded in his name. As the editors of the *STC* acknowledge, "The date of some of Tottell's editions is often repeated in subsequent ones or is entirely erroneous. Although an attempt to establish the true dates has been made with the yearbooks (*STC* numbers between 9551 and 9967), multiple editions of the same date under other headings have not been re-examined" (169).

England.[9] By retaining the original date of the colophon in later reprints of law books, Tottel most likely assumed he was insuring his copyright and providing a sense of authenticity for his reader. One can argue, then, that when Tottel wished to reprint *Songes and Sonettes* after 31 July 1557, and before 1559, a slightly revised Q2 was given to his compositor to reprint, and that following what he took to be the house style in the matter of the colophon, the compositor carefully set the date that was before him.[10]

Following an analysis of the substantive variants, a bibliographical analysis of the three texts was initiated in an attempt to determine the difference in the sequences of printing Q1, Q2, and Q3. David Freeman was a close advisor in this analysis. By a careful reading of the running-titles, folio numbers, catchwords, and signatures of Q2 — which had not been provided in Rollins's edition in 1928/29 — I reconstructed a version of how the pages were printed in the sequences that led to the construction of the various quartos. Eight skeletons in total were used to print Q1. A schedule of the skeletons of the outer and inner formes based on the running-titles suggests that the printing process of the text employed two presses and two compositors. Skeleton I, used for the outer and inner formes, prints two quires for each one pressed by skeleton II. This 2:1 ratio continues until the end of the Wyatt section and the beginning of the Grimald section at M_2^v and M_3^r. Two new skeletons (III and IV) are used for the transition from Wyatt's to Grimald's poems, then two more skeletons (V and VI) continue the regular pattern of printing Grimald's poems in four quires, which the compositor thought consisted only of songs and not of sonnets. The poems by Uncertain Auctours are printed without interruption in skeletons VII and VIII, accommodating the inclusion of the two short clusters of poems by Surrey and Wyatt at the end of Q1.

If the skeletons are loosely related to the sequence of authors in Q1, that sequence reveals an unusual carelessness by the compositors and printer. Poems by Surrey and the Uncertain Auctours conclude on recto leaves, while poems by Wyatt

---

[9] In 1553, four years before the publication of *Songes and Sonettes*, Tottel had secured the license to publish books pertaining to English common law. The income generated by the license would have afforded him the opportunity to publish works of literature for which an audience was less assured.

[10] Tottel did not publish as many yearbooks in 1557 as in 1556, but it was a busy year for the publication of literature. As well as the nine yearbooks published in 1557, Tottel also printed and published two editions of *Songes and Sonettes*; books 2 and 4 of Surrey's translation of Virgil's *Aeneid*; Thomas More's *Works*, a massive project of 1458 leaves, all of which — except the first quire which was produced by the printer Cawood — were printed by Tottel; as well as Rastell's *Correccion of all the Statutes*, amounting to 550 folios.

and again by Surrey near the end of the text begin at the top of verso leaves. It is not good form to begin major sections on verso leaves. A more careful printer would have ensured that authorial sections commenced on recto leaves and concluded on verso leaves, and that the running-titles reflected these changes. Such is not the case with Q1, where the running-titles run along in their curious way with little or no reference to the poems that appear on the pages they head. The evidence, then, supports the claim that once Tottel committed himself to the task of printing a collection of poems, he acquired a number of lyrics by Surrey, Wyatt, and Grimald, then added the lyrics by the Uncertain Auctours before acquiring several more poems by Surrey and Wyatt. No wonder Q2 follows shortly on the heels of Q1; the collection needed an editor to straighten out the compositors' mistakes.

A bibliographical analysis of Q2, based on an analysis of the running titles, with or without points, and on the use of folio references, *Fo* and *Fol,* also with or without points, generally reveals how the printing process provided a more readable text. Nevertheless, it is clear that the missing points after words in the running titles and in the various forms of the abbreviated folio references are caused by idiosyncrasies in composing, which could include inadequate inking. Eight separate skeletons can be identified in Q2, but the skeletons used in the outer and inner formes of A and C are used nowhere else in the text. After sheet A, the compositors apparently had a sense of how the whole text would be impressed. Skeletons III and IV alternate uniformly in the setting of the outer and inner formes of twice as many sheets as skeletons VII and VIII, which were sorted more slowly. Another press was opened for sheet C, of which anomalies include badly inked running titles, missing type from the title of C_3^r, and a crowded text on the left-hand margin on C_3^r and C_4^r. This new press was probably used again, with different compositors and different skeletons, for sheet F. The decision seems to have been made to regularize this second press that was to machine 8 out of the remaining 24 sheets. To achieve a textual sequence from one skeleton to another, casting off — the division of the text into page units before composition began, not necessarily with regard to the poetical content of the poems — would have been desirable. One could surmise, then, that two principal compositors were involved in composing Q2 in a process that was more deliberate than that of Q1.

The editor of Q2 also eliminates many of the inconsistencies in the signatures and running-titles and provides pagination. As a result, the 26 variant signatures in Q1 are reduced to 9 in Q2. There are approximately 50 mispointed running titles in Q1; only 22 in Q2. In Q1, there are 108 leaves and six variant catchwords; while Q2 has 120 leaves and six variant catchwords. Admittedly, the compositors of Q2 had an advantage in that they were able to work with Q1 in mind; nevertheless, given the large number of revisions that were introduced to

Q2, including the rearrangement of numerous lyrics, the vigilance and professionalism of Tottel's editorial staff in regard to Q2 must be recognized. That the arrangement of verses in Q2 was radically altered, and the language in particular poems substantively emended in more than 400 places, suggests that Q2's editor was carefully revising the text even while Q1 was in press. The advantage of a moderate press run would allow Tottel to test the public's interest, which he planned to satisfy expeditiously with "more hereafter," as he states in his preface "to the reader." When the potential readership had been established, he would release an enlarged and revised Q2. This bibliographical analysis then suggests that Q2 printed on 31 July was not a random gathering of miscellaneous poems, as Rollins's 1929 edition of *Tottel's Miscellany* suggests, but a carefully arranged text with a structural and thematic design.

In the Critical Introduction I examine the thematic significance of the structural revisions of poems in Q2. In Q1, the attention of the personae shifts in the poems by Surrey, Wyatt, and Grimald from the self-interested Petrarchan lover to didactic and morally educative poems. The long section of poems by Uncertain Auctours, however, is without a strong sense of closure. This is apparent even though the lyric genres in this section are clustered and arranged according to type and *topoi*. The desire for personal fulfillment in love leads to displays of agony, and fits of despair over the power of beauty. Poems on moderation and the "mean estate" are offered as antidotes to excessive desire, but these are followed by laments for the destructive nature of women and the transience of all earthly things. There is no suggestion here that love can be transformed by virtuous action in the community (as in Surrey's poems) or that sensual love will be rejected and replaced by a spiritual retreat (as in Wyatt's poems) or that love naturally leads to self-sacrifice and martyrdom (as in Grimald's poems). Q1 ends fragmented by several clusters of poems that are obviously out of place.

If Tottel had not been in some way concerned with presenting the 31 July compilation as a unified text, he would have replicated the first edition, simply attaching the small clusters of new poems by Surrey and Wyatt to their respective authorial sections, and the new poems by the Uncertain Auctours, to their section. Instead he incorporated the additions by Surrey and Wyatt into appropriate places, and rearranged a number of poems by the Uncertain Auctours whose section he enlarged by 39 poems. The culling of 30 poems by Grimald also had an impact in the new edition, as did the repositioning of his remaining 10 translations to the end of the volume. By moving the poems of the Uncertain Auctours from the final position in the text to the penultimate position and concluding with Grimald's 10 poems, the editor ensures that Grimald's work has a culminating influence on the compilation and provides an effective closure to the entire text.

Standing back from the entire text of Q2, one can assess the aesthetic effect of the revisions. Surrey's personae praise Wyatt as an exemplar of virtue and criticize the barbarism of the age, which has, from king to courtier, occupied itself with the excessive pursuit of pleasure. Wyatt's personae portray political treachery in the court until in his verse epistles the poet describes his own withdrawal to a quiet life where virtuous action is at least possible. There is a clear moral trajectory in the arrangement of poems by these Henrician poets. In contrast, the voices of the Uncertain Auctours — largely Marian poets, it would seem, who preferred to remain anonymous, or who were granted that privilege by the editor — provide a much less certain view of the world and the place of virtue in it. Some comfort is provided in the numerous encomia of virtuous men and women whose lives are celebrated and praised in this section. Largely from the courts of Henry VIII and Edward VI, these figures remind us of what virtue is and how it should be practiced: Master Devorox, the lord Ferres' son; Sir James Wilforde; Thomas Audley; Philip van Wilder; Lady Anne Wentworth; Sir Anthony Deny; the Countess of Pembroke; Sir Thomas Wyatt the elder; Henry Williams; and Mistress White. These poems are complemented by encomia for the gift of "good will"; the joy that accompanies generosity; the temperament of the "mean estate," the style of Petrarch, and the virtue of Laura; the liberating nature of truth; the comfort of a faithful wife; the wisdom of silence; and the importance of friendship. One could argue that the prominence of these poems in the Uncertain Auctours section of Q2 provides a series of portraits with an educative potential to inspire readers to virtuous action. As moral *exempla*, these lyrics accumulate in effect to provide a measurement against which all examples of self-interested action in the text are judged.

If the revised Grimald section had remained where it is found in Q1, lodged between the long Wyatt section and the even longer section by Uncertain Auctours, it would have been all but invisible to the reader. In their new position in Q2, Grimald's final translations of Beza explore the complex nature of virtuous action, its importance to the survival of the human community, and its relationship to martyrdom and immortality. The thirty poems by Grimald found in Q1 but excluded from Q2 had abbreviated initials for titles addressing close acquaintances, including the Ladies Somerset whose father, Lord Protector of England during the reign of Edward VI, was no friend of Queen Mary's. With their omission the editor ensures that the reader focuses exclusively on Grimald's translations of Beza. The significance of this gesture would not have gone unnoticed. Beza was an active participant in the Reformation; as John N. King points out, "as Calvin's chaplain and the continuator of Marot's French Psalter, Beza was a sanctioned neo-classical model for the Protestant poet."[11] The argument in the final poems in Q2 urges the reader to admire and appreciate the courageous resolve of classical figures who chose the honorable path of martyrdom instead of a life of subjection to the forces of oppression. Tottel's editor anticipates John Foxe's *Acts and Monuments* (1563), which emphasizes the triumphs of faith of the Protestant martyrs.

Grimald's translations also remind us of the difficulties involved in attempting to revive the voices of those trying to contribute to the construction of an improved human community. In spite of the endeavor in the early sixteenth century to inculcate classical ideals in the young through the study of Latin authors, mid-Tudor culture was no less vicious. Parallels can be drawn between the execution of Zoroaster and that of Surrey in 1547, and Cicero's murder and Grimald's brush with public execution at the stake, shortly after Mary assumed the throne in 1553. In these ritual acts of violence, the voice of the poet as prophet and cultural critic is immortalized by the society that he has criticized and helped to sustain. The second edition of *Songes and Sonettes* is a text in which lyric voices explore the volatile and socially unstable world of the Tudor monarchy. The revised arrangement of poems in Q2 suggests that the quest for personal and poetic fulfillment leads not to recantation, as in Petrarch, but to questions about political authority and personal censorship, which set the stage for the cultural criticism of the later Elizabethan period.

Songes and Sonettes provides the first example in English of an editor's canonization in a printed book of poems by a group of authors whose works had been circulating largely in manuscripts. As announced in Tottel's preface, the anthology presents to the reader the "honorable stile of the noble Earle of Surrey and the weightinesse of the depewitted Sir Thomas Wiatt the Elders verse." The book also shows that the works of living authors, reflected in the poems by the Uncertain Auctours and by *N.G.*, could compete with the technical and verbal accomplishments of Latin and Italian verse: "our tong is able in that kinde to do as praise worthelye as the rest," the preface asserts. The careful editing of Q2 and Q3 demonstrates a belief in the value of the anthology as a literary genre and the importance of its aesthetic presentation to the public. In the mid-Tudor period, the advantage of publishing a compilation of poems by other people was that once the poems were arranged, the lyric voices would speak for themselves,

---

[11] J. N. King, *English Reformation Literature: The Tudor Origins of the Protestant Tradition* (Princeton: Princeton Univ. Press, 1995), 243. Also see Hoyt Hopewell Hudson, "Grimald's Translations From Beza," *MLN* 39 (1924): 388–94; and S. Laigneau, "La mort de Cicéron chez Théodore de Bèze (Juvenilia): une silve entre épopée et tragédie," in *Acta Conventus Neo-Latini Bonnensis*, ed. R. Schnur, MRTS 315 (Tempe: ACMRS, 2006), 449–56.

leaving virtually no trace of editorial presence, and thus little room for recrimi-
nation. The arrangement of poems in Q2 traces the plight of the personae from
the private world of courtly love to the public world of politics and religion. But
no one particular position is valorized, for the personae merely record and observe various attitudes towards their relations with others and the political, religious, moral or amoral world in which they live. In the end, however, the new
revised order of Q2 does celebrate the poet for immortalizing the selfless deeds
of those who have suffered injustice in the attempt to construct a more civilized
human community. The editor of Tottel's revised *Songes and Sonettes*, then, assumes the role of the author in the arrangement of a compilation of poems in
which the personae provide cultural commentary on the mid-Tudor world. This
anthology thus anticipated the work of Elizabethan authors and editors who developed the genre of the verse compilation by 31 July 1557.

ST. FRANCIS XAVIER UNIVERSITY

Caelius Secundus Curio
His Historie of the Warr of Malta
Translated by Thomas Mainwaringe, 1579[1]

HELEN L. VELLA BONAVITA

I WOULD LIKE TO BEGIN BY EXPRESSING MY GRATITUDE TO THE RENAISSANCE English Text Society for all of its support in assisting me with the production of this book, and particularly to Professor W. Speed Hill. Speed helped and encouraged me more than I can possibly say. In what turned out to be his final e-mail to me, Speed said: "Ignorance is an acute disease, not a chronic one. Nobody makes the journey down the birth canal with the ability to transcribe secretary hand." I certainly didn't, and it is thanks to Speed and to other members of the Renaissance English Text Society's council that I have gained such knowledge as I now possess, although the birthing process was rather lengthy and a little anaesthetic would not have come amiss on occasion.

The siege of Malta in 1565 was something of a nine days', or at least four months', wonder, particularly within the British context. It was the subject of intense scrutiny while it was going on, but the events faded rapidly in the public memory, and Malta in terms of early modern England is far more likely to be associated with Marlowe than in any other context.[2] It may be worthwhile therefore to attempt a brief summary of the historical, linguistic, and indeed media context in which Thomas Mainwaringe's translation of Caelius Secundus Curio's account of the siege of Malta occurred.

---

[1] This paper was first presented at the 2007 Modern Language Association convention in Chicago, IL, at the RETS Open Business Meeting, Arthur F. Kinney presiding.

[2] See Michael Brennan, "Christopher Marlowe's *The Jew of Malta* and Two Newsletter Accounts of the Siege of Malta (1565)," *Notes and Queries* 40 (1993): 157–60.

Susan Rose uses the term 'thalassocracy', or empire of the sea, to describe Byzantine control over the Mediterranean at the height of its power, and the term could equally be applied to the Ottoman domination of the Eastern Mediterranean in the period between 1453 and 1571, while Spanish forces dominated the west.[3] The island of Malta, lying as it does in the narrow part of the Mediterranean between Sicily and Africa, is on the border of the two territories and thus was a natural focus for the continuation of the Holy War between the Cross and the Crescent: the last battle of the Crusades.

Having lost their island of Rhodes in 1522 after a six-month siege (nothing in the world was ever so well lost as Rhodes, said the young Charles V), the Knights Hospitallers of St. John and of Jerusalem (to give them their full title) spent some years searching for a new base from which they could continue their battle against the Ottoman forces. The island of Malta was not their first choice, and when it was finally made over to them, by Charles V in his capacity of King of Sicily, the small archipelago of islands came with the fortress of Tripoli. Since Tripoli was located on the Libyan coast at some distance from Malta, and was surrounded by hostile Muslim forces, it represented something of a challenging responsibility, and in fact the fortress was lost in 1551. A report on the condition of Malta, written by a commission of Knights in 1524, emphasized Malta's poor fields, lack of water, and unsatisfactory fortifications: "No other fortress than a small construction, ruinous with age, to defend the mouth of the harbor, and little artillery, all in very poor order . . . The island is subject to frequent raids by corsairs who, notwithstanding the harbor defenses, enter whenever they please, carrying off the miserable Maltese population as slaves whenever they choose."[4] An unpromising beginning, then, even allowing for some exaggeration which might have brought in a few extra donations.

On their arrival in Malta in 1530, the Knights made haste to strengthen and extend the existing fortifications, while continuing to supplement their income by carrying out raids on Muslim shipping. It was one particular raid, allegedly, the capture of a vessel in which the seraglio of Suleiman the Magnificent had invested substantially, that made the seemingly invincible sultan of the Ottoman empire declare his intention of completing the task he had begun at Rhodes, and extirpating this breed of pirates from the world:

---

[3] Susan Rose, "Islam Versus Christendom: The Naval Dimension, 1000–1600," *Journal of Military History* 63 (1999): 561–68, at 563.

[4] H. Vella, "The Report of the Knights of St. John's 1524 Commission to Malta and Quintinus' *Insulae Melitae descriptio*," *Melita Historica* 8 (1983): 319–24, at 320.

> . . . when as, therefore these knights had settled them selfs in Malta, and re-
> couered some power, they neuer ceased to annoy the Turkes endeuours, as
> much as in them lay . . . by reason whereof . . . Solyman began to be Vexed
> in mynde, to fret, and haue an ey to these holy knights: and to think how to
> drive and holy banish them from the Sea. [5]

The drama of the siege invited comparison with David and Goliath. Suleiman drew together a massive and well-equipped armada with approximately 36,000 fighting men designed to wipe out the Order once and for all. Against this, the Knights were able to muster about seven hundred knights, two thousand professional soldiers, and five to six thousand local militia. The siege took place largely around the three forts that guarded Malta's chief asset, its deep and spacious harbor, and lasted over four months. After a succession of dramatic battles, Christian fatalities of approximately six thousand, and with much of the island's defenses reduced to rubble, the Ottoman armada was finally driven off. The island's fierce resistance, disease, the advancing autumn with its storms that would place the fleet in great danger, and finally the arrival of a Spanish-led relief force combined to convince the Ottoman leaders that a retreat was necessary. The Ottomans left Malta on 8 September 1565; according to some accounts when they returned to Istanbul they were ordered to do so under cover of night, so as to hide their shame.[6]

To general amazement, not least, it may be imagined, from the knights themselves, a small force had managed to hold its own against overwhelming odds, and in doing so had shaped a narrative which lent itself, with almost remarkable readiness, to the complex semiotics of Christian-pagan narratives. The seemingly miraculous victory reinforced the faith that God could and would support the righteous in their time of need. Some accounts of the siege went so far as to include anecdotes of divine apparitions: St. John the Baptist and the Virgin Mary appearing to strengthen the Christians and terrify the enemy.[7] The events of 1565 and the literary representations of those events confirmed Christian ideology. The politically and doctrinally specific elements of that ideology, however, depended on the particular siege narrative; and the question of who the righteous actually were, of course, depended on the doctrinal inclinations of the writer.

---

[5] Thomas Mainwaringe, *Caelius Secundus Curio his historie of the war of Malta*, ed. H. Vella Bonavita (Tempe: ACMRS for RETS, 2007), 42.

[6] Ernle Bradford, *The Great Siege of Malta 1565* [1ˢᵗ pub. 1961] (London: Wordsworth, 1999), 229.

[7] See, for example, Pietro Gentile de Vendome, *Della Historia di Malta* (Bologna, Giovanni Rossi, 1566).

Accounts of the siege proliferated. Against the background of relentless Ottoman advance, and uncoordinated resistance and internal fighting on the part of Western Christendom which characterized the sixteenth century, it is hardly surprising that the siege of Malta came as a welcome relief. Morale surged, and laudatory accounts of the siege were published by the dozen, particularly on the Continent.[8] Between 1565 and 1570, more than seventy narratives were published in German, French, Latin, and Italian — before the even more dramatic battle of Lepanto in 1571, in which the Ottoman navy was conclusively defeated in the brief space of a few hours, provided still better material for exemplary histories.[9]

The entry of the siege into English literature is somewhat more circumspect. Although prayers for Malta's salvation had been duly read in London, Norwich, and Salisbury, and possibly elsewhere, the news that Malta had survived was met with caution rather than elation. Bishop Grindal reminded William Cecil that in other times celebration had proved premature, such as the (erroneously reported) birth of a son for Queen Mary; perhaps thanksgiving services should be postponed until they were quite sure that such remarkable news was actually true?[10]

A similar reticence seems to have applied when writing accounts of the siege in English. A few newsletters survive offering accounts of episodes within the siege, but aside from that English accounts of the siege exist only within broader histories of the Ottomans. The most influential of these was Richard Knolles' enormously popular *The generall historie of the Turkes*, first published in 1603.[11] This was a compendious work, primarily a translation of Augustine Curio's *Sarracenicae Historiae Libri Tres* or *History of the Saracens* (1568), and it included the 1567 account of the siege of Malta, written by Augustine's father Caelius Secundus Curio, that Mainwaringe had also used for his translation some twenty years earlier. Mainwaringe's account of the siege of Malta is in fact the only siege narrative of the sixteenth and early seventeenth centuries written in English that exists independently of any larger work.

---

[8] The most comprehensive list of siege narratives to date is that of Joseph Galea, *Bibliography of the Great Siege of Malta 1565–1965* (Valletta: n. p., 1965). He also cites many manuscript accounts.

[9] For a useful discussion of Lepanto and its varying interpretations see Robert Appelbaum, "War and Peace in the *Lepanto* of James VI and I," *Modern Philology* 97 (2000): 333–63.

[10] W. Nicholson, ed., *The Remains of Edmund Grindal, D.D.: successively Bishop of London, and Archbishop of York and Canterbury*, Parker Society (Cambridge: Cambridge Univ. Press, 1848), 288.

[11] Richard Knolles, *The generall historie of the Turkes, from the first beginning of that nation to the rising of the Othoman familie* . . . (London: A. Islip, 1603).

It is possible that many potential chroniclers of the siege of Malta who were of the Protestant faith faced the same problem as the one that King James I acknowledged in the preface to his heroic poem, *Lepanto,* in which he wrote that he feared to "penne a worke . . . in praise of a forraine *Papiste* bastard" (the Papist bastard in question being Don John of Austria, an illegitimate son of the Holy Roman Emperor Charles V).[12] In the context of the battle of Lepanto and of the Siege of Malta, celebrating a Muslim defeat ran the risk of implicitly acknowledging a Catholic victory. The Knights of St. John, uncompromisingly Catholic and strongly aligned with Spanish interests, were hardly fit subjects for English praise.

Notwithstanding this problem Thomas Mainwaringe, a student at St. John's College, Oxford, took it upon himself to produce an account of the siege in English, using as his source the respected and eminently respectable Lutheran cleric Caelius Secundus Curio, whose son Augustine was to write the aforementioned *History of the Saracens.* Caelius Secundus Curio's history of the siege was possibly the only siege narrative that would be likely to find favor with a Protestant readership because it did not focus on the victory of Catholic forces, but instead emphasized the dangers of disunity within Christian forces and the threat posed by the Ottomans to the welfare of Christendom as a whole. In order to create such an account, Curio had taken the siege narrative written by Pietro Gentile Vendome (who had been a clerk in Sicily during the siege) in 1565 and published in 1566, *Della Historia di Malta,* and adapted it to his own purposes. Where Vendome's work is unabashedly triumphalist, Curio recasts the narrative into a far more moral and admonitory vein, with much of the Catholic emphasis of Vendome's work removed.

Unfortunately, I have been able to find out very little about Thomas Mainwaringe. It is likely that he came from the large Mainwaringe family in Cheshire, although there is another family in Kent that possesses another possible Thomas Mainwaringe. Along with a Latin obituary which hangs in the chapel of St. John's College, Oxford, the *Historie of the warr of Malta* appears to have been Mainwaringe's only output, and of that, only one copy survives. That copy, dedicated to Sir Henry Lee, a pillar of the Elizabethan court, remained with his estate in Ireland until it was sold to the Folger Shakespeare Library in the 1970s.[13]

Mainwaringe's translation is a reasonably faithful and accurate one. In choosing the least 'Catholic' account of the siege Mainwaringe averted any

---

[12] James I, *Lepanto,* in *The Poems of James VI of Scotland,* ed. James Craigie, 2 vols. (Edinburgh: Blackwood & Sons, 1955), 1:198.

[13] Thomas Mainwaringe, *Caelivs Secvndus Curio his historie of the war of Malta* (1579) (Folger MS. V.a.508 [formerly MS. add. 588]).

imputation of writing Catholic propaganda, instead focusing firmly on the dangers of division within Christendom and the example presented by the events of the siege of heroic valor as an inspiration and direction for others. In this sense, Mainwaringe's *Historie of the Warr of Malta* is a consciously exemplary history, providing a model of good behavior as well as warning explicitly against problems of division that were present during the siege and at the time of Mainwaringe's writing. In *Epic and Empire: Politics and Generic Form from Virgil to Milton*, David Quint distinguishes between "where the text responds to historical occasion and where it repeats a generic convention or commonplace."[14] Curio's account of the siege, and Mainwaringe's translation of it, both respond to the historical occasion — the events of the siege — and also to the conventions of chivalric Christianity which dictate their portrayal of the knights' response to those events. Jean de Valette, the Grand Master of the Knights of St. John during the siege, conforms admirably to the pattern of a military hero, one who leads by example and whose physical presence on the battlefield (as at the breach of the Post of Castille) enables the tide of battle to be turned. However, Mainwaringe's narrative is admonitory as well as exemplary: it concludes not with a triumphal account of the celebrations which accompanied news of the siege in Rome and elsewhere which feature in other siege narratives, but instead with the copy of a letter from the Grand Master, recording the devastation which the island suffered during the siege and the inevitability of a Christian defeat if the Ottomans returned — as seemed not at all improbable in the autumn of 1565.

As I have suggested in my introduction to this edition, Mainwaringe's account of the siege of Malta fell into the genre of exemplary histories which had an overt didactic purpose: to try and demonstrate the dangers of internecine Christian warfare and provide readers with an inspiring model of Christian unity against overwhelming Islamic force. Faith in God and the inspiring, unifying figure of de Valette, whom Mainwaringe writes as *Valeta*, serve to counterbalance the tardy and reluctant assistance from Sicily which nearly results in Malta's downfall. The fact that Mainwaringe records, in his introduction to the translation, that he has dedicated copies of the "warr of Malta" to two Catholic notables, Sir William Catesby and Sir Matthew Arundel, along with the impeccably Protestant Sir Henry Lee, might support the possibility that Mainwaringe was referring obliquely to the danger represented by religious divisions within England as well as more broadly elsewhere. Sadly, there simply is not enough evidence, either within the text or elsewhere, to prove the point more securely.

---

[14] David Quint, *Epic and Empire: Politics and Generic Form from Virgil to Milton* (Princeton: Princeton Univ. Press, 1993), 15.

However, the structure of Curio's narrative and Mainwaringe's translation lend themselves to a classical humanist exemplary history that has the additional advantage of celebrating indisputably Christian values (of whatever denomination) rather than the classical heroes who, along with their manifest virtues, possessed also the occasional flaw. David Quint, in his discussion of *Henry V*, reflects on the problematics of depicting Alexander the Great as a hero. He points out to Alexander's discredit: a drunken Alexander murdered a good friend and counselor, was therefore a problematic model to follow, and figures such as Erasmus were fully aware of this flawed hero.[15] While classical heroes were widely accepted as providing vital exemplars which could inspire readers into learning to love and emulate their virtues, the good Christian, and most of all the Christian Prince, should seek to surpass the classical virtues. The Curio / Mainwaringe *Historie of the Warr of Malta* provides such a model, with de Valette being explicitly compared with ancient heroes. The war in which they fight is, from the Christian perspective, fully justified, for they do not seek to extend their territory but simply to protect what they have. Unlike the Crusades which too often became an excuse to gather funds or extend territory, this was a valid war, and the image of the Knights is untarnished by any hint of internal division or cowardice.

Unlike Alexander or Henry V, there are no moral difficulties to work through when considering de Valette in Curio's narrative. The events of the siege are brought to life through his letters and his reactions, and he is the moral arbiter of events as well as a principal actor. Only once is he moved to violent emotion, and that is on the suggestion that he might accept terms from the Ottomans and surrender. He is also a model of personal bravery: when the battle comes to hand-to-hand fighting he is in the forefront:

> The Master looked to all things, encoraged all partes; praised, exhorted, admonished, them all: fought very much him selfe; performed both the dutie of a valiant soldiour, and a worthi Captein bothe in one.[16]

He is able to inspire and to lead in battle, but he is able also to lament the necessity for that battle, and the weakening of Christian forces by internal divisions. He mourns inwardly over the loss of his men, but maintains a cheerful façade in order to maintain morale:

---

[15] David Quint, "Alexander the Pig: Shakespeare on History and Poetry," *Boundary 2* (1982): 49–67.

[16] Mainwaringe, *Historie*, 92.

Valeta [de Valette] when Saint Hermes castle was loste, although he were greeued at the harte, as good reason was; yet made he shewe of no such thing; least he might discourage his soldiours courage.[17]

I have briefly considered some possible reasons for the muted reception accorded the siege of Malta in England, particularly when compared to the intense emotion that it generated on the continent. To the subsequent impact of the naval triumph of Lepanto and the dangers of appearing to celebrate a Catholic victory may be added the fact that the British Isles were unlikely in the extreme to be themselves the target of an invading Ottoman force (although they were of course to be the target of an armada not many years after Mainwaringe was writing). Judging by the near-perfect condition of the Folger's copy of Mainwaringe's work, Henry Lee was not greatly impressed with the gift; it was certainly presented to him, but he may never even have read it. Had he read it, he would have found that Mainwaringe, following Curio's lead, had provided not a paean in praise of a "forraine *Papiste* bastard," but instead an exemplary epic which neatly sidestepped any doctrinal difficulties in favor of a more generalized call to an end of internecine warfare and a united front against the common enemy: the Ottomans.

Editorial issues

Since Mainwaringe's text is, to the best of my knowledge and belief, unique, issues of copy-text in the usual sense did not arise. Accuracy of transcription was an issue, and in his 1978 article "The Calculus of Error, or Confessions of a General Editor," Speed Hill discussed many issues that are pertinent to my own work, but none more so than his discussion of error. Speed Hill divided error into three categories: that which haunts the editor (error as evil spirit), which creeps into texts (error as vermin) and corrupts them (error as sin).[18]

As Speed notes, absolute accuracy in producing an edition is an impossible ideal, one which it is foolhardy even to attempt. Given the inevitability of human error, total accuracy is not only impossible to achieve, it is impossible to demonstrate. A certain degree of accuracy, however, is achievable, and here I offer the advice that Speed gave me: read the text *backwards*. This practice enables the transcriber to view a collection of letters rather than a word, and renders the transcription of inconsistent spelling, punctuation, and capitalization easier to

---

[17] Mainwaringe, *Historie*, 72.
[18] W. Speed Hill, "The Calculus of Error, or Confessions of a General Editor," *Modern Philology* 75 (1978): 247–60, at 247.

achieve. Nonetheless, errors surely remain; *unperceived error* for, as Speed points out, "perceived error is presumably corrected."[19] I can only be grateful to Speed both for giving me the means to reduce those errors, and for rationalizing so eloquently the impossibility of achieving 100% error-free text.

In creating my edition, the nature and extent of the annotations was a significant issue. Although the copy from which I transcribed Mainwaringe's account is so far as I know unique, his work is a translation, indeed, one stage in a series of translations, since Curio's own work was in large part a translation of another account of the siege. To summarise: Curio's work is an adapted translation of Vendome's account of the siege, and Mainwaringe's work is a faithful translation of Curio. It also has an external set of referents as well: the events of the siege as they were recorded by other sources. As such, although Mainwaringe's text is a unique iteration, it also exists within a network of other texts. While the same could be said for any single text to a certain extent, a translation is more self-evidently part of a textual cosmos than, for example, a novel, however intertextual that novel might be. Thus my work had to encompass not just one but a multiplicity of texts, all of which needed to be taken into account when considering the form of the edition.

Options that I considered included a facing-page edition with Curio's narrative on the one side and Mainwaringe's on the other. This would have involved transcribing Curio's Latin, and would have been useful only to a very limited readership. Another option might have been to provide another English translation of Curio's words, in order to enable comparisons between the two texts. Had there been, so to speak, significant authorial or translator's intervention in Mainwaringe's translation of Curio's work, I might have decided on this option. However, Mainwaringe's translation is reasonably faithful; the major alterations in the narrative were made by Curio when translating from his source, Pietro Gentile de Vendome, as I have discussed elsewhere.[20] To what extent Mainwaringe's selection of the only Protestant siege narrative was ideologically and politically informed, to what extent he might have been aware of other forms of the same history, remain unknown. Therefore to create an edition which enabled comparison among the accounts of Curio, Vendome, and Mainwaringe might have implied a relationship and a degree of conscious selection on the part of Mainwaringe which did not in fact exist. Furthermore, to create an edition which enabled transition among three texts in three different languages was a challenge that

---

[19] Hill, Calculus of Error," 247.

[20] H. Vella Bonavita, "'Base translations and wurthy warrs': The Siege of Malta in Reformation and Counter-Reformation Polemic," *Sixteenth Century Journal* 33 (2002): 1021–24.

defied a print-based edition, and which began to invoke the law of diminishing returns. Using another of Speed's works, Michael Best has set forth, with brevity and elegance, the opportunities that electronic editions offer to enable multiple readings. I was not convinced, and neither were any funding bodies, that such an edition was either possible or worthwhile for this particular, rather obscure, set of translations.[21] After much soul-searching, I decided to keep the edition as clean and simple as possible, allowing its strongest point — Mainwaringe's narrative — to speak for itself.

Mainwaringe's account, following Curio, is not wholly accurate, and in one important section deviates quite significantly from the truth of the events at Malta as they appear in other authoritative accounts of the siege, particularly that of the Order's main historian of this period, Giacomo Bosio. However, since I did not know how many accounts of the siege Mainwaringe had available to him, I had no way of knowing whether he was aware of this. Rather than indicate every point at which Mainwaringe — or his source — departs from historical accuracy, I have, where the matter is significant, indicated the fact in a footnote, and indicated where further information may be found. I have also of course indicated my very minor authorial interventions in the text, although these have amounted to little more than supplying a missing word from the catchword, since the script itself is in very good, clear condition.

My purpose, then, in creating this edition was not to write a new history of the siege of Malta in 1565; other, better, more detailed and more accurate accounts already exist. I set out to enable Mainwaringe's account to reach a wider public than it could do in its present format, and in so doing I believe that the account makes a small but enjoyable contribution to prose history writing in English. Mainwaringe's English is clear and lively; the narrative is well set out and is interspersed with letters from the Grand Master which give de Valette a speaking voice within the text, and give the account as a whole an immediacy and intimacy which might be lacking in other pieces. Mainwaringe's indignant repudiation of the opinions of "coward carpet-knights" — which is actually one of the earliest uses of that term, according to the *Oxford English Dictionary* — that de Valette has risked his own safety in an unjustifiable manner:

> It is an easy thing for him to discredite anothr man, who hath no regarde of
> his owne estimacion: neithr may vnskilful fellows presume to iudge of skill,

---

[21] Michael Best, "Standing in Rich Place: Electrifying the Multiple-Text Edition or, Every Text is Multiple," *College Literature* 36.1 (Winter 2009): 26–39.

> more then the coward carpet knight giue iudgment of the valiaunt attempts
> of soldiours.[22]

is forceful and direct, while de Valette's own pleas to the pope and to the Spanish
viceroy of Sicily render the text accessible and eminently readable.

> I pray god that you send us some succour . . . Oure lyfe and safety is in your
> hands: in whome next vnder god we haue reposed all our trust: I besech you
> hartely that you leave vs not destitute.

I would suggest that this is a text which, as an example of late sixteenth-century
prose, has a very real interest and value to general students of the period as well
as the rather smaller readership interested in the various and varied histories of
Malta, and my annotations are primarily to assist the reader who may not be familiar with the historical and geographical background to the siege.

Curio's work, incorporated by his son Augustine Curio into his history of
the Saracens, was translated again, and more widely published by Francis Knolles
in 1603, but by the early seventeenth century it had lost something of its impact,
particularly I think in Great Britain where concerns over the Ottoman empire
had shifted from fears of invasion to fears of contamination, of "turning Turk",
as Daniel Vitkus, among others, has shown.[23] Lepanto overshadowed Malta, and
continues to do so; a recent article referred to Lepanto as "the singular reference
point" in Christian resistance to the Ottoman empire in the sixteenth century.[24] Both literally in terms of Knolles' edition, and figuratively in terms of the
overarching narrative of Christian-Muslim relations in the early modern period,
the siege of Malta became simply another chapter in a much larger work. Mainwaringe's account of the siege as a single, discrete narrative entity stands as a
record of the very real interest and concern that the siege generated both during
its events and, for a short space of time, afterwards. In choosing to publish it the
Renaissance English Text Society has ensured that, as Speed put it, "Mainwaringe
will get the audience he deserves, and RETS will march out with a really good
read under its banner." Thank you, Speed.

EDITH COWAN UNIVERSITY, WESTERN AUSTRALIA

---

[22] Mainwaringe, *Historie*, 78.

[23] Daniel Vitkus, *Turning Turk: English Theater and the Multicultural Mediterranean,
1570–1630* (New York: Palgrave Macmillan, 2003).

[24] David Bergeron, "Are We Turned Turks?" *Comparative Drama* 44 (2010): 255–75, at 255.

Editing "a mute inglorious Milton" of Gloucestershire: Nicholas Oldisworth[1]

JOHN GOUWS

T HE QUOTATION IN MY TITLE IS OF COURSE FROM THOMAS GRAY'S "ELEGY
Written in a Country Churchyard," and is preceded by the following qua-
train:

Full many a gem of purest ray serene
The dark unfathom'd caves of ocean bear:
Full many a flower is born to blush unseen,
And waste its sweetness on the desert air. (53–56)

There are many early modern poets and writers of poems whose names we shall
never know. There are probably as many whose names we know but whose writings have been lost. And there are some whose names and works have simply
drifted into the abyss or been effaced by traditions and preoccupations whose
light has been bent by the gravity of the dominant imaginary of literary luminar-
ies, constellations and galaxies that have fixed the attention of readers over the
centuries. Oldisworth's dates — 1611–1645 — invite comparison with Milton, but
there is a world of difference between the two. Oldisworth's collection of poems
transcribed in a presentation manuscript for his wife in 1645 shortly before his
death bears no comparison with the collection of poems Milton published in the
same year: his poems disappeared for two and a half centuries, whereas Milton's

---

[1] This paper was first delivered at the 2009 Modern Language Association convention in
Philadelphia, PA, at the RETS Open Business Meeting, Arthur F. Kinney presiding.

ensured that he would be one of the major poets in the language even if he published nothing else. Unlike Milton, Oldisworth was not a man of ambitious intellect, but lived obscurely and modestly in the Cotswolds.

Too many years ago now I sent the late John Buxton[2] part of a poem describing the village of Coln Rogers in Gloucestershire. Buxton, an old-school belletrist
who prided himself on his knowledge of the poets of the English Renaissance and
of Gloucestershire poets in general, did not know the poem. What was even more
surprising was that he did not know that the very house in Coln Rogers which he
and his wife bought after the Second World War had been the parental home of
the poet — Nicholas Oldisworth.

I first encountered Oldisworth while trawling through manuscript miscellanies at the Folger Library for *moriturus* lyrics. My attention was caught by a series
of poems in Folger MS. V.a.170 that were egregious in terms of their quality when
compared with the many unattributed and unattributable poems in so many seventeenth-century poetic miscellanies, and by clearly being the work of one person. The Folger catalogue confirmed this, and provided the author's name, as
well as the information that the Bodleian Library held an autograph manuscript
of Oldisworth's poems, MS. Don. c. 24. All I could discover about Oldisworth
was from a paragraph tacked on to the *DNB* entry for his brother, Giles. I could
connect neither with the world of letters I had been brought up on, apart from the
fact that they were nephews of Sir Thomas Overbury.

Since I happened to be returning to South Africa via London, I used the six
hours between flights to telephone ahead to Duke Humfrey's Library and ask
them to call up the manuscript (those were the days before mobile telephones and
painless internet access, so it was quite an achievement). I also discovered that the
manuscript also contained an incomplete and rather juvenile *roman à clef*, "The
Chronicle of Europe." Having taken one look at the presentation copy the poet
had prepared for his wife a matter of weeks before his own death, I knew I had to
produce an edition of the poems. Little did I know that I would fulfill the advice I
have given my students over the years: "Think of the longest time it will take you
to complete this project; then double it." I thought ten years would suffice. It has
taken twenty, almost to the month. I had not foreseen that I would marry, have
two wonderful children, bury a mother, have the thankless task of Head of a Department of English, be ambushed by ingratitude and live through some of the
gratifyingly momentous, though anticipated, events in my home country South
Africa's at times sad history.

---

[2] John Buxton was a Fellow of New College, Oxford, and a Reader in English Literature
at Oxford, when he supervised my D. Phil.

Normally, when we edit we know, as readers, who and what we are editing, and refine our knowledge through the process of preparing the edition. Our access to the material is conditioned by the information and reading practices we bring with us. When we are faced with an author who in a sense never died because his authorship was unacknowledged, we do not have the ready-made accessibility we all too easily take for granted with authors who already have their allocated places in the literary constellations. It takes a major feat of imagination and will to re-adjust perceptions of authors already known. For people such as Nicholas Oldisworth what is required is the labour of discovering the information of the kind some critical practices of reading authors of name encourage us to pretend are misguided and irrelevant. We also do not have the critical paradigms in terms of which he is to be read (and for that matter, edited). But that is the joy of such a project: one has to discover, invent, and negotiate what will make the literary conduct of a man such as Nicholas Oldisworth accessible. In the process, one will be obliged to challenge and reassess the presuppositions one brings to the whole business of reading and editing. One has to recalibrate and adjust old ways of reading and editing new texts, and finding new ways of reading and editing old texts, all at the same time. What is useful and refreshing about this is that it keeps one mindful of what the editorial enterprise is all about: why we do it; what we want to achieve; its difficulties and challenges, but also its rewards and triumphs.

Oldisworth's case is, of course, not unique.[3] There are many authors who have spun out of the literary gravitational fields, or never been drawn into one. All that is required is that one is aware of the possibility and alert and willing to engage with them on their own terms "like some watcher of the skies / When a new planet swims into his ken" (John Keats, "On First Looking into Chapman's *Homer*," lines 9–10). In the case of Robert Sidney, first earl of Leicester (the brother of Sir Philip Sidney and of Mary Herbert, Countess of Pembroke), whose poems slipped below the horizon in the course of the nineteenth century when the autograph manuscript was re-bound, and "Sonnets by the Earl of Leicester" lettered on the spine, it took the acuity of P. J. Croft to realize that the Earl of Leicester responsible was not the great Elizabethan courtier, Robert Dudley, but his nephew, Robert Sidney.[4] More recently, Stanley Wells encountered William Scott's "The Model of Poesy" (c. 1600), which contains the earliest close criticism

---

[3] A case very similar to Oldisworth's "A Recollection of Certaine Scattered Poëms" (Bodleian MS. Don.c.24) is a near-contemporary work by Cardell Goodman, *Beawty in Raggs or Divine Phancies putt into Broken Verse*, found in two manuscripts, Lambeth MS. 937 and MS. 1063. There is an edition by R. J. Roberts (Reading: Whiteknights Press, 1958).

[4] See P. J. Croft, ed., *The Poems of Robert Sidney* (Oxford: Clarendon Press, 1984), 3–9.

of Shakespeare.[5] The late Jeremy Maule, who assiduously trawled the less frequently examined repositories and archives, was particularly adept at seeing occluded works in their true light.

Who, then, was Nicholas Oldisworth, the agent whose literary conduct is manifest in Bodleian MS. Don. c. 24, and elsewhere? He was born at Bourton-on-the-Hill in Gloucestershire, at the home of his maternal grandfather, Sir Nicholas Overbury, and educated at Westminster School under Lambert Osbaldeston. Some time between Christmas 1628 and Lady Day 1629 he was admitted to Christ Church, Oxford, where he obtained his BA in 1632 (being incorporated at Cambridge in the same year) and his MA in 1635.

At Christ Church we would have known two Old Westminsters of an older generation: Richard Corbett, the Dean from 1620 until 1628, when he was made Bishop of Oxford (until 1632); and Brian Duppa, the Dean from 1628 and Vice-Chancellor of the University in 1632–1633. Corbett already had an established reputation as a poet, and Duppa, though not a regular producer of poems, took an active interest in poetry, and was responsible for the production in 1637 of *Jonsonus Virbius*, the collection of poems commemorating the death of Ben Jonson. Amongst Oldisworth's contemporaries were other known poets: Jasper Mayne and William Cartwright, who arrived from Westminster in the same year (and, as it happens, predeceased Oldisworth by two years). Robert Randolph, the brother of Thomas, arrived at Christ Church from Westminster in 1629.

The connection between Westminster School and Christ Church is important. In terms of the Elizabethan statutes the school had the right annually to elect two scholars to Christ Church, and two to Trinity College, Cambridge. Queen's scholars to Trinity entered the college as undergraduates, but those to Christ Church were made what the College calls "Students"; that is, Fellows, which they remained until they married. William Camden, the headmaster of Westminster when Ben Jonson was at the school, and a great encourager of poetic composition in the vernacular, had arrived as second master of the school from Christ Church, and for much of the seventeenth century Westminster headmasters were products of the School and Christ Church. It is therefore not surprising that the majority of Old Westminsters favoured the Oxford connection, and also not surprising that a large proportion of the surviving poetic miscellanies of the period have a Christ Church connection. What the Cambridge connection lacked in quantity is made up for in quality: George Herbert, Thomas Randolph,

---

[5] Stanley Wells, "By the placing of his words," *TLS*, 26 September 2003: 14–15. The manuscript is now in the British Library (Add. MS. 81983). Gavin Alexander's edition for the Cambridge Univ. Press appeared in November 2013.

Abraham Cowley, and John Dryden were products of Westminster School and Trinity College, Cambridge.

In August 1634, Oldisworth was presented with the living of Bourton-on-the-Hill by his grandfather. In 1640, he married Mary Chamberlayne from Fairford. There were three children: Mary, baptised on 6 January 1641; Frances, baptised 11 June 1642 and buried 28 November 1643; and Margaret, baptised on 8 February 1644. 1644 and 1645 were bad plague years. The parish records for those two years (completed by Giles Oldisworth, his brother's successor as rector of Bourton-on-the-Hill) show that forty-one people died of the plague. Five other deaths are recorded, which is the norm for previous years. One of the victims of the plague was Nicholas Oldisworth himself, who was not buried in his own church. He died at Willington, in Warwickshire (about five miles as the crow flies from Bourton-on-the-Hill). He had probably taken his family there to escape the plague, though he himself continued with his preaching duties at various neighbouring Gloucestershire churches. He was buried in the chancel of the nearby church of Barcheston, but the site has been lost in the obliteration of nineteenth-century church restoration. His wife survived to a long widowhood, dying in 1684 in the village of Batsford, about a mile north of Bourton-on-the-Hill. The elder surviving daughter married a Londoner, Master Sherwood, and the younger, Margaret, who could barely have known her father, married John Mann of Tewkesbury in Gloucestershire. It was she who inherited her father's poetic manuscript and turned it into a recipe book. She records the gift in her own hand: "Margaret Man Her Book Given Me By My Mother." Below this she added a little more formally: "Master Nicholas Oldisworth." Margaret Mann later erected a monument to her mother in Tewkesbury Abbey, a photograph of which appears on the cover of the edition. The inscription reads:

> To the Happy Memory of
> MARY OLDISWORTH
> Daughter of Tho: Chamberlayne of
> Oddington Esqr: Wife to Nicholas Oldis=
> =worth Gent. Son of Robert Oldisworth
> of Fairford Esq. Mother of Mary the
> Wife of John Sherwood Gent. & also
> of Margarite Wife to Iohn Mann Gent.
> She lived a Virgin 29 Yeares a Wife
> 5 & a Widow 39 and Died the 4th
> of August 1684 Aged 73.
> She was a pattern of Piety Charity

Modesty Chastity Temperance &
Frugality of pleasant Conversation
Beloved by all & now Wanted by
many All that was Mortal Lyes
Interred near <thi>s place expecting
a joyful Resurrection.

The discovery of this monument not only allowed me to identify Nicholas Oldisworth's wife, but also confirmed the sense of the marriage as a site of private life
based on mutual respect celebrated in the dedicatory epistle of "A Recollection of
Certain Scattered Poems."

    To his deare Wife, Mar-
    -rie Oldisworth.

Sweet Mall
Wee two have now beene marryed five   5
yeares: and hitherto (praised bee God)
wee have wanted nothing, but Peace.
For my part, I thanke God for those
good dayes, which I have seene in my
youth: wherin I had Leisure to please   10
my owne fancie, and to write such Toyes,
as here doe follow. And I doubt not
but Thou also, in those very dayes,
hadst and didst enjoy thy faire virginlike
contentments; though I then was not   15
so happy, as to know either Them, or Thee.
Time was (Mall) when tabrets and pipes
were more respected, then drummes and
trumpets: which drummes and trumpets
were seldome heard in England, but at   20
a Masque, or at a Play. Time was, when
I could ride from Borton to London, both
without Companie, and without Danger,
and carry my Pockets full of Monie.
But now where is that Monie? My gold-   25
scales (thou knowest) lie uselesse and unemployed:
nor doe I see my Soveraigne's face in silver
at home much oftener, then I see his face

in flesh and blood in Oxford. Yet have I
spent as much, in Contributions and Free-   30
quarters, as would not onely have sett
mee out of debt, but have begunne competent Portions for thy two little daughters.
I pray god send us Patience: for, although
wee are likely to stand in Need of many   35
things, yet are wee likely to stand most
in Neede of Patience. So entreating thee
to bee of good Cheare, and not to trouble
or disquiet thy minde with the Feare
and expectation of those Evils, which per-   40
chance may never come; I rest

From Willington   Thy true Friend   This was written
1644. Febr: 17   Nicolas Oldisworth   in the time
                                                    of the Treaty
                                                    at Uxbridge
                                                    between the
                                                    King's side and
                                                    the Parliament's

What are the challenges of editing Nicholas Oldisworth? One of them is not the problem of establishing the text. The autograph manuscript, as one would expect of a presentation copy prepared for the author's wife, is in an easily readable hand. The other main manuscript, Folger MS. V.a.170, is generally legible, but there are a handful of occasions where it is clear that the copyist is either careless or faced with a problematic source. What is interesting about the Folger manuscript is that in some cases it has variant readings which appear to represent earlier versions derived from a Christ Church contemporary who had access to Oldisworth's working papers. But this can only be a matter of surmise. There are also seven poems of dubious quality which all appear to derive from Oldisworth, but are not represented in the holograph. I have appended these to the edition as "Additional Poems."[6]

Other witnesses to the text are the printed versions of poems written for royal occasions, a scattering of poems found in manuscript miscellanies, and of course the copies of the poem on Ben Jonson "Die Ben Jonson," which the old poet

---

[6] *Nicholas Oldisworth's Manuscript (Bodleian MS. Don.c.24)*, ed. John Gouws, MRTS 380 (Tempe: ACMRS, 2009).

sent to his patron, William Cavendish, Earl of Newcastle. None of these present textual problems. But there will always be manuscript copies that elude an editor. I thought I had traced most of the miscellanies containing poems by Oldisworth, only to discover as I was preparing this discussion, and only two days before printing of the edition was to take place, that there is a copy of the Ben Jonson poem at Yale [Shelfmark: b.356; Folio: p. 316; Ref Nbr: Osborn D0314]. Earlier inquiries had elicited negative responses, but now that the Folger has made available on line its *Union First Line Index of Manuscript Poetry*, I know differently. This research tool will in time be a great boon to scholars working in the field of early modern manuscript poetry, and will allow editors of the future to provide a more comprehensive coverage of manuscript provenance.

If textual problems are not the main concern of an editor working with an authorial fair copy, knowledge of copies and versions in print and manuscript provide insight into the work, and how it should be understood, and require an editor's attention. For instance, in the case of Oldisworth, only a single poem, "Die Ben Jonson," for obvious reasons enjoyed any significant circulation in manuscript and print. A small number of poems is found in another single manuscript, and a handful of other poems appear in various miscellanies. On the one hand this confirms the obvious point that Oldisworth, despite his connection with Sir Thomas Overbury, was not a person whose life and personality rendered him so publicly visible that his poems were worth transcribing or anthologizing in print, and also that the poems themselves were not of a kind which appealed to avid gatherers of other men's flowers in manuscript albums. On the other hand, the restricted circulation might also simply reflect Oldisworth's enactment of himself as a man who flourished in private life and its intimacies. This would be consistent with the gathering of the poems in what was probably a wedding anniversary gift to his wife, and the family's treasuring of the manuscript rather than exposing it on the pillory of print. If this is true, then there is a certain measure of gauche intrusion in seeking to edit and expose to public scrutiny poems which are not simply poems intended for a restricted, private readership, but poems which are also the means by which the writer manifested his self-understanding and conducted his private, though social, life. When poems are, as these clearly were, not simply forms of knowledge, but themselves constituents of a way of life, then they require to be treated with respect and tact. The ethics of editing becomes an issue demanding attention. The editor is no longer the occluded body-slave of the material text at the banquet of "the literary" spread for the delight of the elite.

Editing, especially critical editing, is not merely a matter of locating and presenting a text. The editor is also a reader, a very close reader and scrutinizer who seeks on equal terms with other readers to provide shared access to the work, the literary conduct, of the author. As such, the edition is not the end of a conversation with the author before thrusting him unceremoniously out the door into the cold, but a symposium already in progress requiring an attentive host to usher in from the cold the most recent guest.

This I have learnt from two decades of engagement with Oldisworth, and I have tried already to make a cursory introduction — in the hope that those who might eventually read the introduction of the edition might want to pursue the acquaintance. But a proper introduction requires a great deal of preparation. Oldisworth has not been around to answer questions, and often the records are missing, and this makes it difficult for the first person who takes him seriously. Anyone involved in revealing the biographical details of someone who chose to live in the relative obscurity of rural Gloucestershire in the first half of the seventeenth century must of course be indebted to the International Genealogical Index, and it is appropriate that I express my gratitude to the endeavours of Mormons retrospectively to redeem their ancestors in the Mormon-owned hotel, the Marriott in downtown Philadelphia, where this essay was first presented.

But not even Mormon industry can retrieve church records that have been lost. I went on record in the *Oxford Dictionary of National Biography* entry for Oldisworth saying I could not identify his wife, Mary, because the records of all the churches where I suspected Oldisworth would marry were incomplete. By placing my ignorance in the public sphere, I provoked the research which serendipity cannot replace, and was rewarded by being sought out in Duke Humfrey's Library by a graduate student who had noticed my name in the library day-register and generously shared his discovery with me. Mary Oldisworth had died in Batsford in the northern Cotswolds, near to Bourton-on-the-Hill. I learnt that I should not have looked at marriage or funeral records, but at a list of church monuments in Tewkesbury Abbey. When this was pointed out to me, it made perfect sense, since the Oldisworths' youngest daughter, Margaret, had married John Mann of Tewkesbury. Having an eighteenth-century antiquary's transcription of a memorial tablet in Tewkesbury Abbey was not enough. What was still required was a journey to the far end of the Cotswolds to see whether the memorial still remains. And indeed it does, though worse for wear after more than two centuries of neglect.

There are other persons mentioned in the poems and in Oldisworth's annotations I have not been able to identify, and my hope is that the edition will over time elicit responses to my declarations of ignorance. The most notable are a Mistress Strange, a writer of devotional or theological poems [44];[7] Sir B. R., whose life anticipated *The Compleat Gentleman* [41][8] and B. R, a dissembler [65];[9] Mistress E. W., an enemy of Katherine Bacon, the sister of Richard Bacon, Oldisworth's beloved schoolfriend [20],[10] Mistress Anne Henshaw [55],[11] Squire Burch, who married one of Richard Bacon's sisters [60] and [104];[12] "Mistress Summer" who died in childbed and on whom Oldisworth wrote two poems at the behest of "a Londoner" [74] and [75];[13] a gentleman on behalf of whom Oldisworth wrote one poem (if not two) to Master Henry Gresley [110] and [111].[14] I have also not been able to attach significance to the names of the characters "Tahah" and "Guerim" in a pastoral poem [53], and to "Tharuleot" [66] who runs very fast and is also mentioned in the "Chronicle of Europe."

Making sense of these references requires many hours in archives and libraries, and much serendipity, but as I have already suggested the "new" poet also requires material research in the form of visits to sites, places, and buildings to verify the accuracy of Oldisworth's description of Coln Rogers, or of the Chillings Manor House outside Southampton, for example; to discover if any feature of the church at Bourton-on-the-Hill recalls his presence; or whether his grave in the chancel of the church at Barcheston in Warwickshire still exists. Sometimes the visits did not produce the discoveries I had hoped for. Some did, while others revealed information I had not anticipated. Whatever the outcome, the cumulative experience was a greater sense of accomplishment in retrieving from the past a sense of a life lived on its own terms. I was repeatedly reminded of Wallace Stevens's "A Postcard from the Volcano":

> Children picking up our bones
> Will never know that these were once
> As quick as foxes on the hill;

---

[7] "To the worshipfull, Mistris Strange of Summerfield, a Poëtesse."

[8] "On Sir B.R."

[9] "To B.R. a Dissembler."

[10] "To Mistress E.W."

[11] "To his musicall Valentine Mistris Anne Henshaw."

[12] "Iter Australe, 1632. Or, A journey southwards" lines 99–100, and "To the faire Mistris Burch, at his first sight of her."

[13] "On Mistris Summer, who dyed in child-bedd" and "On the death of both Mistris Summer and her Childe."

[14] "For a Gentleman. On the embracing of his Friend" and "For a Gentleman. To yong Master Henry Gresley."

And that in autumn, when the grapes
Made sharp air sharper by their smell
These had a being, breathing frost;

And least will guess that with our bones
We left much more, left what still is
The look of things, left what we felt

At what we saw. The spring clouds blow
Above the shuttered mansion-house,
Beyond our gate and the windy sky

Cries out a literate despair.
We knew for long the mansion's look
And what we said of it became

A part of what it is . . . Children,
Still weaving budded aureoles,
Will speak our speech and never know,

Will say of the mansion that it seems
As if he that lived there left behind
A spirit storming in blank walls,

A dirty house in a gutted world,
A tatter of shadows peaked to white,
Smeared with the gold of the opulent sun.[15]

My hope, as an editor, is that in attending to the "mansion-house," its look and what Oldisworth said of it to make it become what it is, I would be better enabled to allow the poems to be apprehended as the postcard exchanges constituting the fabric and tissue of his life, rather than their being extraneous and incidental to it.

My work on Oldisworth fortuitously coincided with the emergence of scholarly work on scribal publication and transmission and on poetic communities. Whether this is an instance of synchronicity, I do not know, but being aware of the work of Harold Love and Arthur Marotti, for example, has encouraged me

---

[15] Wallace Stevens, *Collected Poetry and Prose*, ed. Frank Kermode and Joan Richardson (New York: The Library of America, 1997), 128–29.

not to falter in the face of accusations of recidivism from people nurtured on the thin gruel of New Criticism and Literary Theory, where I too would have been marooned, but for the grace of philosophers such as Daantjie Oosthuizen, Ludwig Wittgenstein, Michael Oakeshott, and Charles Taylor; wise teachers such as Guy Butler (a poet whose generous spirit had seen enough of war and suffering to know what was important, and who had been taught by J. B. Leishman), Ruth Harnett (another poet, indomitable spirit, lover of the beautiful and gentle, who had been trained at the University of London — under James Sutherland, and where the influence of W P Ker was still felt), and John Buxton (a writer of poems who never studied English Literature formally, but produced more Professors of English than any of his Oxford contemporaries); and generous scholar-poet friends like Jon Stallworthy.

What is distinctive about Bodleian MS. Don. c. 24, is that it is not simply an autograph manuscript, but a presentation fair copy to the author's wife. We thus have more than a collection of poems, but poems embedded in a personal context which enabled their significance. The manuscript also has marginal comments which supply the kind of socially significant information that is all too often lost in other manuscript collections in general, and in printed ones in particular. The more I lived with these poems and sought ways of rescuing the import of direct, but historically attenuated, references, the oblique allusions and implicit assumptions, the more I realized the need to conceive of the poems as forms of human conduct. Nowhere was this more obvious than in the realization that Oldisworth was part of the Caroline Oxford poetic community, one which was sustained by the interaction between Westminster School and Christ Church, Oxford. But I have also come to realize that this is only the beginning of the story. The full title of the collection is: "A Recollection of Certain Scattered Poems. Written long since by an Undergraduate, being one of the students of Christchurch in Oxford. And now in the yeare 1644 transcribed by the author, and dedicated to his wife. When I was a child, I spake as a child, I understood as a child, I thought as a child: but when I became a man, I put away childish things. 1 Cor. XIII. 11." The gestures of dedication and repudiation indeed have to be given due weight in reading the poems, but we also need to take account not only Oldisworth's act of collecting the poems rather than consigning them to the fire, and to his final poem, in which he does not renounce poetry so much as redirect it. More important even than this, however, is the predicament of the private life in turbulent times that emerges from the dedicatory epistle. Many of the poems are celebrations of social well-being not in metropolitan London, whether at Court or the Inns of Court, nor in the giddy exchanges of undergraduate life in Oxford and Cambridge, but in the homes of the country gentry of Gloucestershire and Wiltshire in particular. This is a different poetic community from the ones which normally receives attention, and in this setting the lyrics, songs, epigrams, epistles, and shape poems we would expect in the period have a greater resonance. This also applies to the "ventriloquist" and prosopopoeic poems, and most especially to what may be called the proxy, surrogate or vicarious poems which Oldisworth writes at the behest of family and friends for their own use.

Dispersed through the collection is a series of poems of intimate friendship entitled "To his Friend beyond sea," which partially suppress the name of the recipient, Richard Bacon, who was at Westminster with Oldisworth before spending a year at Trinity College, Cambridge, and then departing for the English College at Douay. Bacon went on to teach rhetoric at Douay, where he was joined by his brother, Matthew, who removed to Padua to study medicine after the death of his brother from the plague in 1636. Perhaps the most poignant moment in the collection is the last of the poems to his friend "On the death of his deare friend Master Richard Bacon" [172] — a simple blank page. Matthew seems to have inherited Richard's papers, since he appropriated one of Oldisworth's poems to celebrate his own friendship with a fellow Englishman residing in Rome. Oldisworth's thinly veiled relationship with the Bacon family (he visited the sisters at their home in Hampshire) and with other Recusants emerges throughout the collection, and makes us aware of the nuanced complexity of literary social relationships in the period.

Editing Oldisworth has been for me an act of piety, and in the process I have learnt something about the need to attend and to respect, something about the ethics of editing. To end where I began, with Gray's "Elegy":

No farther seek his merits to disclose,
Or draw his frailties from their dread abode
(There they alike in trembling hope repose),
The bosom of his Father and his God. (125–128)

NORTH-WEST UNIVERSITY

On Textual Editing: MA 1057[1]

MICHAEL DENBO

OST LITERARY SCHOLARS ARE CONCERNED WITH THE DEFINITION OF words, and one word—at the very center of our concerns—is the word "text." Peter Beal, in his recent *A Dictionary of English Manuscript Terminology, 1450–2000*, defines the word as follows:

> Derived from the Latin *textum* ('something woven'), which is also related to the words 'textile' and 'texture', the term 'text' means the wording of any piece of writing, manuscript or printed. In a specifically literary context, it denotes the original or main body of wording or verbal structure that constitutes a book or manuscript, or any part of it, excluding subsidiary additions such as preliminaries, notes, and appendices.[2]

This or any other definition of such an elusive term as "text" might foster inquiry, but two aspects of Beal's definition should be questioned. First, why is there any distinction whatsoever between a literary and non-literary text, and, second, what exactly is he referring to when he excludes "subsidiary additions such as preliminaries, notes, and appendices"? Generally, at least today, writers write and rewrite, and I presume, following Beal's definition the text emerges after all preliminaries, notes, and appendices, are tossed in the wastepaper basket. But do these important activities in writing also not constitute a text, and on what basis are they distinguished from the so-called final version, or authorial version of a particular text? All of us know the question I am raising: what exactly

---

[1] This paper was first presented at the RETS Open Business Meeting held at the 2011 MLA Convention in Los Angeles, CA, Arthur F. Kinney presiding.

[2] Peter Beal, *A Dictionary of English Manuscript Terminology, 1450–2000* (Oxford: Oxford Univ. Press, 2008), 414.

defines a text? or from the perspective of this paper, how does the definition of the word 'text' — or the limit of what that word represents in a particular circumstance — affect textual editing? or perhaps even more compelling, does the definition affect anything, least of all the actual editing of the text? To assume it does suggests that the activity of textual editing emanates from the meaning of the word or even the meaning of the word as construed and/or defined by the individual editor. That would assume a kind of definable center around which we, as editors, rotate, that we are somehow influenced by the gravitational pull of this peculiar word or what that word represents. That I have come to believe is not the case. There is a center around which we edit, but it has very little to do with definitions. It has instead to do with how we read, what we see, and how we understand ourselves in the world itself. I also believe that no *one* person actually edits, that instead the project of editing — or writing — or rewriting — involves many people, many ideas, and even more influences than we can ever enumerate. Here part of the definition comes to explain at least something of what it means to edit: the concept of weaving. A text is woven together from many fabrics, many threads, many purposes, and the more of these that can be suggested by an individual edition the better will be that edition — whatever *better* means. More so, no one person edits. Many are involved, either the best or worst example of teamwork in a place where a team is least expected. As multifaceted as editing actually is, equally so, it is a unique and paradoxical activity.

I first encountered the Holgate Miscellany as a graduate student at the City University of New York. W. Speed Hill, my dissertation supervisor and former president of RETS, suggested it to me. He warned me that although an edition would more than likely be published, it would not necessarily lead me to the job that all graduate students want — a job at a well-known university or college. Frankly, I did not believe him about the job, but I did believe him about the project being published, and that it would be a project with a definable limit, i.e., a task, a describable task that that would lead to a completed dissertation. On that basis I accepted the idea and frankly I have never been sorry that I did. I have found it endlessly fascinating and enjoyable.

Speed's first assignment was to read several well-known theories of textual editing. I did so and learned absolutely nothing — at least in terms of the edition. Somehow the manuscript I had already encountered at the Morgan Library had nothing to do with the theoretical strategies outlined by these well-known textual scholars. What was obvious instead was why the Holgate deserved to be edited. It is an early seventeenth-century verse manuscript with poetry by people such as Shakespeare, Donne, Jonson and Carew. It also had a lot of other writing — none of which seemed familiar. There was some prose, but not a lot. There were unascribed poems that seemed odd and confusing. There was one handwriting that predominated, but clearly other writers had added poems and commentary to the manuscript. It is a little book with an original cover. It has a unique smell which I am not able to convey. Both its ink and its paper were differing shades of brown — yes, brown ink. It is a text but it is also many texts — in fact, it seems like one and many texts with each page that's turned. Indeed, there is no way it could have been transcribed in one single sitting. It is a manuscript that someone cared deeply about, but why he or she cared is not obvious to anyone. The transcriber is known as William Holgate, but ensuing attempts to identify him repeatedly led to no positive identification. To this day I am unable to say for sure that one of the several William Holgates considered as the writer of this particular manuscript can be asserted. That fact, more than any single other problem encountered over the long attempt to find him, continues to bother me. In many ways I feel like I know him, but I am always stopped by the fact that his identity continues to escape me. What I have is a text — or perhaps a textile — a garment — a lost glove — unable to tell who its owner was. A curious circumstance.

And there were a mountain of questions: Who wrote which poems? How had they come to be transcribed into this manuscript? What is the meaning of this manuscript? Is it a miscellaneous collection of many poems, or does it by design come together to form something else? How can any individual text, i.e., a particular poem, be a text in and of itself or a part of a much larger text, i.e., the document that has come to be known as the Holgate Miscellany? Who was William Holgate? Where was he educated? Did he have children? Why did he collect these poems? or is it even possible to suggest why he collected them? We can assume — I think — that he liked poetry, but I like poetry too and I never copied this many poems into anything that resembled this manuscript. And — not to be too iconoclastic — what's the big deal? Lots of these poems can be found elsewhere. I had read Donne and Shakespeare. We assume a level of significance that says, somehow, that the texts of these individual poems — not written for this particular manuscript — in their own right are worthy of study. What assumptions do we adapt that make this particular document relevant? We all accept — and therefore know — that someone named John Donne wrote a poem that reads "Go and catch a falling star." Where is the text of that poem? For textual scholars the answer is disconcerting: it's nowhere! Nothing in the hand of John Donne survives that writes out this famous poem, but even if such an artifact did exist, we should still question its status as *the* Donne poem.

Imagine if you will John Donne sitting in a room writing a poem with this first line: "Go and catch a falling star." Assume, too, that he writes out the poem perfectly: there are no emendations, every diacritical mark is exactly what he wants and he is very pleased. Is that the text? Indeed, he likes the poem so much he hands it to his friend, who in turn takes it to a scribe to have it copied. The next day he decides to write out the poem again, but he makes a slight change that even he himself did not notice. Line 14, which only the day before read "Then, when thou retorn'st, wilt tell me" now reads "Thou, when thou retorn'st, wilt tell me". Which of the two is actually the text of this poem? Are they both correct as construed by John Donne, or is neither correct because there cannot be two originals? However, to explore this conceit to its fullest, we must extend it to the week following. No less than Donne himself is handed a copy of the poem which pleases him. It is a copy of the poem that the scribe created using the first exemplar as his copy-text, and as we might expect from this particular narrative, line 14 has once again changed: the comma[3] after 'then' has disappeared as has the comma after 'retorn'st' and the line itself has lost some of its poetic flair; it reads exactly as it does in the Holgate, "then when thou returnst *will* tell me" [italics mine]. We, of course, assume Donne would not be pleased by this particular change. After all, it is not what he wrote, but, in truth, it may not have bothered him. He may have said "Gee, I didn't think of that," or "I'm glad someone reads it a little differently." A playwright cannot predict how a particular actor performs a part, but that does not necessarily mean that a part was performed incorrectly. Whether we like it or not, Donne *may* have considered a text of his poem a kind of performance and a different version of the poem a type of interpretation. Moreover, there is nothing in the early modern literature that I know of writers complaining about altering texts, but there is a great deal in the modern literature that questions this phenomenon. From our scant evidence, Shakespeare himself seemed unconcerned about the validity of his many texts, and as we all know even the correct spelling of his own name seems to have escaped him. Ultimately, every decision an editor makes — or at least an editor of this type of manuscript — assumes a perspective on questions exactly like these; but whether we like it or not the answers to questions of original attitude and perspective are virtually unknowable.

What then is textual editing or textual criticism if we are in any way concerned with textual origins, and do not these textual origins equate with what Beal has already rejected as the "preliminaries, notes, and appendices"? Does not the sense of weaving recognized by Beal also suggest that a text is a three-dimensional — not a two-dimensional — space that the original-text model suggests? Must not these assumptions also be questioned? If so, then lots of us have questions to ask ourselves. I however have no such problem identifying myself as a textual editor because I realize that the term does more for me than I do

---

[3] We would consider a comma an accidental, which would not change meaning.

to the text: nothing that I do or have done alters the Holgate manuscript. One hopes that it will make the manuscript more enjoyable for those who encounter it, through either the edition or a visit to the Morgan Library. Equally, one hopes that it will serve the scholarship community which in many ways has come to value texts such as this manuscript. It may also help those who are interested in various levels or types of interpretation, say of the Donne poem, for surely how a poem was utilized in the time most recent to its own composition is relevant from a variety of critical perspectives, especially gender and historicist studies. Modern scholarship is well served by making texts such as the Holgate available to the academic community. But we still must deal with what textual editing actually is, especially if we retain any problem with the definition of a text. Returning to Peter Beal, his definition of 'textual criticism' certainly describes the activities of a textual editor.

> Textual criticism is a branch of scholarship devoted to the study and analysis of texts, whether extant in printed or in manuscript form. The study involves close scrutiny of every aspect of a text, both its substantive and incidental constituents, as well as its physical embodiment. It also entails detailed collation of the different copies, exempla, or versions of a work in order to understand or reconstruct the process of transmission. While textual criticism is a study in itself, independent of other considerations, it is, in practice, often linked to the requirements of editing in that it may help to determine the accuracy, trustworthiness, or authenticity of different texts; the nature of different readings (whether corruption due to copyists' carelessness or misunderstanding, deliberate scribal emendations, or genuine authorial revisions); the authorship of the work based on stylistic analysis, for instance, if there is evidence of multiple authorship or editions by others; and, possibly, identification of the text that is the earliest or nearest to the author, thereby producing the evidence whereby an editor may restore the text as closely as possible to its original form, free from obtrusive errors and unwarranted alterations and interpolations.[4]

Beal's comprehensive definition is certainly helpful in understanding the task of textual editing but raises several questions for the editor of a manuscript such as the Holgate. Who, for example, is the author of this particular text? Is it William Holgate, the supposed owner and creator of the manuscript, who at the very most wrote seven of the 177 poems found in the manuscript, or is this simply a storehouse (a definition implied by the word 'miscellany') for all the *other* poems

---

[4] Beal, *Dictionary,* 415.

found in the pages of the miscellany? Beal's definition points to an author — and more specifically a literary author — of a particular or specific text, one which, for the present discussion, may be simply a poem known to have been written by someone known as John Donne, which begins, famously, "Go and catch a falling star." But the text itself overwhelmingly points to the creator of the manuscript, for indeed, the definition of text — or a text — as supplied by the field itself is one that suggests a synchronic piece of writing which by itself will not move or change, that the changes required to make virtually every piece of writing occur only before the piece is completed. That is the flat, two-dimensional concept I challenge.

Of course it does not seem a far stretch to argue that any one poem can reflect several purposes, that it is either a part of the entire manuscript, or that any one poem can be an exemplar of something else, i.e., a poem by John Donne. That notion is not hard to grasp or even appreciate, but for the so-called textual editor of this type of multifaceted manuscript, I can assure you that the circumstance is nothing less than schizoid. I say this because every piece of writing — be it poem or cookbook — by necessity has an author, a creator, an authority if you will, as if extending the word 'author' into 'authority' will somehow explain whatever it means to create a text. Lest there be any doubt, when you are reading a manuscript in what is overwhelmingly a single hand, albeit one that comprises many different so-called writers, the author of that manuscript is, simply stated, the author of that manuscript and not the author of the individual poems. Consider the evidence for that statement:

The manuscript itself has been organized. There are large clusters of poems followed by pages that were left blank, and although these unused pages were often filled in by later owners of the manuscript, it is clear that its first owner had a larger concept in mind than just randomly collecting poems and writing them in the book. Moreover, the individual poems were first written over a seventy-year period, the earliest circa 1580, the date of Chiddock Tyckburn's execution for his complicity in a plot to assassinate Elizabeth, and the latest 1649, the year the Duke of Hamilton was executed during the Civil War. These two poems are typical of the manuscript in that they both concern political events. The actual paper that the text (or texts) was written on was first found in England in 1619, so that if the manuscript had been created after all the poems had actually been written, then the compiler found a very old writing book which he/she used to create this manuscript. That, though possible, strains credulity. Manuscript books usually do not lie around for thirty years before someone decides to write in them. More believable is that the manuscript was started around the date of the paper, 1619, when the majority of the poems were indeed were being circulated and written, and that the one owner maintained the book over an extended period of time, occasionally writing new poems in it as they came along to him. That is not a factual statement, but a statement based on probabilities, which, in a sense, goes against the notion that the text is a stable physical artifact. Among the later poems are the eleven by William Strode (1598–1645), the poet who dominates the penultimate section of the book, the final pages essentially devoted to prose, among which can be found sections of John Earle's *Microcosmography*. These dates also agree with the dates of the assumed compiler, William Holgate of Saffron Walden, Essex, born in 1590 and who, based on the Visitation records of Essex, was alive in 1634. This is the same William Holgate who through four centuries has been believed to have created this manuscript, and this is the same William Holgate who — much to my dismay — has left no other document that connects his handwriting with what we see in the text. There is no document existent with his signature, no evidence that he went to school, had children, even that he died (!) except the belief handed down through the family and later owners of the manuscript that this William Holgate is the creator of what has come to be known as the Holgate Miscellany. A fine mess for a textual editor.

This textual enigma, perhaps more than any other, describes the difference between the dissertation and the RETS edition of the Holgate.[5] For obvious reasons, without definitive identification of the compiler/owner/transcriber (whichever of the three functions the person responsible for this document performed or fulfilled), not being able to assert who that person was forces the text into the one definitive area available to me, the editor: the poems themselves, taken as they remain, exemplars of texts somewhat different from other texts — be they print or manuscript — written by someone else. This result is inescapable based on the lack of information revealed by extensive biographic and textual study. What must be appreciated is that the only information we have about the so-called early modern period emanates either from texts (as in the case of the Holgate manuscript) or artifacts (furniture, jars, utensils) that survive from the period. They are all aspects of material culture that represent something other than what they are. An early modern hammer has a hand, a sheath has a sword, a tomb has a body, a manuscript has a scribe, a poem has . . . a poet and a reader, who, exactly like the manuscript, could either be its creator or its reader, depending on how we view the creative process itself. The RETS edition of the Holgate identifies the predominant italic hand that created the manuscript as 'the scribe'. Beal is quite careful *not* to separate a professional from an amateur writer.

---

[5] *The Holgate Miscellany*, ed. M. Denbo, MRTS 438/RETS35 (Tempe: ACMRS, 2012).

Deriving from the Latin *scriba*, the term 'scribe' denotes a person responsible for the writing of a manuscript text. The term is commonly used to denote a professional clerk or copyist, in the sense of one who is a reasonably accomplished penman, whose employment it is to write or copy out documents, and who is likely to be attached, possibly as part of a team, to some kind of office or institution (ecclesiastical, royal, legal, academic, commercial, etc.), or else employed in the shop of a stationer or scrivener. The term may, however, just as readily be applied to amateurs, such as a member of someone's family, household, or social circle who makes copies of that person's writings, or to anyone else who copies out a text for whatever reason.[6]

In Beal's terminology, 'scribe' attempts to be a neutral term, but I don't think it is. Whoever reads this text, or any text, imagines the hand that creates it. To say otherwise would be to deny the reason we read. Moreover, if indeed this manuscript was created by its owner, I doubt very much if he or she would have referred to him/herself as a 'scribe'. The nature of the artifact is clearly otherwise.

Thus, at least two unanswerable questions characterize the RETS edition of the Holgate. Who actually created the manuscript and why, and how do the individual texts found in the manuscript help us understand the history of a particular poem? Without being able to answer fully either question — at least to my own satisfaction — the edition will leave open many questions for the individual reader. But perhaps that's as it should be. Reading is an endless series of interpretations, and who am I as the editor to tell my reader how he/she should read this particular text? I can certainly advise or suggest, but ultimately the creative act is left up to the reader. I can only supply what is known (or what I have been able to find out); my hand cannot reach out of the pages and manipulate the reaction of any given reader. Indeed, I question the difference between reading and writing: is the only text the text that the writer writes? Or is the text somewhere in the mind of the reader, far beyond the grasp of any reader or editor?

A recent example from film also illustrates my point. Juan José Campanella's *El secreto de sus ojos (The Secret in Their Eyes)* concerns a retired judicial investigator who writes a novel based on a murder he investigated twenty years ago. Typical of a writer, he wakes in the middle of the night to write down an idea, 'Te mo' (I fear); however, when, upon rising the next morning, he looks at 'Te mo', he does not seem to understand what it is he meant — also typical of a writer. The end of the film solves the mystery of this two-word text, either a text by itself or part of a much larger text, the screenplay. Now, after re-living the

---

[6] Beal, *Dictionary*, 361.

actual nightmare that will become the novel, he looks at the same piece of paper and inserts an 'A' between the two words, which now read 'Te amo' (I love you). If we were to somehow look at the new text without any knowledge of the text's history — even as simple as it is — we would never understand how one meaning was embedded in the other, nor if the first mistake and its later correction were made consciously or unconsciously. Was this a so-called 'slip' in the language, a concept to my knowledge unknown to early modern culture, or is this a case of the changes language can have on reality itself, i.e., the writer through the writing has overcome his fear and now is able to say, simply, elegantly, 'Te amo' (I love you; I used to fear you but now I love you, a theme common to both the film and early modern writing)? Whichever, or whichever other, the writer him/herself may not know the answer to this question, thus destroying the concept of writer's intention, or, even more significantly, collapsing the difference between writing and interpretation, not to mention the idea that a writer is nothing other than an imaginative reader. Of course, looking back to the early seventeenth century when poems circulated in manuscript, we have no knowledge of how much they would have approved this slippage, but we also have no knowledge to the contrary, and in a period when themes of mutability, paradox, and innate messiness were so prevalent, it is hard to imagine that there was not some discussion for the problems I am describing.

But one last note on the RETS edition. Synchronically, Beal's definition of 'text' relies on a sense of weaving, combining different threads and patterns into a larger, stronger, ultimately more meaningful fabric of ideas. So it is with the RETS edition, which has been assisted so diligently by the committee that has guided this very complex document to fruition. The committee has been led by Steven May, and includes Arthur Marotti, Elizabeth Hageman, and Roy Flannagan. I am deeply appreciative of all their kind support and help through this difficult process. I hope they will be pleased with the result.

BRONX COMMUNITY COLLEGE
CITY UNIVERSITY OF NEW YORK

Index

(Proper names and topics that appear in the text and cited *anywhere* in the notes are included. Proper names that appear *only* in the notes are omitted. An asterisk after the name indicates a contributor to this volume.)

A

Acquisti, Alessandro, 29, 40
Adams, Thomas, 235
Alexander, Bryan, 31, 38
Alexander, Gavin, 247, 247n4, 251n15, 325n5
Alleyn, Edward, 71–80
Amelang, James, 270, 270nn29–30
Andrewes, Lancelot, 283n21, 284, 285n27
Anne, Queen of England, 73, 78
Aristotle, 259, 262, 266n18
Arundel, Sir Matthew, 314
Aubrey, John, 287, 287n37, 288, 288n42
Audley, Thomas, 306
Austin, David, 38

B

Bacon, Sir Francis, 71, 76, 255–71, 273–290
    Advancement of Learning (AL), 259, 259n3, 260, 270, 272, 281, 284, 285
    De sapientia veterum, 279
    Essayes, 284
    Instauratio magna, 284, 286, 289, 291
    New Atlantis, 283, 288, 289n44, 290
    Novum Organon (NO), 259, 259n2, 260, 261, 263, 273
    Redargutio philosophiarum, 277, 277n2, 294
    Sylva sylvarum, 283, 289n44
Bacon, Katherine, 330

Bacon, Richard, 330, 333
Baker, Father Augustine, 195, 195n8, 196, 207
Baker, Herschel, xi
Bailey, Walter, 271, 271n39
Baranzano, Redemptus, 285, 285n28, 290, 290n46, 291, 291n47
Bate, Jonathan, 82, 84, 100, 101
Beal, Peter, 75, 235nn2–3, 292, 292n49, 335, 335n2, 338, 339, 339n4, 340, 341, 342, 342n6, 343
Beale, Mary, 198, 202
Bell, Ilona*, 236, 247–58
Bellasys, Margaret, 235–45
Berger, Thomas L., 92, 108
Best, Michael*, 7, 40, 91–112, 318, 318n22
Bevington, David, 81, 82, 104, 111
Bickley, Francis, 74, 74n3
Birch, Thomas, 281
Bistué, Belén, 211, 212, 212n9, 214, 216, 216n12
Blair, Ann, 261, 261n4
Blayney, Peter W. M., 108, 302n7
Boener, Peter, 287, 287n39, 288
Bolton, Edmund, 287
Bolton, Whitney, 14n18, 38
Bonavita, Helen L. Vella*, 309–319
Boot, Peter, 38
Booty, John, xiii

Bosio, Girolamo, 318
Bourdieu, Pierre, 273, 273n49, 274
Bourgeois, Louise, 270, 270n31
Bowen, William R., 26n28, 39, 44, 57n13,
    58, 114n5
Bowers, Fredson, xii, xviii, 89n13
Bowsher, Julian, 74n6, 75
Bowyer, Ann, 236
Boyd, Danah, 29, 39, 41
Braithwaite, Richard, 173
Braunmuller, A. R., 95, 108, 167n6
Brown, Susan, 39, 44
Buc, George, 73
Burbage, Richard, 72
Burre, Walter, 86, 90
Bushell, Thomas, 287, 288
Buxton, John, 322, 322n2, 332

C

Caesar, Sir Julius, 73
Calahorra, Diego Ortúñez de, 209–217
Calaluca, Eric, 7
Camden, William, 87, 324
Campanella, Juan José, 342
Canadian Research Knowledge Network
    / Réseau Canadien de Docu-
    mentation pour la Recherche
    (CRKN/RCDR), 11, 23, 39
Capito, Wolfgang, 183, 189, 191
Carew, Thomas, 235, 336
Carey, Henry, 73
Cartwright, William, 72, 318
Cary, Dame Clementia, 193–207
Cary, Dame Elizabeth, 193, 194, 195,
    196n11, 198n20, 205n34
Cary, Dame Magdalene (Lucy), 196, 206
Cary, Dame Mary, 194, 194n4, 196, 205, 206
Catesby, Sir William, 314
Cavanagh, Sheila T.*, 61–69, 154
Cavendish, Charles, 283
Cavendish, William, 328
Cecil, Sir Robert, 73
Cecil, William (Lord Burghley), 172, 312
Cerasano, S. P. 75, 76

Chapman, George, 72, 98
Charles V, 310
Charles VIII, 221, 225, 225nn11–12, 227,
    231, 231n37, 232, 232n41
Chettle, Henry, 72
Clare, Robert, 95, 108
Clayton, Thomas, 96n10, 109
Clegg, Cyndia S., 98, 109
Coates, Tom, 29, 39
Coke, Sir Edward, 73
*College Learning for the New Global Cen-
    tury*, 63, 64nn2–4
Collex, 11, 39
Collier, John Payne, 73
Cooper, David, 75, 79, 80
Cooper, Gill, 80
Corbett, Richard, 324
Cosin, John
    A Collection of Private Devotions, xi
Coverdale, Miles, 182
Cowley, Abraham, 325
Craig, Hugh, 109
Cranmer, Thomas, 182, 187, 190, 187 n28
Croft, P. J., 323, 323n4
Croll, Morris W., 268, 268n23, 269, 270, 275
Curio, Caelius Secundus, 309–319

D

d'Angoulême, Charles, 221, 222n7,
    225n12, 226n14, 228
Daniel, Samuel, 250, 250n13, 251, 251n15
Data Fountains, 26, 39
Davidson, Adele, 93n4, 109
Davidson, Peter, 193, 193n2
Dawson, Anthony, 84, 85
Dawson, Giles, 89, 89n16
Day, John, 98
de Beaujeu, Anne, 222n7, 227n20, 228,
    230n33, 230n35
de Bretagne, Anne, 225, 225nn12–13,
    227n18, 228, 229, 230n33
de France, Jeanne (*aka* Jeanne de Valois),
    227–233, 227n20, 228n21,
    229n24, 229n28, 232n41,

232n42, 232n45, 233n46, 233nn48–50
de Grazia, Margreta, 13n16, 39, 107n23, 109
de Savoie, Charlotte, 222nn7–9, 228, 230n35
de Savoie, Louise, 225, 225n12, 228
de Valette, Jean, 314, 315, 316, 318, 319
de Vendome, Pietro Gentile, 311n7, 317
Dekker, Thomas, 72, 89n13
Delany, Paul, 13, 39
Deloney, Thomas, 270, 270nn34–35, 271, 271n36
Denbo, Michael*, ix, xv–xxi, 335–43
Deny, Sir Anthony, 306
Derrida, Jacques, 81, 267, 268n22
Devorox, Master, 306
Dobson, Michael, 95, 109
d'Orléans, Louis, 228
Donaldson, Ian, 287, 287n36
Donath, Judith, 29, 39
Donne, Constance, 78
Donne, John, 15n26, 73, 78, 193, 200, 235, 249, 252, 255, 256, 286n30, 336, 337, 338, 340
Donne Variorum, xvii, 256, 256n32
Drucker, Johanna, 39, 42
Dryden, John, 325
Dubrow, Heather, 247, 247n4
DuBruck, Edelgard E., 27, 27nn30–31, 27n39
Dudley, Guildford, 182
Dudley, Robert, 323
Duppa, Brian, 324
Duthie, George Ian, 93n4, 109

E

Eamon, William, 265, 265n15
Earle, John, 341
Early English Books Online (*EBBO*), 7, 8, 50, 53, 210, 215n11, 216, 217, 243n19
Early Modern English Dictionaries Database, 6, 39
East, Thomas, 209n3, 215, 216
Edelen, Georges, xii, xiii

Edward VI, 135, 300, 306
Eisenberg, Daniel, 210, 210n5
Eld, George, 86, 87, 90
Electronic Textual Cultures Laboratory (ETCL), 4, 44
Elizabeth I, xiii, 73, 281, 282, 288, 300, 340
Elizabeth II, xiii
Ellis, Robert Leslie, 277n2, 279
Ellison, Nicole B., 29, 39
Emory Women Writers Resource Project (EWWRP), 61–69, 160, 161, 209–218
Erasmus, Desiderius, 173, 182, 185, 189, 315
Erickson, Peter, 3n2, 37
Erne, Lukas, 95, 109
Estill, Laura*, 235–44
eXist, 40
eXist XML-RPC, 40
Ezell, Margaret, 114n4, 141, 142n62, 143, 143n65, 169, 170, 170n13, 200n23, 257, 257nn36–37

F

Farr, Erika*, 63, 153–61
Farrington, Benjamin, 263, 263n10, 277, 277n2, 278nn3–6, 279n8
Faulhaber, Charles B. 14n19, 40
Fedora, 40
Felch, Susan F.*, 181–92
Ferrabosco, Alfonso, 241, 243n17
Field, Nathan, 72
Fiormonte, Domenico, 154, 155, 156, 160
Fisher, Bishop John, 183, 185, 189
Fitzpatrick, Kathleen, 30, 40, 48n4, 58
Flanders, Julia, 154, 155, 156, 160
Flannagan, Roy, 6n6, 343
Foakes, R. A., 72, 72nn4–5, 73, 99, 100, 109
Fortier, Paul, 11n12, 40
Foucault, Michel, 99, 103, 103n19, 109
Fowler, Constance Aston, 236
Foxe, John, 181, 181n2, 182, 307
Franco, Veronica, 257
Freeman, David, ix, 298, 303

G

Gardiner, Richard, 272, 272n43
Gardiner, Stephen, 182
Gardner, Helen, xi
Gascoigne, George, 250, 250n10, 251, 297
Genette, Garard, 155–61
Girgensohn, Andreas, 29, 40
Goldring, Beth, 107, 109
Gondomar, Count, 73, 77
Goodrich, Jamie*, 193–207
Google Book Search, 8, 40
Gorges, Arthur, 283
Gosson, Stephen, 73
Gouws, John*, 321–33
Grafton, Anthony, 261, 261n4
Gray, Thomas, 321, 333
Greetham, D. C., 5n4, 40
Greg, W. W., xii, xviii, xix, 88, 89, 89n12,
    302n6
Gresley, Master Henry, 330
Greville, Fulke, 281, 281nn14–15
Grey, Lady Jane, 182
Griffin, Andrew, 96, 109
Grimald, Nicholas, 299–307
Grindal, Bishop Edmund, 312 n10
Gross, Ralph, 29, 40
Guillory, John, 10, 40, 289, 290n45

H

Hacket, John, 286–87
Hackett, Helen, 142, 142n63
Hageman, Elizabeth H., 298, 343
Halio, Jay, 98, 100, 103, 111
Hall, Bishop Joseph, 235
Hall, Kim F., 5, 40
Hall, Rupert, 259, 259n11
Halliwell-Phillips, J. O., 73
Hammer, Paul, 281, 281nn14–15, 283
Hannaway, Owen, 261, 261n4
Hannay, Margaret, 236, 236nn5–6,
    251n14, 251n16, 251n17, 254n24,
    254n26, 257n38
Hardison, O. B., xii
Harley, Brilliana, 165–80

Harley, Edward 'Ned', 165–80
Harley, Sir Robert, 166, 166n3, 171n16, 174
Harrier, Richard, 115n8, 116, 116n13
Harris, Johanna*, 165–80
Hatton, Christopher, 73
Hayashi, Tetsumaro, 24, 40
Heale, Elizabeth, 117n15, 118n19, 132,
    132nn50–51, 134, 134n53, 142,
    143, 143n64, 195n6
Heath, Douglas Denon, 277n2, 279
Henry V, 315
Henry VIII, 116, 119n20, 119n23, 121,
    135, 136, 181, 181n2, 188,
    188n22, 306
Henslowe-Alleyn Digitisation Project, 71–80
Henslowe, Philip, 71, 72, 76
Herbert, George, 235, 285, 286, 286nn30–
    33, 293, 324
Herbert, Mary Sidney, 250, 254
Herbert, Susan, 254
Herbert, William, 73, 247, 251, 254,
    254nn26–27, 256
Heywood, Thomas, 72
Hill, Thomas, 271, 271n38
Hill, W. Speed, ix–xxi, 113n6, 298, 309, 336
    "The Calculus of Error", xx, xxn6,
    316, 316n18, 317n19
    "Editing Nondramatic Texts", xvi
    Works of Richard Hooker, xi–xiv,
    xx, xxi
Hiltner, Ken*, 259–75
Hoadley, Christopher M., 30, 40
Hobbes, Thomas, 268, 287, 288, 291, 293
Hockey, Susan, 11n13, 38
Holgate, William, xvi, 336–42
Holland, John, 194
Honigmann, Ernst, 101, 105n21, 109
Howard, Charles, 73
Howard, Henry (Surrey), 115, 116, 229, 301
Howard, Jean E., 5n3, 40
Howard, Sir Thomas, 73, 77, 115–23,
    127n44, 129n48, 135n54, 137,
    137n57, 144
Hughey, Ruth, 62

I

Internet Shakespeare Editions, 7, 40, 104, 109
Ioppolo, Grace*, 71–80, 96, 98, 109
Iter, 3, 26, 26n28, 27, 38, 39, 40, 44, 57n13, 58

J

Jackson, MacDonald P., 97, 110
Johnson, Richard, 270, 270n33
Jones, R. F., 269, 269n24
Jonson, Ben, 72, 79, 93, 98, 231, 239,
    239n12, 252, 282, 287, 324, 327,
    328, 336
    Cynthia's Revels, 81–90
    Entertainment through London, 90
    Epicoene, 236, 239, 241
    Every Man in his Humour, 87
    Forest, The, 241, 243
    Neptune's Triumph, 87, 87n10
    Volpone, 236, 237, 241, 243
Juxta, 11, 40,

K

Kastan, David Scott, 83–84, 84n2, 110
Keble, John, xx
Kemp, Anne, 157, 158, 159, 160
Kemp, Will, 72
Kerrigan, John, 96n10, 98, 110
Kilner, Peter G., 30, 40
King, Johnn, 306, 307n11
Kinney, Arthur, 6n6, 98, 109, 110, 297
Kirby, Torrance, xiv
Kliman, Bernice, 104, 110
Knolles, Francis, 319
Knolles, Richard, 312, 312n11
Knowles, Richard, 93n4, 94, 98, 102n18, 110
Krontiris, Tina, 21n8, 217, 217n13
Kuhn, Thomas, 263, 263n12, 265, 266n18

L

Labé, Louise, 257, 257n39
Lachmann, Karl, xii, xvi, xvii
Lamb, Mary Ellen, 253, 253n22, 254n27
Lancashire, Ian, 6n6, 7, 11n12, 14n18, 39, 41
Latimer, Hugh, 182

Latz, Dorothy L., 196, 196n12, 197,
    197n14, 197nn16–17, 198,
    198n22, 200, 200n24
Lavagnino, John, 75, 79, 238n10
Lavin, J. A., 86, 86n8
Lee, Alison, 29, 40
Lee, Anthony, 115, 121, 133, 147
Lee, Sir Henry, 313, 314, 316
Leitch, Cara, 3, 16n25, 28, 41, 44, 45, 113
Lemon8-XML, 41
Lexicons of Early Modern English, 7, 18, 41
Literature Online, 7, 41
Locke, John, 268, 274, 274nn51–52, 275
Love, Harold, 136, 136n55, 331
Lucene, 41, 42, 45
Lucy, Calista, 75, 80

M

Machan, Tim William, 41
Madden, Mary, 29, 41
Mainwaringe, Thomas, 309–319
Malone, Edmond, 73, 94
Mann, Margaret, 325, 329
Manners, Roger, 281
Many Eyes (IBM), 11, 41
Marcus, Leah S., 13n15, 41, 244, 244n24
Markham, Gervase, 271, 271n41
Marlow, Cameron, 31, 41
Marlowe, Christopher, 309, 309n2
Marotti, Arthur, ix, xviii, 118n16, 141n60,
    201nn27–28, 197n28, 209n2,
    331, 343
Marquis, Paul A.*, 297–308
Martin, Shawn*, 47–59
Massai, Sonia, 86n7, 93, 110
Massey, Charles, 77
Massinger, Philip, 72, 98
Masten, Jeffrey, 201n27, 209n2, 210,
    210n7, 212
Matthew, Tobie, 286, 286n34
Maule, Jeremy, 324
May, Steven W., 131n15, 248, 255, 255n31,
    343
Mayne, Jasper, 324

McCanles, Michael, 267, 268n22
McCann, Dom Justin, 197
McCarty, Willard, 6n6, 9, 10n10, 14n22, 42, 48n5, 58
McGann, Jerome, xviii, 5, 42, 54n10, 58, 59, 92, 110, 117n14, 201n27
McGrade, Arthur Stephen, xiii
McKellen, Ian, 95
McKenzie, D. F., xviii, 5, 42, 92, 110, 117, 117n14, 170, 170n14
McKerrow, R. B., 99
McLeod, Randall, 13n15, 42, 94n8, 105n22, 110
McMullan, Gordon, 98, 110
Merrick, James, 207
Metadata Offer New Knowledge (MONK), 11, 42
Miall, David S., 11n11, 42
Michigan Early Modern English Materials, 6n5, 4042
Middleton, Irene J.*, 209–18
Middleton, Thomas, 72, 238, 238n10
    The Widow, 236, 237, 238n10, 239, 239n11
Millman, Jill Seal, 257, 257n35
Milton, John, 321–22
Mitchell, Steve, 26n29, 42
Montaigne, Michel de, 264, 268, 269, 269 nn27–28, 270, 270n32
More, Dame Gertrude, 195, 196, 196nn8–9, 197n16, 206
More, Sir Thomas, 181–92
Morley, George, 202
Moulton, Ian Frederick, 235n4, 236, 236n6, 244 , 244n20
Mowat, Barbara, 6n6, 99, 100, 100n15, 101, 101n17, 110, 111
Mozart, Wolfgang Amadeus, 96
Mueller, Janel, 181–91
Mueller, Martin, 12, 42, 53, 53n9, 58
Muir, Carolyn Diskant*, 219–33
Murphy, J. Stephen, 159, 161
Murphy, Patiricia, 7

N
Nalanda iVia Focused Crawler, 26, 42
Neuman, Michael, 6, 6nn6–7, 43
Nietzsche, Friedrich, 274, 274n50
Nott, G. F., 116, 116n10
Nutch, 26, 42

O
Oldisworth, Giles, 322, 325
Oldisworth, Margaret, 325, 329
Oldisworth, Mary Chamberlayne, 325, 329
Oldisworth, Nicholas, 321–33
Open Access Text Archive, 8, 43
Open Journal Systems, 11, 37, 43
Open Monograph Press, 11, 43
Orland, Charles, 232
Osbaldeston, Lambert, 324
Overbury, Sir Nicholas, 324
Overbury, Sir Thomas, 322, 328
Oxford English Dictionary Online, 18, 43
Oxford Text Archive, 6n5, 17n27, 43

P
Paley, W. Bradford, 125
Parr, Katherine, 181–92
Peacham, Henry, 172, 172n18, 173
Pechter, Edward, 5n3, 43
Pérez-Ramos, Antonio, 265, 265n16, 266, 266nn17–18, 267n19
Phelippes, Thomas, 282
Piggott, Jan, 75, 80
Pigman, G. W., 250, 250n10
Plat, Sir Hugh, 271, 271n42, 272, 272nn44–45, 273, 273n46
Plato, 259, 260, 262, 262n8, 266n18, 273
Playfere, Dr. Thomas, 284, 284n22, 284n26, 291
Pole, Reginald Cardinal, 185, 188
Pope, Alexander, 93, 93n7, 101, 269n24
PostgreSQL, 43
Professional Reading Environment (PReE), 3–46
Public Knowledge Project, 8, 28, 37, 39, 41, 43

Pudsey, Edward, 237, 237n8
Pullen, Benjamin, xii–xiii

Q

Quint, David, 314, 314n14, 315, 315n15

R

Rabb, Melinda Alliker, 114n2, 143, 143n66
Randolph, Robert, 324
Randolph, Thomas, 324
Rasmussen, Eric*, 81–90, 95, 100, 101, 110
Rawley, William, 280, 286, 287, 287n40,
        288, 288n41, 289, 289n43, 293,
        293n59
Read, Richard, 86, 87, 87n11, 88, 89,
        89n14, 89n16, 90
Rees, Graham, 279, 280n11
Reinventing Undergraduate Education
        (Boyer Report), 64, 65, 65n5
Remley, Paul, 16, 43, 115, nn7–8, 116n9,
        116n12, 117n15, 118n19, 119n22,
        123, 127n44, 137n57
Renaissance English Knowledgebase
        (*REKn*), 3–46
Richardson, David A., 6nn6–7, 43
Roberts, Josephine, 248, 248n6, 249,
        249n7, 249n9, 251, 252, 252n20,
        253, 254n23, 254n27, 255,
        255n30, 256, 257
Roberts, Sasha, 236, 236n7, 244, 244n21
Robinson, Ralph, 185
Rockwell, Geoffrey, 9n8, 14n22, 39, 43, 45
Rollins, Hyder E., 297, 299, 299n3, 301,
        302n6, 303, 305
Rooks, Mark, 7
Rose, Susan, 310, 310n3
Rossi, Paolo, 262, 262nn6–8, 263, 263n9,
        264nn13–14, 265, 267n21
Ruby on Rails, 43
RubyFedora, 43
Ruecker, Stan, 15n23, 39, 43
Rushdie, Salman, 63, 155

S

Sackville, Thomas, 73
Sanders, Julie, 141, 141n61
Schreibman, Susan, 12, 42, 44, 45
Scott, William, 323
Seaton, Ethel, 116, 116n13
Sessions, W. A., 268n22, 286n31, 286n33,
        301, 301n5
Shakespeare Database Project, 6n5, 44
Shakespeare, William, 24, 72, 80, 85n5,
        89, 91–112, 252, 255, 297, 313,
        324, 336, 336–38
Shapin, Steven, 265, 265n15
Sidney, Sir Philip, 250, 254, 254n27, 251, 323
Sidney, Sir Robert, 78, 255n29, 323
Siemens, Raymond G.*, 3–46, 113–51,
        195n6
Simmes, Valentine, 89, 89n14, 90
Simpson, Percy, 87, 87n9, 88
Simson, Francis, 86, 87
Simson, Gabriel, 86
Sinclair, Stéfan, 14n22, 44, 45
Slights, Camille, 95, 111
Smith, Bruce R., 236, 236n7
Smith, Pamela H., 265, 265n15
Solr, 45
Southall, Raymond, 16, 45, 115, 115n6,
        115n8, 116, 116n13, 118n18, 121n34
Spedding, James, 277n2, 279, 279n10, 281,
        282n20, 285n28, 290n46
Spenser, Edmund, 52, 255, 297
Sprat, Thomas, 273, 273nn47–48
Stallybrass, Peter, 13n16, 39, 107n23, 109
Stanley, Ferdinando, 73
Stanwood, P. G.*, xi–xiv
Stevens, John, 116, 116n13, 135
Stevenson, Jane, 193, 193n2
Stewart, Alan*, 277–94
Strange, Mistress, 330, 330n7
Strode, William, 341
Suleiman the Magnificent, 310, 311
Suso, Henry, 221
Sutherland, Kathryn, 5, 13n16, 45

Sydenham, Cuthbert, 197, 197n15
Synergies, 11, 37, 45

T
Tanselle, G. Thomas, xviii, xix, 5n4, 45
TAPoR Tools, 3, 11, 18, 37, 45
Taverner, Richard, 184 , 184n7, 189, 191
Taylor, Gary, 94, 97, 98, 107, 109, 110, 111,
        112, 236n4, 236n7, 238n10
Taylor, Jeremy, xi, xii
Taylor, John, 78
Taylor, Neil, 100, 101
Tenison, Thomas, 280, 284, 284n23,
        284n25, 285, 285n29, 286, 287,
        287n35, 297n38, 293
Text Encoding Initiative (TEI), 49, 56,
        153–61
Textbase of Early Tudor English, 6, 7, 45
Thompson, Ann, 100, 101
Thrall, Margaret E., 176, 176n22, 179,
        180n26
Tilney, Sir Edmund, 73
Tottel, Richard, 143
        Songes and Sonettes, 297–308
Tourneur, Cyril, 72
Tudor, Mary, 185, 191, 300, 301
Tusser, Thomas, 271, 271n37
Tyckburn, Chiddock, 340
Tyler, Margaret, 209–16
Tyndale, William, 176
Tyrwhit, Elizabeth, 181n2, 189, 190, 191,
        191nn29–30, 192, 192n34

U
Udall, Nicholas, 182
Uman, Deborah, 211, 212, 212n9, 214,
        216, 216n12
Unsworth, John, 9, 12n14, 45, 47n1, 59
Urkowitz, Steven, 93, 93n7, 94, 95, 96n10,
        101n16, 102, 103n20, 106, 111

V
Van Wilder, Philip, 306
Vandendorpe, Christian, 9, 44

Vander Wal, Thomas, 31, 45
Vavasour, Anne, 256
Vérard, Antoine, 219–33
Vetch, Paul, 75, 79, 80
Vickers, Brian, 259n3, 267, 267n20, 269,
        269n25, 281, 281nn16–17
Villiers, George, 73, 78
Vitkus, Daniel, 319, 319n24

W
Walker, Claire, 195n7, 201, 201n28, 203n32
Walker, Kim, 140, 140n59
Walsingham, Francis, 282
Walton, Izaak, 285, 286n30
Warkentin, Germaine, 255, 255n29
Warner, George, 74, 74n2
Warren, Michael J., 94, 96n10, 100, 102,
        109, 110, 111, 112
Warren, Roger, 97n12, 109
Warwick, Claire, 10n9, 45
Watt, Ian, 275, 275n53
Wayne, Valerie, 127, 127nn45–46
Webster, John, 72, 98
Weis, René, 100, 111
Weiss, Adrian, 89n14, 90
Wells, Stanley, 94, 100, 107, 111, 112, 323,
        324n5
Wentworth, Lady Anne, 306
Werstine, Paul, 92, 93n5, 97, 99, 101,
        101n17, 104, 111, 112
White, Mistress, 306
Wilforde, Sir James, 306
Williams, George W., 298
Williams, Henry, 306
Williams, John, 287
Wolfe, Heather, 194, 194n3, 196nn10–
        11, 197, 197n18, 198n20, 201,
        201n28
Women Writers Project, 6n5, 17n27, 46
Woodford, Samuel, 194–207
Woudhuysen, H. R., 75, 104, 112, 251n18,
        255n28, 256n34
Wright, Gillian, 257, 257n35
Wriothesley, Thomas, 182

Wroth, Mary, 62
    Pamphilia to Amphilanthus, 247–58
Wroth, Robert, 254, 256
Wyatt, Thomas, 16, 45, 115–23, 129nn48–
    49, 133, 134, 140, 143, 299–306
Wynne-Davies, Marion, 197, 197n19,
    198n20, 200, 200n25, 201

Y
Yeandle, Laetitia, xiii

Z
Zilsel, Edgar, 261, 262n5, 263, 264n14, 265
Zotero, 46

RETS Panels and Papers
(printed in this volume)

The Josephine A. Roberts Forums, MLA

2007: *E-Editing in Corpora*
chair, Michael Denbo

Underpinnings of the Social Edition? A Brief Narrative, 2004–9, for
The Renaissance English Knowledgebase (REKn) and Professional
Reading Environment (PReE) Projects
RAYMOND G. SIEMENS

Providing a Base for E-Editing: The Text Creation Parnership Project
SHAWN MARTIN

The Emory Women Writers Resource Project: Teaching Students,
Training Students
SHEILA T. CAVANAGH

2008: *Digital Technology and Manuscript Study*
chairs, Arthur F. Marotti and Steven May

Drawing Networks in the Devonshire Manuscript (BL Add.
MS. 17492): Toward Visualizing a Writing Community's Shared
Apprenticeship, Social valuation, and Self-Validation
RAYMOND G. SIEMENS

2009: *Early Modern Women's Manuscripts*
       chair, Margaret P. Hannay

       Reforming Sir Thomas More in the Court of Katherine Parr
       SUSAN F. FELCH

       Monastic Authorship, Protestant Poetry, and the Psalms Attributed to
       Dame Clementia Cary
       JAIME GOODRICH

2010: *Bacon in the Twenty-First Century*
       chair, Arthur F. Marotti

       Sixteenth-Century Artisanal Practices and Baconian Prose
       KEN HILTNER

       Francis Bacon in Collaboration
       ALAN STEWART

              (There was no MLA convention in 2011.)

                    Open Business Meetings, MLA

2007: Editing Richard Tottel's *Songes and Sonettes*
       PAUL A. MARQUIS

       Cælivs Secvndus Curio His Historie of the Warr of Malta: Translated by
       Thomas Mainwaringe, 1579
       HELEN L. VELLA BONAVITA

2008: In Memoriam — W. Speed Hill
       PAUL STANWOOD
       MICHAEL DENBO

2009: Editing "a mute inglorious Milton" of Gloucestershire:
       Nicholas Oldisworth
       JOHN GOUWS

2010: On Textual Editing: MA 1057
MICHAEL DENBO

Renaissance Society of America

2008: *New Technologies and Renaissance Studies II: RETS, The Henslowe-Alleyn Digitisation Project*
chair, Michael Denbo

> The Henslowe-Alleyn Digitisation Project: Past, Present and Future
> GRACE IOPPOLO

2010: *Early Modern Women's Manuscripts*
chair, Margaret Hannay

> The Woman in Black: The Patron of Antoine Vérard's Edition of the *Horloge de Sapience* (PML 17591)
> CAROLYN DISKANT MUIR

The Medieval Congress at Kalamazoo

2008: *Electronic Shakespeare*
chair, Michael Denbo

> Brave New World or Dumping Ground? Electronic Supplements and the Printing of Jonson's *Cynthia's Revels*
> ERIC RASMUSSEN

> Mutability and Variation: A Digital Response to Complex Texts
> MICHAEL BEST

2009: *Electronic Editing of Medieval and Renaissance Texts*: The Emory Women Writers Research Project
chair, Sheila T. Cavanagh

> Paratext and Pointy Brackets: How Early Modern Archives Can Inform Digital Collections
> ERIKA FARR

"Who am I?": Exploring Questions of Authorship Using Digital Texts
IRENE J. MIDDLETON

2010:   *Early Modern Women's Manuscripts*
         chair, Margaret P. Hannay

"All the Adulteries of Art": The Dramatic Excerpts of Margaret
Bellasys's BL MS. Add. 10309
LAURA ESTILL

The Autograph Manuscript of Mary Wroth's *Pamphilia to Amphilanthus*
ILONA BELL